# The Oxford Book of Verse
# in English Translation

# The Oxford Book of Verse in English Translation

Chosen and Edited by
Charles Tomlinson

Oxford  New York  Toronto  Melbourne
OXFORD UNIVERSITY PRESS
1980

*Oxford University Press, Walton Street, Oxford* OX2 6DP

OXFORD   LONDON   GLASGOW
NEW YORK   TORONTO   MELBOURNE   WELLINGTON
KUALA LUMPUR   SINGAPORE   HONG KONG   TOKYO
DELHI   BOMBAY   CALCUTTA   MADRAS   KARACHI
NAIROBI   DAR ES SALAAM   CAPE TOWN

*British Library Cataloguing in Publication Data*

The Oxford book of verse in English
translation.
1 Poetry – Collections
I. Tomlinson, Charles
808.81          PN6101          79–42643

*First published 1980*
*First issued as an Oxford University Press paperback 1983*

*ISBN 0–19–281426–5 pbk*

*Filmset by Northumberland Press Ltd,
Gateshead, Tyne and Wear
Printed in Great Britain by
Richard Clay (The Chaucer Press) Ltd,
Bungay, Suffolk*

TO BRENDA

# INTRODUCTION

## The Poet as Translator

'With Poesie to open Poesie'—thus George Chapman on his aim as a translator of Homer. All good translators of verse seem to have worked in this spirit. Chapman having fallen foul of scholars who imagined only they could possess a definitive idea of what Homer was at, Dryden wrote in his defence, 'They neither knew good verse nor loved it.' It was out of this knowledge and this love that Rossetti declared, 'The life-blood of rhymed translation is this,—that a good poem shall not be turned into a bad one. The only true motive for putting poetry into a fresh language must be to endow a fresh nation, as far as possible, with one more possession of beauty.' To which Pasternak adds that a translation should 'stand on a level with the original and in itself be unrepeatable'. So the anthologist who goes to work in the light of such remarks will turn first to the great poets—say Wyatt, Jonson, Dryden, Pope, Pound—and establish his scale of values by seeing what they have made of translation.

Where to begin his choice? My own starts with Gavin Douglas's *Aeneid*, completed in 1513. If it seems tendentious to open *The Oxford Book of Verse in English Translation* with a Scot, I can only reply that it was Douglas's work which first established on this island the level at which great poetry can be translated. And why not Chaucer? If Chaucer was 'grant translateur', he translated mostly by incorporating and transforming other men's work in poems that are ultimately great originals. One could, of course, assemble fragments from here and there, including an early example of Petrarch in his *Song of Troylus*, but the results would be scrappy.[1] Perhaps only once do we find a stretch of translation as neatly excerptable as his free version in *The Legend of Good Women* of this passage from Virgil's first book, where Aeneas and Achates meet with Venus:

> So longe he walketh in this wildernesse,
> Til at the laste he mette an hunteresse.
> A bowe in hande and arwes hadde she;
> Hire clothes cutted were unto the kne.
> But she was yit the fayreste creature
> That evere was yformed by Nature;
> And Eneas and Achates she grette,

[1] One might say the same of trying to extricate Ovid from Spenser's *Muiopotmos*.

vii

And thus she to hem spak, whan she hem mette;
'Saw ye,' quod she, 'as ye han walked wyde,
Any of my sustren walke yow besyde
With any wilde bor or other best,
That they han hunted to, in this forest,
Ytukked up, with arwes in hire cas?'
'Nay, sothly, lady,' quod this Eneas:
'But by thy beaute, as it thynketh me,
Thow myghtest nevere erthly woman be,
But Phebus syster art thow, as I gesse.
And, if so be that thow be a goddesse,
Have mercy on oure labour and oure wo.'
'I n'am no goddesse, sothly,' quod she tho;
'For maydens walken in this contre here,
With arwes and with bowe, in this manere.
This is the reyne of Libie, there ye ben,
Of which that Dido lady is and queen'...

'My mastir Chauser', writes Gavin Douglas, who knew this passage, as can be seen by comparing it with his own translation of the same incident (No. 2), where, once more, poesie opens poesie, in spite of Robert Frost's dictum, 'Poetry is what gets lost in translation'.

I admire the way George Steiner, in the introduction to *The Penguin Book of Modern Verse Translation*, finds a reply to that depressing, even self-satisfied, adage of Frost's. As Steiner says, 'Arguments against verse translation are arguments against all translation', since 'There can be no exhaustive transfer from language A to language B, no meshing of nets so precise that there is identity of conceptual content, unison of undertone, absolute symmetry of aural and visual association. This is true', Steiner concludes, 'of a simple prose statement and of poetry.'

Side by side with Frost's dictum, two other threats have persisted to admonish the translator of poetry. Both of them seem to be products of the academic milieu, distrustful still of the way the non-expert—usually meaning the poet—might set to work as translator. The first of these threats hints that the only true translation would be a kind of mirror image of the original, and therefore it is either best not to try, or best to leave it to the experts in the field of French, Russian or whatever. The second threat is the outwardly bullying, inwardly fearful child of the first—the preference for a rather staid but 'accurate' rendering into tame iambics of, say, Pushkin, so that nothing extraneous, as it were, should come between the reader and the original.

Dryden long ago took on this argument when he wrote: '...a good poet is no more like himself in a dull translation than his carcass would be to his living body.' And Dryden, being a poet and a person, not a mirror, admits with candour of his own translations—some of the greatest in the language: 'I have both added and omitted, and even sometimes very boldly made such expositions of my authors, as no Dutch commentator will forgive me'.

Dryden early in his career had entered into a debate on translation begun by the Royalist group of poets—Denham, Cowley, Fanshawe, Sherburne, and Stanley—who had been in French exile after the defeat of Charles I and thus had particular and daily reason to think in terms of translation. Sir John Denham, in congratulating Fanshawe on his version of Guarini's *Il Pastor Fido*, contrasted his achievement with the pedantry of those who stuck too closely to the original text:

> That servile path thou nobly dost decline,
> Of tracing word by word, and line by line ...
> A new and nobler way thou dost pursue,
> To make Translations and Translators too:
> They but preserve the Ashes, thou the Flame,
> True to his sense, but truer to his fame.

Dryden had been at pains to draw out some distinctions from Denham's poem and also from the preface to his version of Virgil's second book, in which Denham had written, 'Poetry is of so subtile a spirit, that, in pouring out of one language into another, it will all evaporate; and, if a new spirit be not added in the transfusion, there will remain nothing but a caput mortuum.' What troubled Dryden was just how much should be added. Perhaps one could defend Cowley's free imitations of so 'wild and ungovernable' a poet as Pindar, but what of 'any regular intelligible authors' such as Virgil and Ovid? Dryden joined with Denham in refusing to trace 'word by word, and line by line'—metaphrase, as he calls this. He distrusts imitation, or adaptation as we should say, and chooses 'paraphrase, or translation with latitude, where the author is kept in view by the translator, so as never to be lost, but his words are not so strictly followed as his sense; and that too is admitted to be amplified, but not altered'. Once one has put things like this, it is, as Dryden was to find, difficult in practice to limit the element of adaptation: 'I have both added and omitted', as he later confesses. Thus in his translation of Boccacio's *Cymon and Iphigenia* appears the splendid interpolation about the Militia of Rhodes ('Mouths without hands, maintained at vast expense,/ In peace a charge, in war a weak defence'); Vulcan in *The Iliad* Book I becomes 'the rude Skinker' (a phrase purloined from a marginal gloss of Chapman's); memories of *Macbeth* are called on to describe the feast of the gods ('But Mirth is marr'd, and the good Chear is lost'); Vulcan pours and Crashaw's twenty-third psalm ('How my cup orelooks her brims') reinforces the result: 'The laughing Nectar overlook'd the Lid'. Here Dryden appears to have advanced beyond the modesty of Fanshawe's 'a Translation at the best is but a mock Rainbow in the clouds imitating a true one' towards Cowley's, 'I am not so enamoured of the Name Translator, as not to wish to be Something Better, though it want yet a Name'. Indeed, throughout the Augustan era, a philosophy of translation prevailed that permitted a wide freedom in abstracting from one's original and drew attention to its general nature rather than its local details, so that Stephen Barrett, whose *Ovid's Epistles* appeared in 1759, could write: '. . . if you take care to make sure of the true outlines, and strong likeness of your picture; the remainder is only drapery, and of no great consequence, whether exactly copied or not'.

In the present anthology, I have excluded large-scale works of imitation like Johnson's *Vanity of Human Wishes* and Pope's *Imitations of Horace*—works that bear out Johnson's own definition of imitation, 'A method of translating looser than paraphrase, in which modern examples and illustrations are used for ancient, domestick for foreign.'[1] At the same time I have, from early on, included poems—Wyatt and Surrey are cases in point—where a foreign original is 'imitated' in terms of personal feeling and new possibilities have come into the language by way of the tension. However freely our older authors appropriated their originals, I can, at this point in history, see good reason for having at least a working definition of the word 'translation'. This is what Donald Davie calls for in a tightly argued paper for the Open University, 'Poetry in Translation'. He comes up with the formula: 'Translation is something which takes more liberties (i.e., takes on more responsibilities) than the "trot", but denies itself the liberties of the imitation and of other relations more tenuous still.' Davie is arguing against George Steiner's willingness to 'consider as "translation" any poem which makes a sustained allusion to a previous poem'. One sees the good sense in Davie's desire for clarity here and one admires the conduct of his argument. Among his examples of poetic translations appear two versions of part of Baudelaire's *Le Cygne*

---

[1] A shorter example of this comes in C. H. Sisson's imitation of Horace's *Carmen Saeculare* (No. 536), which forces one to ask oneself whether a closer translation of this poem could even begin to exist *as poetry* in our own time, and whether Sisson's is not perhaps the only way of remaining true to certain elements in Horace. Such 'straight' renderings as come to hand (from Bulwer Lytton to James Michie) suggest only the unbridgeable distance between us and the original.

—one by Lowell and one by himself. The Lowell contains some very free and sometimes very odd inventions (from 'when Racine's tirades scourged our greasy Seine' to 'greening horses' teeth') and is surely a work of adaptation. Davie's own version is more literal, but where Baudelaire has the swan stretching its head towards the ironic sky 'Comme s'il adressait des reproches à Dieu', Davie writes 'as if to sue / (Its neck all twisted) God for damages'. Is not that phrase also adaptation in its purely fanciful relation to the original? And so one is back with the perhaps insoluble question of what degree of adaptation is necessary or desirable in a creative translation.

One thing is certain—translation of poetry is essentially a compromise between the original texts and the present interests and capacities of a given writer. Dryden says that the writer must be a poet. There is a difficulty here, in that some translators have shown no particular capacity as poets outside their translations, and others, like Gavin Douglas or Golding, are famous for a single extended work of translation—Douglas for his Virgil and Golding for his Ovid. Certainly our great poets have often been great translators, but perhaps the safest minimum prescription is that the translator of poetry must be a poet so long as he is engaged in that act and art.

In speaking of translation as a compromise between his original and the interests and capacities of a writer, I trust the word 'compromise' carries over no sense of timidity. Dryden's interests and capacities were those of a man in 'his great climacteric' who had written the masterpieces of his age. One of his modern admirers, the poet Charles Sisson, introducing his own translations, draws from Dryden's example what he calls 'an ineluctable law', namely 'that a verse translation has to be done in the only verse that the translator, at the time of writing, can make; and that if he could not make verse before he will not suddenly become so gifted because he is faced with a classical text'.

How elementary and yet how salutory such a reminder is when one thinks of the enormous number of translations from classical texts, ranging from the marmoreal to the mushy, in which Greece and Rome were industriously buried by earnest but untalented people—people who 'could not make verse', people on whom the judgement of Sisson's 'ineluctable law' would be that no inner pressure of their own lives had revealed in them the gift of art.

It is the sense of inner pressure that makes vivid those versions of Marina Tsvetayeva done by another British contemporary, Elaine Feinstein—translations that embody for us the tortured years of pre- and post-revolutionary Russia, and the way they were suffered by a very un-English sensibility but a sensibility that has, at last, found for itself a style in English. Like Sisson, Mrs Feinstein knows there is no ideal mode of translation and that it is undertaken in the course of a life and amid contingencies. She is even frank enough to say: 'I am not sure . . . how far a discussion of methods of translation attracts much useful reflection. . . . Poems are not translated *consistently*. Every line proposes a new set of possibilities.' What Mrs Feinstein aimed at, while facing this challenge, was, she says, 'to be sure the total movement had been sustained'. In similar vein, Henry Gifford has said that translation is resurrection, but not of the body. Introducing those versions from the nineteenth-century Russian, Fyodor Tyutchev, in which we both collaborated, he speaks of the flight or track a poem makes through the mind. 'Every real poem', he says, 'starts from a given ground and carries the reader to an unforeseen vantage-point, whence he views differently the landscape over which he has passed. What the translator must do is to recognise these two terminal points, and to connect them by a coherent flight. This will not be exactly the flight of the original, but no essential reach of the journey will have been left out.' So, in the end, for any live translator, it is not a question of approaching a text with a defined method, but of eliciting definition from, and restoring to clarity that chaos which occurs, as, line by line, the sounds and patterns of the original crumble to pieces in the mind of the translator. Davie catches the challenge of that disconcerting moment brilliantly when, in his *The Poems of Dr. Zhivago*, he writes of the professional poet as translator realizing that 'in translating rhymed verse the rhyme is the first thing to go, and metre the second: whereas the amateur, wretched sceptic that he is, cannot be sure of having poetry at all unless he has these external features of it'. Predictably, Mrs Feinstein's versions when they first appeared were criticized for her neglect of Tsvetayeva's stanza schemes, yet by neglecting what cannot be convincingly reproduced in English the Feinstein versions went immediately to the heart of what can— that jagged, breathless, self-wearing tone of Tsvetayeva's poems.

Clearly there was common ground, a common sense of impending inner chaos perhaps, that drew Elaine Feinstein to Tsvetayeva. This personal aspect is a paramount one. Verse translation is not just a job to be got through. In the best translations there is an area of agreement between translator and translated, something they have spiritually in sympathy. The Earl of Roscommon in that very sensible poem, *An Essay on Translated Verse*, of 1684, puts it like this:

> Examine how your Humour is inclin'd,
> And which the Ruling Passion of your Mind;
> Then seek a Poet who *your* way do's bend,

And Chuse an Author as you chuse a friend:
United by this Sympathetick Bond,
You grow Familiar, Intimate and Fond;
Your thoughts, your Words, your Stiles, your Souls agree,
No longer his Interpreter, but He.

Pound himself possessed this kind of ability. I am thinking of his versions of Li Po—Li Po seen as the outsider like himself—where he enters into the skin of his original through one of those combinations of the fortuitous and the creative that make art possible. In Pound's case the fortuitous aspect, the historic chance that deepened his very creativeness lay also in the fact of the First World War. Pound admired the implicitness of Chinese poetry—the silent eloquence underlying 'The Jewel Stairs' Grievance', for example—and those poems of parting and frontier service which make up *Cathay* clearly had their implicit link for him with the present campaigns in France. '*Cathay*', in Hugh Kenner's words, 'is largely a war-book, using Fenollosa's notes much as Pope used Horace or Johnson Juvenal, to supply a system of parallels and a structure of discourse ... the *Cathay* poems paraphrase, as it were, an elegiac war poetry nobody wrote.' This confrontation, deepened by history between the personal and a text in a language distant in time and place, was of a kind that had happened to one of Pound's acknowledged forebears, Gavin Douglas. Out of the conditions of a Scotland in turmoil, Douglas had brought imaginative recognition to that sense of instability and threat to civilized values that gives an undertow to Virgil's cadences. Again, it is a story of the man and the moment—a time of imminent chaos and daily insecurities culminating in the Battle of Flodden in 1513 and the destruction of Scotland's youth. It was in that very year that Douglas completed his *Aeneid*, a year whose train of disasters involved not only the spirit of that undertaking but his ultimate exile and death.

The success of translation depends, then, on a writer's confrontation with his given moment. It depends also on his capacity and readiness to undertake it and is thus, in some sense, a self-interested undertaking. In the doing of it, that writer is thrown up against a new scale of things, adding to his awareness of alternatives in literary expression, an awareness which carries over to his reader. This is what happened in the august cases from Wyatt to Ezra Pound. In their 'opening Poesie with Poesie', one hears English being drawn into a dialogue with other cultures, as when Pound, in Canto LII, translating the Chinese Book of Rites, gives us in magnificent processional rhythms something English and something irreducibly foreign and distant:

Know then:
    Toward summer when the sun is in Hyades
Sovran is Lord of the Fire
        to this month are birds
with bitter smell and with the odour of burning
To the hearth god, lungs of the victim
        The green frog lifts up his voice
        and the white latex is in flower
In red car with jewels incarnadine
        to welcome the summer

Thus, in all the great examples of how to do it, the matter is two way—the poet-translator is extending his own voice, is sometimes writing his finest work, and is performing a transmission of civilization in the process of extending his own voice. Wyatt found his personal voice to some extent through Seneca, Petrarch, and the Psalms, Marlowe through Ovid—a voice that Donne seems to have learned from in the *Songs and Sonnets*. Where Wyatt was thought once to be most bluntly English, as in 'Madame withouten many words', it now turns out he was translating from the Italian of Dragonetto Bonifacio. And all the time English was gaining by these interchanges.

Think how Ben Jonson brings over the very cleanliness of Latin when he refleshes Catullus in 'Come, my Celia, let us prove / While we can, the sports of love', where the famous *Nox est perpetua una dormienda* gets translated as:

> But if once we lose this light
> Tis with us perpetual night.

And here the loss of *dormienda* is made up for, by the succinct suggestiveness of the couplet and its brisk conclusive rhyming. Without these examples of intermarriage, English poetry would be the poorer—and so, in a sense, would Latin. Dryden talks about French having the nimbleness of a greyhound and English the bulk and body of a mastiff. And, very differently from Jonson, he sets precisely that bulk and body at the service of Latin when he translates Juvenal's *Sixth Satire*:

> In Saturn's Reign, at Nature's Early Birth,
> There was that Thing call'd Chastity on Earth ...
> Those first unpolisht Matrons, Big and Bold,
> Gave Suck to Infants of Gygantick Mold;
> Rough as their Savage Lords who Rang'd the Wood,
> And Fat with Acorns Belcht their windy Food.

In all these examples the first thing one sees is the way that, having rejected the metres of their originals, these translators do not stop at a merely literal rendering of the unmetred words. Octavio Paz clinches our point about their opening of Poesie in an essay about translation where he says: '...literal translation in Spanish we call, significantly, *servil*. I am not saying that literal translation is impossible, only that it is not translation. It is a device, generally composed of a string of words, to aid us in reading the text in its original language. It is somewhat closer to a dictionary than to translation, which is always a literary operation.'[1] Our examples have invented a linguistic system as strongly organized as that of their originals, different as it must be in terms of music and metre, but comparable in terms of literary vitality—and, in Pasternak's word 'unrepeatable'. They have 'made it new' in the phrase Ezra Pound was so fond of. And to any discussion of translation Pound must sooner or later be admitted. He is significant in the way he has extended the resources of English in his handling of the Chinese, for instance, and he is significant also for his very active awareness of the creative problem— the transformation of the literal into the literary.

In an early essay, *I gather the limbs of Osiris*, Pound speaks about the way words transmit an electricity among themselves, generate and intergenerate certain qualities and combinations of energy by their very positions in a work. 'Three or four words', he says, 'in exact juxtaposition are capable of radiating this energy at a very high potentiality ... [The] peculiar energy which fills [words] is the power of tradition, of centuries of race consciousness, of agreement, of association....'

What Pound's essay implies for a translator of poetry is that he must find a way of so placing his substituted words that the electric current flows and that there is no current wasted. If you fail *here*, at the level of the electric interchange of the words, you fail badly and this is the most common failure in translated poetry, even though you avoid howlers like 'le peuple ému répondit' Englished as 'the purple emu laid another egg'.

Pound was thinking particularly about the translation of Chinese poetry at that time. Now in H. A. Giles's *A History of Chinese Literature* of 1901, a book current, that is, during Pound's formative

---

[1] Aurelian Townshend (fl. 1601–43), in 'To the Right Honorable, The Lord Cary ...', reflects:

> Verball Translators sticke to the bare Text,
> Sometimes so close, the Reader is perplext,
> Finding the words, to finde the wit that sprung
> From the first writer in his native tongue.

years, the reader was asked to believe that the great poet, Wang Wei, wrote the following:

> Dismounted, o'er wine
>   we had our last say;
> Then I whisper, 'Dear friend,
>   tell me whither away.'
> 'Alas,' he replied,
>   'I am sick of life's ills
> And I long for repose
>   on the slumbering hills
> But oh seek not to pierce
>   where my footsteps may stray:
> The white cloud will soothe me
>   for ever and ay.'

Funnily enough, sinologists seem to have complained less about this kind of thing than about Pound's subsequent remarkable but free translations. Indeed, Arthur Waley praises Giles for uniting 'rhyme and literalness with wonderful dexterity'. His version has been thought presumably to be what is called 'accurate'. Half the trouble in this Wang Wei piece is the absurd tripping metre. In the last analysis the whole thing is a failure of ear, 'the ear', as Charles Olson says in his essay, *Projective Verse*, 'which is so close to the mind that it *is* the mind's, that it has the mind's speech'. For the mind's speech, surely, is what the translator is always seeking to catch *in his own language*, however much he may sacrifice the original metre and stanza form. And only according to the degree of his success in this attempt will his words carry the conviction of 'a man speaking to men'.

It remains for an editor to offer a little guidance to his reader and to explain one or two of his predilections. This choice does not include drama except for some choruses. If an author translated Virgil and Homer then Homer will come first. However, in the case of Pound, whose style undergoes such vast changes, I have abandoned this chronological arrangement to reveal something of the chronology of his stylistic development. There would be, of course, some excuse for doing likewise in the cases of Wyatt, Milton, and Dryden, but perhaps less. In the case of Sidney, his contribution to the great psalter completed by his sister (a work that seems to have influenced both Donne and Herbert) stands next to hers. The Bible also required some readjustment of position as far as the dates go. Later on, come a block of translations from the American Indian: though I have been forced to ignore further developments, those I have chosen begin at an interesting moment when, in the late nineteenth century, American ethnologists were often writing better than the poets. It is curious that Ezra Pound, looking to Chinese and Japanese sources for a poetry of emotional compactness, should have been so unaware of the native product. After 1910 a translation explosion takes place, and one can present nothing like the homogeneity of early phases of culture. Perhaps the chief problem here is just how much one has been forced to leave out. There is room for a whole volume, or perhaps an extended reprint, that would bring George Steiner's anthology of 1966 up to date.

In making my choice, I began with the great and worked my way down, but trust I have kept out of the *bas fonds* created by the no doubt inevitable but in some ways depressing translation boom of recent years. I did, however, spend more time than I enjoyed wading about down there. I have put in a few oddities and there are versions by different hands of the same text. If I had to give my vote to our greatest translator, it would go to Dryden. Had he lived to complete his *Iliad*, that would perhaps have made the future of English poetry a very different thing. If Pope looks down today on our literary doings he must think our relegation of his Homer very odd, and I have tried to atone for this. No anthology, however, would be big enough to hold all of his best feats of narrative skill (I should have liked all of Juno's deception of Jove in Book XIV, for example). The Bible, of course, forces the anthologist to similar arbitrarinesses of exclusion. And the same is true of all the major translators. What, briefly, I have tried to do is reveal some of the outlines of an immense and, as far as past centuries are concerned, a largely forgotten literature.

# PERSONAL ACKNOWLEDGEMENTS

In preparing this anthology, I was particularly indebted to the knowledge and kindness of John Burrow, John Carey, August Closs, Donald and Mark Davie, Michael Dibb, Michael Edwards, Miriam Emery, Alastair Fowler, Ronald Gaskell, Henry Gifford, David Holloway, David Hopkins, Ted Hughes, Aubrey Johnson, Hugh Kenner, Frank Kermode, Q. D. Leavis, Elisabeth S. Leedham-Green, Peter Porter, F. T. Prince, Christopher Ricks, Pat Rogers, John Scattergood, Michael Schmidt, Eric Southworth, Jon Stallworthy, W. M. Stewart, Peter Tomlinson, Gael Turnbull, Joachim Utz. I must also thank the Leverhulme Trust for financial assistance in helping to make possible the year's leave of absence that the University of Bristol generously granted me in order to extend my reading in the vast literature of translation. I owe especial gratitude to Judith Chamberlain for her editorial care.

# CONTENTS

xix

# CONTENTS

# CONTENTS

# CONTENTS

# CONTENTS

# CONTENTS

# CONTENTS

# CONTENTS

xxvi

# CONTENTS

# CONTENTS

# CONTENTS

# CONTENTS

# CONTENTS

# CONTENTS

# CONTENTS

# CONTENTS

# CONTENTS

# CONTENTS

# CONTENTS

# CONTENTS

# CONTENTS

# CONTENTS

xl

# CONTENTS

# CONTENTS

# CONTENTS

# CONTENTS

# CONTENTS

xlv

# CONTENTS

# CONTENTS

# CONTENTS

# GAVIN DOUGLAS

## 1474/5–1522

### FROM THE LATIN OF VIRGIL

## The Aeneid

I

### '*The Rubric*'

Cp.
Stanyhurst
Dryden

The batellis and the man I will descrive,
Fra Troys boundis first that fugitive,
By fait to Itale coyme and coist Lavyne;
Our land and see cachit with mekle pyne,
By force of goddis abuif, fro every steid,
Of cruell Juno throw ald ramembrit feid.
Greit pane in batell sufferit he also,
Or he his goddis brocht in Latio,
And belt the ciete, fra quhame, of noble fame,
The Latyne peple takin hes thair name,
And eik the faderis, princis of Alba
Come, and the valleris of greit Rome alswa.

  O thou my muse, declair the causis quhy,
Quhat maiestie offendit, schaw quham by,
Or ʒit of goddis quharfor the drery quene
Sa feill dangeris, sic travell maid sustene
Ane worthy man fulfillit of piete;
Is thair sic greif in hevinlie myndis hie?


2    '*Aeneas (with Achates) meets his Mother, Venus*'

Cp.
Chaucer
(Intro-
duction)

Amyd the wod his modir met thame tway,
Semand ane maid in visage and array,
With wapinnis like the virginis of Spartha,

coist] coast    Lavyne] Lavinium, near mouth of the Tiber    our] over
cachit] driven    mekle pyne] much pain    steid] place
feid] feud, hatred    Latio] Latium    faderis] fathers
valleris] those who built the walls    ʒit] yet
sa feill dangeris] so many dangers    fulfillit] endued with

2  wapinnis] weapons

I

Or the stowt wenche of Traice, Harpalica,
Haistand the hors hir fadir to reskew,
Spediar than Hebrun, the swift flude, did persew.
For Venus, eftir the gise and maneir thair,
An active bow apon hir schuldir bair
As scho had bene ane wild hunteres,
With wynd waving hir haris lowsit of tres,
Hir skirt kiltit till hir bair kne,
And, first of other unto thame spak sche:
How, say me, ȝonkeris, saw ȝe walkand heir,
By aventure ony of my sisteres deir,
The cace of arrowis taucht by hir syde,
And cled into the spottit linx hyde,
Or with lowde cry followand the chace
Eftir the fomy bair, in ther solace?
Thus said Venus. And hir sone agane
Answeris and saide: Trewlie, maidin, in plane
Nane of thi sisteris did I heir ne se;
Bot, O thou virgine, quham sall I call the?
Thi visage semis na mortale creature;
Nor thi voce soundis nocht lik to humane nature;
A goddes art thou suithlie to my sycht.
Quhiddir thou be Dyane, Phebus sister brycht,
Or than sum goddes of the nymphis kynd,
Mastres of woddis, beis to ws happy and kynd,
Releif our lang travell quhat evir thou be,
And, wnder quhat art of the hevin so hie,
Or at quhat coist of the warld finalie
Sall we arrive, thou teich ws by and by;
Of men and land unknaw, we ar driv will
By wynd and storme of see cachit hiddertill;
And mony fair sacrifice and offerand
Befoire thine altair sall dee with my rycht hand.
Venus answered, I denȝe nocht to resave
Sic honour certes, quhilk feris me nocht to have;
For to the madinnis of Tire this is the gise,
To beir ane caice of arrowis on this wise,

       hors] horse     lowsit of tres] unconfined
ȝonkeris] youngmen    taucht] fastened    cled] clad    bair] boar
suithlie] certainly    mastres] powers    art] quarter    will] astray
    denȝe] deign    resave] receive    feris] becomes

# GAVIN DOUGLAS

With rede botynis on thair schankis hie.
This is the realme of Pwnice quhilk thow se,
The peple of Tire, and the ciete, but moir,
Belt by the folk descend frome Agenoir.


3                  *'The Building of Carthage'*

Dryden

Eneas wonderit the greitnes of Cartaige,
Quhilk laite befoir hed bene ane small cottage;
The fare portis also he farleit fast,
And of the brute of peple thairat inpast,
The large stretis pathit by and by,
The besy Tirianis lauborand ardently;
Ane part haistis to beild the wallis wicht,
And sum to raise the greit castell on hicht,
And wolt wp stanes to the werk on hie;
Sum graithis fast the thak and rufe of tree,
And sum about delvis the fowssy deip;
Sum chesis officiaris the lawis for to keip,
With conselouris and senatouris, wise folkis;
3onder wther sum the new havin holkis,
And heir also, ane wther end fast by,
Lais the fundament of the theatry;
And wtheris eik the huge pillaris greit
Out of the querillis can to hew and beit,
For to adorne that place in all degre,
In tyme cuming quhar greit tryumph suld be.
Lyke to the beis, on feildis flurest new,
Gadering thair werk of mony divers hew,
In soft somer the brycht son hait schyning,
Quhen of thair kynd thaim list swarmis furth bring,
Or in camys incluse the hwny clene,
And with sweit liquor stuffis ther cellis schene,
Or ressavis the birdingis frome wther thairout,

botynis] buskins      Pwnice] Carthage

3 farleit] wondered at      brute] clamour      wicht] strong      wolt] rolled
graithis] prepare      thak] thatch      fowssy] ditch      havin] port
holkis] excavate      querillis] quarries      beis] bees      flurest] beflowered
camys] combs      stuffis] supplies      ressavis] receive
birdingis] burdens

3

Or fra thair hife togiddir in a rout
Expellis the bowbart beist, the faynt drone be;
Thair labour is besy and fervent for to se,
The hwny smellis of the sweit tyme seid.

4       *'The Wooden Horse is brought into Troy'*

Onto the hallowit steid bryng in, thai cry,
The greite figure, and lat ws sacrify
The halie goddes, and magnify hir mycht
With orisonis and offerandis day and nycht.
Quhat will ȝe mair? the barmekin down we rent,
And wallis of our cietie we made patent;
Onto thair werk all sped thame beselie;
Turnand quhelis thai set in, by and by,
Under the feit of this ilk bisnyng jaip;
About the nek knyt mony bassyn raip:
The fatale monstour clame our the wallis then,
Greit wamit and stuffit full of armyt men;
And thair about ran childring and maidis ȝing,
Singand carellis and dansand in a ring;
Full wele was thame, and glaid was every wycht,
That with thair handis anis twich the cordis mycht.
Furtht drawin haldis this subtell hors of tree,
And manysand strydis throw the myd cietie.
O native cuntre, and ryall realme of Troy!
O goddis hous Ilion full of joy!
O worthy Troiane wallis chevalrus!
Four tymes stoppit that monster perellus,
Evin at the entre of the portis wyde,
And four sise the armour, that ilk tyde,
Clinkit and rang amyd the large belly.
Bot notheles, intill our blind fury,
Forȝetting this, instantlie we wyrk,
And for to drug and draw wald never irk,
Quhill that myschancy monstir, quentlie bet,

bowbart] lazy

4 barmekin] rampart     patent] open     ilk] same     bisnyng] terrible
jaip] mock, jest     bassyn raip] bast rope     greit wamit] with a great belly
anis] once     twich] touch     manysand] menacing     sise] times
quentlie] knowingly     bet] built

4

Amyd the hallowit temple wp was set.
Cassandra than the faitis to cum tald plane,
Bot, by command of Phebus, all was in vane;
For thocht scho spayit the suitht, and maid na bourd,
Quhatevir scho said, Troianis trowit nevir a wourd.
The tempillis of goddis and sanctuaris all,
We fey peple, allace! quhat say I sall?
Quham till this was the dulefull lettir day,
With festuall flouris and bewis, as in May,
Did weill annorne, and feist and riot maid
Throwout the towne, and for myscheif was glaid.

5                    *'Aeneas' Image of War'*

Affrayit, I glistnyt of sleip, and stert on feit;
Syne to the hous heid ascendis anone,
With eris prest stude thair als still as stone.
A sownd or soucht I hard thair at the last,
Lyke quhen the fyre, be felloun wyndis blast,
Is drevin amyd the flate of cornys rank;
Or quhen the burne on spait hurlis doun the bank,
Othir throw a water brek, or spait of fluide,
Ryvand wp reid erd as it war wouide,
Downe dingand cornys, all the plewch labour at anis,
And drivis on swiftlie stoikis, treis and stanis:
The sely hyrd, seand this griselie sycht,
Set on ane pinnakle of sum craigis hycht,
All abaisit, not knawand quhat this ma mene,
Wounderis of the sownd and ferly at he hes sene.

spayit] foretold     suitht] truth
bourd] jest     trowit] trusted     bewis] boughs     annorne] adorn

5 glistnyt] blinked like one newly wakened     prest] ready
soucht] rushing sound     felloun] dreadful     flate] plain
on spait] in flood     othir] either     Ryvand] tearing     erd] earth
wouide] mad, wild     plewch] plough     at anis] at once
sely] simple, innocent     hyrd] shepherd     griselie] terrible
ferly] wonder     at] that

6                        *'The Sybil'*

... quhen thou art careit to that cuntree,
And cumin is to the citie of Cumas,
And by the lakis dedicat to goddis doith pas
Outthrow the soundand forest of Averne,
Under ane roche, law within a caverne,
Thair sall thou fynd the godly prophetes,
Full of the spreit divine, that schawis expres
The revelationis and fatis for to cum,
In palme tree leifis thame notand all and sum,
Writand wp every worde as sal betyde,
Direckand the leifis per ordour furth on syde.
Quhat evir this virgine descrive in hir endyte,
Without the cave closit sche layis the wryte:
Thai leifis remainis onsterit of thair place,
Ne partis nocht furth of reule, quhill percace
The pipand wynd blaw wp the dur on char,
And drife the levis, and blaw thame out of har
In at the entre of the cave agane,
That all hir first laubour was in vane ...


7                      *'Dido's Suicide'*

Bot now the haisty, egir, and wild Dido,
Into hir cruell purpos enragit so,
The bludy ene rolling in hir heid,
Wan and full pale for feir of the neir deid,
With cheikis freklit, and all of tichwris bysprent,
Quaking throw dreid, ruschit furth, or sche wald stent,
Onto the innar wardis of hir place,
As wod woman clam on the bing, allace!
And furth scho drew the Troiane swerd, fute hait,


onsterit] not stirred      dur] door      on char] ajar      reule] order
                           har] order

        7 egir] eager      deid] death      tichwris] small spots
    or sche wald stent] rather than restrain herself      wardis] rooms
        wod] mad      bing] pyre      fute hait] hot foot, straightway

6

A wappin was nevir wrocht for sic a nate.
And sone as scho beheld Eneas clething,
And eke the bed bekend, a quhile weping,
Stude musing in hir mynd; and syne, but baid,
Fell in the bed, and thir last wordis said:
   O sweit habit, and likand bed, quod sche,
Sa lang as God list suffir and destanye,
Ressave my blud, and this saull that on flocht is,
And me deliver from thir hevy thochtis.
Thus lang I leiffit have, and now is spent
The terme of lif that fortoun has me lent;
For now my gret gost ondir the erth man go.
A rycht fair cite haif I beild also;
Myne awin werk and wallis behald have I;
My spous wrokin of my brothir enemy,
Fra hym byreft his tressour, and quyt hym weill.
Happy, allace! our happy, and full of seill
Had I bene, only geif that nevir nane
At our cost had arrivit schip Troiane.
And saying thus, hir mouth fast thristis sche
Doun in the bed: Onwrokin sall we de?
De ws behuffis, sche said, and quhou, behald!
And gan the scharp swerd to hir breist wphald;
3a, thus, thus likis ws to sterf and depart:
And, with that word, raif hir self to the hart.
Now lat 3one cruell Troiane swelly and see
This our fyre funerall from the deip see;
And of our deid turs with hym fra Cartage
This takin of mischeif in his vayage.
   Quod sche: and, thairwith, gan hir servandis behald
Hir fallin and stekit on the irn cald;
The blud outbullerand on the nakit swerd,
Hir handis furthsprent.

nate] purpose     bekend] familiar    but baid] without delay
  ressave] receive    on flocht] in dismay    wrokin] revenged
  seill] happiness    geif] if    de] die    behuffis] behoves
quhou] how   3a] yes    sterf] die    raif] rent    3one] yon
   swelly] drink in    deid] death    turs] carry away
        outbullerand] bubbling out

# GAVIN DOUGLAS

8                         *'Charon'*

Cp.
Dryden

Thir riveris and thir watteris kepit war
By ane Charon, a grislie ferriar,
Terrible of schap, and sluggert of array:
Apon his chin feill cannos haris gray,
Lyart feltat tatis; with birnand ene reid,
Like tua fire blesis fixit in his heid.
His smotterit habit, our his schulderis lidder,
Hang prevagely knyt with a knot togiddir.
Hymself the cobil did with his bolm furth schow,
And, quhen hym list, halit wp salis fow.
This ald hasard careis our fludis hoit
Spretis and figuris in his irn hewit boit,
Allthocht he eildit was, or step in age,
Als fery and als swippir as a page;
For in a god the age is fresche and grene,
Infatigable and immortale as thai mene.
  Thiddir to the bray swarmit all the rout
Of deid gaistis, and stud the bank about;
Baith matrouns, and thair husbandis, all yferis,
Ryall princis, and nobill chevaleris,
Small childrin, and ȝoung damicellis unwed,
And fair springaldis laitlie deid in bed,
In fader and in moderis presens laid on beir.
Als gret number thiddir thikkit in feir,
As in the first frost eftir hervist tyde,
Levis of treis in the wod doith slyde;
Or birdis flokkis our the fludis gray,
Onto the land seikand the nerrest way,
Quhom the cald sesoun cachis our the see,
Into sum benar realm and warm countre.

thir] these     feill] many     cannos] hoary
lyart feltat tatis] grey matted locks     smotterit] besmeared     lidder] loose
prevagely] carelessly     cobil] flat bottomed boat     bolm] waterman's pole
schow] shove     halit] hauled     fow] full     hasard] dotard     our] over
     hoit] hot     hewit] coloured     fery] vigorous     swippir] nimble
          bray] bank     yferis] together     springaldis] striplings
               thikkit] crowded     benar] pleasanter

Thair stud thai praying sum support to gett,
That thai mycht with the formast our be sett,
And gan wphevin petuuslie handis tuay,
Langing to be apon the forthir bray.

9     'Turnus summons his Allies, Aeneas is "perturbit
wyth gret thochtis"'

As this convine and ordinance was mayd
Of Latium throu out the boundis braid,
Quhilk every poynt this Troiane lord anon,
Cumin of the hous of king Laomedon,
In hevy curis flowand all on flocht,
Avisis weill, hou all this thing was wrocht;
And haistilly in mynd on every sydis
Nou for this purpos, nou for that, providis,
Nou heyr, nou there, revist in syndry partis,
And seirsis, turnand to and fro all artis.
Lik as the radius sonnis bemys brycht,
Or than the glymmerand monis schaddowis lycht,
Reflexit from the brasin veschell, we se,
Fillit wyth watter to the cirkill on hie,
Our all the hous reboundis and dois spreyd
Schynand, and sersis every steyd on breid,
Quhill in the ayr upgois the tuynkilland lycht,
Glytterand on every spar and ruf on hycht.

10            'Turnus and the Courser'

Cp.      As, sum tyme, dois the curser stert and ryn,
Dryden   That brokin hes his band, furth of his stall,
Now gois at large out our the feyldis all,
And haldis towart the studys in a rage,
Quhar meris rakis in thar pasturage;
Or than onto the deip rynnand ryver,
Quhar he was wont to drynk the watir cler:

9 curis] cares       revist] seized       seirsis, sersis] searches
on breid] widely     quhill] until        tuynkilland] twinkling

10 studys] breeding grounds     meris] mares     rakis] range

He sprentis furth, and full proud walxis he,
Heich strekand up his hed with mony a ne;
Out our his spaldis and nek lang, by and by,
His lokkyrrit mayn schakand wantounly.
Siklyke this Turnus semis, quhair he went...

<br>

11          *'The Defeat of Turnus'*

And Turnus than, quhar he at erth dyd ly,
Addressis furth full humyll and lawly
Towart Ene hys sycht and ene tway,
And strekis eik hys rycht hand him to pray.
And thus he said: forsuyth, I have deserve
The deid, I knaw, and of thy hand to sterve,
Ne will I nocht beseik the me to spayr;
Oys furth thy chance: quhat nedis proces mar?
Bot gif that ony cuir or thocht quod he,
Of ony wofull parent may tuiche the,
Have rewth and mercy of kyng Dawnus the auld;
Thou had forsuyth, as I have hard betald,
Anchises, sik a fader as is he;
And me, or than, gif bettyr likis the,
My body, spulȝeit and the life byreft,
Onto my folkis thou may rendir eft.
Thou hes me venquyst, I grant, and me ourcum.
Italian pepill present all and sum
Hes sene streik furth my handis humely;
Lavinia is thy spows, I nocht deny:
Extend na forthir thy wraith and matalent.
   Eneas stern in armis tho present
Rolland hys ene towart Turnus dyd stand,
And lyst nocht stryke, bot can withdraw his hand;
And mor and mor thir wordis, by and by,
Begouth inclyne hym to reuth and mercy,
Abydand lang in hovir quhat he suld do:

---

     spaldis] shoulders      lokkyrrit] curled     siklyke] suchlike

11 deid] death    sterve] die    oys] use    gif] if    cuir] care
   spulȝeit] spoiled    eft] after    matalent] rage    lyst] desire
        hovir] indecision

Quhen, at the last, on Turnus schuldir, lo!
The fey gyrdill hie set dyd appeyr,
With stuthis knaw and pendeis schynand cleyr,
The belt or tysche of the child Pallas,
Quhilk by this Turnus laitly venquyst was,
As we have said, and wyth a grevus wound
Slane in the feld, bet doun, and brocht to ground;
And Turnus, in remembrans of this thing,
Abowt his schuldris bayr this onfrendly sing.
  Bot eftir that Eneas wyth his ene
Sa cruell takynnys of dyseis hes sene,
And can sik weid byreft thar aspy,
All full of furor kyndillis he in hy,
Full brym of ire and terribill thus can say:
Sall thou eschape me of this sted away,
Cled with the spulȝe of my freindis deyr?
Pallas, Pallas, with this wond rycht heyr
Of the ane offerand to the Goddis makis,
And of thy wikkit blude punytioun takis.
And sayand thus, full fers, with all his mayne,
Law in his breist or cost, lay hym forgayne,
Hys swerd hes hyd full hait; and tharwythall
The cald of deid dissoluit his membris all,
The spreit of lyfe fled murnand wyth a grone,
And with disdeyn under dyrk erd is gone.

          fey] fated       stuthis] studs       knaw] famous
    pendeis] pendants       tysche] girdle       child] youth of gentle birth
sing] sign       dyseis] uneasiness       weid] article of wear       spulȝe] spoil
                    forgayne] against

# WILLIAM TYNDALE

## ?1494–1536

### FROM THE HEBREW

## The Bible

12  *Genesis 27: 27–9: 'Isaac's Blessing'*

See, the smell of my sone is as the smell of a feld which the lorde hath blessed. God geve the of the dewe of heaven and of the fatnesse of the erth and plentie of corne and wyne. People be thy servauntes and nations bowe unto the. Be lorde over thy brethren, and thy mothers children stoupe unto the. Cursed be he that curseth the, and blessed be he that blesseth the.

13  *Numbers 6: 24–7: 'The Priestly Blessing'*

The lorde blesse the and kepe the.

The lorde make his face shyne apon the and be mercyfull unto the.

The lorde lifte upp his countenaunce apon the, and geve the peace. For ye shall put my name apon the childern of Ysrael, that I maye blesse them.

14  *Numbers 24: 5–9:*
*'Balam's Prophecy of the Happiness of Israel'*

How goodly are the tentes of Jacob and thine habitacions Israel, even as the brode valeyes and as gardens by the ryvers syde, as the tentes which the Lorde hath pitched and as ciperstrees apon the water. The water shall flowe out of his boket and his feed shall be many waters, and his kynge shalbe hyer then Agag. And his kyngdome shalbe exalted. God that broughte him out of Egipte is as the strenght of an unycorne unto him, and he shall eate the nacions that are his enemies and breake their bones and perse them thorow with his arowes. He couched him selfe and laye doune as a lion and as a lyonesse, who shall stere him up? blessed is he that blesseth the, and cursed is he that curseth the.

15      *Exodus 15: 1–8:*
*'The Song of Moses and the Children of Israel'*

Let us synge unto the Lorde, for he is become glorious, the
horse and him that rode upon him hath he overthrowne in the see.

The Lorde is my strength and my songe, and is become my
salvation.

He is my God and I will glorifie him, he is my fathers God and
I will lifte him up an hie.

The Lorde is a man off warre, Jehovah ys his name: Pharaos
charettes and his hoste hath he cast in to the see.

His jolye captaynes are drowned in the red see, the depe waters
have covered them: thei soncke to the botome as a stone.

Thine hande Lorde is glorious in power, thine hande Lord hath
all to dashed the enemye.

And with thy great glorie thou hast destroyed thine adversaries,
thou sentest forth thy wrath and it consumed them: even as
stobell.

With the breth off thine anger the water gathered together and
the flodes stode styll as a rocke and the depe water congeled
together in the myddest off the see.

16      *Deuteronomy 32: 9–15: 'The Song of Moses'*

For the Lordes parte is his folke, and Israel is the porcion of his
enheritaunce.

He founde him in a deserte londe, in a voyde ground and a
rorynge wildernesse. He led him aboute and gave him
understondynge, and kepte him as the aple of his eye.

As an egle that stereth upp hyr nest and flotereth over hyr
younge, he stretched oute his wynges and toke hym upp and bare
hym on his shulders.

The Lorde alone was his guyde, and there was no straunge God
with him.

He sett him upp apon an hye londe, and he ate the encrease of
the feldes. And he gave him honye to sucke out of the rocke, and
oyle out of the harde stone.

With butter of the kyne and mylke of the shepe, with fatt of the

15 jolye] spirited, brave      stobell] stubble

13

lambes and fatt rammes and he gootes with fatt kydneyes and with whete. And of the bloude of grapes thou dronkest wyne.

And Israel waxed fatt and kyked. Thou wast fatt, thicke and smothe, And he let God goo that made him and despysed the rocke that saved him.

# MILES COVERDALE*

## 1488–1568

### FROM THE HEBREW VIA LATIN AND GREEK

## The Bible

17                           *Psalm 8*

Cp.
Smart

O Lorde oure governoure, howe excellent is thy name in all the world, thou that hast sett thy glory above the heavens? Out of the mouth of very babes and sucklynges hast thou ordeyned strength because of thyne enemyes, that thou myghtest still the enemye and the avenger. For I wyll consydre thy heavens, even the worcke of thy fyngers: the moone and the starres which thou hast ordeyned. What is man, that thou art myndfull of him? and the sonne of man, that thou visyteth hym? Thou madest him lower then the aungels, to crowne him with glory and worshippe. Thou makest him to have domynion in the workes of thy handes: and thou hast put all thynges in subjeccion under his fete. All shepe and oxen, yee and the beastes of the felde. The foules of the ayre, and the fysch of the see and whatsoever walcketh thorow the pathes of the sees. O Lorde oure governoure, how excellent is thy name in all the worlde.

16 kyked] kicked

* Coverdale appears out of chronology and after Tyndale because Tyndale's Pentateuch (1530) predates these psalms (1539)

## 18 *Psalm 19*

Cp.
Sidney

The heavens declare the glory of God, and the
firmament sheweth hys handye worcke. One daye telleth
another, and one nyght certifyeth another. There is nether
speach ner language, but their voyces are herde among
them.

Their sounde is gone out in to all landes, and their
wordes in to the endes of the worlde. In them hath he sett
a tabernacle for the Sunne, which commeth forth as a
brydegrome out of his chambre, and rejoyseth as a giaunt
to runne his course. It goeth forth from the uttemost
parte of the heaven, and runneth about unto the ende of it
agayne, and there is nothinge hyd from the heate therof.

The law of the Lord is a undefyled law converting the
soule. The testimony of the Lord is sure, and geveth
wisdome unto the symple. The statutes of the Lord are
right and rejoyce the herte: the commaundement of the
Lorde is pure, and geveth lyght unto the eyes. The feare
of the Lord is cleane, and endureth for ever: the
judgmentes of the Lorde are true and ryghteous all
together.

More to be desyred are they then golde, yee then moch
fyne golde: sweter also then hony, and the hony combe.
Morover, by them is thy servaunt taught, and in keping of
them there is greate rewarde. Who can tell, how oft he
offendeth? Oh clense thou me fro my secrete fautes. Kepe
thy servaunt also from presumptuous synnes, lest they get
the dominion over me: so shall I be undefyled, and
innocent from the greate offence. Let the wordes of my
mouth, and the meditacion of my herte be allwaye
acceptable in thy sight, O Lord, my strength and my
redemer.

## 19 *Psalm 23*

The Lorde is my shepherde, therfore can I lack nothing. He
shall fede me in a grene pasture, and leade me forth besyde the
waters of comforte. He shall converte my soule, and bryng me
forth in the pathes of ryghteousnes for hys names sake. Yee though

I walke thorow the valley of the shadow of death, I will feare no evell, for thou art with me: thy rodde and thy staffe comforte me.

Thou shalt prepare a table before me agaynst them that trouble me: thou hast anoynted my head with oyle, and my cuppe shalbe full.

But thy lovynge kyndnes and mercy shall folowe me all the dayes of my lyfe: and I will dwell in the house of the Lord for ever.

20                          *Psalm 90*

Lorde, thou hast bene oure refuge from one generacion to another.

Before the mountaynes were brought forth, or ever the earth and the worlde were made, thou art God from everlastyng and worlde without ende.

Thou turnest man to destruccion. Agayne, thou sayest: come agayne ye chyldren of men. For a thousande yeares in thy syght are but as yesterdaye, seynge that is past as a watch in the nyght. As sone as thou scatrest them, they are even as a slepe, and fade awaye sodenly lyke the grasse.

In the mornyng it is grene and groweth up, but in the evenynge it is cut downe dryed up and withered. For we consume awaye in thy displeasure, and are afrayed at thy wrathfull indignacyon. Thou hast set oure misdedes before the, and oure secrete synnes in the lyght of thy countenaunce. For when thou art angrye, all oure dayes are gone: we brynge oure yeares to an ende, as it were a tale that is tolde.

The dayes of our age are thre score yeares and ten: and though men be so stronge that they come to foure score yeares, yet is theyr strength then but laboure and sorowe: so soone passeth it awaye, and we are gone.

But who regardeth the power of thy wrath, for even therafter as a man feareth, so is thy displeasure. O teach us to nonbre oure dayes, that we maye applye oure hertes unto wysdome. Turne the agayne (O Lorde) at the last, and be gracious unto thy servauntes. O satisfie us with thy mercy, and that soone: so shall we rejoyce and be glad all the dayes of oure lyfe.

Comforte us agayne, now after the tyme that thou hast plagued us, and for the yeares wherin we have suffred adversyte.

Shewe thy servauntes thy worcke, and theyr children thy glory.

And the gloryous majesty of the Lorde oure God be upon us: prospere thou the worcke of our handes upon us, O prospere thou oure handy worcke.

21 *Psalm 133*

Beholde, how good and joyfull a thinge it is, brethren to dwell to gether in unitye. It is lyke the precyous oyntement upon the heade that ranne downe unto the beerd: even unto Aarons beerd, and wente downe to the skyrtes of his clothinge. Like the dewe of Hermon which fell upon the hyll of Sion. For there the Lorde promised hys blessynge, and lyfe for evermore.

22 *Psalm 137*

By the waters of Babylon we sat downe and weapte, when we remembred the, O Syon. As for our harpes, we hanged them up upon the trees, that are therin. For they that led us awaye captyve, required of us then a songe and melody in our hevynes: synge us one of the songes of Sion. How shall we synge the Lordes songe in a straunge lande. If I forget the, O Jerusalem, let my right hande be forgotten. If I do not remembre the, let my tongue cleve to the rofe of my mouth: yee yf I preferre not Jerusalem in my myrth. Remembre the chyldren of Edom, O Lorde, in the daye of Jerusalem, how they sayd: downe with it, downe with it: even to the grounde. O daughter of Babylon, thou shalt come to misery thy selfe: yee, happye shall he be, that rewardeth the as thou hast served us. Blessed shall he be, that taketh thy chyldren, and throweth them agaynst the stones.

# SIR THOMAS WYATT

?1503–1542

PARAPHRASED FROM THE LATIN VULGATE
as illuminated by Fisher, Tyndale, Joye, Luther, Zwingli,
incorporating also paraphrases by Aretino and Campensis.

23                    Penitential Psalms

from *Psalm 6*

O lord, I dred, and that I did not dred
    I me repent, and evermore desyre
The, the to dred. I open here and spred
    My fawte to the, but thou, for thi goodnes,
    Mesure it not in largenes nor in bred,
Punish it not, as askyth the grettnes
    Off thi furour, provokt by my offence.
    Tempre, O lord, the harme of my excesse
With mendyng will, that I for recompense
    Prepare agayne; and rather pite me,
    For I ame wek and clene withowt defence:
More is the nede I have of remede,
    For off the hole the lech takyth no cure.
    The shepe that strayth the sheperd sekes to se:
I lord ame strayd: I, sek withowt recure,
    Fele al my lyms, that have rebelld for fere,
    Shake in dispayre, onles thou me assure.

24                    from *Psalm 102*

Lord here my prayre and let my crye passe
    Unto the lord withowt impediment.
    Do not from me torne thy mercyfull fase,
Unto my sellff leving my government.
    In tyme off troble and adversitye
    Inclyne to me thyn ere and thyn Intent;
And when I call help my necessitye;

23  bred] breadth    hole] whole    sek] sick

18

Redely graunt th'effect off my desyre.
  Thes bold demaundes do plese thy maiestye,
And ek my Case such hast doth well require.
  Ffor like as smok my days bene past awaye,
  My bonis dryd up as forneis with the fyre.
My hert, my mynd is wytherd up like haye,
  By cawse I have forgot to take my brede,
  My brede off lyff, the word off trowthe, I say.
And ffor my plaintfull syghes, and my drede,
  My bonis, my strenght, my very force of mynde
  Cleved to the flesh, and from thi spryte were flede,
As dispairate thy mercy for to fynd.
  So made I me the solaine pelycane,
  And lyke the owle that fleith by propre kynd
Lyght of the day and hath her sellff betane
  To ruyne lyff owt of all companye.
  With waker care that with this wo bygane,
Lik the sparow was I solytarye,
  That sittes alone under the howsis effes.
  This while my foes conspird continually,
And did provoke the harme off my dises.

25                    *Psalm 130*

Ffrom depth off sinn and from a diepe dispaire,
  Ffrom depth off deth, from depth off hertes sorow,
  From this diepe Cave off darknes diepe repayre,
The have I cald o lord to be my borow;
  Thow in my voyce o lord perceyve and here
  My hert, my hope, my plaint, my overthrow,
My will to ryse, and let by graunt apere
  That to my voyce, thin eres do well entend.
  No place so farr that to the it is not nere;
No depth so diepe that thou ne maist extend
  Thin ere therto; here then my wofull plaint.
  Ffor, lord, if thou do observe what men offend
And putt thi natyff mercy in restraint,
  If just exaction demaund recompense,
  Who may endure o lord? who shall not faynt

hast] haste    solaine] solitary    waker] wakeful    effes] eaves
                25 borow] bail, ransom

# SIR THOMAS WYATT

At such acompt? dred, and not reverence,
    Shold so raine large. But thou sekes rather love,
    Ffor in thi hand is mercys resedence,
By hope wheroff thou dost our hertes move.
    I in the, lord, have set my confydence;
    My sowle such trust doth evermore approve
Thi holly word off eterne excellence,
    Thi mercys promesse, that is alway just,
    Have bene my stay, my piller and pretence;
My sowle in god hath more desyrus trust
    Then hath the wachman lokyng for the day,
    By the releffe to quenche of slepe the thrust.
Let Israell trust unto the lord alway,
    Ffor grace and favour arn his propertie;
    Plenteus rannzome shall com with hym, I say,
And shall redeme all our iniquitie.

## FROM THE LATIN OF SENECA

26          Chorus from *Thyestes*, Act II

Cp.
Heywood
Hale
Cowley
Marvell

Stond who so list upon the Slipper toppe
Of courtes estates, and lett me heare rejoyce;
And use me quyet without lett or stoppe,
Unknowen in courte, that hath suche brackish joyes.
In hidden place, so lett my dayes forthe passe,
That when my yeares be done, withouten noyse,
I may dye aged after the common trace.
For hym death greep'the right hard by the croppe
That is moche knowen of other, and of him self alas,
Doth dye unknowen, dazed with dreadfull face.

## FROM THE ITALIAN OF PETRARCH

27          *Rime 49*
[The poet is addressing his tongue-tied tongue]

Bicause I have the still kept fro lyes and blame
    And to my power alwaies have I the honoured,

26 slipper] slippery       greep'the] grips

Unkynd tong right ill hast thou me rendred
For suche deserft to do me wrek and shame.
In nede of succour moost when that I ame
To aske reward, then standest thou like oon aferd
Alway moost cold, and if thou speke towerd,
It is as in dreme unperfaict and lame.
And ye salt teres again my will eche nyght
That are with me when fayn I would be alone,
Then are ye gone when I should make my mone;
And you so reddy sighes to make me shright,
Then are ye slake when that ye should owtestert,
And onely my loke declareth my hert.

28

## *Rime 57*

Ever myn happe is slack and slo in commyng,
Desir encresing, myn hope uncertain,
That leve it or wayt it doeth me like pain,
And Tigre like, swift it is in parting.
Alas, the snow shalbe black and scalding,
The See waterles, fisshe in the moyntain,
The Tamys shall retorne back into his fountain,
And where he rose the sonne shall take lodging,
Ere that I in this fynde peace or quyetenes,
Or that love or my lady rightwisely
Leve to conspire again me wrongfully;
And if that I have after suche bitternes
Any thing swete, my mouth is owte of tast,
That all my trust and travaill is but wast.

29

## *Rime 134*

I fynde no peace and all my warr is done;
I fere and hope I burne and freise like yse;
I fley above the wynde yet can I not arrise;
And noght I have and all the worold I seson.

27 shright] shriek     owtestert] spring out     loke] look
     29 seson] seize on, embrace

That loseth nor locketh holdeth me in prison
    And holdeth me not, yet can I scape no wise;
    Nor letteth me lyve nor dye at my devise,
    And yet of deth it gyveth me occasion.
Withoute Iyen, I se; and withoute tong I plain;
    I desire to perisshe and yet I aske helthe;
    I love an othre and thus I hate my self;
I fede me in sorrowe and laugh in all my pain;
    Likewise displeaseth me boeth deth and lyffe;
    And my delite is causer of this stryff.

30

## Rime 140

Cp.
Surrey

The longe love, that in my thought doeth harbar
    And in myn hert doeth kepe his residence
    Into my face preseth with bold pretence,
    And therin campeth, spreding his baner.
She that me lerneth to love and suffre
    And will that my trust, and lustes negligence
    Be rayned by reason, shame, and reverence
    With his hardines taketh displeasure.
Wherewithall, unto the hertes forrest he fleith,
    Leving his entreprise with payne and cry
    And there him hideth and not appereth.
What may I do when my maister fereth,
    But, in the felde, with him to lyve and dye?
    For goode is the liff, ending faithfully.

31

## Rime 189

My galy charged with forgetfulnes
    Thorrough sharpe sees in wynter nyghtes doeth pas
    Twene Rock and Rock; and eke myn ennemy, Alas,
    That is my lorde, sterith with cruelnes;
And every owre a thought in redines,
    As tho that deth were light in suche a case;
    An endles wynd doeth tere the sayll a pase
    Of forced sightes and trusty ferefulnes.

30 my maister] love

31 a pase] apace

A rayn of teris, a clowde of derk disdain
   Hath done the wered cordes great hinderaunce,
   Wrethed with errour and eke with ignoraunce.
The starres be hid that led me to this pain;
   Drowned is reason that should me confort,
   And I remain dispering of the port.

32        Imitated from *Rime 190*

Who so list to hounte I know where is an hynde;
   But as for me, helas, I may no more:
   The vayne travaill hath weried me so sore,
   I ame of theim that farthest cometh behinde;
Yet may I by no meanes my weried mynde
   Drawe from the Diere: but as she fleeth afore
   Faynting I folowe; I leve of therefore,
   Sithens in a nett I seke to hold the wynde.
Who list her hount I put him owte of dowbte,
   As well as I may spend his tyme in vain:
   And graven with Diamondes in letters plain
There is written her faier neck rounde abowte:
   'Noli me tangere for Cesars I ame,
   And wylde for to hold though I seme tame'.

33        Imitated from *Rime 269*

The piller pearisht is whearto I Lent
   The strongest staye of myne unquyet mynde;
   The lyke of it no man agayne can fynde
   From East to west still seking though he went.
To myne unhappe, for happe away hath rent
   Of all my joye the vearye bark and rynde;
   And I (alas) by chaunce am thus assynde
   Dearlye to moorne till death do it relent.
But syns that thus it is by destenye
   What can I more but have a wofull hart,
   My penne in playnt, my voyce in wofull crye,
My mynde in woe, my bodye full of smart,
   And I my self my self alwayes to hate
   Till dreadfull death do ease my dolefull state?

31 wered] weried

# SIR THOMAS WYATT

## FROM THE ITALIAN OF SERAFINO

34    He is not ded that somtyme hath a fall.
The Sonne retorneth that was under the clowd
And when fortune hath spitt oute all her gall
I trust good luck to me shalbe allowd.
For I have sene a shippe into haven fall
After the storme hath broke boeth mast and shrowd;
And eke the willowe that stowpeth with the wynde
Doeth ryse again, and greater wode doeth bynd.


35    What nedeth these thretning wordes and wasted wynde?
All this cannot make me restore my pray.
To robbe your good, I wis, is not my mynde,
Nor causeles your faire hand did I display.
Let love be judge, or els whome next we meit,
That may boeth here what you and I can say.
She toke from me an hert and I a glove from her:
Let us se nowe, if th'one be wourth th'othre.


## FROM THE ITALIAN OF BONIFACIO

36    Madame, withouten many wordes,
Ons I am sure ye will or no:
And if ye will, then leve your bordes,
And use your wit and shew it so.

And with a beck ye shall me call,
And if of oon that burneth alwaye
Ye have any pitie at all,
Aunswer him faire with yea or nay.

Yf it be yea, I shalbe fayne;
If it be nay, frendes as before;
Ye shall an othre man obtain,
And I myn owne and yours no more.

34 stowpeth] stoopeth

36 bordes] games, bantering

## IMITATED FROM THE ITALIAN OF ALAMANNI

37                   *Satires*, X

Myne owne John Poyntz, sins ye delight to know
  The cawse why that homeward I me draw,
  And fle the presse of courtes wher soo they goo
Rather then to lyve thrall under the awe
  Of lordly lookes, wrappid within my cloke,
  To will and lust lerning to set a lawe,
It is not for becawsse I skorne or moke
  The power of them to whome fortune hath lent
  Charge over us, of Right, to strike the stroke;
But trew it is that I have allwais ment
  Lesse to estime them then the common sort
  Off owtward thinges that juge in their intent
Withowte Regarde what dothe inwarde resort.
  I grawnt sumtime that of glorye the fyar
  Dothe touche my hart: me lyst not to report
Blame by honowr and honour to desyar;
  But how may I this honour now atayne
  That cannot dy the coloure blake a lyer?
My Poyntz, I cannot frame my tonge to fayne
  To cloke the trothe for praisse, withowt desart,
  Of them that lyst all vice for to retayne.
I cannot honour them that settes their part
  With Venus and Baccus all their lyf long,
  Nor holld my pece of them alltho I smart.
I cannot crowche nor knelle, nor do so great a wrong
  To worship them like God on erthe alone,
  That ar as wollffes thes sely lambes among.
I cannot with my wordes complayne and mone
  And suffer nought; nor smart wythout complaynt,
  Nor torne the worde that from my mouthe is gone.
I cannot speke and lok lyke a saynct,
  Use wyles for witt and make deceyt a plesure,
  And call crafft counsell, for proffet styll to paint.
I cannot wrest the law to fill the coffer,
  With innocent blode to fede my sellff ffat,
  And doo most hurt where most hellp I offer.

I am not he that can alow the state
   Off highe Cesar and dam Cato to dye,
   That with his dethe dyd skape owt off the gate
From Cesares handes, if Lyvye do not lye,
   And wolld not lyve whar lyberty was lost:
   So did his hart the commonn wele aplye.
I am not he suche eloquence to boste,
   To make the crow singing as the swanne,
   Nor call the lyon of cowarde bestes the moste,
That cannot take a mows as the cat can:
   And he that diethe for hunger of the golld
   Call him Alessaundre, and say that Pan
Passithe Apollo in musike manyfolld;
   Praysse Syr Thopas for a noble tale,
   And skorne the story that the knyght tolld;
Praise him for counceill that is droncke of ale;
   Grynne when he laugheth, that bereth all the swaye,
   Frowne when he frowneth and grone when he is pale;
On othres lust to hang boeth nyght and daye:
   None of these poyntes would ever frame in me.
   My wit is nought, I cannot lerne the waye:
And much the lesse of thinges that greater be,
   That asken helpe of colours of devise
   To joyne the mene with eche extremitie,
With the neryst vertue to cloke always the vise;
   And as to pourpose like wise it shall fall
   To presse the vertue that it may not rise;
As dronkenes good felloweshippe to call,
   The frendly ffoo with his dowble face
   Say he is gentill and courtois therewithall;
And say that Favell hath a goodly grace
   In eloquence, and crueltie to name
   Zele of Justice and chaunge in tyme and place;
And he that sufferth offence withoute blame
   Call him pitefull and him true and playn
   That raileth rekles to every mans shame.
Say he is rude that cannot lye and fayn,
   The letcher a lover, and tirannye
   To be the right of a prynces reigne.

        colours of devise] false appearances
          Favell] duplicity, flattery

## SIR THOMAS WYATT

I cannot, I; no, no, it will not be,
    This is the cause that I could never yet
    Hang on their slevis that way as thou maist se
A chippe of chaunce more then a pownde of witt.
    This maketh me at home to hounte and hawke
    And in fowle weder at my booke to sitt.
In frost and snowe then with my bow to stawke;
    No man doeth marke where so I ride or goo;
    In lusty lees at libertie I walke,
And of these newes I fele nor wele nor woo,
    Sauf that a clogg doeth hang yet at my hele:
    No force for that for it is ordered so,
That I may lepe boeth hedge and dike full well.
    I ame not now in Fraunce to judge the wyne,
    With saffry sauce the delicates to fele;
Nor yet in Spainge where oon must him inclyne
    Rather then to be owtewerdly to seme.
    I meddill not with wittes that be so fyne,
Nor Flaunders chiere letteth not my sight to deme
    Of black and white, nor taketh my wit awaye
    With bestlynes, they beestes do so esteme;
Nor I ame not where Christe is geven in pray
    For mony, poisen and traison at Rome,
    A commune practise used nyght and daie:
But here I ame in Kent and Christendome
    Emong the muses where I rede and ryme;
    Where if thou list, my Poynz, for to come,
Thou shalt be judge how I do spend my tyme.


way] weigh

# HENRY HOWARD, EARL OF SURREY

?1517–1547

## FROM THE LATIN OF VIRGIL

## The Aeneid

38

### '*Laocoön*'

Loe! formest of a rout that followd him,
Kindled Laocoon hasted from the towre,
Crieng far of: 'O wreched citezens,
What so great kind of frensie freteth you?
Deme ye the Grekes our enemies to be gone?
Or any Grekish giftes can you suppose
Devoid of guile? Is so Ulysses known?
Either the Grekes ar in this timber hid,
Or this an engin is to anoy our walles,
To view our toures, and overwhelme our towne.
Here lurkes some craft. Good Troyans, geve no trust
Unto this horse, for, what so ever it be,
I dred the Grekes; yea! when they offer gyftes!'

39

### '*Dido to her Sister Anna*'

'To my prowd foe thus, sister, humblie saye:
I with the Grekes in the port Aulide
Conjured not, the Troianes to destroie;
Nor to the walls of Troie yet sent my fleete;
Nor cynders of his father Anchises
Disturbed, aye owt of his sepulture.
Whie lettes he not my wordes synk in his eares
So hard for to intreat? whither whorles he?
This last boone yet graunte he to wretched love:
Prosperous windes for to depart with ease
Let him abide. The foresaid marriage now,
That he betraide, I do not him requyer,
Nor that he shuld faire Italie forgoe;
Nether I woold he shuld his kingdome leave;
Quiet I aske, and a tyme of delaye,

And respite eke my furie to aswage,
Till my mishappe teach me, all comefortles,
How for to waile my greif. This latter grace,
Sister, I crave; have thow remorse of me!
Which, if thow shalt vouchsafe, with heapes I shall
Leave by my dethe well rendred unto the.'

40          *'Dido by Night'*

And oft the owle with rufull song complaind
From the howse topp, to drawe his plaining tunes.
And manie thinges, forspoke by prophetes past,
Of dreddfull warninges gan her now afraye,
And sterne Aeneas semed in her slepe
To chase her still abowt, bestraught in rage.
And still her thowght that she was left alone
Unwaited on great voiages to wende,
In desert land her Tyrian folke to seke.
Like Pentheus, that in his maddnes sawe
Swarminge in flockes the furies all of hell,
Two souns remove, and Thebes towne showde twaine...

FROM THE LATIN OF MARTIAL

41         *Epigrams*, Book X, 47

Cp.
Jonson
Fanshawe
Fenton

Marshall, the thinges for to attayne
The happy life be thes, I fynde:
The riches left, not got with payne;
The frutfull grownd; the quyet mynde;
The equall freend; no grudge, nor stryf;
No charge of rule nor governance;
Without disease, the helthfull life;
The howshold of contynuance;
The meane dyet, no delicate fare;
Wisdom joyned with simplicitye;
The night discharged of all care,
Where wyne may beare no soveranty;
The chast wife, wyse, without debate;
Suche sleapes as may begyle the night;
Contented with thyne owne estate,
Neyther wisshe death, nor fear his might.

## FROM THE LATIN OF HORACE

**42** *Odes*, Book II, 10

Cp.
Sidney
Cowper

Of thy lyfe, Thomas, this compasse well mark:
Not aye with full sayles the hye seas to beat;
Ne by coward dred, in shonning stormes dark,
On shalow shores thy keel in perill freat.
Who so gladly halseth the golden meane,
Voyde of dangers advisdly hath his home
Not with lothsom muck, as a den uncleane,
Nor palacelyke, wherat disdayn may glome.
The lofty pyne the great winde often rives;
With violenter swey falne turrets stepe;
Lightninges assault the hye mountains and clives.
A hart well stayd, in overthwartes depe,
Hopeth amendes; in swete, doth feare the sowre.
God, that sendeth, withdrawth winter sharp.
Now ill, not aye thus: once Phebus to lowre
With bow unbent shall cesse, and frame to harp
His voyce. In straite estate appere thou stout;
And so wisely, when lucky gale of winde
All thy puft sailes shall fil, loke well about,
Take in a ryft; hast is wast, profe doth finde.

## FROM THE ITALIAN OF PETRARCH

**43** Imitated from *Sonetto in Vita* 113

Alas! so all thinges nowe doe holde their peace:
Heaven and earth disturbed in nothing;
The beastes, the ayer, the birdes their song doe cease;
The nightes chare the starres aboute dothe bring.
Calme is the sea, the waves worke lesse and lesse;
So am not I, whom love, alas! doth wring;
Bringing before my face the great encrease
Of my desires, whereat I wepe and syng,
In joye and wo, as in a doubtful ease:

42 halseth] call upon    overthwartes] difficulties    ryft] gust

For my swete thoughtes sometyme doe pleasure bring,
But, by and by, the cause of my disease
Geves me a pang that inwardly dothe sting,
When that I thinke what griefe it is againe
To live and lacke the thing should ridde my paine.

44　　　　Imitated from *Sonetto in Morte* 42

The soote season, that bud and blome furth bringes,
With grene hath clad the hill and eke the vale;
The nightingale with fethers new she singes;
The turtle to her make hath tolde her tale.
Somer is come, for every spray nowe springes;
The hart hath hong his olde hed on the pale;
The buck in brake his winter cote he flings;
The fishes flote with newe repaired scale;
The adder all her sloughe awaye she slinges;
The swift swalow pursueth the flyes smale;
The busy bee her honye now she minges.
Winter is worne, that was the flowers bale.
And thus I see among these pleasant thinges
Eche care decayes, and yet my sorow springes.

45　　　　　*Rime 140*

Cp.　　Love that doth raine and live within my thought,
Wyatt　And buylt his seat within my captyve brest,
　　　　Clad in the armes wherein with me he fowght,
　　　　Oft in my face he doth his banner rest.
　　　　But she that tawght me love and suffre paine,
　　　　My doubtful hope and eke my hote desire
　　　　With shamfast looke to shadoo and refrayne,
　　　　Her smyling grace convertyth streight to yre.
　　　　And cowarde Love, then, to the hart apace
　　　　Taketh his flight, where he doth lurke and playne
　　　　His purpose lost, and dare not shew his face.
　　　　For my lordes gilt thus fawtles byde I payine;
　　　　Yet from my lorde shall not my foote remove:
　　　　Sweet is the death that taketh end by love.

44　minges] mixes

45　my lorde] love

# JASPER HEYWOOD

## 1535–1598

### FROM THE LATIN OF SENECA

46       Chorus from *Hercules Furens*, Act IV

[The Chorus addresses first Hercules, who has slain
his children, and then the children's spirits.]

Let oken club now strike, and poast of might
With knots ful hard his brestee load all aboute.
Let even his weapons so great woes complayne
Not you pore babes mates of your fathers praise,
With cruell wound revenging kinges agayne:
Not you your lims in Argos barriars playes,
Are taught to turne with weapons strong to smite
And strong of hand yet even now daring loe
The weapons of the Scithian quiver light
With stedy hand to paise set out from bow.
And stags to perce that save them selves by flight
And backes not yet ful maend of cruel beast.
To Stigian havens goe ye of shade and night
Goe hurtles soules, whom mischiefe hath opprest
Even in fyrst porch of lyfe but lately had,
And fathers fury goe unhappy kind
O litle children, by the way ful sad
    Of journey knowen.
    Goe see the angry kynges.

47       Chorus from *Thyestes*, Act II

Cp.
Wyatt
Hale
Cowley
Marvell

Let who so lyst with mighty mace to raygne,
In tyckle toppe of court delight to stand
Let mee the sweete and quiet rest obtayne.
So set in place obscure and lowe degree,
Of pleasaunt rest I shall the sweetnesse knoe.
My lyfe unknowne to them that noble bee,
Shall in the steppe of secret sylence goe.

46 barriars] the palisades enclosing a tournament      maend] maned
angry kynges] the lords of death angered by Hercules' defiance

Thus when my dayes at length are over past,
And tyme without all troublous tumult spent,
An aged man I shall depart at last,
In meane estate, to dye full well content.
But greevuous is to him the death, that when
So farre abroade the bruite of him is blowne,
That knowne hee is to much to other men:
Departeth yet unto him selfe unknowne.

## 48    Chorus from *Thyestes*, Act III

O yee, whome lorde of lande and waters wyde,
Of Lyfe and death grauntes here to have the powre,
Lay yee your proude and lofty lookes aside:
What your inferiour feares of you amis,
That your superiour threats to you agayne.
To greater kyng, eche kyng a subject is.
Whom dawne of day hath seene in pryde to raygne,
Hym overthrowne hath seene the evening late.
Let none rejoyce to much that good hath got,
Let none dispayre of best in worst estate.
For Clotho myngles all, and suffreth not
Fortune to stande: but Fates about doth drive.
Such friendship finde wyth Gods yet no man myght,
That he the morowe might be sure to lyve.
The God our things all tost and turned quight
    Rolles with a whyrle wynde.

47  bruite] renown

48   Clotho] one of the three Fates. She spins the thread of human life.

# JOHN STUDLEY

?1545–1590

**FROM THE LATIN OF SENECA**

49        Chorus from *Medea*, Act III

### 'The Deaths of Orpheus and Hercules'

That Orpheus Calliops sonne who stayde the running Brooke,
Whyle he recordes on heavenly Harpe with twanckling finger fine,
The wynde layde downe his pipling blastes: his harmony divine
Procurde the woods to styr them selves, and trees in traynes along
Came forth with byrds that held their layes and listned to his song.
With lims on sunder rent in fielde of Thrace he lyeth dead.
Up to the top of Heber floude, eke haled was his head.
Gone downe he is to Stygian dampes, which seene hee had before,
And Tartar boyling pits, from whence returne hee shall no more.
Alcydes banging bat did bringe the Northern laddes to grounde.
To Achelo of sundry shapes he gave his mortall wounde.
Yet after he could purchase peace both unto sea and land,
And after Ditis dungeon blacke rent open by his hand,
He lyving spred himselfe along on burning Oetas hill:
His members in his proper flame the wretche did thrust to spill:
His bloud he brewd with Nestors bloud, and lost his lothsome lyfe
By traytrous gyft that poysoned shyrt receaved of his wyfe.


50        Chorus from *Medea*, Act IV

### 'Medea's Frenzy'

Her chaunging lookes no colour longe can holde,
Her shifting feete still travasse to and froe.
Even as the fearce and ravening Tyger olde
That doth unware his sucking whelpes forgoe,
Doth rampe, and rage, most eger ferce and wood,
Among the shrubs and bushess that doe growe
On Ganges stronde that golden sanded flood,
Whose silver streame through India doth flowe.

50  wood] mad, wild

34

Even so Medea sometime wantes her wits
To rule the rage of her unbrydeled ire,
Nowe Venus Sonne, wyth busie froward fits,
Nowe Wrath, and Love enkyndle both the fire.
What shall shee doe? when will this heynous wyght
With forwarde foote bee packing hence away
From Greece? to ease our Realme of terrour quight,
And prynces twayne whom she so sore doth fray.

51      Chorus from *Hercules Oetaetus*, Act II

Let other mount aloft, let other sore,
As happy men in great estate to sitte.
By flattring name of Lord I set no store:
For under shore my little keele shall flitt:
    And from rough wyndes my sayles fayne would I kepe,
    Least I be driven into the daungerous deepe.
Prowde Fortunes rage doth never stoupe so low
As litle roades, but them shee overflyes
And seekes amid mayne seas her force to shew
On argosies, whose toppes do reach the skyes.
    But lo, here comes our Lady Deianire,
    Straught of her wits, and ful of furious yre.

# RICHARD STANYHURST

## 1536–1618

### FROM THE LATIN OF VIRGIL

## from *The Aeneid*

52      Now manhood and garbroyls I chaunt, and martial horror.
     I blaze thee captayne first from Troy cittye repairing,
Cp.   Lyke wandring pilgrim too famosed Italie trudging,
Douglas
Dryden  And coast of Lavyn: soust wyth tempestuus hurlwynd,
     On land and sayling, bi Gods predestinat order:

    52 garbroyls] tumult, confusion

35

But chiefe through Junoes long fostred deadlye revengment.
Martyred in battayls, ere towne could statelye be buylded,
Or Gods theare setled: thence flitted thee Latin ofspring,
Thee roote of old Alban: thence was Rome peereles inhaunced.
My muse shew the reason, what grudge or what furye
    kendled
Of Gods thee Princesse, through so cursd mischevus
    hatred,
Wyth sharp sundrye perils too tugge so famus a captayne.
Such festred rancoure doo Sayncts celestial harbour?
   A long buylt citty theare stood, Carthago so named,
From the mouth of Tybris, from land eke of Italye
    seaverd,
Possest wyth Tyrians, in streingh and ritches abounding.
Theare Juno, thee Princes her Empyre wholye reposed,
Her Samos owtcasting, heere shee dyd her armonye settle,
And warlick chariots, heere chiefly her joylitye raigned.
This towne shee labored too make thee gorgeus empresse,
Of towns and regions, her drift yf destenye furthred.
But this her hole meaning a southsayd mysterie letted
That from thee Troians should branch a lineal ofspring,
Which would thee Tyrian turrets quite batter a sunder,
And Libye land likewise wyth warlick victorye conquoure.

## 53 'Aeneas sails from Crete to the Island of the Harpies'

Wee leave Creete Country; and our sayls unwrapped uphoysing,
With woodden vessel thee rough seas deepelye we furrowe.
When we fro land harbours too mayne seas gyddye dyd enter
Voyded of al coast sight with wild fluds roundly bebayed,
A watrye clowd gloomming, ful above mee clampred, apeered,
A sharp storme menacing, from sight beams soonye rejecting:
Thee flaws with rumbling, thee wroght fluds angrye doe jumble:
Up swel thee surges, in chauffe sea plasshye we tumble:
With the rayn, is daylight through darcknesse mostye bewrapped,
And thundring lightbolts from torneclowds fyrye be flasshing.

52 letted] prevented

Wee doe mis oure passadge through fel fluds boysterus erring,
Oure pilot eke, Palinure, through dymnesse clowdye bedusked
In poinccts of coompasse dooth stray with palpabil erroure.
Three dayes in darcknesse from bright beams soony repealed,
And three nights parted from lightning starrye we wandered,
The fourth day foloing thee shoare, neere setled, apeered
And hils uppeaking; and smoak swift steamed to the skyward.
Oure sayls are strucken, we roa furth with speedines hastye,
And the sea by our mariners with the oars cleene canted is
   harrowd
On shoars of strophades from storme escaped I landed,
For those plats Strophades in languadge Greekish ar highted,
With the sea coucht Islands. Where foule bird foggye Celaeno
And Harpy is nestled: sence franckling Phines his housroume
From theym was sunderd, and fragments plentye remooved.
No plage more perilous, no monster grislye more ouglye,
No stigian vengaunce lyke too theese carmoran haggards.
Theese fouls lyke maydens are pynde with phisnomye palish;
With ramd cramd garbadge, thire gorges draftye· be gulled,
With tallants prowling, theire face wan withred in hunger,
With famin upsoaken.

# ARTHUR GOLDING

## ?1536–?1605

### FROM THE LATIN OF OVID

## Metamorphoses

54      *'Daphne and Apollo'*

I pray thee Nymph Penæis stay, I chase not as a fo:
Stay Nymph: the Lambes so flee the Wolves, the Stags the
   Lions so:
With flittring fethers sielie Doves so from the Gossehauke flie,
And every creature from his foe. Love is the cause that I

---

53  plats] places, spots    Celaeno] a harpy    franckling] too outspoken
  Phines] Phineus, who revealed the gods' secrets. The harpies tormented
    him by removing his food.

Do followe thee: alas alas how woulde it grieve my heart,
To see thee fall among the briers, and that the bloud should start
Out of thy tender legges, I wretch the causer of thy smart.
The place is rough to which thou runst, take leysure I thee pray,
Abate thy flight, and I my selfe my running pace will stay.
Yet would I wishe thee take advise, and wisely for to viewe
What one he is that for thy grace in humble wise doth sewe.
I am not one that dwelles among the hilles and stonie rockes,
I am no sheepehearde with a Curre, attending on the flockes:
I am no Carle nor countrie Clowne, nor neathearde taking charge
Of cattle grazing here and there within this Forrest large.
Thou doest not know poore simple soule, God wote thou dost
    not knowe,
From whome thou fleest. For if thou knew, thou wouldste not flee
    me so.
In Delphos is my chiefe abode, my Temples also stande
At Glaros and at Patara within the Lycian lande.
And in the Ile of Tenedos the people honour mee.
The king of Gods himself is knowne my father for to bee.
By me is knowne that was, that is, and that that shall ensue,
By mee men learne to sundrie tunes to frame sweete ditties true.
In shooting I have stedfast hand, but surer hand had hee
That made this wound within my heart that heretofore was free.
Of Phisicke and of surgerie I found the Artes for neede
The powre of everie herbe and plant doth of my gift proceede.
Nowe wo is me that neare an herbe can heale the hurt of love
And that the Artes that others helpe their Lord doth helpelesse
    prove.
        As Phœbus would have spoken more, away Penæis stale
        With fearefull steppes, and left him in the midst of all
            his tale.
And as shee ran the meeting windes hir garments backewarde
    blue,
So that hir naked skinne apearde behinde hir as she flue,
Hir goodly yellowe golden haire that hanged loose and slacke,
With every puffe of ayre did wave and tosse behind hir backe.
Hir running made hir seeme more fayre. The youthfull God
    therefore
Coulde not abyde to waste his wordes in dalyance any more.

neathearde] cowherd

But as his love advysed him he gan to mende his pace,
And with the better foote before the fleeing Nymph to chace.
And even as when the greedie Grewnde doth course the sielie Hare
Amiddes the plaine and champion fielde without all covert bare,
Both twaine of them do straine themselves and lay on footemanship,
Who may best runne with all his force the tother to outstrip,
The tone for safetie of his lyfe, the tother for his pray,
The Grewnde aye prest with open mouth to beare the Hare away,
Thrusts forth his snoute, and gyrdeth out, and at hir loynes
   doth snatch,
As though he would at everie stride betweene his teeth hir latch:
Againe in doubt of being caught the Hare aye shrinking slips,
Upon the sodaine from his Jawes, and from betweene his lips:
So farde Apollo and the Mayde: hope made Apollo swift,
And feare did make the Mayden fleete devising how to shift.
Howebeit he that did pursue of both the swifter went,
As furthred by the feathred wings that Cupid had him lent:
So that he would not let hir rest, but preased at hir heele
So neere that through hir scattred haire she might his breathing
   feele.
But when she sawe hir breath was gone and strength began
   to fayle,
The colour faded in hir cheekes, and ginning for to quayle,
Shee looked too Penæus streame, and sayde, nowe Father dere,
And if yon streames have powre of Gods, then help your
   daughter here.
O let the earth devour me quicke, on which I seeme to fayre,
Or else this shape which is my harme by chaunging straight
   appayre.
This piteous prayer scarsly sed: hir sinewes waxed starke,
And therewithall about hir breast did grow a tender barke.
Hir haire was turned into leaves, hir armes in boughes did growe,
Hir feete that were ere while so swift, now rooted were as slowe.
Hir crowne became the toppe, and thus of that she earst had beene,
Remayned nothing in the worlde, but beautie fresh and greene.
Which when that Phœbus did beholde (affection did so move)
The tree to which his love was turnde he coulde no lesse but love.
And as he softly layde his hand upon the tender plant,
Within the barke newe overgrowne he felt hir heart yet pant.


Grewnde] greyhound

39

And in his armes embracing fast hir boughes and braunches lythe,
He proferde kisses too the tree: the tree did from him writhe.
Well (quoth Apollo) though my Feere and spouse thou can not bee,
Assuredly from this time forth yet shalt thou be my tree.
Thou shalt adorne my golden lockes, and eke my pleasant Harpe,
Thou shalt adorne my Quyver full of shaftes and arrowes sharpe,
Thou shalt adorne the valiant knyghts and royall Emperours:
When for their noble feates of armes like mightie conquerours,
Triumphantly with stately pompe up to the Capitoll,
They shall ascende with solemne traine that doe their deedes
    extoll.
Before Augustus Pallace doore full duely shalt thou warde,
The Oke amid the Pallace yarde aye faythfully to garde,
And as my heade is never poulde nor never more without
A seemely bushe of youthful haire that spreadeth rounde about:
Even so this honour give I thee continually to have
Thy braunches clad from time to tyme with leaves both fresh
    and brave.
Now when that Pean of this talke had fully made an ende,
The Lawrell to his just request did seeme to condescende,
By bowing of hir newe made boughes and tender braunches
    downe,
And wagging of hir seemely toppe, as if it were hir crowne.


55               *'Address to Bacchus'*

To thee obeyeth all the East as far as Ganges goes,
Which doth the scorched land of Inde with tawnie folke enclose.
Lycurgus with his twibill sharpe, and Penthey who of pride
Thy Godhead and thy mightie power rebelliously denide,
Thou right redowted didst confounde: Thou into Sea didst send
The Tyrrhene shipmen. Thou with bittes the sturdy neckes doste
    bend
Of spotted Lynxes: Throngs of Frowes and Satyres on thee tend,
And that olde Hag that with a staffe his staggering limmes doth stay
Scarce able on his Asse to sit for reeling every way.
Thou commest not in any place but that is hearde the noyse

Feere] spouse, mate
55  twibill] double-bladed axe      Frowes] Bacchantes

Of gagling womens tatling tongues and showting out of boyes.
With sound of Timbrels, Tabors, Pipes, and Brazen pannes and pots
Confusedly among the rout that in thine Orgies trots.


56 *'Prosperpine and Dis'*

Neare Enna walles there standes a Lake Pergusa is the name
Cayster heareth not mo songs of Swannes than doth the same.
A wood environs everie side the water round about,
And with his leaves as with a veyle doth keepe the Sunne heate out.
The boughes do yeelde a coole fresh Ayre: the moystnesse of the
　　grounde
Yeeldes sundrie flowres: continuall spring is all the yeare there
　　founde.
While in this garden Prosperpine was taking hir pastime,
In gathering eyther Violets blew, or Lillies white as Lime,
And while of Maidenly desire she fillde hir Maund and Lap,
Endevoring to outgather hir companions there. By hap
Dis spide hir: lovde hir: caught hir up: and all at once well neere:
So hastie, hote, and swift a thing is Love, as may appeare.
The Ladie with a wailing voyce afright did often call
Hir Mother and hir waiting Maides, but Mother most of all
And as she from the upper part hir garment would have rent,
By chaunce she let her lap slip down, and out the flowres went.
And such a sillie simplenesse hir childish age yet beares,
That even the verie losse of them did move hir more to teares.


57 *'Medea's Incantation'*

Ye Ayres and windes: ye Elves of Hilles, of Brookes, of Woods
　　alone,
Of standing Lakes, and of the Night approach ye every chone.
Through helpe of whom (the crooked bankes much wondring at
　　the thing)
I have compelled streams to run cleane back ward to their spring.
By charmes I make the calme seas rough, and make the rough
　　Seas plaine
And cover all the Skie with Cloudes, and chase them thence again.
By charmes I rayse and lay the windes, and burst the Vipers jaw,

56 Cayster] a river of Asia Minor　　　Maund] basket

And from the bowels of the Earth both stones and trees doe drawe.
Whole woods and Forestes I remove: I make the Mountaines
   shake,
And even the earth it selfe to grone and fearfully to quake.
I call up dead men from their graves: and thee O lightsome
   Moone
I darken oft, though beaten brasse abate thy perill soone
Our Sorcerie dimmes the Morning faire, and darkes the Sun at
   Noone.


58             *'Daedalus and Icarus'*

Now in this while gan Dædalus a wearinesse to take
Of living like a banisht man and prisoner such a time
In Crete, and longed in his heart to see his native Clime.
But Seas enclosed him as if he had in prison be.
Then thought he: though both Sea and land King Minos
   stop fro me,
I am assurde he cannot stop the Aire and open Skie:
To make my passage that way then my cunning will I trie.
Although that Minos like a Lord held all the world beside:
Yet doth the Aire from Minos yoke for all men free abide.
This sed: to uncoth Arts he bent the force of all his wits
To alter natures course by craft. And orderly he knits
A rowe of fethers one by one, beginning with the short,
And overmatching still eche quill with one of longer sort,
That on the shoring of a hill a man would thinke them grow.
Even so the countrie Organpipes of Oten reedes in row
Ech higher than another rise. Then fastned he with Flax
The middle quilles, and joyned in the lowest sort with Wax.
And when he thus had finisht them, a little he them bent
In compasse, that the verie Birdes they full might represent.
There stoode me by him Icarus his sonne a pretie Lad:
Who knowing not that he in handes his owne destruction had,
With smiling mouth did one while blow the fethers to and fro
Which in the Aire on wings of Birds did flask not long ago:
And with his thumbes another while he chafes the yelow Wax
And lets his fathers wondrous worke with childish toyes and knax.
Assoone as that the worke was done, the workman by and by

flask] flutter

42

Did peyse his bodie on his wings, and in the Aire on hie
Hung wavering: and did teach his sonne how he should also flie.
I warne thee (quoth he) Icarus a middle race to keepe.
For if thou hold to low a gate, the dankenesse of the deepe
Will overlade thy wings with wet. And if thou mount to hie,
The Sunne will sindge them. Therefore see betweene them
   both thou flie.
I bid thee not behold the Starre Boötes in the Skie,
Nor looke upon the bigger Beare to make thy course thereby,
Nor yet on Orions naked sword. But ever have an eie
To keepe the race that I doe keepe, and I will guide thee right.
In giving counsell to his sonne to order well his flight,
He fastned to his shoulders twaine a paire of uncoth wings.
And as he was in doing it and warning him of things,
His aged cheekes were wet, his handes did quake, in fine he gave
His sonne a kisse the last that he alive should ever have.
And then he mounting up aloft before him tooke his way
Right fearfull for his followers sake: as is the Bird the day
That first she tolleth from hir next among the braunches hie
Hir tender yong ones in the Aire to teach them for to flie.
So heartens he his little sonne to follow teaching him
A hurtfull Art. His owne two wings he waveth verie trim,
And looketh backward still upon his sonnes. The fishermen
Then standing angling by the Sea, and shepeherdes leaning then
On sheepehookes, and the Ploughmen on the handles of their
   Plough,
Beholding them, amazed were: and thought that they that through
The Aire could flie were Gods. And now did on their left side
   stand
The Iles of Paros and of Dele, and Samos, Junos land:
And on their right, Lebinthos, and the faire Calydna fraught
With store of honie: when the Boy a frolicke courage caught
To flie at randon. Whereupon forsaking quight his guide,
Of fond desire to flie to Heaven, above his boundes he stide.
And there the nerenesse of the Sunne which burnd more hote
   aloft,
Did make the Wax (with which his wings were glewed) lithe and
   soft.
Assoone as that the Wax was molt, his naked armes he shakes,
And wanting wherewithall to wave, no helpe of Aire he takes.

tolleth] lures     stide] rose

But calling on his father loud he drowned in the wave:
And by this chaunce of his, those Seas his name for ever have.
His wretched Father (but as then no father) cride in feare
O Icarus O Icarus where art thou? tell me where
That I may finde thee Icarus. He saw the fethers swim
Upon the waves, and curst his Art that so had spighted him.
At last he tooke his bodie up and laid it in a grave,
And to the Ile the name of him then buried in it gave.


59                              *'Atalanta'*

And from the Citie Tegea there came the Paragone
Of Lycey forrest, Atalant, a goodly Ladie, one
Of Schœnyes daughters, then a Maide. The garment she did weare
A brayded button fastned at hir gorget. All hir heare
Untrimmed in one only knot was trussed. From hir left
Side hanging on hir shoulder was an Ivorie quiver deft:
Which being full of arrowes, made a clattring as she went.
And in hir right hand shee did beare a Bow already bent.
Hir furniture was such as this. Hir countnance and hir grace
Was such as in a Boy might well be cald a Wenches face,
And in a Wench be cald a Boyes.


60                    *'Atalanta and Hippomenes'*

                              Now whyle Hippomenes
Debates theis things within himselfe and other like to these,
The Damzell ronnes as if her feete were wings. And though that
   shee
Did fly as swift as arrow from a Turkye bowe: yit hee
More woondred at her beawtye than at swiftness of her pace:
Her ronning greatly did augment her beawtye and her grace.
The wynd ay whisking from her feete the labells of her socks
Uppon her back as whyght as snowe did tosse her golden locks,
And eeke thembroydred garters that were tyde beneathe her ham.
A rednesse mixt with whyght uppon her tender bodye cam,
As when a scarlet curtaine streynd ageinst a playstred wall
Dooth cast like shadowe, making it seeme ruddye therwithall.


60 labells] tassels

44

61        *'Polypheme woos Galatea'*                    Cp.
                                                        Elizabeth
More whyght thou art then Primrose leaf my Lady Galatee,   Barrett
More fresh than meade, more tall and streyght than lofty Aldertree,  Browning's
More bright than glasse, more wanton than the tender kid forsooth,   version
Than Cockleshelles continually with water worne, more smoothe,   from
More cheerefull than the winters Sun, or Sommers shadowe cold,   Theocritus
More seemely and more comly than the Planetree too behold,
Of valew more than Apples bee although they were of gold:
More cleere than frozen yce, more sweete than Grape through rype
  .  ywis,
More soft than butter newly made, or downe of Cygnet is;
And much more fayre and beawtyfull than gardein too myne eye,
But that thou from my companye continually doost flye.
And thou the selfsame Galate, art more tettish for too frame
Than Oxen of the wildernesse whom never wyght did tame:
More fleeting than the waves, more hard than warryed Oke too twyne,
More tough than willow twiggs, more lyth than is the wyld whyght
  vyne:
More than this rocke unmovable, more violent than a streame,
More prowd than Peacocke praysd, more feerce than fyre and
  more extreeme:
More rough than Breers, more cruell than the new delivered Beare,
More mercilesse than troden snake, than sea more deafe of eare:
And which (and if it lay in mee I cheefly would restrayne)
Not only swifter paced than the stag in chace on playne,
But also swifter than the wynd and flyghtfull ayre But if
Thou knew me well, it would thee irke to flye and bee a greef
Too tarrye from mee. Yea thou wouldst endevor all thy powre
Too keepe mee wholly too thy self. The Quarry is my bowre
Heawen out of whole mayne stone. No Sun in sommer there can
  swelt,
No nipping cold in wintertyme within the same is felt.
Gay Apples weying downe the boughes have I, and Grapes like gold,
And purple Grapes on spreaded Vynes as many as can hold,
Bothe which I doo reserve for thee. Thyself shalt with thy hand
The soft sweete strawbryes gather, which in wooddy shadowe stand.
The Cornell berryes also from the tree thy self shalt pull,

tettish] captions        frame] direct

45

And pleasant plommes, sum yellow lyke new wax, sum blew, sum full
Of ruddy jewce. Of Chestnutts eeke (if my wyfe thou wilt bee)
Thou shalt have store: and frutes all sortes: All trees shall serve for
   thee.
This Cattell heere is all myne owne. And many mo besyde
Doo eyther in the bottoms feede, or in the woodes them hyde,
And many standing at theyr stalles doo in my Cave abyde.
The number of them (if a man should ask) I cannot showe.
Tush, beggars of theyr Cattell use the number for too knowe.
And for the goodnesse of the same, no whit beleeve thou mee,
But come thyself (and if thou wilt) the truth thereof too see.
See how theyr udders full doo make them straddle. Lesser ware
Shet up at home in cloce warme peends, are Lambes. There also are
In other pinfolds Kidds of selfsame yeaning tyme. Thus have
I alwayes mylke as whyte as snow, wherof I sum doo save
Too drink, and of the rest is made good cheese. And furthermore
Not only stale and common gifts and pleasures wherof store
Is too bee had at eche mannes hand, (as Leverets, Kidds, and Does,
A payre of pigeons, or a nest of birds new found, or Roes),
Shall untoo thee presented bee. I found this toother day
A payre of Bearewhelpes, eche so lyke the other as they lay
Uppon a hill, that scarce yee eche discerne from other may.
And when that I did fynd them I did take them up, and say
Theis will I for my Lady keepe for her therwith too play.
Now put thou up thy fayre bryght head good Galat I thee pray
Above the greenish waves: now come my Galat, come away,
And of my present take no scorne. I know my selfe too bee
A jollye fellow. For even now I did behold and see
Myne image in the water sheere, and sure mee thought I tooke
Delyght too see my goodly shape and favor, in the brooke.
Behold how big I am, not Jove in heaven (for so you men
Report one Jove too reigne, of whom I passe not for too ken)
Is howger than this doughty corce of myne. A bush of heare
Dooth overdreepe my visage grim, and shadowes as it were
A grove uppon my shoulders twayne. And think it not too bee
A shame for that with bristled heare my body rough yee see.
A fowle ilfavored syght it is too see a leavelesse tree,
A lothely thing it is, a horse without a mane too keepe.
As fethers doo become the birdes, and wooll becommeth sheepe,
Even so a beard and bristled skin becommeth also men.

I have but one eye, which dooth stand amid my frunt: what then?
This one round eye of myne is lyke a myghty target. Why?
Vewes not the Sun all things from heaven? Yit but one only eye
Hath hee: moreover in your Seas my father beares the sway.
Him will I make thy fathrinlaw. Have mercy I the pray,
And harken too myne humble sute. For only untoo thee
Yeeld I. Even I of whom bothe heaven and Jove despysed bee
And eeke the percing thunderbolt, doo stand in awe and feare
Of thee O Nerye. Thyne ill will is greevouser too beare
Than is the deadly Thunderclappe. Yit could I better fynd
In hart too suffer this contempt of thyne with pacient mynd,
If thou didst shonne all other folk as well as mee. But why
Rejecting Cyclops doost thou love dwarf Acis? why say I
Preferst thou Acis untoo mee? well let him liked bee
Both of himself, and also (which I would be lothe) of thee.
And if I catch him he shall feele that in my body is
The force that should bee. I shall paunch him quicke. Those limbes
    of his
I will in peeces teare, and strew them in the feeldes, and in
Thy waters, if he doo thee haunt. For I doo swelt within,
And being chaafte the flame dooth burne more feerce too my unrest.
Mee thinks mount Aetna with his force is closed in my brest.


62                    *'The Conclusion'*

Now have I brought a woork too end which neither Joves feerce
    wrath,
Nor swoord, nor fyre, nor freating age with all the force it hath
Are able too abolish quyght. Let comme that fatall howre
Which (saving of this brittle flesh) hath over mee no powre,
And at his pleasure make an end of myne uncerteyne tyme.
Yit shall the better part of mee assured bee too clyme
Aloft above the starry skye. And all the world shall never
Be able for too quench my name. For looke how farre so ever
The Romane Empyre by the ryght of conquest shall extend,
So farre shall all folke reade this woork. And tyme without all end
(If Poets as by prophesie about the truth may ame)
My lyfe shall everlastingly bee lengthened still by fame.

# GEORGE TURBERVILLE

?1540–?1610

## FROM THE LATIN OF OVID

## Heroides

63                    from *Oenone to Paris*

To Paris that was once her owne though now it be not so,
From Ida, Oenon greeting sendes as these hir letters show,
May not thy novell wife endure that thou my Pistle reade?
That they with Grecian fist were wrought thou needste not stand
    in dreade.
Pegasian nymph renounde in Troie, Oenone hight by name,
Of thee (that were mine owne) complaine if thou permit the same.
What froward God doth seeke to barre Oenone to be thine?
Or by what guilt have I deservde that Paris should decline?
Take paciently deserved wo and never grutch at all:
But undeserved wrongs will grieve a woman at the gall.
Scarce were thou of so noble fame, as platly doth appeare:
When I (the offspring of a floud) did choose thee for my feere.
And thou, who now art Priams sonne, (all reverence layd apart)
Were tho a Hyard to beholde when first thou wanste my heart.
How oft have we in shaddow laine whylst hungrie flocks have
    fedde?
How oft have we of grasse and greaves preparde a homely bed?
How oft on simple stacks of strawe and bennet did we rest?
How oft the dew and foggie mist our lodging hath opprest?
Who first discoverde thee the holtes and lawndes of lurcking
    game?
Who first displaid thee where the whelps lay sucking of their
    Dame?
I sundrie tymes have holpe to pitch thy toyles for want of ayde:
And forst thy Hounds to climbe the hilles that gladly would have
    stayde.
One boysteous Beech Oenones name in outward barke doth beare:
And with thy carving knife is cut OENON, every wheare.

platly] flatly    offspring of a floud] daughter of a river god, Cebren
      feere] spouse, mate    tho] then    Hyard] hireling
          greaves] branches, twigs

And as the trees in tyme doe ware so doth encrease my name:
Go to, grow on, erect your selves helpe to advance my fame.
There growes (I minde it verie well) upon a banck, a tree
Whereon ther doth a fresh recorde and will remaine of mee,
Live long thou happie tree, I say, that on the brinck doth stande:
And hast ingraved in thy barke these wordes, with Paris hande:
'When Pastor Paris shall revolte, and Oenons love forgoe:
Then Xanthus waters shall recoile, and to their Fountaynes floe.'
Now Ryver backward bend thy course, let Xanthus streame retier:
For Paris hath renounst the Nymph and proovde himself a lier.
That cursed day bred all my doole, the winter of my joy,
With cloudes of froward fortune fraught procurde me this annoy;
When cankred craftie Juno came with Venus (Nurce of Love)
And Pallas eke, that warlike wench, their beauties pride to prove.

# EDMUND SPENSER

?1552–1599

### FROM THE FRENCH OF DU BELLAY

## *Antiquitez de Rome*

64
Cp.
Cunningham

Thou stranger, which for Rome in Rome here seekest,
And nought of Rome in Rome perceiv'st at all,
These same olde walls, olde arches, which thou seest,
Olde Palaces, is that which Rome men call.
    Behold what wreake, what ruine, and what wast,
And how that she, which with her mightie powre
Tam'd all the world, hath tam'd herselfe at last,
The pray of time, which all things doth devowre.
    Rome now of Rome is th'onely funerall,
And onely Rome of Rome hath victorie;
Ne ought save Tyber hastning to his fall
Remaines of all: O worlds inconstancie.
      That which is firme doth flit and fall away,
      And that is flitting, doth abide and stay.

65      Who list the Romane greatnes forth to figure,
Him needeth not to seeke for usage right
Of line, or lead, or rule, or squaire, to measure
Her length, her breadth, her deepnes, or her hight:
    But him behooves to vew in compasse round
All that the Ocean graspes in his long armes;
Be it where the yerely starre doth scortch the ground,
Or where colde *Boreas* blowes his bitter stormes.
    Rome was th'whole world, and al the world was Rome,
And if things nam'd their names doo equalize,
When land and sea ye name, then name ye Rome;
And naming Rome ye land and sea comprize:
    For th'auncient Plot of Rome displayed plaine,
    The map of all the wide world doth containe.


FROM THE ITALIAN OF TASSO

## from *Gerusalemme Liberata*

66      The whiles some one did chaunt this lovely lay;
Cp.         Ah see, who so faire thing doest faine to see,
Fairfax     In springing flowre the image of thy day;
Ah see the Virgin Rose, how sweetly shee
Doth first peepe forth with bashfull modestee,
That fairer seemes, the lesse ye see her may;
Lo see soone after, how more bold and free
Her bared bosome she doth broad display;
Loe see soone after, how she fades, and falles away.

So passeth, in the passing of a day,
    Of mortall life the leafe, the bud, the flowre,
    Ne more doth flourish after first decay,
    That earst was sought to decke both bed and bowre,
    Of many a Ladie, and many a Paramowre:

EDMUND SPENSER

Gather therefore the Rose, whilest yet is prime,
For soone comes age, that will her pride deflowre:
Gather the Rose of love, whilest yet is time,
Whilest loving thou mayst loved be with equall crime.


# SIR WALTER RALEGH

?1552–1618

## FROM THE LATIN OF CATULLUS

67 *Carmina*, V. 4–6

Cp.
Jonson
Crashaw
Wordsworth
Landor

The Sunne may set and rise:
But we contrariwise
Sleepe after our short light
One everlasting night.


## FROM THE LATIN OF VIRGIL

### from *The Aeneid*

68 The heaven, the earth, and all the liquid mayne,
The Moones bright Globe, and Starres Titanian,
A Spirit within maintaines: and their whole Masse,
A Minde, which through each part infus'd doth
    passe,
Fashions, and workes, and wholly doth transpierce
All this great body of the Universe.


## FROM THE LATIN OF LUCAN

### from *Pharsalia*

69 O wastfull Riot, never well content
With low-priz'd fare; hunger ambitious

51

Of cates by land and sea farre fetcht and sent:
Vaine glorie of a table sumptuous,
Learne with how little life may be preserved.
In Gold and Myrrhe they neede not to carrouse,
But with the brooke the peoples thirst is served:
Who fedde with bread and water are not sterved.

FROM THE LATIN OF AUSONIUS

70                    *Epigrams*, CXVIII

I am that Dido which thou here do'st see,
Cunningly framed in beauteous Imagrie.
Like this I was, but had not such a soule,
As Maro fained, incestuous and foule.
Æneas never with his Troian host
Beheld my face, or landed on this coast.
But flying proud Iarbas villanie,
Not mov'd by furious love or jealousie;
I did with weapon chast, to save my fame,
Make way for death untimely, ere it came.
This was my end; but first I built a Towne,
Reveng'd my husbands death, liv'd with renowne.
Why did'st thou stirre up Virgil, envious Muse,
Falsely my name and honour to abuse?
Readers, beleeve Historians; not those
Which to the world Joves thefts and vice expose.
Poets are liers, and for verses sake
Will make the Gods of humane crimes partake.

70 Maro] Virgil

52

# SIR PHILIP SIDNEY

## 1554–1586

### FROM THE GREEK OF SAPPHO

[This lyric that Catullus translated came to Sidney via the Anacreontea
probably read in a Latin version.]

**71**

Cp.
W. C. Williams

My muse, what ails this ardour?
My eys be dym, my lymns shake,
My voice is hoarse, my throte scorcht,
My tong to this roofe cleaves,
My fancy amazde, my thoughtes dull'd,
My head doth ake, my life faints,
My sowle begins to take leave,
So greate a passion all feele,
To think a soare so deadly
I should so rashly ripp up.

### FROM THE LATIN OF CATULLUS

[A metrical experiment and the first Catullus in English]

**72**            *Carmina*, LXX

Cp.
Lovelace

Unto no body my woman saith she had rather a wife be,
    Then to my selfe, not though Jove grew a suter of hers.
These be her words, but a woman's words to a love that
        is eager,
    In wind or water streame do require to be writ.

### FROM THE LATIN OF HORACE

**73**            *Odes*, Book II, 10

Cp.
Surrey
Cowper

You better sure shall live, not evermore
    Trying high seas, nor while Sea rage you flee,
    Pressing too much upon ill harbourd shore.

53

The golden meane who loves, lives safely free
   From filth of foreworne house, and quiet lives,
   Releast from Court, where envie needes must be.

The wynde most oft the hugest Pine-tree greeves:
   The stately towers come downe with greater fall:
   The highest hills the bolt of thunder cleeves:

Evill happes do fill with hope, good happes appall
   With feare of change, the courage well preparde:
   Fowle Winters as they come, away they shall.

Though present times and past with evils be snarde,
   They shall not last: with Citherne silent muse
   Apollo wakes, and bow hath sometime sparde.

In hard estate with stowt shew valor use,
   The same man still in whom wysdome prevailes,
   In too full winde draw in thy swelling sailes.

### FROM THE HEBREW

via Coverdale's Prayer Book with aid from the Geneva, the Bishops' and
the Tremellius Bibles, the French psalter of Marot and Bèze and the
commentaries of Bèze and Calvin.

**74**                   *Psalm 11*

Since I do trust Jehova still,
   Your fearfull words why do you spill
   That like a byrd to some strong hill
      I now should Fall aflying?
Behold the evill have bent their bow
   And set their arrows in a rowe
   To give unwares a Mortall blow
      To hearts that hate all lying.

But that in building they begunne
   With ground plot's fall shall be undone:
   For what, alas, have just men done?
      In them no cause is growing.

God in his Holy Temple is,
   The throne of Heav'n is only His:
   Naught his allseing sight can miss,
      His eyelidds peyse our going.

The lord doth search the just man's reines,
   But hates, abhorrs the wycked braines,
   On them storms, brimstone, coales he raines,
      That is their share assigned.
But so of happy other side
   His lovely face on them doth bide
   In race of life their Feet to guide
      Who be to God enclined.

75                 *Psalm 13*

How long, O Lord, shall I forgotten be?
       What? ever?
How long wilt Thou Thy hidden face from me
       Dissever?

How long shall I consult with carefull sprite
       In anguish?
How long shall I with foes' triumphant might
       Thus languish?

Behold me, lord, let to Thy hearing creep
       My crying:
Nay give me eyes, and light, least that I sleep
       In dying.

Least my Foe bragg, that in my ruin hee
       Prevailed,
And at my fall they joy that, troublous, me
       Assailed.

No, No, I trust on thee, and joy in Thy
       Great Pity.
Still therfore of Thy Graces shall be my
       Song's Ditty.

76 *Psalm 17*

My suite is just, just lord to my suite hark;
I plain sweet Lord, my plaint for pitty mark;
  And since my lipps feign not with Thee,
  Thyne Ears voutchsafe to bend to me.
O let my sentence passe from Thyne own face;
Show that Thy eyes respect a faithfull case;
  Thou that by proofe acquainted art
  With Inward secrets of my heart.
When silent night might seeme all faults to hide,
Then was I by thy searching insight try'd,
  And then by Thee was guiltless found
  From Ill word, and ill meaning sound.
Not weighing ought how fleshly fancys run,
Led by Thy Word the Rav'ner's stepps I shun,
  And pray that still Thou guide my way
  Least yet I slip or go astray.
I say again that I have calld on Thee
And boldly say Thou wilt give eare to me,
  Then let my Words, my Crys ascend,
  Which to Thy self my soul will send.
Shew then O Lord Thy wondrous kindness show,
Make us in mervailes of Thy mercy know
  That Thou by Faithfull Men wilt stand
  And save them from rebellious hand.
Then keep me as the Apple of an Eye,
In Thy wings' shade then let me hidden ly
  From my destroying Wicked Foes
  Who for my Death still me enclose.
Their eyes do swim, their face doth shine in fatt,
And cruel Words their swelling tongues do chatt,
  And yet their high hearts look so low
  As how to watch our overthrow,
Now like a lion gaping to make preyes,
Now like his Whelp in den that lurking stayes.
  Up lord prevent those gaping jawes
  And bring to naught those watching pawes.
Save me from them Thou usest as thy blade,
From men I say, and from men's worldly trade,

Whose life doth seeme most greatly blest
And count this life their Portion best,
Whose bellyes so with daintys Thou dost fill
And so with hidden treasures grant their Will,
    That they in riches flourish do
    And children have to leave it to.
What would they more? And I would not their case.
My joy shall be pure to enjoy thy face,
    When waking of this sleep of mine
    I shall see Thee in likeness Thine.

## 77          from *Psalm 19*

Cp.
Coverdale

The heavnly Frame sets forth the Fame
    Of him that only thunders;
The firmament, so strangely bent,
    Shewes his handworking wonders.

Day unto day doth it display,
    Their Course doth it acknowledg,
And night to night succeding right
    In darkness teach cleere knowledg.

There is no speech, no language which
    Is so of skill bereaved,
But of the skyes the teaching cryes
    They have heard and conceived.

\*

Is not he blind that doth not find
    The tabernacle builded,
There by his Grace for sun's fair face
    In beams of beauty guilded.

Who forth doth come like a bridegrome
    From out his veiling places,
As glad is he, as Giants be
    To runne their mighty races.

His race is even from ends of heaven
    About that Vault he goeth,

There be no Rea'ms hidd from his beames,
  His heat to all he throweth.

O law of his How perfect 'tis
  The very soul amending,
God's witness sure for aye doth dure
  To simplest Wisdom lending.

God's doomes be right, and cheer the sprite,
  All his commandments being
So purely wise it gives the eyes
  Both light and force of seing.

Of him the Feare doth cleaness beare
  And so endures for ever,
His judgments be self verity,
  They are unrighteous never.

Then what man would so soon seek gold
  Or glittering golden mony?
By them is past in sweetest taste
  Hony or Comb of hony.


# MARY HERBERT,
# COUNTESS OF PEMBROKE

## 1561–1621

[At the death of her brother, Sir Philip Sidney, the
psalms were completed by her, possibly with other collaborators.]

78                  *Psalm 52*

Tyrant, why swel'st thou thus,
  Of mischief vaunting?
Since helpe from God to us,
  Is never wanting?

Lewd lies thy tongue contrives,
  Lowd lies it soundeth:
Sharper than sharpest knives
  With lies it woundeth.

Falshood thy witt approves,
    All truth rejected:
Thy will all vices loves,
    Vertue neglected.

Not wordes from cursed thee,
    But gulfes are powred;
Gulfes wherin daily bee
    Good men devoured.

Think'st thou to beare it soe?
    God shall displace thee;
God shall thee overthrow,
    Crush thee, deface thee.

The just shall fearing see
    These fearefull chaunces:
And laughing shoote at thee
    With scornfull glances.

Loe, loe, the wretched wight,
    Who God disdaining,
His mischief made his might,
    His guard his gaining.

I as an olive tree,
    Still green shall flourish:
Gods house the soile shall bee
    My rootes to nourish.

My trust on his true love
    Truly attending,
Shall never thence remove,
    Never see ending.

Thee will I honor still
    Lord, for this justice:
There fix my hopes I will
    Where thy saincts trust is.

Thy saints trust in thy name,
    Therin they joy them:
Protected by the same
    Nought can annoy them.


79                       from *Psalm 55*

My God most glad to look, most prone to heere,
    An open eare O let my praier find,
And from my plaint turne not thy face away.
Behold my gestures, harken what I say
    While uttering mones with most tormented mind.
My body I no lesse torment and teare,
For loe, their fearful threatnings wound mine eare,
Who griefs on griefs on me still heaping laie,
    A mark to wrath and hate and wrong assign'd,
    Therefore my hart hath all his force resign'd
To trembling pants, Deaths terrors on me pray,
I feare, nay shake, nay quiv'ring quake with feare.

Then say I, O might I but cutt the wind,
    Born on the wing the fearfull dove doth beare:
Stay would I not, till I in rest might stay.
Far hence, O far, then would I take my way
    Unto the desert, and repose me there,
These stormes of woe, these tempests left behind:
But swallow them, O Lord, in darkness blind,
Confound their councells, leade their tongues astray,
    That what they meane by wordes may not appeare;
    For Mother Wrong within their towne each where,
And daughter Strife their ensignes so display,
As if they only thither were confin'd.

These walk their cittie walles both night and day,
    Oppressions, tumults, guiles of ev'ry kind
Are burgesses, and dwell the midle neere:
About their streetes his masking robes doth weare
    Mischief, cloth'd in deceit, with treason lin'd,
Where only hee, hee only beares the sway.
But not my foe with mee this pranck did play,

For then I would have borne with patient cheere
   An unkind part from whom I know unkind;
   Nor hee whose forhed Envies mark had sign'd,
His trophes on my ruins sought to reare,
From whom to fly I might have made assay.

But this to thee, to thee impute I may,
   My fellow, my companion, held most deere,
My soule, my other self, my inward frend:
Whom unto me, me unto whom did bind
   Exchanged secrets, who together were
Gods temple wont to visit, there to pray.
O lett a soddaine death work their decay,
Who speaking faire, such canckred malice mind,
   Let them be buried breathing in their beir.
   But purple morn, black ev'n, and midday cleare,
Shall see my praying voice to God enclin'd,
Rowzing him up; and nought shall me dismay.

80            from *Psalm 72*

Looke how the woods, where enterlaced trees
   Spread frendly armes each other to embrace,
Joyne at the head, though distant at the knees,
   Waving with wind, and lording on the place:
         So woods of corne
         By mountaynes borne
      Shall on their showlders wave:
         And men shall passe
         The numbrous grasse,
      Such store each town shall have.

Looke how the sunne, soe shall his name remayne;
   As that in light, so this in glory one:
All glories that, at this all lights shall stayne:
   Nor that shall faile, nor this be overthrowne.
         The dwellers all
         Of earthly ball
      In hym shall hold them blest:
         As one that is
         Of perfect blisse
      A patterne to the rest.

O God who art, from whom all beings be;
   Eternall Lord, whom Jacobs stock adore,
And wondrous works are done by only thee,
   Blessed be thou, most blessed evermore.
       And lett thy name,
       Thy glorious fame,
    No end of blessing know:
       Lett all this Round
       Thy honor sound,
    So Lord, O be it so.

81                 from *Psalm 78*

There where the deepe did show his sandy flore,
   And heaped waves an uncouth way enwall:
Whereby they past from one to other shore,
   Walking on seas, and yet not wett at all:
He ledd them so; a cloud was them before
   While light did last: when night did darkness call,
A flaming piller glitt'ring in the skies
Their load starr was, till sunne again did rise.

He rift the Rocks and from their perced sides,
   To give them drinck, whole seas of water drew:
The desert sand no longer thirst abides;
   The trickling springs to such huge rivers grew.
Yet not content their furie further slides;
   In those wild waies they anger God anew.
As thirst before, now hunger stirrs their lust
To tempting thoughtes, bewraying want of trust;

*

Yet he unclos'd the garners of the skies,
   And bade the cloudes Ambrosian manna rain:
As morning frost on hoary pasture lies,
   So strawed lay each where this heav'nly grain
The finest cheat that dearest princes prise,
   The bread of heav'n could not in fineness stain:
Which he them gave, and gave them in such store,
Each had so much, he wish't to have no more.

    81  cheat] (1) wheaten bread   (2) booty, prize

But that he might them each way satisfie,
    He slipt the raines to east and southerne wind;
These on the cloudes their uttmost forces try,
    And bring in raines of admirable kind.
The dainty Quailes that freely wont to fly,
    In forced showers to dropp were now assign'd:
And fell as thick as dust on sunn-burnt field,
Or as the sand the thirsty shore doth yeeld.


82                    from *Psalm 139*

Each inmost peece in me is thine:
    While yet I in my mother dwelt,
            All that me cladd
            From thee I hadd.
    Thou in my frame hast strangly delt:
Needes in my praise thy workes must shine
    So inly them my thoughts have felt.

Thou, how my back was beam-wise laid,
    And raftring of my ribbs, dost know:
            Know'st ev'ry point
            Of bone and joynt,
    How to this whole these partes did grow,
In brave embrod'ry faire araid,
    Though wrought in shopp both dark and low.

Nay fashionless, ere forme I tooke,
    Thy all and more beholding ey
            My shapelesse shape
            Could not escape:
    All these tyme fram'd successively
Ere one had beeing, in the booke
    Of thy foresight, enrol'd did ly.

My God, how I these studies prize,
    That doe thy hidden workings show!
            Whose summ is such,
            Noe suume soe much:
    Nay summ'd as sand they summlesse grow.
I lye to sleepe, from sleepe I rise,
    Yet still in thought with thee I goe.

# GEORGE CHAPMAN

?1559–?1634

FROM THE GREEK OF HOMER

## The Iliad

SOME SIMILES

83            *'The Greeks like Bees'*

                             As when of frequent Bees
Swarmes rise out of a hollow rocke, repairing the degrees
Of their egression endlesly with ever rising new
From forth their sweet nest, as their store, still as it faded, grew
And never would ceasse, sending forth her clusters to the spring
They still crowd out so—this flocke here, that there, belabouring
The loaded flowres: so from the ships and tents the armie's store
Troopt to these Princes and the Court along th'unmeasur'd
    shore . . .

84    *'The Greeks like the Sea, the Trojans like Ewes'*

Cp.    And as when with the West-wind's flawes the sea thrusts
Pope      up her waves
        One after other, thicke and high, upon the groning shores,
        First in her selfe lowd (but opposd with banks and Rocks)
          she rores
        And (all her backe in bristles set) spits everie way her fome:
        So (after Diomed) instantly the field was overcome
        With thicke impressions of the Greekes and all the noise
          that grew
        (Ordring and chearing up their men) from onely leaders flew.
        The rest went silently away, you could not heare a voice,
        Nor would have thought in all their breasts they had one in
          their choice—
        Their silence uttering their awe of them that them contrould,
        Which made ech man keep bright his arms, march, fight still
          where he should.
        The Troyans (like a sort of Ewes pend in a rich man's fold,
        Close at his dore till all be milkt, and never baaing hold,

Hearing the bleating of their lambs) did all their wide
host fill
With showts and clamors, nor observ'd one voice, one
baaing still
But shew'd mixt tongs from many a land of men cald to their
aid.

85                    *'The Greeks like Clouds'*

Cp.                              Their ground they stil made good,
Pope      And (in their silence and set powers) like faire still clouds they
stood,
With which Jove crownes the tops of hils in any quiet day,
When Boreas and the ruder winds (that use to drive away
Aire's duskie vapors, being loose, in many a whistling gale)
Are pleasingly bound up and calme, and not a breath exhale:
So firmely stood the Greeks, nor fled for all the Ilians' ayd.

86                       *'Men like Leaves'*

Cp.                              'Why dost thou so explore,'
Ecclesiasticus   Said Glaucus, 'of what race I am, when like the race
Pope                 of leaves
Johnson
The race of man is, that deserves no question? Nor
receives
My being any other breath. The wind in Autumne
strowes
The earth with old leaves; then the Spring the woods
with new endowes—
And so death scatters men on earth, so life puts out
againe
Man's leavie issue.

87                    *'Paris and the Courser'*

Cp.                              And now was Paris come
Pope      From his high towres, who made no stay when once he had
put on
His richest armour, but flew forth; the flints he trod upon

Sparkled with luster of his armes; his long-ebd spirits now flowd
The higher for their lower ebbe. And as a faire Steed, proud
With ful-given mangers, long tied up and now (his head-stall
    broke)
He breakes from stable, runnes the field and with an ample
    stroke
Measures the center, neighs and lifts aloft his wanton head,
About his shoulders shakes his Crest, and where he hath bene
    fed
Or in some calme floud washt or (stung with his high plight)
    he flies
Amongst his femals, strength puts forth, his beautie beautifies,
And like Life's mirror beares his gate—so Paris from the towre
Of loftie Pergamus came forth ...

## 88      *'Jove's cold-sharpe javelines'*

Cp.
Pope
Diaper's Oppian
Cowper

And as in winter time when Jove his cold-sharpe
    javelines throwes
Amongst us mortals and is mov'd to white earth
    with his snowes
(The winds asleepe) he freely poures, till highest
    Prominents,
Hill tops, low meddowes and the fields that crowne
    with most contents
The toiles of men, sea ports and shores are hid,
    and everie place
But floods (that snowe's faire tender flakes, as their
    owne brood, embrace):
So both sides coverd earth with stones, so both for
    life contend
To shew their sharpnesse.

## 89      *'The two Ajaxes compared to Oxen'*

Cp.
Pope
Cowper

Oileus by his brother's side stood close and would not
    thence
For any moment of that time. But as through fallow fields
Blacke Oxen draw a well-joyn'd plough and either evenly
    yeelds
His thriftie labour, all heads couch so close to earth they
    plow

The fallow with their hornes, till out the sweate begins
  to flow,
The stretcht yokes cracke, and yet at last the furrow forth
  is driven:
So toughly stood these to their taske and made their worke
  as even.

90      *'Paris and Menelaus'*

Cp.
Pope

But ere sterne conflict mixt both strengths, faire Paris stept
  before
The Troyan host. Athwart his backe a Panther's hide he wore,
A crooked bow and sword, and shooke two brazen-headed
  darts,
With which well-arm'd, his tongue provok't the best of Grecian
  hearts
To stand with him in single fight. Whom when the man,
  wrong'd most
Of all the Greekes, so gloriously saw stalke before the host,
As when a Lion is rejoyc't (with hunger halfe forlorne)
That finds some sweet prey (as a Hart, whose grace lies
  in his horne,
Or Sylvane Goate) which he devours, though never so pursu'd
With dogs and men, so Sparta's king exulted when he view'd
The faire-fac'd Paris so exposde to his so thirsted wreake—
Whereof his good cause made him sure. The Grecian front did
  breake
And forth he rusht, at all parts arm'd, leapt from his chariot
And royally prepar'd for charge. Which seene, cold terror shot
The heart of Paris, who retir'd as headlong from the king
As in him he had shund his death. And as a hilly spring
Presents a serpent to a man full underneath his feete,
Her blew necke (swolne with poison) raisd and her sting out,
  to greet
His heedlesse entrie, sodainely his walke he altereth,
Starts backe amaz'd, is shooke with feare and lookes as pale
  as death;
So Menelaus Paris scar'd, so that divine-fac't foe
Shrunke in his beauties.

91 *'The old Trojan Chiefs see Helen'*

Cp.
Pope

All grave old men, and souldiers they had bene, but for age
Now left the warres; yet Counsellors they were exceeding sage.
And as in well-growne woods, on trees, cold spinie
    Grashoppers
Sit chirping and send voices out that scarce can pierce our eares
For softnesse and their weake faint sounds; so (talking on
    the towre)
These Seniors of the people sate, who, when they saw the
    powre
Of beautie in the Queene ascend, even those cold-spirited
    Peeres,
Those wise and almost witherd men, found this heate in
    their yeares
That they were forc't (though whispering) to say: 'What man
    can blame
The Greekes and Troyans to endure, for so admir'd a Dame,
So many miseries, and so long? In her sweet countenance
    shine
Lookes like the Goddesses'. And yet (though never so divine)
Before we boast, unjustly still, of her enforced prise
And justly suffer for her sake, with all our progenies,
Labor and ruine let her go: the profit of our land
Must passe the beautie.'

92 *'Hector's Child and the Plume'*

This said, he reacht to take his sonne, who (of his armes afraid,
And then the horse-haire plume, with which he was so overlaid,
Nodded so horribly) he clingd backe to his nurse and cride.
Laughter affected his great Sire, who doft and laid aside
His fearfull Helme, that on the earth cast round about it light.
Then tooke and kist his loving sonne and (ballancing his weight
In dancing him) these loving vowes to living Jove he usde
And all the other bench of Gods: 'O you that have infusde
Soule to this infant, now set downe this blessing on his starre.
Let his renowne be cleare as mine, equall his strength in warre.'

93     '*Night Piece: the Trojans outside Troy*'

Cp.
Pope
Cowper
Tennyson

This speech all Troyans did applaud, who from their
    traces losde
Their sweating horse, which severally with headstals they
    reposde
And fastned by their chariots; when others brought from
    towne
Fat sheepe and oxen instantly, bread, wine, and hewed
    downe
Huge store of wood. The winds transferd into the friendly
    skie
Their supper's savour, to the which they sate delightfully
And spent all night in open field. Fires round about them
    shinde.
As when about the silver Moone, when aire is free from
    winde
And stars shine cleare, to whose sweete beames high
    prospects and the brows
Of all steepe hils and pinnacles thrust up themselves for
    showes
And even the lowly vallies joy to glitter in their sight,
When the unmeasur'd firmament bursts to disclose her
    light
And all the signes in heaven are seene that glad the
    shepheard's hart;
So many fires disclosde their beames, made by the Troyan
    part,
Before the face of Ilion and her bright turrets show'd.
A thousand courts of guard kept fires, and every guard
    allow'd
Fiftie stout men, by whom their horse eate oates and hard
    white corne,
And all did wishfully expect the silver-throned morne.

# The Odyssey

## 94 'Mercury is sent by Jupiter to Calypso, to command Ulysses' return'

Cp.
Pope
Cowper

Thus charg'd he; nor Argicides denied,
But to his feete his faire wingd shooes he tied,
Ambrosian, golden, that in his command
Put either sea or the unmeasur'd land
With pace as speedie as a puft of wind.
Then up his Rod went, with which he declin'd
The eyes of any waker, when he pleasd,
And any sleeper, when he wisht, diseasd.
    This tooke, he stoopt Pieria, and thence
Glid through the aire, and Neptune's Confluence
Kist as he flew, and checkt the waves as light
As any Sea-Mew in her fishing flight,
Her thicke wings soucing in the savorie seas.
Like her, he past a world of wildernesse,
But when the far-off Ile he toucht, he went
Up from the blue sea to the Continent,
And reacht the ample Caverne of the Queene,
Whom he within found—without, seldome seene.
A Sun-like fire upon the harth did flame,
The matter precious, and divine the frame,
Of Cedar cleft, and Incense was the Pile,
That breath'd an odour round about the Ile.
Her selfe was seated in an inner roome,
Whom sweetly sing he heard, and at her loome
About a curious web, whose yarne she threw
In with a golden shittle. A Grove grew
In endlesse spring about her Caverne round,
With odorous Cypresse, Pines, and Poplars crownd,
Where Haulks, Sea-owles, and long-tongu'd Bittours
    bred,
And other birds their shadie pinions spred—
All Fowles maritimall; none roosted there
But those whose labours in the waters were.
A Vine did all the hollow Cave embrace,
Still greene, yet still ripe bunches gave it grace.

Haulks] hawks    Bittours] bitterns

Foure Fountaines one against another powrd
Their silver streames, and medowes all enflowrd
With sweete Balme-gentle and blue Violets hid,
That deckt the soft brests of each fragrant Mead.
Should any one (though he immortall were)
Arrive and see the sacred objects there,
He would admire them and be over-joyd.
And so stood Hermes' ravisht powres employd.

95          *'Ulysses builds his Ship'*

Cp.
Pope

The Nymph turnd home. He fell to felling downe,
And twentie trees he stoopt in litle space,
Plaind, usde his Plumb, did all with artfull grace.
In meane time did Calypso wimbles bring.
He bor'd, closde, naild, and orderd every thing.
And looke how much a ship-wright will allow
A ship of burthen (one that best doth know
What fits his Art), so large a Keele he cast—
Wrought up her decks and hatches, side-boords, mast,
With willow watlings armd her to resist
The billowes' outrage, added all she mist—
Sail-yards and sterne for guide. The Nymph then brought
Linnen for sailes, which with dispatch he wrought—
Gables, and halsters, tacklings. All the Frame
In foure dayes' space to full perfection came.
The fifth day they dismist him from the shore,
Weeds, neate and odorous, gave him, victles' store,
Wine and strong waters, and a prosperous wind.
To which Ulysses (fit to be divin'd)
His sailes exposd, and hoised. Off he gat . . .

96          *'The Wrecking of the Ship'*

Cp.
Pope

This spoke, a huge wave tooke him by the head
And hurld him o're-boord: ship and all it laid
Inverted quite amidst the waves, but he
Farre off from her sprawld, strowd about the sea,
His Sterne still holding, broken off; his Mast
Burst in the midst, so horrible a blast

Of mixt winds strooke it. Sailes and saile-yards fell
Amongst the billowes, and himselfe did dwell
A long time under water, nor could get
In haste his head out—wave with wave so met
In his depression, and his garments too
(Given by Calypso) gave him much to do,
Hindring his swimming; yet he left not so
His drenched vessell, for the overthrow
Of her nor him, but gat at length againe
(Wrestling with Neptune) hold of her, and then
Sate in her Bulke, insulting over Death—
Which (with the salt streame prest to stop his breath)
He scap't and gave the sea againe to give
To other men. His ship so striv'd to live,
Floting at randon, cufft from wave to wave,
As you have seene the Northwind when he drave
In Autumne heapes of thorne-fed Grashoppers
Hither and thither; one heape this way beares,
Another that, and makes them often meete
In his confusde gales; so Ulysses' fleete
The winds hurl'd up and downe: now Boreas
Tost it to Notus, Notus gave it passe
To Eurus; Eurus Zephyr made pursue
The horrid Tennis.

## 97    *'The Garden of Alcinous, King of Phaecea'*

Cp.
Pope

Without the Hall, and close upon the Gate,
A goodly Orchard ground was situate
Of neare ten Acres, about which was led
A loftie Quickset. In it flourished
High and broad fruit trees that Pomegranats bore;
Sweet Figs, Peares, Olives, and a number more
Most usefull Plants did there produce their store,
Whose fruits the hardest Winter could not kill,
Nor hotest Summer wither. There was still
Fruite in his proper season all the yeare.
Sweet Zephyr breath'd upon them blasts that were
Of varied tempers: these he made to beare
Ripe fruites, these blossomes; Peare grew after Peare,
Apple succeeded apple, Grape the Grape,
Fig after Fig came; Time made never rape

Of any daintie there. A spritely vine
Spred here his roote, whose fruite a hote sun-shine
Made ripe betimes. Here grew another, greene.
Here some were gathering, here some pressing scene.
A large-allotted severall each fruite had;
And all th'adornd grounds their apparance made
In flowre and fruite, at which the King did aime
To the precisest order he could claime.

    Two Fountaines grac't the garden; of which, one
Powrd out a winding streame that over-runne
The grounds for their use chiefly, th'other went
Close by the loftie Pallace gate, and lent
The Citie his sweet benefit. And thus
The Gods the Court deckt of Alcinous.

98        *'Ulysses and his Mother's Spirit'*

    'She thus; when I had great desire to prove
My armes the circle where her soule did move.
Thrice prov'd I, thrice she vanisht like a sleepe
Or fleeting shadow, which strooke much more deepe
The wounds my woes made, and made aske her why
She would my Love to her embraces flie,
And not vouchsafe that even in hell we might
Pay pious Nature her unalterd right,
And give Vexation here her cruell fill?
"Should not the Queene here, to augment the ill
Of every sufferance (which her office is),
Enforce thy idoll to affoord me this?"
    '"O Sonne," she answerd, "of the race of men
The most unhappy, our most equall Queene
Will mocke no solide armes with empty shade,
Nor suffer empty shades againe t'invade
Flesh, bones, and nerves; nor will defraud the fire
Of his last dues, that, soone as spirits expire
And leave the white bone, are his native right,
When, like a dreame, the soule assumes her flight.
The light then of the living with most haste,
O Sonne, contend to: this thy little taste
Of this state is enough; and all this life
Will make a tale fit to be told thy wife."

# GEORGE CHAPMAN

99          *'Penelope fetches Ulysses' Bow'*

Cp.          And now the Queene of women had intent
Pope       To give it use; and therefore made ascent
Up all the staire's height to the chamber dore,
Whose shining leaves two bright Pilasters bore
To such a Close, when both together went,
It would resist the Aire in their consent.
The Ring she tooke then, and did draw aside
A barre that ran within, and then implide
The Key into the Locke—which gave a sound
(The Bolt then shooting) as in pasture ground
A Bull doth Low and make the valleys ring:
So loud the Locke humm'd, when it loosd his Spring,
And ope the doores flew. In she went along
The lofty chamber, that was boorded strong
With heart of Oake, which many yeares ago
The Architect did smooth and polish so
That now as then he made it freshly shine,
And tried the evennesse of it with a Line.

There stood in this roome Presses that enclos'd
Robes odoriferous, by which repos'd
The Bow was upon pins, nor from it farre
Hung the round Quiver, glittering like a Starre—
Both which her white extended hand tooke downe.
Then sate she low, and made her lap a Crowne
Of both those Reliques, which she wept to see,
And cried quite out with loving memory
Of her deare Lord: to whose worth paying then
Kinde debts enow, she left, and to the men
Vow'd to her wooing brought the crooked Bow
And shaft-receiving Quiver, that did flow
With arrowes, beating sighes up where they fell.
Then with another Chist, repleate as well
With Games won by the King of Steele and Brasse,
Her Maids attended—past whom making passe
To where her wooers were, she made her stay
Amids the faire Hall doore, and kept the ray
Of her bright count'nance hid with veyles so thin
That, though they seem'd t'expose, they let love in.

100 ### 'The Flight of the Wooers'

And now man-slaughtering Pallas tooke in hand
Her Snake-fring'd shield, and on that beam took stand
In her true forme, where Swallow-like she sat.
And then in this way of the house and that
The wooers (wounded at the heart with feare)
Fled the encounter. As in Pastures, where
Fat Herds of Oxen feede, about the field
(As if wilde madnesse their instincts impeld)
The high-fed Bullockes flye, whom in the Spring
(When dayes are long) Gadbees or Breezes sting,
Ulysses and his sonne the Flyers chac'st;
As when with crooked Beakes and Seres a cast
Of hill-bred Eagles, cast off at some game,
That yet their strengths keepe, but (put up) in flame
The Eagles' stoopes—from which along the field
The poore Foules make wing, this and that way yield
Their hard-flowne Pinions, then the clouds assay
For scape or shelter, their forlorne dismay
All spirit exhaling all wings' strength to carry
Their bodies forth; and (trust up) to the Quarry
Their Faulconers ride in, and rejoyce to see
Their Hawkes performe a flight so fervently:
So (in their flight) Ulysses with his Heire
Did stoope and cuffe the wooers, that the aire
Broke in vaste sighes—whose heads they shot and cleft,
The Pavement boyling with the soules they reft.

101 ### 'Pallas glorifies Ulysses'

And now Eurynome had bath'd the King,
Smooth'd him with Oyles, and he himselfe attir'd
In vestures royall. Her part then inspir'd
The Goddesse Pallas, deck't his head and face
With infinite beauties, gave a goodly grace
Of stature to him, a much plumper plight
Through all his body breath'd. Curles soft and bright

100 Seres] talons

75

Adorn'd his head withall, and made it show
As if the flowry Hyacinth did grow
In all his pride there, in the generall trim
Of every locke, and every curious lim.
Looke how a skilfull Artizan, well seene
In all Arts Metalline, as having beene
Taught by Minerva and the God of fire,
Doth Gold with Silver mix so that entire
They keepe their selfe distinction, and yet so
That to the Silver from the Gold doth flow
A much more artificiall luster than his owne,
And thereby to the Gold it selfe is growne
A greater glory than if wrought alone,
Both being stuck off by either's mixtion:
So did Minerva hers and his combine;
He more in Her, She more in Him did shine.


# SIR JOHN HARINGTON

## 1561–1612

### FROM THE ITALIAN OF ARIOSTO

## Orlando Furioso

102 *'Alcyna, "a famous witch or faerie", leads astray the
Hero, Rogero'*

Alcyna met them at the outer gate
And came before the rest a little space,
And with a count'nance full of high estate
Salutes Rogero with a goodly grace,
And all the other courtiers in like rate
Do bid Rogero welcome to the place
With so great showes of duetie and of love
As if some god descended from above,

Nor onely was this pallace for the sight
Most goodly, faire, and stately to behold,
But that the peoples courtsie bred delight

Which was as great as could with tongue be told.
All were of youth and beautie shining bright,
Yet to confirme this thing I dare be bold:
That faire Alcyna past the rest as farre
As doth the Sunne an other little starre.

A shape whose like in waxe tweare hard to frame
Or to expresse by skill of painters rare.
Her heare was long and yellow to the same
As might with wire of beaten gold compare.
Her lovely cheekes with shew of modest shame
With roses and with lillies painted are.
Her forhead faire and full of seemely cheare
As smoth as pullisht Ivorie doth appeare.

Within two arches of most curious fashion
Stand two black eyes that like two cleare suns shind,
Of stedie looke but apt to take compassion,
Amid which lights the naked boy and blind
Doth cast his darts that cause so many a passion
And leave a sweete and curelesse wound behind;
From thence the nose in such good sort descended
As envie knowes not how it may be mended,

Conjoynd to which in dew and comly space
Doth stand the mouth staind with Vermillion hew;
Two rowes of precious perle serve in their place
To show and shut, a lip right faire to vew.
Hence come the courteous words and ful of grace
That mollifie hard harts and make them new;
From hence proceed those smilings sweet and nice
That seeme to make an earthly paradice.

Her brests as milke, her necke as white as snow,
Her necke was round, most plum and large her brest,
Two Ivory apples seemed there to grow,
Full tender, smooth, and fittest to be prest,
They wave like seas when winds most calm doth blow;
But Argos selfe might not descerne the rest,
Yet by presumption well it might be gest
That that which was concealed was the best.

Her armes due measure of proportion bare,
Her faire white hand was to be vewed plaine,
The fingers long, the joynts so curious are
As neither knot appeard nor swelling vaine,
And full to perfect all those features rare.
The foote that to be seene doth sole remaine,
Both slender, short, little it was and round:
A finer foote might no where well be found....

\*

Now as abrode the stately courts did sound
Of trumpets, shagbot, cornets, and of flutes,
Even so within there wants no pleasing sound
Of virginals, of vials, and of lutes,
Upon the which persons not few were found
That did record their loves and loving sutes,
And in some song of love and wanton verse
Their good or ill successes did reherse.

As for the sumptuous and luxurious fare,
I thinke not they that Nynus did succeed
Nor Cleopatra faire whose riot rare
To Antonie such love and losse did breed
Might with Alcynas any way compare
Whose love did all the others farre exceed,
So deepely was she ravisht in the sight
Of this so valiant and so comly knight.

The supper done and tables tane away,
To purposes and such like toyes they went,
Each one to other secretly to say
Some word by which some pretie toy is ment.
This helpt the lovers better to bewray
Each unto other what was their intent,
For when the word was hether tost and thither
Their last conclusion was to lie togither.

These pretie kinds of amorous sports once ended,
With torches to his chamber he was brought.
On him a crew of gallant squires attended
That everie way to do him honor sought.

The chambers furniture could not be mended.
It seemd Arachne had the hangings wrought.
A banket new was made, the which once finished,
The companie by one and one diminished.

Now was Rogero couched in his bed
Betweene a paire of cambricke sheetes perfumed,
And oft he harkens with his wakefull hed
For her whose love his hart and soule consumed.
Each little noise hope of her comming bred,
Which finding false against himselfe he fumed
And curst the cause that did him so much wrong
To cause Alcina tarrie thence so long.

Sometime from bed he softly doth arise
And looke abroad if he might her espie.
Sometime he with himselfe doth thus devise:
Now she is comming, now she drawes thus nie.
Sometime for verie anger out he cries:
What meaneth she, she doth no faster hie?
Sometimes he casts least any let should be
Betweene his hand and this desired tree;

But faire Alcina, when with odors sweete
She was perfumd according to her skill,
The time once come she deemed fit and meete
When all the house were now asleepe and still,
With rich embroderd slippers on her feete,
She goes to give and take of joyes her fill
To him whom hope and feare so long assailed
Till sleepe drew on and hope and feare both failed.

Now when Astolfos successor espide
Those earthly starres, her faire and heav'nly eies,
As sulphur once inflamed cannot hide
Even so the mettell in his veines that lies
So flam'd that in the skin it scant could bide,
But of a sodaine straight he doth arise,
Leapes out of bed and her in armes embraced,
Ne would he stay till she her selfe unlaced.

So utterly impacient of all stay
That though her mantell was but cyprous light
And next upon her smocke of lawne it lay,
Yet so the champion hasted to the fight
The mantell with his furie fell away,
And now the smocke remain alone in sight,
Which smock as plaine her beauties all discloses
As doth a glasse the lillies faire and roses.

103 *'The Archangel Michael, ordered to find Silence and Discord, sets out'*

The blessed Angell not a word replies
But doth his makers holy will obay.
Foorthwith ev'n in a moment downe he flies,
And where he goes the clouds do fleet away,
But by the way he thinks and doth devise
Of ev'rie place where Silence find he may:
Though he an Angell were he could not tell
Where this same enemie of speech doth dwell.

At last he fully doth him selfe perswade
To find him in some houses of devocion
That first for life monasticall were made,
Where godly men, despisers of promocion,
Dwell far from all this worldly wicked trade
With minds abhorring flesh and fleshly motion,
Where idle words should counted be a shame
And where on ev'rie wall they write his name.

Wherefore into an Abbey he doth go,
And makes no question Silence there to find
And Peace and Charitie and Love also
And lowly thoughts and well contented mind,
But soone he was aware it was not so.
All contrarie their humors were enclind,
For Silence in that Abbey doth not host:
His name was onely writ upon a post.

Nor Quietnesse, nor Humblenesse, nor Peace,
Nor Charitie, nor godly love was here.

They wer somtimes, but now those times do cease.
Now Covetise and Ease and Belly chere,
Pride, Envie, Slouth, and Anger so increase,
That Silence banisht is and comes not nere.
With wonder great the Angell them doth vew
And findeth Discord in this cursed crew.

*

He knew her by her weed of sundrie hew,
All patcht with infinit unequall lists.
Her skin in sundrie places naked vew
At divers rents and cuts, he may that lists.
Her haire was gray and red and blacke and blue
And hard and soft; in laces some she twists;
Some hangeth down; upright some standeth staring
As if each haire with other had bene squaring.

Her lap was full of writs and of citations,
Of processes, of actions and arrests,
Of bill, of answers, and of replications
In courts of Delegats and of Requests,
To grieve the simple sort with great vexations.
She had resorting to her as her guests,
Attending on her circuits and her journeys,
Scriv'ners and clarks, and lawyers and atturneys.

104 '*Ariosto celebrates the Martyrdom of Isabella at the
Hands of Rodomont, King of Algiers*'

Go soule, go sweetest soule for ever blest,
So may my verse please those whom I desire,
As my poore Muse shall ever do her best
As farre as pen can paint and speech aspire,
That thy just prayses may be plaine exprest
To future times. Go soule to heaven or hyer,
And if my verse can graunt to thee this chartir,
Thou shalt be calld of chastitie the Martir.

At this her deed so straunge and admirable
He that above all heav'ns doth ay remaine
Lookt down and said it was more comendable

Then hers for whom Tarquino lost his raigne,
And strait an ordinaunce inviolable
Ay to be kept on earth he doth ordaine,
And thus he said: ev'n by my selfe I sweare,
Whose powre heav'n, earth, sprits, men, and Angels feare,

That for her sake that dy'd of this name last,
Who ever shall hereafter beare that name
Shal be both wise and continent and chast,
Of faultlesse manners and of spotlesse fame;
Let writers strive to make their glorie last
And oft in prose and verse record the same;
Let Hellicon, Pindus, Parnassus hill
Sound Isabella, Isabella still.

# CHRISTOPHER MARLOWE

## 1564–1593

### FROM THE LATIN OF OVID

105                    *Elegies*, Book I, 5

In summers heate and mid-time of the day
To rest my limbes upon a bed I lay,
One window shut, the other open stood,
Which gave such light as twincles in a wood,
Like twilight glimps at setting of the Sunne
Or night being past, and yet not day begunne.
Such light to shamefast maidens must be showne,
Where they may sport, and seeme to bee unknowne.
Then came Corinna in a long loose gowne,
Her white neck hid with tresses hanging downe:
Resembling fayre Semiramis going to bed
Or Layis of a thousand wooers sped.
I snacht her gowne, being thin, the harme was small,
Yet striv'd she to be covered there withall.
And striving thus as one that would be cast,

105 cast] chaste

Betray'd her selfe, and yelded at the last.
Starke naked as she stood before mine eye,
Not one wen in her body could I spie.
What armes and shoulders did I touch and see,
How apt her breasts were to be prest by me?
How smooth a belly under her wast saw I?
How large a legge, and what a lustie thigh?
To leave the rest, all lik'd me passing well,
I cling'd her naked body, downe she fell,
Judge you the rest: being tirde she bad me kisse,
Jove send me more such after-noones as this.

106                 *Elegies*, Book I, 13

Now ore the sea from her old Love comes she
That drawes the day from heavens cold axletree.
Aurora whither slidest thou? downe again
And birdes for Memnon yearely shal be slaine.
Now in her tender armes I sweetly bide,
If ever, now well lies she by my side.
The aire is cold, and sleepe is sweetest now
And birdes send forth shrill notes from every bough:
Whither runst thou, that men, and women love not?
Hold in thy rosy horses that they move not.
Ere thou rise, starres teach sea-men where to saile,
But when thou commest they of their courses faile.
Poore travailers though tierd, rise at thy sight,
And souldiours make them ready to the fight.
The painefull hinde by thee to field is sent,
Slowe Oxen early in the yoake are pent.
Thou cousenst boyes of sleepe, and doest betray them
To Pedants that with cruell lashes pay them.
Thou mak'st the surety of the Lawyer runne,
That with one word hath nigh himselfe undone.
The Lawyer and the client hate thy view,
Both whom thou raisest up to toyle anew.
By thy meanes women of their rest are bard,
Thou setst their labouring hands to spin and card.
All could I beare, but that the wench should rise
Who can endure save him with whom none lyes?

How oft wisht I, night would not give thee place,
Nor morning starres shunne thy uprising face.
How oft that either winde would breake thy coach,
Or steeds might fall forc'd with thick clouds approach.
Whether goest thou hatefull Nimph? Memnon the elfe
Receiv'd his cole-black colour from thy selfe.
Say that thy love with Cæphalus were not knowne,
Then thinkest thou thy loose life is not showne?
Would Tithon might but talke of thee a while,
Not one in heaven should be more base and vile.
Thou leavest his bed, because hee's faint through age,
And early mountest thy hatefull carriage.
But heldst thou in thine armes some Cephalus,
Then wouldst thou cry, stay night and runne not thus.
Doest punish me, because yeares make him waine?
I did not bid thee wed an aged swaine.
The Moone sleepes with Endymion every day,
Thou art as faire as she, then kisse and play.
Jove that thou shoulst not hast but waite his leasure,
Made two nights one to finish up his pleasure.
I chid no more, she blusht and therefore heard me,
Yet lingered not the day, but morning scard me.

107                    *Elegies*, Book II, 1

I Ovid Poet of my wantonnesse,
Borne at Peligny, to write more addresse.
So Cupid wills, farre hence be the severe,
You are unapt my looser lines to heare.
Let Maydes whom hot desire to husbands leade,
And rude boyes toucht with unknowne love me reade,
That some youth hurt as I am with loves bowe
His owne flames best aquainted signes may knowe,
And long admiring say, by what meanes learnd
Hath this same Poet my sad chaunce discernd?
I durst the great celestiall battells tell,
Hundred-hand Gyges, and had done it well,

scard] scared

107 Peligny] Paeligni—a tribe, not a place

With earthes revenge and how Olimpus toppe
High Ossa bore, mount Pelion up to proppe.
Jove and Joves thunderbolts I had in hand
Which for his heaven fell on the Gyants band.
My wench her dore shut, Joves affares I left,
Even Jove himselfe out off my wit was reft.
Pardon me Jove, thy weapons ayde me nought,
Her shut gates greater lightning then thyne brought.
Toyes, and light Elegies my darts I tooke,
Quickly soft words hard dores wide open strooke.
Verses reduce the horned bloudy moone
And call the sunnes white horses backe at noone.
Snakes leape by verse from caves of broken mountaines
And turned streames run back-ward to their fountaines.
Verses ope dores, and lockes put in the poast,
Although of oake, to yeeld to verses boast.
What helpes it me of fierce Achill to sing?
What good to me wil either Ajax bring?
Or he who war'd and wand'red twenty yeare?
Or wofull Hector whom wilde jades did teare?
But when I praise a pretty wenches face
Shee in requitall doth me oft imbrace.
A great reward: Heroes, O famous names
Farewel, your favour nought my minde inflames.
Wenches apply your faire lookes to my verse
Which golden love doth unto me rehearse.

108                    *Elegies*, Book III, 6

Either she was foule, or her attire was bad,
Or she was not the wench I wisht t'have had.
Idly I lay with her, as if I lov'd not,
And like a burthen griev'd the bed that mov'd not.
Though both of us perform'd our true intent,
Yet could I not cast anckor where I meant.
She on my neck her Ivory armes did throwe,
Her armes farre whiter, then the Sythian snow.
And eagerly she kist me with her tongue,
And under mine her wanton thigh she flung.
Yea, and she soothd me up, and calld me sire,
And usde all speech that might provoke, and stirre.

85

Yet like as if cold Hemlock I had drunke,
It mocked me, hung downe the head, and sunke.
Like a dull Cipher, or rude block I lay,
Or shade, or body was I who can say?
What will my age do, age I cannot shunne,
When in my prime my force is spent and done?
I blush, that being youthfull, hot, and lustie,
I prove neither youth nor man, but old and rustie.
Pure rose she, like a Nunne to sacrifice,
Or one that with her tender brother lyes.
Yet boorded I the golden Chie twise,
And Libas, and the white cheekt Pitho thrice.
Corinna crav'd it in a summers night,
And nine sweete bowts we had before day-light.
What, wast my limbs through some Thessalian charmes?
May spells, and drugges do silly soules such harmes?
With virgin waxe hath some imbast my joynts?
And pierc'd my liver with sharpe needles points?
Charmes change corne to grasse and make it die.
By charmes are running springs and fountaines dry.
By charmes mast drops from oakes, from vines grapes fal,
And fruite from trees when ther's no winde at all.
Why might not then my sinewes be inchaunted,
And I growe faint as with some spirit haunted?
To this adde shame: shame to performe it quaild me
And was the second cause why vigour failde me.
My idle thoughts delighted her no more,
Then did the robe or garment which she wore.
Yet might her touch make youthfull Pylius fire
And Tithon livelier then his years require.
Even her I had, and she had me in vaine,
What might I crave more, if I aske againe?
I thinke the great gods griev'd they had bestow'd
The benefit: which lewdly I for-slow'd.
I wisht to be receiv'd in, in I get me,
To kisse, I kisse: to lie with her, she let me.
Why was I blest? why made King to refuse it?
Chuffe-like had I not gold and could not use it?
So in a spring thrives he that told so much,
And lookes upon the fruits he cannot touch.
Hath any rose so from a fresh yong maide,
As she might straight have gone to church and praide?

Well I beleeve, she kist not as she should,
Nor us'd the sleight and cunning which she could,
Huge oakes, hard adamants might she have moved,
And with sweet words cause deafe rocks to have loved.
Worthy she was to move both gods and men,
But neither was I man nor lived then.
Can deafe eare take delight when Phæmius sings?
Or Thamiras in curious painted things?
What sweete thought is there but I had the same?
And one gave place still as an other came.
Yet not-withstanding like one dead it lay,
Drouping more then a rose puld yester-day.
Now when he should not jette, he boults upright,
And craves his taske, and seekes to be at fight.
Lie downe with shame, and see thou stirre no more,
Seeing thou wouldst deceive me as before.
Thou cousenest me: by thee surpriz'd am I,
And bide sore losse with endlesse infamy.
Nay more, the wench did not disdaine a whit,
To take it in her hand, and play with it.
But when she sawe it would by no meanes stand,
But still droupt downe, regarding not her hand,
Why mockst thou me? she cryed, or being ill
Who bad thee lie downe heere against thy will?
Either th'art witcht with bloud of frogs newe dead
Or jaded camst thou from some others bed.
With that her loose gowne on, from me she cast her,
In skipping out her naked feete much grac'd her.
And least her maide should know of this disgrace,
To cover it, spilt water on the place.

109      *Elegies*, Book III, 13

Seeing thou art faire, I barre not thy false playing,
But let not me poore soule know of thy straying.
Nor do I give thee counsell to live chaste,
But that thou wouldst dissemble, when 'tis paste.
She hath not trod awry, that doth deny it.
Such as confesse have lost their good names by it.
What madnesse ist to tell nights pranckes by day?
And hidden secrets openly to bewray?

The strumpet with the stranger will not doo,
Before the roome be cleere, and dore put too.
Will you make ship-wrack of your honest name,
And let the world be witnesse of the same?
Be more advisde, walke as a puritan,
And I shall thinke you chaste, do what you can.
Slip still, onely deny it, when 'tis done,
And before folke immodest speeches shunne.
The bed is for lascivious toyings meete,
There use all tricks, and tread shame under feete.
When you are up, and drest, be sage and grave,
And in the bed hide all the faults you have.
Be not asham'de to strip you being there,
And mingle thighes yours ever mine to beare.
There in your Rosie lips my tongue in-tombe,
Practise a thousand sports when there you come.
Forbeare no wanton words you there would speake,
And with your pastime let the bed-stead creake.
But with your robes put on an honest face,
And blush, and seeme as you were full of grace.
Deceive all, let me erre, and thinke I am right,
And like a Wittal thinke thee voide of slight.
Why see I lines so oft receiv'd, and given?
This bed and that by tumbling made uneven?
Like one start up your haire tost and displac'd,
And with a wantons tooth your neck new rac'd?
Graunt this, that what you doe I may not see,
If you weigh not ill speeches, yet weigh mee.
My soule fleetes, when I thinke what you have done,
And thorough every veine doth cold bloud runne.
Then thee whom I must love, I hate in vaine,
And would be dead, but dead with thee remaine.
Ile not sift much, but holde thee soone excusde,
Say but thou wert injuriously accusde.
Though while the deed be dooing you be tooke,
And I see when you ope the two leav'd booke,
Sweare I was blinde, deny, if you be wise,
And I will trust your words more then mine eyes.

Wittall] cuckold

88

# CHRISTOPHER MARLOWE

From him that yeelds the palme is quickly got,
Teach but your tongue to say, I did it not,
And being justifide by two words thinke,
The cause acquits you not, but I that winke.


# THOMAS UNDERDOWNE
*fl.* 1566–1587

### FROM THE LATIN OF OVID

110                      from *Invective Against Ibis*

While Thracians shal with arrowes war, Iaziges with bowe:
While Ganges shalbe luke warme felt, and Ister colde as snowe.
While mountaines hye great trees shal bear, in fields while grasse
    shal grow:
While Tibris shal through Tuscan land with any water flow.
I wyl make warres with thee, not death shall bryng my wrath to
    ende:
But wyll geve weapons to my ghostes against thy sprytes to sende.
And then also when into ayre, my selfe shall turned be:
My lyvelesse shadow shall with hate, pursue the gostes of thee.
Then also myndefull of thy deedes, I wyll thy shadowes chase:
And I a bony forme wylbe, with thee in every place.
Whether I by yeares consumed long (which I would not) shall dye:
Or else shalbe by force of hand resolved by and by.
Or whether tost amyd the Seas, shall suffer wrack with greefe:
And Fyshes strange upon my corse, shall seeke to fynde releefe.
Or whether that the Ravens shall, make of my fleshe theire foode:
Or greedy Wolves shal have their lyps embrewed with my blood.
Or whether some may wel vouchsafe, me under ground to laye:
Or cast me into flaming fyre, when lyfe is gone away.
What so I bee, I mynde to come from Hell, that ugly place:
And then with colde (revenging) hands, wyll scratch thee by the
    face.
Thou waking shalt me see, with gostes, my selfe Ile secret keepe:
Then wyll I seeme t'appeare to thee, to wake thee from thy sleepe.

---

110 Iaziges] a tribe bordering on Thrace    Ister] the Danube

And last what so thou dost, before thy face and eyes, Ile flee:
And wyll complaine, so that no where, in quiet thou shalt bee.
The cruell strokes wherewith I wyll thee smite shal sownd againe:
And hellish brandes before thee styll, shall smoke unto thy payne.
Alive the furyes shall the vexe, and after Death also:
So that thy lyfe shall shorter be, than either payne or wo.
To thee shal nether Death rytes hap, nor frendly teares befall:
Thy body shalbe cast abroade, bewayled nought at all.
Thou shalt with cruell hang mans hand be drawne to all mens
    joye:
The hooke hard fastened to thy bones, unto thy more annoye.
Also the fyre that all consumes, from thee alone shall flye:
The just earth shal not grant thy corps, a place wherein to lye.
The Ravens shall with crooked beak, and talons draw a part
Thy entrayles, and the greedy Dogs, devoure thy faithlesse heart.
And though this praise do make thee prowde, that Wolves insatiate:
About thy caryan corps shall have, continuall debate.


# THOMAS CAMPION

## 1567–1619

### IMITATED FROM THE LATIN OF CATULLUS

III                          *Carmina*, V

Cp.          My sweetest Lesbia let us live and love,
Ralegh       And though the sager sort our deedes reprove,
Jonson       Let us not way them: heav'ns great lampes doe dive
Crashaw      Into their west, and strait againe revive,
Wordsworth   But soone as once set is our little light,
             Then must we sleepe one ever-during night.

             If all would lead their lives in love like mee,
             Then bloudie swords and armour should not be,
             No drum nor trumpet peaceful sleepes should move,
             Unles alar'me came from the campe of love:
             But fooles do live, and wast their little light,
             And seeke with paine their ever-during night.

When timely death my life and fortune ends,
Let not my hearse be vext with mourning friends,
But let all lovers rich in triumph come,
And with sweet pastimes grace my happie tombe;
And Lesbia close up thou my little light,
And crowne with love my ever-during night.

112 ## *Carmina*, VIII

Harden now thy tyred hart, with more then flinty rage;
Ne'er let her false teares henceforth thy constant griefe asswage.
Once true happy dayes thou saw'st when shee stood firme and
    kinde,
Both as one then liv'd and held one eare, one tongue, one
    minde:
But now those bright houres be fled, and never may returne;
What then remaines but her untruths to mourne?

Silly Traytresse, who shall now thy carelesse tresses place?
Who thy pretty talke supply, whose eare thy musicke grace?
Who shall thy bright eyes admire? what lips triumph with thine?
Day by day who'll visit thee and say 'th'art onely mine'?
Such a time there was, God wot, but such shall never be:
Too oft, I feare, thou wilt remember me.

IMITATED FROM THE LATIN OF PROPERTIUS

113 ## *Carmina*, II. 28

When thou must home to shades of under ground,
And there ariv'd, a newe admired guest,
The beauteous spirits do ingirt thee round,
White Iope, blith Hellen, and the rest,
To heare the stories of thy finisht love
From that smoothe toong whose musicke hell can move;

Then wilt thou speake of banqueting delights,
Of masks and revels which sweete youth did make,
Of Turnies and great challenges of knights,
And all these triumphes for thy beauties sake:
When thou hast told these honours done to thee,
Then tell, O tell, how thou didst murther me.

# THE AUTHORIZED VERSION OF
# THE BIBLE (1611)

## FROM THE HEBREW

### 114 *2 Samuel 1 : 19–27: David lamenteth the death of Jonathan*

The beauty of Israel is slaine upon thy high places: how are the mightie fallen!

Tell it not in Gath, publish it not in the streetes of Askelon: lest the daughters of the Philistines rejoyce, lest the daughters of the uncircumcised triumph.

Yee mountaines of Gilboa, let there bee no dewe, neither let there be raine upon you, nor fields of offerings: for there the shield of the mightie is vilely cast away, the shield of Saul, as though hee had not beene annointed with oile.

From the blood of the slaine, from the fat of the mightie, the bow of Jonathan turned not backe, and the sword of Saul returned not emptie.

Saul and Jonathan were lovely and pleasant in their lives, and in their death they were not divided: they were swifter then Eagles, they were stronger then Lions.

Yee daughters of Israel, weepe over Saul, who clothed you in scarlet, with other delights, who put on ornaments of golde upon your apparell.

How are the mightie fallen in the midst of the battell! O Jonathan, thou wast slaine in thine high places.

I am distressed for thee, my brother Jonathan, very pleasant hast thou been unto mee: thy love to mee was wonderfull, passing the love of women.

How are the mightie fallen, and the weapons of warre perished!

## *Job 3:3–26: Job curseth the day, and services of his birth.*

Let the day perish, wherein I was borne, and the night in which it was said, There is a man-childe conceived.

Let that day bee darkenesse, let not God regard it from above, neither let the light shine upon it.

Let darkenes and the shadowe of death staine it, let a cloud dwell upon it, let the blacknes of the day terrifie it.

As for that night, let darkenesse seaze upon it, let it not be joyned unto the dayes of the yeere, let it not come into the number of the moneths.

Loe, let that night be solitarie, let no joyfull voice come therein.

Let them curse it that curse the day, who are ready to raise up their mourning.

Let the starres of the twilight thereof be darke, let it looke for light, but have none, neither let it see the dawning of the day:

Because it shut not up the doores of my mothers wombe, nor hid sorrowe from mine eyes.

Why died I not from the wombe? why did I not give up the ghost when I came out of the bellie?

Why did the knees prevent mee? or why the breasts, that I should sucke?

For now should I have lien still and beene quiet, I should have slept; then had I bene at rest,

With Kings and counsellers of the earth, which built desolate places for themselves,

Or with Princes that had golde, who filled their houses with silver:

Or as an hidden untimely birth, I had not bene; as infants which never saw light.

There the wicked cease from troubling: and there the wearie be at rest.

There the prisoners rest together, they heare not the voice of the oppressour.

The small and great are there, and the servant is free from his master.

Wherefore is light given to him that is in misery, and life unto the bitter in soule?

Which long for death, but it commeth not, and dig for it more then for hid treasures:

Which rejoice exceedingly, and are glad when they can finde the grave?

Why is light given to a man, whose way is hid, and whom God hath hedged in?

For my sighing commeth before I eate, and my roarings are powred out like the waters.

For the thing which I greatly feared is come upon me, and that which I was afraid of, is come unto me.

I was not in safetie, neither had I rest, neither was I quiet: yet trouble came.

116                                    *Job 14*

Man that is borne of a woman, is of few dayes, and full of trouble.

Hee commeth forth like a flower, and is cut downe: he fleeth also, as a shaddow and continueth not.

And doest thou open thine eies upon such an one, and bringest me into judgment with thee?

Who can bring a cleane thing out of an uncleane? not one.

Seeing his daies are determined, the number of his moneths are with thee, thou hast appointed his bounds that he cannot passe.

Turne from him that hee may rest, till he shall accomplish, as an hireling, his day.

For there is hope of a tree, if it be cut downe, that it will sprout againe, and that the tender branch thereof will not cease.

Though the roote thereof waxe old in the earth, and the stocke thereof die in the ground:

Yet through the sent of water it will bud, and bring forth boughes like a plant.

But man dyeth, and wasteth away; yea, man giveth up the ghost, and where is hee?

As the waters faile from the sea, and the floud decayeth and dryeth up:

So man lyeth downe, and riseth not, till the heavens be no more, they shall not awake; nor bee raised out of their sleepe.

O that thou wouldest hide mee in the grave, that thou wouldest keepe me secret, untill thy wrath bee past, that thou wouldest appoint me a set time, and remember me.

If a man die, shall he live againe? All the dayes of my appointed time will I waite, till my change come.

Thou shalt call, and I will answer thee: thou wilt have a desire to the worke of thine hands.

For nowe thou numbrest my steppes, doest thou not watch over my sinne?

My transgression is sealed up in a bagge, and thou sowest up mine iniquitie.

And surely the mountaine falling commeth to nought: and the rocke is removed out of his place.

The waters weare the stones, thou washest away the things which growe out of the dust of the earth, and thou destroyest the hope of man.

Thou prevailest for ever against him, and hee passeth: thou changest his countenance, and sendest him away.

His sonnes come to honour, and he knoweth it not; and they are brought lowe, but he perceiveth it not of them.

But his flesh upon him shall have paine, and his soule within him shall mourne.

117     *Job 38: 'God answers Job'*

Then the Lord answered Job out of the whirlewind, and sayd,

Who is this that darkneth counsell by words without knowledge?

Gird up nowe thy loines like a man; for I will demaund of thee, and answere thou me.

Where wast thou when I layd the foundations of the earth? declare, if thou hast understanding.

Who hath layd the measures thereof, if thou knowest? or who hath stretched the line upon it?

Whereupon are the foundations thereof fastened? or who layd the corner stone thereof?

When the morning starres sang together, and all the sonnes of God shouted for joy.

Or who shut up the sea with doores, when it brake foorth as if it had issued out of the wombe?

When I made the cloud the garment thereof, and thicke darkness a swadling band for it,

And brake up for it my decreed place, and set barres and doores,

And said, Hitherto shalt thou come, but no further: and heere shall thy proud waves be stayed.

Hast thou commaunded the morning since thy daies? and caused the day-spring to know his place,

That it might take hold of the endes of the earth, that the wicked might be shaken out of it?

It is turned as clay to the seale, and they stand as a garment.

And from the wicked their light is withholden, and the high arme shalbe broken.

Hast thou entred into the springs of the sea? or hast thou walked in the search of the depth?

Have the gates of death bene opened unto thee? or hast thou seene the doores of the shadow of death?

Hast thou perceived the breadth of the earth? Declare if thou knowest it all.

Where is the way where light dwelleth? and as for darknesse, where is the place thereof?

That thou shouldest take it to the bound thereof, and that thou shouldest know the pathes to the house thereof.

Knowest thou it, because thou wast then borne? or because the number of thy daies is great?

Hast thou entred into the treasures of the snowe? or hast thou seene the treasures of the haile,

Which I have reserved against the time of trouble, against the day of battaile and warre?

By what way is the light parted? which scattereth the East wind upon the earth.

Who hath divided a water-course for the overflowing of waters? or a way for the lightning of thunder,

To cause it to raine on the earth, where no man is: on the wildernesse wherein there is no man?

To satisfie the desolate and waste ground, and to cause the bud of the tender herbe to spring forth.

Hath the raine a father? or who hath begotten the drops of dew?

Out of whose wombe came the yce? and the hoary frost of heaven, who hath gendred it?

The waters are hid as with a stone, and the face of the deepe is frozen.

Canst thou bind the sweete influences of Pleiades? or loose the bands of Orion?

Canst thou bring forth Mazzaroth in his season, or canst thou guide Arcturus with his sonnes?

Knowest thou the ordinances of heaven? canst thou set the dominion thereof in the earth?

Canst thou lift up thy voice to the cloudes, that abundance of waters may cover thee?

Canst thou send lightnings, that they may goe, and say unto thee, Here we are?

Who hath put wisedome in the inward parts? or who hath given understanding to the heart?

Who can number the cloudes in wisedome? or who can stay the bottles of heaven,

When the dust groweth into hardnesse, and the clods cleave fast together?

Wilt thou hunt the pray for the lyon? or fill the appetite of the young lyons,

When they couch in their dennes, and abide in the covert to lie in waite?

Who provideth for the raven his foode? when his young ones cry unto God, they wander for lacke of meate.

118                           *Job 39*

Knowest thou the time when the wild goates of the rocke bring forth? or canst thou marke when the hindes doe calve?

Canst thou number the moneths that they fulfill? or knowest thou the time when they bring forth?

They bowe themselves, they bring forth their young ones, they cast out their sorrowes.

Their yong ones are in good liking, they grow up with corne: they go forth, and returne not unto them.

Who hath sent out the wild asse free? or who hath loosed the bands of the wild asse?

Whose house I have made the wildernesse, and the barren lande his dwellings.

He scorneth the multitude of the citie, neither regardeth he the crying of the driver.

The range of the mountaines is his pasture, and hee searcheth after every greene thing.

Will the Unicorne be willing to serve thee? or abide by thy cribbe?

Canst thou binde the Unicorne with his band in the furrow? or will he harrow the valleyes after thee?

Wilt thou trust him because his strength is great? or wilt thou leave thy labour to him?

Wilt thou beleeve him that hee will bring home thy seed? and gather it into thy barne?

97

Gavest thou the goodly wings unto the peacocks, or wings and feathers unto the Ostrich?

Which leaveth her egges in the earth, and warmeth them in dust,

And forgetteth that the foot may crush them, or that the wilde beast may breake them.

She is hardened against her yong ones, as though they were not hers: her labour is in vaine without feare.

Because God hath deprived her of wisedome, neither hath he imparted to her understanding.

What time she lifteth up her selfe on high, she scorneth the horse and his rider.

Hast thou given the horse strength? hast thou clothed his necke with thunder?

Canst thou make him afraid as a grashopper? the glory of his nostrils is terrible.

He paweth in the valley, and rejoyceth in his strength: hee goeth on to meet the armed men.

He mocketh at feare, and is not affrighted; neither turneth he backe from the sword.

The quiver ratleth against him, the glittering speare and the shield.

He swalloweth the ground with fiercenesse and rage: neither beleeveth he that it is the sound of the trumpet.

He saith among the trumpets, Ha, ha: and he smelleth the battaile afarre off, the thunder of the captaines, and the shouting.

Doeth the hawke flie by thy wisedome, and stretch her wings toward the South?

Doeth the Eagle mount up at thy commaund? and make her nest on high?

She dwelleth and abideth on the rocke, upon the cragge of the rocke, and the strong place.

From thence she seeketh the pray, and her eyes behold a farre off.

Her yong ones also suck up blood: and where the slaine are, there is she.

119 *Job 40*

Moreover the Lord answered Job, and said,

Shall hee that contendeth with the Almightie, instruct him? he that reproveth God, let him answere it.

Then Job answered the LORD, and said,

Behold, I am vile, what shall I answere thee? I will lay my hand upon my mouth.

Once have I spoken, but I will not answere: yea twise, but I will proceed no further.

Then answered the LORD unto Job out of the whirlewinde, and said:

Gird up thy loynes now like a man: I will demaund of thee, and declare thou unto me,

Wilt thou also disanul my judgement? wilt thou condemne mee, that thou mayest be righteous?

Hast thou an arme like God? or canst thou thunder with a voyce like him?

Decke thy selfe now with Majestie, and excellencie, and aray thy selfe with glory, and beautie.

Cast abroad the rage of thy wrath: and behold every one that is proud, and abase him.

Looke on every one that is proud, and bring him low: and tread downe the wicked in their place.

Hide them in the dust together, and binde their faces in secret.

Then will I also confesse unto thee, that thine owne right hand can save thee.

Beholde now Behemoth which I made with thee, hee eateth grasse as an oxe.

Loe now, his strength is in his loynes, and his force is in the navell of his belly.

Hee moveth his taile like a Cedar: the sinews of his stones are wrapt together.

His bones are as strong pieces of brasse: his bones are like barres of iron.

Hee is the chiefe of the wayes of God: he that made him, can make his sword to approach unto him.

Surely the mountaines bring him foorth foode: where all the beasts of the field play.

He lieth under the shady trees, in the covert of the reede, and fennes.

The shady trees cover him with their shaddow: the willowes of the brooke compasse him about.

Behold, he drinketh up a river, and hasteth not: he trusteth that he can draw up Jordan into his mouth.

He taketh it with his eyes: his nose pearceth through snares.

Canst thou draw out Leviathan with an hooke? or his tongue with a corde which thou lettest downe?

Canst thou put an hooke into his nose? or bore his jawe through with a thorne?

Will he make many supplications unto thee? will he speake soft words unto thee?

Will he make a covenant with thee? wilt thou take him for a servant for ever?

Wilt thou play with him as with a birde? wilt thou binde him for thy maydens?

Shall the companions make a banquet of him? shall they part him among the merchants?

Canst thou fill his skinne with barbed irons? or his head with fish-speares?

Lay thine hand upon him, remember the battell: doe no more.

Behold, the hope of him is in vaine: shall not one be cast downe even at the sight of him?

None is so fierce that dare stirre him up: who then is able to stand before me?

Who hath prevented me that I should repay him? whatsoever is under the whole heaven, is mine.

I will not conceale his parts, nor his power, nor his comely proportion.

Who can discover the face of his garment? or who can come to him, with his double bridle?

Who can open the doores of his face? his teeth are terrible round about.

His scales are his pride, shut up together as with a close seale.

One is so neere to another, that no ayre can come betweene them.

They are joyned one to another, they sticke together, that they cannot be sundred.

By his neesings a light doth shine, and his eyes are like the eye-liddes of the morning.

Out of his mouth goe burning lampes, and sparkes of fire leape out.

---

neesings] i.e. sneezings. The spray breathed through his nostrils flashes in the sunlight.

Out of his nostrels goeth smoke, as out of a seething pot or caldron.

His breath kindleth coales, and a flame goeth out of his mouth.

In his necke remaineth strength, and sorrowe is turned into joy before him.

The flakes of his flesh are joyned together: they are firme in themselves, they cannot be moved.

His heart is as firme as a stone, yea as hard as a peece of the nether mil-stone.

When he rayseth up himselfe, the mightie are afraid: by reason of breakings they purifie themselves.

The sword of him that layeth at him cannot hold: the speare, the dart, nor the habergeon.

He esteemeth iron as straw, and brasse as rotten wood.

The arrow cannot make him flee: sling-stones are turned with him into stubble.

Darts are counted as stubble: he laugheth at the shaking of a speare.

Sharpe stones are under him: he spreadeth sharpe pointed things upon the mire.

He maketh the deepe to boyle like a pot: hee maketh the sea like a pot of oyntment.

Hee maketh a path to shine after him; one would thinke the deepe to bee hoarie.

Upon earth there is not his like: who is made without feare.

He beholdeth all high things: he is a king over all the children of pride.

121                    *Ecclesiastes 3:1–8*

To every thing there is a season, and a time to every purpose under the heaven.

A time to be borne, and a time to die: a time to plant, and a time to pluck up that which is planted.

A time to kill, and a time to heale: a time to breake downe, and a time to build up.

A time to weepe, and a time to laugh: a time to mourne, and a time to dance.

A time to cast away stones, and a time to gather stones together: a time to imbrace, and a time to refraine from imbracing.

120 breakings] later emended to consternation

A time to get, and a time to lose: a time to keepe, and a time to cast away.

A time to rent, and a time to sow: a time to keepe silence, and a time to speake.

A time to love, and a time to hate: a time of warre, and a time of peace.

122          *Ecclesiastes 11:1–8*

Cast thy bread upon the waters: for thou shalt find it after many dayes.

Give a portion to seven and also to eight; for thou knowest not what evill shall be upon the earth.

If the clouds be full of raine, they emptie themselves upon the earth: and if the tree fall toward the South, or toward the North, in the place where the tree falleth, there it shall be.

He that observeth the wind, shall not sow: and hee that regardeth the clouds, shall not reape.

As thou knowest not what is the way of the spirit, nor how the bones doe growe in the wombe of her that is with child: even so thou knowest not the workes of God who maketh all.

In the morning sowe thy seede, and in the evening withhold not thine hand: for thou knowest not whether shall prosper, either this or that, or whether they both shall be alike good.

Truly the light is sweet, and a pleasant thing is it for the eyes to behold the sunne.

But if a man live many yeeres, and rejoyce in them all; yet let him remember the dayes of darkenesse, for they shall be many. All that commeth is vanitie.

123          *Ecclesiastes 12: 1–8*

Remember now thy Creatour in the days of thy youth, while the evil daies come not, nor the yeeres drawe nigh, when thou shalt say, I have no pleasure in them:

While the Sunne, or the light, or the moone, or the starres be not darkened, nor the cloudes returne after the raine:

In the day when the keepers of the house shall tremble, and the strong men shall bowe themselves, and the grinders cease, because they are fewe, and those that looke out of the windowes be darkened:

And the doores shal be shut in the streets, when the sound of the grinding is low, and he shall rise up at the voice of the bird, and all the daughters of musicke shall be brought low.

Also when they shalbe afraid of that which is high, and feares shall bee in the way, and the Almond tree shall flourish, and the grashopper shall be a burden, and desire shall faile: because man goeth to his long home, and the mourners goe about the streets:

Or ever the silver corde be loosed, or the golden bowle be broken, or the pitcher be broken at the fountaine, or the wheele broken at the cisterne.

Then shall the dust returne to the earth as it was: and the spirit shall returne unto God who gave it.

Vanitie of vanities (saith the preacher) all is vanitie.

## 124 *The Song of Solomon 1*

The song of songs, which is Solomons.

Let him kisse mee with the kisses of his mouth: for thy Love is better then wine.

Because of the savour of thy good ointments, thy name is as ointment powred forth, therefore doe the virgins love thee.

Draw me, we will runne after thee: the king hath brought me into his chambers: we will be glad and rejoyce in thee, we wil remember thy love more then wine: the upright love thee.

I am blacke, but comely, (O ye daughters of Jerusalem) as the tents of Kedar, as the curtaines of Solomon.

Looke not upon me because I am blacke, because the Sunne hath looked upon me: my mothers children were angry with me, they made me the keeper of the vineyards, but mine owne vineyard have I not kept.

Tell me, (O thou whom my soule loveth) where thou feedest, where thou makest thy flocke to rest at noone: for why should I be as one that turneth aside by the flockes of thy companions?

If thou know not (O thou fairest among women) goe thy way forth by the footsteps of the flocke, and feede thy kiddes beside the shepheards tents.

I have compared thee, O my love, to a company of horses in Pharaohs chariots.

Thy cheekes are comely with rowes of jewels, thy necke with chaines of golde.

Wee will make thee borders of golde, with studdes of silver.

While the king sitteth at his table, my spikenard sendeth foorth the smell thereof.

A bundle of myrrhe is my welbeloved unto me; he shall lie all night betwixt my breasts.

My beloved is unto me, as a cluster of Camphire in the vineyards of Engedi.

Behold, thou art faire, my love: behold, thou art faire, thou hast doves eyes.

Behold, thou art faire, my beloved; yea pleasant: also our bedde is greene.

The beames of our house are Cedar, and our rafters of firre.

125        *The Song of Solomon 2*

I am the rose of Sharon, and the lillie of the valleys.

As the lillie among thornes, so is my love among the daughters.

As the apple tree among the trees of the wood, so is my beloved among the sonnes. I sate downe under his shadow with great delight, and his fruit was sweete to my taste.

Hee brought me to the banketting house, and his banner over mee, was love.

Stay me with flagons, comfort me with apples, for I am sicke of love.

His left hand is under my head, and his right hand doeth imbrace me.

I charge you, O ye daughters of Jerusalem, by the Roes, and by the hindes of the field, that ye stirre not up, nor awake my love, till she please.

The voice of my beloved! behold! hee commeth leaping upon the mountaines, skipping upon the hils.

My beloved is like a Roe, or a young Hart: behold, he standeth behind our wall, he looketh foorth at the windowe, shewing himselfe through the lattesse.

My beloved spake, and said unto me, Rise up, my Love, my faire one, and come away.

For loe, the winter is past, the raine is over, and gone.

The flowers appeare on the earth, the time of the singing of birds is come, and the voice of the turtle is heard in our land.

The fig tree putteth foorth her greene figs, and the vines with the tender grape give a good smell. Arise, my love, my faire one, and come away.

O my dove! that art in the clefts of the rocke, in the secret places of the staires: let me see thy countenance, let me heare thy voice, for sweet is thy voice, and thy countenance is comely.

Take us the foxes, the litle foxes, that spoile the vines: for our vines have tender grapes.

My beloved is mine, and I am his: he feedeth among the lillies.

Untill the day breake, and the shadowes flee away: turne my beloved and be thou like a Roe, or a yong Hart, upon the mountaines of Bether.

126                    *The Song of Solomon 5*

I am come into my garden, my sister, my spouse, I have gathered my Myrrhe with my spice, I have eaten my honie combe with my hony, I have drunke my wine with my milke: eate, O friends, drinke, yea drinke abundantly, O beloved!

I sleepe, but my heart waketh: it is the voyce of my beloved that knocketh, saying, Open to me, my sister, my love, my dove, my undefiled: for my head is filled with dewe, and my lockes with the drops of the night.

I have put off my coate, how shall I put it on? I have washed my feete, how shall I defile them?

My beloved put in his hand by the hole of the dore, and my bowels were moved for him.

I rose up to open to my beloved, and my hands dropped with myrrhe, and my fingers with sweete smelling myrrhe, upon the handles of the locke.

I opened to my beloved, but my beloved had with drawen himselfe, and was gone: my soule failed when hee spake: I sought him, but I could not find him: I called him, but he gave me no answere.

The watchmen that went about the citie, found me, they smote me, they wounded me, the keepers of the walles tooke away my vaile from me.

I charge you, O daughters of Jerusalem, if ye find my beloved, that yee tell him, that I am sicke of love.

What is thy beloved more then another beloved, O thou fairest among women? what is thy beloved more then another beloved, that thou doest so charge us?

My beloved is white and ruddy, the chiefest among tenne thousand.

His head is as the most fine gold, his locks are bushy, and blacke as a Raven.

His eyes are as the eyes of doves by the rivers of water, washed with milk, and fitly set.

His cheekes are as a bed of spices, as sweete flowers: his lippes like lillies, dropping sweete smelling myrrhe.

His hands are as gold rings set with the Berill: His belly is as bright ivorie, overlayd with Saphires.

His legges are as pillars of marble, set upon sockets of fine gold: his countenance is as Lebanon, excellent as the Cedars.

His mouth is most sweete, yea he is altogether lovely. This is my beloved, and this is my friend, O daughters of Jerusalem.

127 *Isaiah 11: 1—11*

And there shall come forth a rod out of the stemme of Jesse, and a branch shal grow out of his rootes.

And the Spirit of the LORD shall rest upon him, the spirit of wisedome and understanding, the spirit of counsell and might, the spirit of knowledge, and of the feare of the LORD:

And shal make him of quicke understanding in the feare of the LORD, and he shall not judge after the sight of his eyes, neither reprove after the hearing of his eares.

But with righteousnesse shall he judge the poore, and reproove with equitie, for the meeke of the earth: and he shall smite the earth with the rodde of his mouth, and with the breath of his lips shall he slay the wicked.

And righteousnesse shalbe the girdle of his loines, and faithfulnesse the girdle of his reines.

The wolfe also shall dwell with the lambe, and the leopard shall lie downe with the kid: and the calfe and the yong lion, and the fatling together, and a litle child shall lead them.

And the cow and the beare shall feed, their yong ones shall lie downe together: and the lyon shall eate straw like the oxe.

And the sucking childe shall play on the hole of the aspe, and the weaned childe shall put his hand on the cockatrice denne.

They shall not hurt nor destroy in all my holy mountaine: for the earth shall bee full of the knowledge of the LORD, as the waters cover the sea.

And in that day there shall bee a roote of Jesse, which shall stand for an ensigne of the people; to it shall the Gentiles seeke, and his rest shall bee glorious.

And it shall come to passe in that day, that the Lord shall set

his hande againe the second time, to recover the remnant of his
people which shalbe left, from Assyria, and from Egypt, and from
Pathros, and from Cush, and from Elam, and from Shinar, and
from Hamath, and from the ylands of the Sea.

## 128 *Isaiah 35*

The wildernesse and the solitarie place shall be glad for them: and
the desert shall rejoyce and blossome as the rose.

It shall blossome abundantly, and rejoyce even with joy and
singing: the glory of Lebanon shal be given unto it, the excellencie
of Carmel and Sharon: they shall see the glory of the LORD, and
the excellencie of our God.

Strengthen yee the weake hands, and confirme the feeble knees.

Say to them that are of a fearefull heart; Be strong, feare not:
behold, your God will come with vengeance, even God with a
recompence, he will come and save you.

Then the eyes of the blind shall be opened, and the eares of the
deafe shalbe unstopped.

Then shall the lame man leape as an Hart, and the tongue of the
dumbe sing: for in the wildernesse shall waters breake out, and
streames in the desert.

And the parched ground shall become a poole, and the thirstie
land springs of water: in the habitation of dragons, where each lay,
shalbe grasse with reeds and rushes.

And an high way shalbe there, and a way, and it shall be called
the way of holinesse, the uncleane shall not passe over it, but it
shall be for those: the wayfaringmen, though fooles, shall not erre
therein.

No lyon shalbe there; nor any ravenous beast shall goe up
thereon, it shall not be found there: but the redeemed shall walke
there.

And the ransomed of the LORD shall returne and come to Zion
with songs, and everlasting joy upon their heads: they shall obtaine
joy and gladnesse, and sorrow and sighing shall flee away.

## 129 *Isaiah 40: 1–8*

Comfort ye, comfort ye my people, sayth your God.

Speake ye comfortably to Jerusalem, and cry unto her, that her
warrefare is accomplished, that her iniquitie is pardoned: for shee
hath received of the LORDS hand double for all her sinnes.

The voyce of him that cryeth in the wildernesse, Prepare yee the way of the LORD, make straight in the desert a high way for our God.

Every valley shalbe exalted, and every mountaine and hill shalbe made low: and the crooked shall be made straight, and the rough places plaine.

And the glory of the LORD shall be revealed, and all flesh shall see it together: for the mouth of the LORD hath spoken it.

The voyce sayd; Cry. And hee sayd; What shall I cry? All flesh is grasse, and all the goodlinesse thereof is as the flowre of the field.

The grasse withereth, the flowre fadeth; because the spirit of the LORD bloweth upon it: surely the people is grasse.

The grasse withereth, the flowre fadeth: but the word of our God shall stand for ever.


130                  *Jeremiah 4: 3–31*

For thus saith the LORD to the men of Judah and Jerusalem; Breake up your fallow ground, and sow not among thornes.

Circumcise your selves to the LORD, and take away the foreskinnes of your heart, ye men of Judah, and inhabitants of Jerusalem, lest my furie come forth like fire, and burne that none can quench it, because of the evill of your doings.

Declare ye in Judah, and publish in Jerusalem, and say, Blow yee the Trumpet in the land: cry, gather together, and say, Assemble your selves, and let us goe into the defenced cities.

Set up the standards toward Zion: retyre, stay not; for I wil bring evil from the North, and a great destruction.

The Lion is come up from his thicket, and the destroyer of the Gentiles is on his way; hee is gone foorth from his place to make thy land desolate, and thy cities shall be layed waste, without an inhabitant.

For this gird you with sackcloth; lament and howle: for the fierce anger of the LORD is not turned backe from us.

And it shall come to passe at that day, saith the LORD, that the heart of the King shall perish, and the heart of the Princes: and the Priests shalbe astonished, and the prophets shall wonder.

Then said I, Ah Lord GOD, surely thou hast greatly deceived this people, and Jerusalem, saying, Ye shall have peace, whereas the sword reacheth unto the soule.

At that time shall it bee said to this people, and to Jerusalem; A dry winde of the high places in the wildernes toward the daughter of my people, not to fanne, nor to cleanse,

Even a full winde from those places shall come unto mee: now also will I give sentence against them.

Behold, hee shall come up as cloudes, and his charets shall bee as a whirlewinde: his horses are swifter then Eagles: woe unto us, for wee are spoiled.

O Jerusalem, wash thine heart from wickednesse, that thou mayest bee saved: how long shall thy vaine thoughts lodge within thee?

For a voice declareth from Dan, and publisheth affliction from mount Ephraim.

Make ye mention to the nations, behold, publish against Jerusalem, that watchers come from a farre countrey, and give out their voice against the cities of Judah.

As keepers of a fielde are they against her round about; because shee hath bene rebellious against mee, saith the LORD.

Thy way and thy doings have procured these things unto thee, this is thy wickednes because it is bitter, because it reacheth unto thine heart.

My bowels, my bowels, I am pained at my very heart, my heart maketh a noise in mee, I cannot hold my peace, because thou hast heard, O my soule, the sound of the Trumpet, the alarme of warre.

Destruction upon destruction is cried, for the whole land is spoiled: suddenly are my tents spoiled, and my curtaines in a moment.

How long shal I see the standard and heare the sound of the Trumpet?

For my people is foolish, they have not knowen me, they are sottish children, and they have none understanding: they are wise to doe evill, but to doe good they have no knowledge.

I beheld the earth, and loe, it was without forme and void: and the heavens, and they had no light.

I beheld the mountaines, and loe they trembled, and all the hilles mooved lightly.

I behelde, and loe, there was no man, and all the birdes of the heavens were fled.

I beheld, and loe, the fruitfull place was a wildernesse, and all the cities thereof were broken downe at the presence of the LORD, and by his fierce anger.

For thus hath the LORD said; The whole land shall be desolate; yet will I not make a full ende.

For this shall the earth mourne, and the heavens above be blacke: because I have spoken it, I have purposed it, and will not repent, neither will I turne backe from it.

The whole citie shall flee, for the noise of the horsemen and bowmen, they shall goe into thickets, and climbe up upon the rockes: every city shall be forsaken, and not a man dwell therein.

And when thou art spoiled, what wilt thou doe? though thou clothest thy selfe with crimsin, though thou deckest thee with ornaments of golde, though thou rentest thy face with painting, in vaine shalt thou make thy selfe faire, thy lovers will despise thee, they will seeke thy life.

For I have heard a voice as of a woman in travel, and the anguish as of her that bringeth foorth her first childe, the voice of the daughter of Zion, that bewaileth her selfe, that spreadeth her hands, saying; Woe is me now, for my soule is wearied because of murderers.

### FROM THE HEBREW VIA THE GREEK

131                 *Ecclesiasticus 14: 17–18*

Cp. Pope's and Johnson's Homer

All flesh waxeth old as a garment: for the covenant from the beginning is; thou shalt die the death.

As of the greene Leaves on a thicke tree, some fall, and some grow; so is the generation of flesh and blood, one commeth to an end, and another is borne.

132                 *Ecclesiasticus 43: 13–26*

By his commandement hee maketh the snow to fall apace, and sendeth swiftly the lightnings of his judgment.

Through this the treasures are opened, and clouds flie forth as foules.

By his great power hee maketh the cloudes firme, and the hailestones are broken small.

At his sight the mountaines are shaken, and at his will the South wind bloweth.

The noise of the thunder maketh the earth to tremble: so doth the Northren storme, and the whirlewinde: as birds flying he scattereth the snow, and the falling downe thereof, is as the lighting of grashoppers.

The eye marveileth at the beauty of the whitenesse thereof, and the heart is astonished at the raining of it.

The hoare frost also as salt hee powreth on the earth, and being congealed, it lieth on the toppe of sharpe stakes.

When the colde North-winde bloweth, and the water is congealed into yce, it abideth upon every gathering together of water, and clotheth the water as with a brestplate.

It devoureth the mountaines, and burneth the wildernesse, and consumeth the grasse as fire.

A present remedy of all is a miste comming speedily: a dew coming after heate, refresheth.

By his counsell he appeaseth the deepe, and planteth Ilands therein.

They that saile on the Sea, tell of the danger thereof, and when wee heare it with our eares, wee marveile thereat.

For therein be strange and wonderous workes, varietie of all kindes of beasts, and whales created.

By him the ende of them hath prosperous successe, and by his word all things consist.


133        *Ecclesiasticus 44: 1–15*

Let us now praise famous men, and our Fathers that begat us.

The Lorde hath wrought great glory by them, through his great power from the beginning.

Such as did beare rule in their kingdomes, men renowmed for their power, giving counsell by their understanding, and declaring prophecies:

Leaders of the people by their counsels, and by their knowledge of learning meet for the people, wise and eloquent in their instructions.

Such as found out musical tunes, and recited verses in writing.

Rich men furnished with abilitie, living peaceably in their habitations.

All these were honoured in their generations, and were the glory of their times.

There be of them, that have left a name behind them, that their praises might be reported.

And some there be, which have no memorial, who are perished as though they had never bene, and are become as though they had never bene borne, and their children after them.

But these were mercifull men, whose righteousness hath not beene forgotten.

With their seed shall continually remaine a good inheritance, and their children are within the covenant.

Their seed stands fast, and their children for their sakes.

Their seed shall remaine for ever, and their glory shall not be blotted out.

Their bodies are buried in peace, but their name liveth for evermore.

The people will tell of their wisdome, and the congregation will shew forth their praise.


## FROM THE GREEK OF THE NEW TESTAMENT

134          *Matthew 5: 3–16*

Blessed are the poore in spirit: for theirs is the kingdome of heaven.

Blessed are they that mourne: for they shall be comforted.

Blessed are the meeke: for they shall inherit the earth.

Blessed are they which doe hunger and thirst after righteousnesse: for they shall be filled.

Blessed are the mercifull: for they shall obtaine mercie.

Blessed are the pure in heart: for they shall see God.

Blessed are the peacemakers: for they shall bee called the children of God.

Blessed are they which are persecuted for righteousnesse sake: for theirs is the kingdome of heaven.

Blessed are ye, when men shall revile you, and persecute you, and shal say all manner of evill against you falsly for my sake.

Rejoyce, and be exceeding glad: for great is your reward in heaven: For so persecuted they the Prophets which were before you.

Yee are the salt of the earth: But if the salt have lost his savour, wherewith shall it bee salted? It is thenceforth good for nothing, but to be cast out, and to be troden under foote of men.

Yee are the light of the world. A citie that is set on an hill, cannot be hid.

Neither doe men light a candle, and put it under a bushell: but on a candlesticke, and it giveth light unto all that are in the house.

Let your light so shine before men, that they may see your good workes, and glorifie your father which is in heaven.

135                     *Matthew 6: 24–9*

No men can serve two masters: for either he will hate the one and love the other, or else hee will holde to the one, and despise the other. Ye cannot serve God and Mammon.

Therfore I say unto you, Take no thought for your life, what yee shall eate, or what ye shall drinke, nor yet for your body, what yee shall put on: Is not the life more then meate? and the body then raiment?

Behold the foules of the aire: for they sow not, neither do they reape, nor gather into barnes, yet your heavenly father feedeth them. Are yee not much better then they?

Which of you by taking thought, can adde one cubite unto his stature?

And why take ye thought for raiment? Consider the lillies of the field, how they grow: they toile not, neither doe they spinne.

And yet I say unto you, that even Solomon in all his glory, was not arayed like one of these.

136                     *Mark 4: 26–32*

And he said, So is the kingdome of God, as if a man should cast seede into the ground,

And should sleepe, and rise night and day, and the seed should spring, and grow up, he knoweth not how.

For the earth bringeth foorth fruite of herselfe, first the blade, then the eare, after that the full corne in the eare.

But when the fruite is brought foorth, immediately he putteth in the sickle, because the harvest is come.

And he said, Wherunto shal we liken the kingdome of God? Or with what comparison shall we compare it?

It is like a graine of mustard seed: which when it is sowen in the earth, is lesse then all the seedes that be in the earth.

But when it is sowen, it groweth up, and becommeth greater then all herbes, and shooteth out great branches, so that the fowles of the aire may lodge under the shadow of it.

137 *Luke 1: 46–55*

And Marie said, My soule doth magnifie the Lord.

And my spirit hath rejoyced in God my saviour.

For hee hath regarded the low estate of his handmaiden: for behold, from hencefoorth all generations shall call me blessed.

For he that is mighty hath done to mee great things, and holy is his Name.

And his mercy is on them that feare him, from generation to generation.

Hee hath shewed strength with his arme, he hath scattered the proud, in the imagination of their hearts.

He hath put downe the mighty from their seates, and exalted them of low degree.

Hee hath filled the hungry with good things, and the rich hee hath sent emptie away.

Hee hath holpen his servant Israel, in remembrance of his mercy,

As he spake to our fathers, to Abraham, and to his seed for ever.

138 *Luke 12: 32–40*

Feare not, litle flocke, for it is your fathers good pleasure to give you the kingdome.

Sell that yee have, and give almes: provide your selves bagges which waxe not old, a treasure in the heavens that faileth not, where no theefe approcheth, neither moth corrupteth.

For where your treasure is, there will your heart be also.

Let your loines be girded about, and your lights burning,

And ye your selves like unto men that waite for their Lord, when he will return from the wedding, that when he commeth and knocketh, they may open unto him immediately.

Blessed are those servants, whom the Lord when he commeth, shall find watching: Verily, I say unto you, That he shall girde himselfe, and make them to sit downe to meate, and will come foorth and serve them.

And if he shall come in the second watch, or come in the third watch, and find them so, blessed are those servants.

And this know, that if the good man of the house had knowen what houre the theefe would come, he would have watched, and not have suffred his house to be broken thorow.

Be yee therefore ready also: for the sonne of man commeth at an houre when yee thinke not.

139                     *John 15: 1–8*

I am the true vine, and my Father is the husbandman.

Every branch in me that beareth not fruit, hee taketh away: and every branch that beareth fruit, he purgeth it, that it may bring foorth more fruit.

Now ye are cleane through the word which I have spoken unto you.

Abide in me, and in you: As the branch cannot beare fruit of it selfe, except it abide in the vine: no more can ye, except ye abide in me.

I am the vine, ye are the branches: He that abideth in me, and I in him, the same bringeth forth much fruit: for without me ye can doe nothing.

If a man abide not in me, he is cast forth as a branch, and is withered, and men gather them, and cast them into the fire, and they are burned.

If ye abide in me, and my words abide in you, ye shall aske what ye will, and it shall be done unto you.

Herein is my Father glorified, that ye beare much fruit, so shall ye bee my Disciples.

# JOHN DONNE

## 1572–1631

### FROM THE LATIN OF GAZAEUS

140          *Vota Amico Facta*, Fol. 160

God grant thee thine own wish, and grant thee mine,
Thou, who dost, best friend, in best things outshine;
May thy soul, ever chearfull, nere know cares,
Nor thy life, ever lively, know gray haires.
Nor thy hand, ever open, know base holds,
Nor thy purse, ever plump, know pleits, or folds.
Nor thy tongue, ever true, know a false thing,

Nor thy word, ever mild, know quarrelling.
Nor thy works, ever equall, know disguise,
Nor thy fame, ever pure, know contumelies.
Nor thy prayers, know low objects, still Divine;
God grant thee thine own wish, and grant thee mine.

## FROM HIS OWN LATIN

141            *To Mr George Herbert,*
*with one of my seals, of the anchor and Christ*

A sheafe of Snakes used heretofore to be
My Seal, The Crest of our poore Family.
Adopted in Gods Family, and so
Our old Coat lost, unto new armes I go.
The Crosse (my seal at Baptism) spred below,
Does, by that form, into an Anchor grow.
Crosses grow Anchors; Bear, as thou shouldst do
Thy Crosse, and that Crosse grows an Anchor too.
But he that makes our Crosses Anchors thus,
Is Christ, who there is crucifi'd for us.
Yet may I, with this, my first Serpents hold,
God gives new blessings, and yet leaves the old;
The Serpent, may, as wise, my pattern be;
My poison, as he feeds on dust, that's me.
And as he rounds the Earth to murder sure,
My death he is, but on the Crosse, my cure.
Crucifie nature then, and then implore
All Grace from him, crucified there before;
When all is Crosse, and that Crosse Anchor grown,
This Seal's a Catechism, not a Seal alone.
Under that little Seal great gifts I send,
[Wishes,] and prayers, pawns, and fruits of a friend.
And may that Saint which rides in our great Seal,
To you, who bear his name, great bounties deal.

# EDWARD FAIRFAX

d. 1635

## FROM THE ITALIAN OF TASSO

## Godfrey of Bulloigne or
## The Recoverie of Jerusalem

142    *'Armida, Niece to the Wizard who rules
Damascus, sets out to undo the Crusaders'*

The sweet Armida tooke this charge on hand,
A tender peece, for beautie, sexe and age,
The sunne was sunken underneath the land
When she began her wanton pilgrimage,
In silken weedes she trusteth to withstand,
And conquer knights, in warlike equipage,
  Of their night ambling dame, the Syrians prated
  Some good, some bad, as they her lov'd or hated.

Within few daies, the Nymph arrived theare
Where puissant Godfrey had his tents ipight;
Upon her strange attire, and visage cleare,
Gazed each soldier, gazed everie knight,
As when a comet doth in skies appeare,
The people stand amazed at the light,
  So wondred they, and each at other sought,
  What mister wight she was, and whence ibrought.

Yet never eie to Cupids service vow'd
Beheld a face of such a lovely pride,
A tinsell vaile her amber locks did shrowd,
That strove to cover what it could not hide,
The golden sunne, behinde a silver cloud,
So streameth out his beames on everie side,
  The marble goddesse, set at Guidos, naked,
  She seem'd, were she uncloath'd, or that awaked.

mister] kind, sort of

117

The gamesome winde among her tresses plaies,
And curleth up, those growing riches, short;
Her sparefull eie to spread his beames denaies,
But keepes his shot, where Cupid keepes his fort;
The rose and lillie on her cheeke, assaies
To paint true fairenesse out, in bravest sort,
   Her lips, where bloomes nought but the single rose,
   Still blush, for still they kisse, while still they close.

Her breasts, two hils orespred with purest snow,
Sweet, smooth and supple, soft and gently swelling,
Betweene them lies a milken dale below,
Where love, youth, gladnes, whitenes make their dwelling,
Her brests halfe hid, and halfe were laid to show;
Her envious vesture greedie sight repelling,
   So was the wanton clad, as if thus much
   Should please the eie, the rest unseene, the tuch.

As when the sun-beames dive through Tagus wave,
To spie the store-house of his springing gold,
Love pearsing thought so through her mantle drave,
And in her gentle bosome wandred bold:
It view'd the wondrous beautie virgins have,
And all to fond desire (with vantage) told,
   Alas what hope is left, to quench his fire
   That kindled is, by sight; blowne, by desire.

143                 *'In Armida's Garden'*

The joyous birds, hid under greenewood shade,
Sung merrie notes on every branch and bow,
The winde (that in the leaves and waters plaid)
With murmur sweete, now song, and whistled now,
Ceased the birds, the winde loud answere made:
And while they sung, it rumbled soft and low;
   Thus, were it happe or cunning, chance or art,
   The winde in this strange musicke bore his part.

With partie coloured plumes and purple bill,
A woondrous bird among the rest there flew,
That in plaine speech sung lovelaies loud and shrill,

Her leden was like humaine language trew,
So much she talkt and with such wit and skill,
That strange it seemed how much good she knew,
　　Her feathred fellowes all stood husht to heare,
　　Dombe was the winde, the waters silent weare.

Cp.
Spenser

The gentlie budding rose (quoth she) behold,
That first scant peeping foorth with virgin beames,
Halfe ope, halfe shut, her beauties doth upfold
In their deare leaves, and lesse seene, fairer seames,
And after spreeds them foorth more broad and bold,
Then languisheth and dies in last extreames,
　　Nor seemes the same, that decked bed and boure
　　Of many a ladie late, and paramoure:

So, in the passing of a day, doth pas
The bud and blossome of the life of man,
Nor ere doth flourish more, but like the gras
Cut downe, becommeth withred, pale and wan:
O gather then the rose while time thou has,
Short is the day, done when it scant began,
　　Gather the rose of love, while yet thou mast
　　Loving, belov'd; embrasing, be embrast.


# BEN JONSON

## 1572–1637

### IMITATED FROM THE LATIN OF CATULLUS

144　　　　　　　Carmina, V

*To Celia*

Cp.
Ralegh
Crashaw
Wordsworth
Landor

Come my Celia, let us prove,
While we may, the sports of love;
Time will not be ours, for ever:
He, at length, our good will sever.
Spend not then his guifts in vaine.

143 leden] language

Sunnes, that set, may rise againe:
But if once we loose this light,
'Tis, with us, perpetuall night.
Why should we deferre our joyes?
Fame, and rumor are but toyes.
Cannot we delude the eyes
Of a few poore houshold spyes?
Or his easier eares beguile,
So removed by our wile?
'Tis no sinne, loves fruit to steale,
But the sweet theft to reveale:
To be taken, to be seene,
These have crimes accounted beene.

145          Carmina, V and VII

*To the Same*

Cp.
Ralegh
Crashaw
Wordsworth
Landor

Kisse me, sweet: The warie lover
Can your favours keepe, and cover,
When the common courting jay
All your bounties will betray.
Kisse againe: no creature comes.
Kisse, and score up wealthy summes
On my lips, thus hardly sundred,
While you breath. First give a hundred,
Then a thousand, then another
Hundred, then unto the tother
Adde a thousand, and so more:
Till you equall with the store,
All the grasse that Rumney yeelds,
Or the sands in Chelsey fields,
Or the drops in silver Thames,
Or the starres, that guild his streames,
In the silent sommer-nights,
When youths ply their stolne delights.
That the curious may not know
How to tell'hem, as they flow,
And the envious, when they find
What their number is, be pin'd.

## FROM THE LATIN OF HORACE

146                Epodes, II

### *The Praises of a Countrie Life*

Happie is he, that from all Businesse cleere,
    As the old race of Mankind were,
With his owne Oxen tills his Sires left lands,
    And is not in the Usurers bands:
Nor Souldier-like started with rough alarmes,
    Nor dreads the Seas inraged harmes:
But flees the Barre and Courts, with the proud bords,
    And waiting Chambers of great Lords.
The Poplar tall, he then doth marrying twine
    With the growne issue of the Vine;
And with his hooke lops off the fruitless race,
    And sets more happy in the place:
Or in the bending Vale beholds a-farre
    The lowing herds there grazing are:
Or the prest honey in pure pots doth keepe
    Of Earth, and sheares the tender Sheepe:
Or when that Autumne, through the fields lifts round
    His head, with mellow Apples crown'd,
How plucking Peares, his owne hand grafted had,
    And purple-matching Grapes, hee's glad!
With which, Priapus, he may thanke thy hands,
    And, Sylvane, thine that keptst his Lands!
Then now beneath some ancient Oke he may,
    Now in the rooted Grasse, him lay,
Whilst from the higher Bankes doe slide the floods,
    The soft birds quarrell in the Woods,
The Fountaines murmure as the streames doe creepe,
    And all invite to easie sleepe.
Then when the thundring Jove, his Snow and showres
    Are gathering by the Wintry houres;
Or hence, or thence, he drives with many a Hound
    Wild Bores into his toyles pitch'd round:
Or straines on his small forke his subtill nets
    For th'eating Thrush, or Pit-falls sets:
And snares the fearfull Hare, and new-come Crane,
    And 'counts them sweet rewards so ta'en:

Who (amongst these delights) would not forget
   Loves cares so evill, and so great?
But if, to boot with these, a chaste Wife meet
   For houshold aid, and Children sweet;
Such as the Sabines, or a Sun-burnt-blowse,
   Some lustie quick Apulians spouse,
To deck the hallow'd Harth with old wood fir'd
   Against the Husband comes home tir'd;
That penning the glad flock in hurdles by
   Their swelling udders doth draw dry:
And from the sweet Tub Wine of this yeare takes,
   And unbought viands ready makes:
Not Lucrine Oysters I could then more prize,
   Nor Turbot, nor bright Golden eyes:
If with East floods, the Winter troubled much,
   Into our Seas send any such:
Th'Ionian God-wit, nor the Ginny hen
   Could not goe downe my belly then
More sweet then Olives, that new gather'd be
   From fattest branches of the Tree:
Or the herb Sorrell, that loves Meadows still,
   Or Mallowes loosing bodyes ill:
Or at the Feast of Bounds, the Lambe then slaine,
   Or Kid forc't from the Wolfe againe.
Among these Cates how glad the sight doth come
   Of the fed flocks approaching home!
To view the weary Oxen draw, with bare
   And fainting necks, the turned Share!
The wealthy houshold swarme of bondmen met,
   And 'bout the steeming Chimney set!
These thoughts when Usurer Alphius, now about
   To turne mere farmer, had spoke out,
'Gainst th'Ides, his moneys he gets in with paine,
   At th'Calends, puts all out again.

> God-wit] a marsh bird    Ginny] guinea
> Mallowes] plant used medicinally

## 147 Odes, Book IV, 1

### *To Venus*

Venus againe thou mov'st a warre
      Long intermitted, pray thee, pray thee spare:
   I am not such, as in the Reigne
Of the good Cynara I was: Refraine,
      Sower Mother of Sweet Loves, forbeare
To bend a man now at his fiftieth yeare
      Too stubborne for Commands, so slack:
Goe where Youths soft intreaties call thee back.
      More timely hie thee to the house,
With thy bright Swans, of Paulus Maximus:
      There jest, and feast, make him thine host,
If a fit livor thou dost seeke to toast;
      For he's both noble, lovely, young,
And for the troubled Clyent fyl's his tongue,
      Child of a hundred Arts, and farre
Will he display the Ensignes of thy warre.
      And when he smiling finds his Grace
With thee 'bove all his Rivals gifts take place,
      He will thee a Marble Statue make
Beneath a Sweet-wood Roofe, neere Alba Lake:
      There shall thy dainty Nostrill take
In many a Gumme, and for thy soft eares sake
      Shall Verse be set to Harpe and Lute,
And Phrygian Hau'boy, not without the Flute.
      There twice a day in sacred Laies,
The Youths and tender Maids shall sing thy praise:
      And in the Salian manner meet
Thrice 'bout thy Altar with their Ivory feet.
      Me now, nor Wench, nor wanton Boy,
Delights, nor credulous hope of mutuall Joy,
      Nor care I now healths to propound;
Or with fresh flowers to girt my Temple round.
      But, why, oh why, my Ligurine,
Flow my thin teares, downe these pale cheeks of mine?

livor] liver (the seat of love)      Salian] like the Salii, priests of Mars
                              propound] propose

123

Or why, my well-grac'd words among,
With an uncomely silence failes my tongue?
  Hard-hearted, I dreame every Night
I hold thee fast! but fled hence, with the Light,
  Whether in Mars his field thou bee,
Or Tybers winding streames, I follow thee.


## Ars Poetica

148    *'Words like the Woods'* [revised version]

                As woods whose change appeares
Still in their leaves, throughout the sliding yeares,
The first borne dying; so the aged state
Of words decay, and phrases borne but late
Like tender buds shoot up, and freshly grow.
Our selves, and all thats ours, to death we owe:
Whether the Sea receiv'd into the shore,
That from the North, the Navie safe doth store,
A kingly worke; or that long barren fen
Once rowable, but now doth nourish men
In neighbour-townes, and feeles the weightie plough:
Or the wilde river, who had changed now
His course so hurtfull both to graine, and seedes,
Being taught a better way. All mortall deeds
Shall perish: so farre off it is, the state,
Or grace of speech, should hope a lasting date.
Much phrase that now is dead, shall be reviv'd;
And much shall dye, that now is nobly liv'd,
If Custome please; at whose disposing will
The power, and rule of speaking resteth still.


### FROM THE LATIN

[ascribed to Petronius in the 1585 edition of his work]

149        Doing, a filthy pleasure is, and short;
        And done, we straight repent us of the sport:
        Let us not then rush blindly on unto it,
        Like lustfull beasts, that onely know to doe it:
        For lust will languish, and that heat decay,
        But thus, thus, keeping endlesse Holy-day,

Let us together closely lie, and kisse,
There is no labour, nor no shame in this;
This hath pleas'd, doth please, and long will please; never
Can this decay, but is beginning ever.


FROM THE LATIN OF LUCAN

150             from *Pharsalia*

[Photinus is speaking to Ptolemy at Alexandria]

Just and fit actions Ptolemey (he saith)
Make many, hurt themselves; a praysed faith
Is her owne scourge, when it sustaines their states
Whom fortune hath deprest; come nere the fates
And the immortall gods; love only those
Whom thou seest happy; wretches flee as foes:
Looke how the starres from earth, or seas from flames
Are distant, so is proffitt from just aymes.
The mayne comaund of scepters, soone doth perishe
If it begyn religious thoughts to cherish;
Whole armyes fall swayd by those nyce respects
It is a lycense to doe ill, protectes,
Even states most hated, when no lawes resist
The sword but that it acteth what it list.
Yet ware; thou mayst do all things cruellie:
Not safe; but when thou dost them thoroughlie:
He that will honest be may quitt the Court,
Virtue, and Soveraigntie, they not consort.
That prince that shames a tyrants name to beare,
Shall never dare do any thing but feare.


FROM THE LATIN OF MARTIAL

151             *Epigrams*, Book X, 47

Cp.
Surrey
Fanshawe
Fenton
     The things that make the happier life, are these,
Most pleasant Martial; Substance got with ease,
Not labour'd for, but left thee by thy Sire;
A Soyle, not barren; a continewall fire;

Never at Law; seldome in office gown'd;
A quiet mind; free powers; and body sound;
A wise simplicity; freindes alike-stated;
Thy table without art, and easy-rated:
Thy night not dronken, but from cares layd wast;
No sowre, or sollen bed-mate, yet a Chast;
Sleepe, that will make the darkest howres swift-pac't;
Will to bee, what thou art; and nothing more:
Nor feare thy latest day, nor wish therfore.


ADAPTED FROM THE GREEK OF PHILOSTRATUS

[A mosaic from his prose *Epistles*,
possibly influenced by Bonfini's Latin translation of their Greek.]


152           *To Celia*

Drinke to me, onely, with thine eyes,
   And I will pledge with mine;
Or leave a kisse but in the cup,
   And Ile not looke for wine.
The thirst, that from the soule doth rise,
   Doth aske a drinke divine:
But might I of Jove's Nectar sup,
   I would not change for thine.
I sent thee, late, a rosie wreath,
   Not so much honoring thee,
As giving it a hope, that there
   It could not withered bee.
But thou thereon did'st onely breath,
   And sent'st it backe to mee:
Since when it growes, and smells, I sweare,
   Not of it selfe, but thee.

# SIR JOHN BEAUMONT

## 1582–1628

### FROM THE LATIN OF VIRGIL

153 *Eclogues*, IV

[The poem celebrates the birthday of Saloninus, son of the consul Pollio]

Sicilian Muses, sing we greater things;
All are not pleas'd with shrubs and lowly springs;
More fitly to the consull, woods belong.
Now is fulfild Cumaean sibyl's song:
Long chaines of better times begin againe;
The Maide returnes, and brings backe Saturne's raigne;
New progenies from lofty Heav'n descend;
Thou chaste Lucina, be this Infant's friend,
Whose birth the days of ir'n shall quite deface,
And through the world the golden age shall place;
Thy brother Phoebus weares his potent crowne.
And thou—O Pollio—know thy high renowne—
Thy consulship this glorious change shall breed,
Great months shall then endeavour to proceed:
Thy rule the steps of threatening sinne shall cleare,
And free the Earth from that perpetuall feare.
He with the gods shall live, and shall behold,
With heavenly spirits noble souls enroll'd;
And, seene by them, shall guide this worldly frame,
Which to His hand His father's strength doth tame.
To Thee—sweet child—the Earth brings native dowres,
The wandring ivy, with faire bacchar's flowres,
And colocasia, sprung from Egypt's ground,
With smiling leaves of greene acanthus crown'd;
The goats their swelling udders home shall beare,
The droves no more shall mighty lions feare:
For Thee, Thy cradle, pleasing flowres shall bring;
Imperious Death shall blunt the serpent's sting;
No herbes shall with deceitfull poyson flow,
And sweet amomum ev'ry where shall grow.
But when Thou able art to reade the facts
Of worthies, and thy father's famous acts,

127

To know what glories Vertue's name adorne,
The fields to ripeness bring the tender corne;
Ripe grapes depend on carelesse brambles' tops,
Hard oakes sweat hony, form'd in dewy drops.
Yet some few steps of former fraudes remaine,
Which men to trie, the sea with ships constraine,
With strengthening walles their cities to defend,
And on the ground long furrows to extend;
A second Tiphys, and new Argo then,
Shall leade to brave exploits the best of men;
The war of Troy that town againe shall burne,
And great Achilles thither shall returne:
But when firm age a perfect man Thee makes,
The willing sayler straight the seas forsakes;
The pine no more the use of Trade retaines;
Each country breeds all fruits, the Earth disdaines
The harrowes weight, and vines the sickle's strokes;
Strong ploughmen let their bulls go free from yokes;
Wooll feares not to dissemble colours strange,
But rams their fleeces then in pastures change
To pleasing purple, or to saffron dye,
And lambes turn ruddy, as they feeding lie.
The Fates—whose wills in stedfast end agree,
Command their wheels to run such daies to see—
Attempt great honours, now the time attends;
Dear Childe of Gods, whose line from Jove descends.
See how the world with weight declining lies;
The Earth, the spacious seas, and arched skies:
Behold againe, how these their grief asswage
With expectation of the future age:
O that my life and breath so long would last
To tell Thy deeds! I should not be surpast
By Thracian Orpheus, nor if Linus sing,
Though they from Phœbus and the muses spring:
Should Pan—Arcadia judging—strive with me,
Pan by Arcadia's doome would conquer'd be.
Begin Thou, little Childe; by laughter owne
Thy mother, who ten months hath fully knowne
Of tedious houres: begin, Thou little Childe,
On Whom as yet thy parents never smil'd;
The God with meate hath not Thy hunger fed,
Nor goddesse laid thee in a little bed.

# DRUMMOND OF HAWTHORNDEN

## 1585–1649

### FROM THE FRENCH OF JEAN PASSERAT

154            *Song*

DAPHNÈ
Shephard loveth thow me vell?

AMINTAS
So vel that I cannot tell.

DAPHNÈ
Like to vhat, good shephard, say?

AMINTAS
Like to thee, faire cruell May.

DAPHNÈ
Ah! how strange thy vords I find!
But yet satisfie my mind;
Shephard vithout flatterie,
Beares thow any love to me,
Like to vhat, good shephard, say?

AMINTAS
Like to thee, faire cruell May.

DAPHNÈ
Better answer had it beene
To say, I love thee as mine eyne.

AMINTAS
Voe is me, I love them not,
For be them love entress got
At the time they did behold
Thy sveet face and haire of gold.

May] Maid      entress] entrance

#### DAPHNÈ
Like to vhat, good shephard, say?

#### AMINTAS
Like to thee, faire cruelle May.

#### DAPHNÈ
But, deare shephard, speake more plaine,
And I sal not aske againe;
For to end this gentle strife,
Doth thow love me as thy life?

#### AMINTAS
No, for it doth eb and flow
Vith contrare tides of grief and voe;
And now I through loves strange force
A man am not, but a dead corse.

#### DAPHNÈ
Like to vhat, good shephard, say?

#### AMINTAS
Like to thee, faire cruell May.

#### DAPHNÈ
This 'like to thee' O leave, I pray,
And as my selfe, good shephard, say.

#### AMINTAS
Alas! I do not love my selff,
For I me split on beuties shelf.

#### DAPHNÈ
Like to vhat, good shephard, say?

#### AMINTAS
Like to thee, faire cruell May.

# ANONYMOUS

## Published 1588

### FROM THE GREEK OF THEOCRITUS

<sup>1</sup>55

*Idylls*, XX

#### ARGUMENT

A Neteheard is brought in, chafing that EUNICA, a Maid of the cittie, disdained to kisse him. Whereby it is thought that THEOCRITUS seemeth to checke them that thinke this kinde of writing in Poetry to be too base and rustical. And therefore this Poeme is termed NETEHEARD.

#### NETEHEARD

Eunica skornde me, when her I would have sweetly kist,
And railing at me said, Goe with a mischiefe, where thou list!
Thinkst thou, a wretched Neteheard, mee to kisse? I have no will
After the Countrie Guise to smouch; of Cittie lips I skill.
My lovely mouth so much as in thy dreame thou shalt not touch.
How dost thou look! How dost thou talke! How plaiest thou the
    slouch!
How daintilie thou speakst! What courting words thou bringest
    out!
How soft a beard thou hast! How faire thy locks hang round
    about!
Thy lips are like a sickmans lips! thy hands, so black they bee,
And rankely thou dost smel, awaie, lest thou defilest me!
    Having thus sed, she spatterd on her bosome twise or thrise;
And, still beholding me from top to toe in skorneful wise,
She mutterd with her lips, and with her eies she lookte aside,
And of her beutie wondrous coy she was; her mouth she wride,
And proudly mockt me to my face. My blud boild in each vaine,
And red I woxe for griefe as doth the rose with dewye raine.
Thus leaving me, awaie she flung, since when, it vexeth me
That I should be so skornde of such a filthie drab as she.
    Ye Shepeheards, tel me true, am not I fair as any swan?
Hath of a sodaine anie God made me another man?
For well I wote, before a cumlie grace in me did shine,
Like ivy round about a tree, and dekt this bearde of mine.

Neteheard] cowherd

<sup>1</sup>31

My crisped lockes like Parslie, on my temples wont to spred;
And on my eiebrowes black, a milke white forhed glistered:
More seemelie were mine eies than are MINERVAS eies, I know.
My mouth for sweetnes passed cheese, and from my mouth did
    flow
A voice more sweete than hunniecombes. Sweete is my rundelaie,
When on the whistle, flute or pipe, or cornet I do plaie.
And all the weemen on our hills, do saie that I am faire,
And all do love me well: but these that breathe the citty air
Did never love me yet. And why? The cause is this, I know,
That I a Neteheard am. They heare not how, in vales below
Fair BACCHUS kept a heard of beastes. Nor can these nice ones tell
How VENUS, raving for a Neteheards love, with him did dwell
Upon the hills of Phrygia; and how she lovde againe
ADONIS in the woods, and mournde in woods when hee was slaine.
What was ENDYMION? Was he not a Neteheard? Yet the Moone
Did love this Neteheard so, that from the heavens descending
    soone,
She came to Latmos grove where with the daintie lad she laie.
And RHEA, thou a Neteheard dost bewaile, and thou, al daie
O mighty JUPITER but for a shepeheardes boy didst straie.
EUNICA only, dained not a Neteheard for to love:
Better, forsooth, than CYBEL, VENUS, or the Moone above.
And VENUS, thou hereafter must not love thy faire ADONE
In cittie nor on hill, but all the night must sleep alone.


# ROBERT HERRICK

1591–1674

## FROM THE GREEK

### Anacreontea

156      *The Wounded Cupid. Song*

Cupid as he lay among
Roses, by a Bee was stung.
Whereupon in anger flying
To his Mother, said thus crying;

Help! O help! your Boy's a dying.
And why, my pretty Lad, said she?
Then blubbering, replyed he,
A winged Snake has bitten me,
Which Country people call a Bee.
At which she smil'd; then with her hairs
And kisses drying up his tears:
Alas! said she, my Wag! if this
Such a pernicious torment is:
Come, tel me then, how great's the smart
Of those, thou woundest with thy Dart!

157   *The Cheat of Cupid: or, The Ungentle Guest*

One silent night of late,
   When every creature rested,
Came one unto my gate,
   And knocking, me molested.

Who's that (said I) beats there,
   And troubles thus the Sleepie?
Cast off (said he) all feare,
   And let not Locks thus keep ye.

For I a Boy am, who
   By Moonlesse nights have swerved;
And all with showrs wet through,
   And e'en with cold half starved.

I pittifull arose,
   And soon a Taper lighted;
And did my selfe disclose
   Unto the lad benighted.

I saw he had a Bow,
   And Wings too, which did shiver;
And looking down below,
   I spy'd he had a Quiver.

I to my Chimney's shine
   Brought him, (as Love professes)
And chaf'd his hands with mine,
   And dry'd his dropping Tresses:

But when he felt him warm'd,
   Let's try this bow of ours,
And string if they be harm'd,
   Said he, with these late showrs.

Forthwith his bow he bent,
   And wedded string and arrow,
And struck me that it went
   Quite through my heart and marrow.

Then laughing loud, he flew
   Away, and thus said flying,
Adieu, mine Host, Adieu,
   Ile leave thy heart a dying.

FROM THE GREEK OF MELEAGER

158      *Upon a Maid that Dyed*
*the Day She Was Marryed*

That Morne which saw me made a Bride,
The Ev'ning witnest that I dy'd.
Those holy lights, wherewith they guide
Unto the bed the bashfull Bride;
Serv'd, but as Tapers, for to burne,
And light my Reliques to their urne.
This Epitaph, which here you see,
Supply'd the Epithalamie.

## FROM THE LATIN OF HORACE

159       Odes, Book III, 9

*A Dialogue Betwixt Horace and Lydia*

HORACE

While, Lydia, I was lov'd of thee,
Nor any was preferr'd 'fore me
To hug thy whitest neck: Then I,
The Persion King liv'd not more happily.

LYDIA

While thou no other didst affect,
Nor Cloe was of more respect;
Then Lydia, far-fam'd Lydia,
I flourish't more then Roman Ilia.

HORACE

Now Thracian Cloe governs me,
Skilfull i' th' Harpe, and Melodie:
For whose affection, Lydia, I
(So Fate spares her) am well content to die.

LYDIA

My heart now set on fire is
By Ornithes sonne, young Calaïs;
For whose commutuall flames here I
(To save his life) twice am content to die.

HORACE

Say our first loves we sho'd revoke,
And sever'd, joyne in brazen yoke:
Admit I Cloe put away,
And love againe love-cast-off Lydia?

LYDIA

Though mine be brighter then the Star;
Thou lighter then the Cork by far:
Rough as th' Adratick sea, yet I
Will live with thee, or else for thee will die.

## FROM THE LATIN OF MARTIAL

160 ## Epigrams, Book XI, 16: 9–10

### *Another*

To read my Booke the Virgin shie
May blush, (while Brutus standeth by:)
But when He's gone, read through what's writ,
And never staine a cheeke for it.


# THOMAS CAREW

?1598–?1639

## FROM THE ITALIAN OF
## GIOVANNI BATTISTA GUARINI

161 ### *A Ladies prayer to Cupid*

Since I must needes into thy schoole returne
Be pittifull (O Love) and doe not burne
Mee with desier of cold, and frozen age,
Nor let me follow a fond boy or page:
But gentle Cupid give mee if you can,
One to my love, whom I may call a man,
Of person comely, and of face as sweete,
Let him be sober, secret, and discreete,
Well practis'd in love's schoole, let him within
Weare all his beard, and none uppon his chinn.


## FROM THE ITALIAN OF GIOVAN BATTISTA MARINO

162 ### *Lips and Eyes*

In Celia's face a question did arise
Which were more beautifull, her lips or eyes:
We (said the eyes,) send forth those poynted darts
Which pierce the hardest adamantine hearts.

From us (replyd the lips,) proceed those blisses
Which lovers reape by kind words and sweet kisses.
Then wept the eyes, and from their springs did powre
Of liquid orientall pearle a shower.
Whereat the lips, mov'd with delight and pleasure,
Through a sweete smile unlockt their pearlie treasure;
And bad Love judge, whether did adde more grace:
Weeping or smiling pearles to Celia's face.


# WILLIAM STRODE

### ?1600–?1645

#### FROM THE LATIN OF FAMIANUS STRADA

163         *The Nightingale*

Now the declining sun 'gan downwards bend
From higher heavens, and from his locks did send
A milder flame, when near to Tiber's flow
A lutinist allay'd his careful woe
With sounding charms, and in a greeny seat
Of shady oake took shelter from the heat.
A Nightingale oreheard him, that did use
To sojourn in the neighbour groves, the muse
That fill'd the place, the Syren of the wood;
Poore harmless Syren, stealing neare she stood
Close lurking in the leaves attentively
Recording that unwonted melody:
Shee cons it to herselfe and every strayne
His finger playes her throat return'd again.
The lutinist perceives an answeare sent
From th' imitating bird and was content
To shewe her play; more fully then in hast
He tries his lute, and (giving her a tast
Of the ensuing quarrel) nimbly beats
On all his strings; as nimbly she repeats,
And (wildely ranging ore a thousand keys)
Sends a shrill warning of her after-layes.
With rolling hand the Lutinist then plies
His trembling threads; sometimes in scornful wise

He brushes down the strings and keemes them all
With one even stroke; then takes them severall
And culles them ore again. His sparkling joynts
(With busy descant mincing on the points)
Reach back with busy touch: that done hee stayes,
The bird replies, and art with art repayes,
Sometimes as one unexpert or in doubt
How she might wield her voice, shee draweth out
Her tone at large and doth at first prepare
A solemne strayne not weav'd with sounding ayre,
But with an equall pitch and constant throate
Makes clear the passage of her gliding noate;
Then crosse division diversly shee playes,
And loudly chanting out her quickest layes
Poises the sounds, and with a quivering voice
Falls back again: he (wondering how so choise,
So various harmony should issue out
From such a little throate) doth go about
Some harder lessons, and with wondrous art
Changing the strings, doth upp the treble dart,
And downwards smites the base; with painefull stroke
Hee beats, and as the trumpet doth provoke
Sluggards to fight, even so his wanton skill
With mingled discords joynes the hoarse and shrill:
The Bird this also tunes, and while she cutts
Sharp notes with melting voice, and mingled putts
Measures of middle sound, then suddenly
Shee thunders deepe, and juggs it inwardly,
With gentle murmurs, cleare and dull shee sings,
By course, as when the martial warning rings:
Beleev't the minstrel blusht; with angry mood
Inflam'd, quoth hee, thou chauntresse of the wood,
Either from thee Ile beare the prize away,
Or vanquisht break my lute without delay.
Inimitable accents then hee straynes;
His hand flyes ore the strings: in one hee chaynes
Four different numbers, chasing here and there,
And all the strings belabour'd everywhere:
Both flatt and sharpe hee strikes, and stately grows
To prouder straynes, and backwards as he goes

keemes] combs

138

Doubly divides, and closing upp his layes
Like a full quire a shouting consort playes;
Then pausing stood in expectation
If his corrival now dares answeare on;
But shee when practice long her throate had whett,
Induring not to yield, at once doth sett
Her spiritt all of worke, and all in vayne;
For while shee labours to express againe
With nature's simple touch such diverse keyes,
With slender pipes such lofty noates as these,
Orematcht with high designes, orematcht with woe,
Just at the last encounter of her foe
Shee faintes, shee dies, falls on his instrument
That conquer'd her; a fitting monument.
 So far even little soules are driven on,
 Struck with a vertuous emulation.


# SIR RICHARD FANSHAWE

## 1608–1666

### FROM THE LATIN OF HORACE

**164**

Cp.
Milton
Cowley
Horneck
Smart

## *Odes*, Book I, 5

What Stripling now Thee discomposes,
In Woodbine Rooms, on Beds of Roses,
 For whom thy Auburn Haire
 Is spread, Unpainted Faire?
How will he one day curse thy Oaths
And Heav'n that witness'd your Betroaths!
 How will the poor Cuckold,
 That deems thee perfect Gold,
Bearing no stamp but his, be mas'd
To see a suddain Tempest rais'd!
 He dreams not of the Windes,
 And thinks all Gold that shines.
For me my Votive Table showes
That I have hung up my wet Clothes
 Upon the Temple Wall
 Of Seas great Admirall.

165 *Odes*, Book I, 8

Lydia, in Heavens Name
  Why melts yong Sybaris in thy Flame?
Why doth he bed-rid lie
  That can indure th' intemp'rate Skie?
Why rides he not and twits
  The French great Horse with wringled bits?
Why shuns he Tybur's Flood,
  And wrastlers Oyle like Vipers Blood?
Nor hath His Flesh made soft
  With bruising Arms; having so oft
Been prais'd for shooting farre
  And clean delivered of the Barre?
For shame, why lies he hid
  As at Troy's Siege Achilles did,
For fear lest Mans Array
  Should Him to Manly Deeds betray?

166 Odes, Book I, 9

*To Thaliarchus*

Cp.
Dryden

Thou seest the Hills candied with Snow
Which groaning Woods scarce undergo,
  And a stiff Ice those Veins
  Congeals which Branch the Plains,
Dissolve the Frost with Logs pil'd up
To th' Mantle-Tree; let the great Cup
  Out of a larger Sluice
  Poure the reviving Juice.
Trust Jove with other things; when He
The fighting Winds takes up at Sea,
  Nor speared Cypress shakes,
  Nor Aged Elme Tree quakes.
Upon to Morrow reckon not,
Then if it comes 'tis clearly got:
  Nor being young despise
  Or Dancings, or Loves Joies.
Till testy Age gray Hairs shall Snow
Upon thy Head, loose Mask, nor Show:

Soft whispers now delight
At a sett hour by Night:
And Maids that gigle to discover
Where they are hidden to a Lover;
And Bracelets or some toy
Snatcht from the willing Coy.


OUT OF THE LATIN OF MARTIAL

**167**  Epigrams, Book X, 47
*A Happy Life*

Cp.
Surrey
Jonson
Fenton

The things that make a life to please
(Sweetest Martiall) they are these:
Estate inherited, not got:
A thankfull Field, Hearth always hot:
City seldome, Law-suits never:
Equall Friends agreeing ever:
Health of Body, Peace of Minde:
Sleepes that till the Morning binde:
Wise Simplicitie, Plaine Fare:
Not drunken Nights, yet loos'd from Care:
A Sober, not a sullen Spouse:
Cleane strength, not such as his that Plowes:
Wish onely what thou art, to bee;
Death neither wish, nor feare to see.


FROM THE PORTUGUESE OF LUIS VAZ DE CAMOËNS

## The Luciad

**168**  *'Dione (Venus) and the Sea-Nymphs prevent
da Gama from landing, to save him from the Moors of
Mombassa'*

Now through the ocean in great haste they flunder,
Raising the white foam with their silver Tayles.
Cloto with bosom breaks the waves in sunder,
And, with more fury then of custom, sayles;

Nise runs up an end, Nerine (younger)
Leaps o're them; frizled with her touching Scales,
   The crooked Billows (yielding) make a lane
    For the feard Nymphs to post it through the Maine.

Upon the Triton's back, with kindled Face,
The beauteous Ericyna furious rode.
He, to whose fortune fell so great a grace,
Feels not the Rider, proud of his fair load.
Now were they almost come upon the place
Where a stiff gale the warlike Navy blow'd.
   Here they devide, and in an instant cast
    Themselves about the Ships advancing fast.

The Goddess, with a party of the rest,
Lays her self plum against the Am'ral's Prow,
Stopping her progress with such main contest
That the swoln sayl the Wind in vain doth blow.
To the hard Oak she rivets her soft Brest,
Forcing the strong ship back again to go.
   Others (beleagu'ring) lift it from the Wave,
    It from the Bar of Enemies to save.

As to their Store-House when the Houswife Ants,
Carrying th'unequal Burthens plac't with slight
To their small shoulders (lest cold Winter's wants
Surprize them helpless) exercise their might;
This tugs, that shoves, one runs, another pants;
Strength far above their size, they All unite;
   So toyl the Nymphs, to snatch and to defend
    The men of Lusus from a dismal end.

169   *'The Moors of Melinde welcome the Portuguese'*

The shores are crown'd with people (of a fire
To be Spectators onely of the show):
The Scarlet Coates flame with the dye of Tyre:
The glossie Silks with all May's flow'rs do blow.
Instead of Arrows (part of Warr's Attire)
And of the horn'd Moon-imitating Bow,
   Palm in their hands, in sign of Peace, they bear:
    Which on their Heads victorious Heroes wear.

In a Canoe (which was both long and broad,
And glissend in the Sun with Cov'rings, made
Of mixed Silks) Melinde's King is row'd,
Wayted by Princes 'mongst their own obay'd.
In rich Attire (according to the mode
And custom of that Land) he comes arayd.
  Upon his Head he weares a Terbant, roll'd,
  Of silk and Cotton, with a Crown of gold.

A Roabe, of Scarlet-damask, (high-extold
By Them, and worth the wearing of a King)
About his Neck a Collar of pure gold:
The work worth twice the substance of the Thing.
A Velvet sheath a dagger keen did hold,
With Diamond-hilt, hang'd by a golden string.
  Sandals of Velvet on his Feet he wore,
  With gold and pearl imbroydred richly o're.

O're Him a round Silk-Canopy he had
Advanc't aloft upon a gilded Pole;
With which a Boy behind to burn forbad
Or trouble the Great King, the beams of Sol.
Musick ith'Prow, so merry that 'twas mad,
Grating the Eare with a harsh noise. The whole
  Consort is onely crooked Horns, wreath'd round,
  Which keep no time, but make a dismal sound.

No less adorn'd, the Lusitanian
From the Armada in his Boats doth dance,
To meet Him of Melinde with a Train
Whom much their cloaths, but more their deeds advance:
Gama comes clad after the use of Spain,
But wears a Cassock ala mode de France:
  The Stuff, a Florence-Satin; and the dye,
  A perfect Crimson, glorious in their Eye.

The Sleeves have golden Loops, which the Sun-shine
Makes too too bright and slippry for the Eyes:
His close Camp-Trowzes lac't with the same myne,
Which Fortune to so many men denyes:
Poynts likewise of the same, and Tagging fine,
With which his Doublet to his Hose he tyes.

A Sword of massive Gold, in Hanger tyde:
A Cap and Plume; the Cap set at one side.

Mong'st his Camrades, the noble Tyrian dye
(Not liv'ry-wise, but) sparcled here, and there,
The sev'ral Colours recreate the Eye:
So do the diff'rent Fashions which they weare.
Such their inamel'd Cloathes Varietie
(Compriz'd in one survey) as doth appear
    The painted Bow, in water-colours laid,
    Of Juno's Minion, the Thaumantian Mayd.

The ratling Trumpets, now, their joy augment
As, other times, they had their courage done.
The Moorish Boats cover'd the Sea, and went
Sweeping the Water with their silks Anon.
The Clowds of Heav'n the thund'ring Cannon rent,
And with new Clowds of Smoak put out the Sun.
    Before the Blow the winged lightning flies:
    The Moors's hands stop their Eares, the lids their Eyes.

FROM THE ITALIAN OF
GIOVANNI BATTISTA GUARINI

## Il Pastor Fido

170    *'The Speech of Corsica, a wanton Nymph*
*in love with Mirtillo'*

Learn women all from this housewifery,
Make you conserve of Lovers to keep by.
Had I no Sweet-heart but this sullen Boy,
Were I not well provided of a joy?
To extreme want how likely to be hurl'd
Is that ill houswife, who in all the world
But one Love onely, but one Servant hath?
Corsica will be no such fool. What's faith?
What's constancy? Tales which the jealous feign
To awe fond girls: names as absurd as vain.
Faith in a woman (if at least there be
Faith in a woman unreveal'd to me)

169 the Thaumantian Mayd] Iris (the rainbow), daughter of Thaumas

Is not a vertue, nor a heavenly grace,
But the sad penance of a ruin'd face,
That's pleas'd with one, cause it can please no more.
A handsome woman sought unto by store
Of gallant youths, if pleas'd with one alone
No woman is, or is a foolish one.
What's beauty (tell me) if not view'd? or view'd,
If not pursu'd? or if pursu'd, pursu'd
By one alone? Where Lovers frequent are,
It is a signe the partie lov'd is rare,
Glorious and bright. A womans honour is
T' have many Servants: Courtly Dames know this,
Who live in Towns, and those most practise it
Who have most wealth, most beauty, and most wit.
'Tis clownishnesse (say they) to reject any,
And folly too, since that's perform'd by many,
One cannot do: One Officer to wait,
A second to present, a third to prate,
A fourth for somewhat else; so it doth fall
Out oft, that favours being generall
No favours seem: or jealousie thus throwne
To whet them, all are easier kept then one.
This merry life is by great Ladies led
In Towns, and 'twas my fortune to be bred
With one of them; by whose example first,
Next by her rules, I in Loves art was nurst
Up from my childhood: she would often say,
'Corsica, thou must use another day
Thy Lovers like thy garments, put on one,
Have many, often shift, and wear out none.
For daily conversation breeds distast,
Distast contempt, and loathing at the last.
Then get the start, let not the servant say,
H' as turnd his Mistresse, not she him, away.

171        *'Kissing Chorus'*

   Well may that kisse be sweet that's giv'n t' a sleek
And fragrant rose of a vermilion cheek;
And understanding tasters (as are true
And happy Lovers) will commend that too.
'Tis a dead kisse, say I, and must be poor,
Which the place kist hath no means to restore.

But the sweet ecchoing, and the Dove-like billing
Of two encountring Mouthes, when both are willing;
And when at once both Loves advance their bows,
Their shafts drawn home, at once sound at the loose,
(How sweet is such Revenge!) This is true kissing,
Where there is one for t' other without missing
A minute of the time, or taking more
Then that which in the taking they restore.
Where by an interchange of amorous blisses
At the same time they sow and gather kisses.
Kisse a red swelling lip, then kisse a wrist,
A brest, a forehead, or what else thou list,
No part of a fair Nymph so just will be,
Except the lip, to pay this kisse to thee.
Thither your souls come sallying forth, and they
Kisse too, and by the wandring pow'rs convey
Life into smacking Rubies, and transfuse
Into the live and sprightly kisse their use
Of reason; so that yee discourse together
In kisses, which with little noyse deliver
Much matter; and sweet secrets, which hee spels,
Who is a Lover; Gibbrish to all else.
    Like life, like mutuall joy they feel, where Love
With equall flames as with two wings doth move.
And as where lips kisse lips is the best Kisse:
So where one's lov'd, to love, best loving is.


172        *Corsica encourages Amarillis to love*

        Our beauty is to us that which to men
        Wit is, or strength unto the lion. Then
        Let us use it whilst wee may;
        Snatch those joyes that haste away.
        Earth her winter-coat may cast,
        And renew her beauty past;
        But, our winter come, in vain
        We sollicite spring again:
        And when our furrows snow shall cover,
        Love may return, but never Lover.*

    * Guarini has a note on his debt to Catullus V.

146

173 *Chorus*

Fair golden Age! when milk was th' onely food,
And cradle of the infant-world the wood
(Rock'd by the windes); and th' untoucht flocks did bear
Their deer young for themselves! None yet did fear
The sword or poyson: no black thoughts begun
T' eclipse the light of the eternall Sun:
Nor wandring Pines unto a forreign shore
Or War, or Riches, (a worse mischief) bore.
That pompous sound, Idoll of vanity,
Made up of Title, Pride, and Flattery,
Which they call Honour whom Ambition blindes,
Was not as yet the Tyrant of our mindes,
But to buy reall goods with honest toil
Amongst the woods and flocks, to use no guile,
Was honour to those sober souls that knew
No happinesse but what from vertue grew.
Then sports and carols amongst Brooks and Plains
Kindled a lawfull flame in Nymphs and Swains.
Their hearts and Tongues concurr'd, the kisse and joy
Which were most sweet, and yet which least did cloy
Hymen bestow'd on them. To one alone
The lively Roses of delight were blown;
The theevish Lover found them shut on triall,
And fenc'd with prickles of a sharp denyall.
Were it in Cave or Wood, or purling Spring,
Husband and Lover signifi'd one thing.
  Base present age, which dost with thy impure
Delights the beauty of the soul obscure:
Teaching to nurse a Dropsie in the veins:
Bridling the look, but giv'st desire the reins.
Thus, like a net that spread and cover'd lies
With leaves and tempting flowrs, thou dost disguise
With coy and holy arts a wanton heart;
Mak'st life a Stage-play, vertue but a part:
Nor thinkst it any fault Love's sweets to steal,
So from the world thou canst the theft conceal.
  But thou that art the King of Kings, create
In us true honour: Vertue's all the state
Great souls should keep. Unto these cels return
Which were thy Court, but now thy absence mourn:

147

From their dead sleep with thy sharp goad awake
Them who, to follow their base wils, forsake
Thee, and the glory of the ancient world.
Let's hope: our ills have truce till we are hurld
From that: Let's hope; the sun that's set may rise,
And with new light salute our longing eyes.

## FROM THE SPANISH OF GÓNGORA

174      *A Great Favorit Beheaded*

The bloudy trunck of him who did possesse
    Above the rest a haplesse happy state,
    This little Stone doth Seale, but not depresse,
    And scarce can stop the rowling of his fate.

Brasse Tombes which justice hath deny'd t'his fault,
    The common pity to his vertues payes,
    Adorning an Imaginary vault,
    Which from our minds time strives in vaine to raze.

Ten yeares the world upon him falsly smild,
    Sheathing in fawning lookes the deadly knife
    Long aymed at his head; That so beguild
    It more securely might bereave his Life;

Then threw him to a Scaffold from a Throne,
Much Doctrine lyes under this little Stone.

# JOHN MILTON

### 1608–1674

## FROM THE HEBREW

175      *Psalm 2*

Why do the Gentiles tumult, and the Nations
    Muse a vain thing, the Kings of th'earth upstand
    With power, and Princes in their Congregations

Lay deep their plots together through each Land,
    Against the Lord and his Messiah dear
    Let us break off, say they, by strength of hand
Their bonds, and cast from us, no more to wear,
    Their twisted cords: he who in Heaven doth dwell
    Shall laugh, the Lord shall scoff them, then severe
Speak to them in his wrath, and in his fell
    And fierce ire trouble them; but I saith hee
    Anointed have my King (though ye rebell)
On Sion my holi'hill. A firm decree
    I will declare; the Lord to me hath say'd
    Thou art my Son I have begotten thee
This day; ask of me, and the grant is made;
    As thy possession I on thee bestow
    Th'Heathen, and as thy conquest to be sway'd
Earths utmost bounds: them shalt thou bring full low
    With Iron Scepter bruis'd, and them disperse
    Like to a potters vessel shiver'd so.
And now be wise at length ye Kings averse
    Be taught ye Judges of the earth; with fear
    Jehovah serve, and let your joy converse
With trembling; kiss the Son least he appear
    In anger and ye perish in the way
    If once his wrath take fire like fuel sere.
Happy all those who have in him their stay.


176            *Psalm 3*

Lord how many are my foes
    How many those
   That in arms against me rise
    Many are they
  That of my life distrustfully thus say,
No help for him in God there lies.
But thou Lord art my shield my glory,
    Thee through my story
  Th'exalter of my head I count
    Aloud I cry'd
  Unto Jehovah, he full soon reply'd
And heard me from his holy mount.

I lay and slept, I wak'd again,
　　　　For my sustain
　　　Was the Lord. Of many millions
　　　　The populous rout
　　I fear not though incamping round about
They pitch against me their Pavillions.
Rise Lord, save me my God for thou
　　　　Hast smote ere now
　　　On the cheek-bone all my foes,
　　　　Of men abhor'd
　　Hast broke the teeth. This help was from the Lord
Thy blessing on thy people flows.

FROM THE LATIN OF HORACE

177　　　　*Odes*, Book I, 5

Rendred almost word for word without Rhyme according to the Latin
Measure, as near as the Language will permit

Cp.
Fanshaw
Cowley
Horneck
Smart

What slender Youth bedew'd with liquid odours
　　Courts thee on Roses in some pleasant Cave,
　　Pyrrha for whom bindst thou
　　In wreaths thy golden Hair,
Plain in thy neatness; O how oft shall he
On Faith and changed Gods complain: and Seas
　　Rough with black winds and storms
　　Unwonted shall admire:
Who now enjoyes thee credulous, all Gold,
Who alwayes vacant always amiable
　　Hopes thee; of flattering gales
　　Unmindfull. Hapless they
To whom thou untry'd seem'st fair. Me in my vow'd
Picture the sacred wall declares t'have hung
　　My dank and dropping weeds
　　To the stern God of Sea.

# SIR MATTHEW HALE

## 1609–1676

### FROM THE LATIN OF SENECA

178              Chorus from *Thyestes*, Act II

Cp.
Wyatt
Heywood
Cowley
Marvell

Let him that will, ascend the tottering Seat
Of Courtly Grandeur, and become as great
As are his mountain Wishes; as for me,
Let sweet Repose, and Rest my portion be;
Give me some mean obscure Recess, a Sphere
Out of the road of Business, or the fear
Of Falling lower, where I sweetly may
My Self, and dear Retirement still enjoy.
Let not my Life, or Name, be known unto
The Grandees of the Times, tost to and fro
By Censures, or Applause; but let my Age
Slide gently by, not overthwart the Stage
Of Publick Interest; unheard, unseen,
And unconcern'd, as if I ne're had been,
And thus while I shall pass my silent days
In shady Privacy, free from the Noise
And busles of the World, then shall I
A good old Innocent Plebeian dy.
Death is a mere Surprize, a very Snare,
To him that makes it his lifes greatest care
To be a publick Pageant, known to All,
But unacquainted with Himself, doth fall.

# RICHARD CRASHAW

## 1612/13–1649

### FROM THE LATIN OF CATULLUS

Cp.
Ralegh
Jonson
Wordsworth
Landor

179

## *Carmina*, V

Come and let us live my Deare,
Let us love and never feare,
What the sowrest Fathers say:
Brightest Sol that dyes to day
Lives againe as blith to morrow,
But if we darke sons of sorrow
Set; ô then, how long a Night
Shuts the Eyes of our short light!
Then let amorous kisses dwell
On our lips, begin and tell
A Thousand, and a Hundred, score
An Hundred, and a Thousand more,
Till another Thousand smother
That, and that wipe of another.
Thus at last when we have numbered
Many a Thousand, many a Hundred;
Wee'l confound the reckoning quite,
And lose our selves in wild delight:
While our joyes so multiply,
As shall mocke the envious eye.

### FROM THE LATIN OF THOMAS OF CELANO

180

## *The Day of Judgment*

Hears't thou, my soul, what serious things
Both the Psalm and sybyll sings
Of a sure judge, from whose sharp Ray
The world in flames shall fly away.

O that fire! before whose face
Heavn and earth shall find no place.
O those eyes! whose angry light
Must be the day of that dread Night.

O that trump! whose blast shall run
An even round with the circling Sun.
And urge the murmuring graves to bring
Pale mankind forth to meet his king.

Horror of nature, hell and Death!
When a deep Groan from beneath
Shall cry we come, we come and all
The caves of night answer one call.

O that Book! whose leaves so bright
Will sett the world in severe light.
O that Judge! whose hand, whose eye
None can indure; yet none can fly.

Ah then, poor soul, what wilt thou say?
And to what Patron chuse to pray?
When starres themselves shall stagger; and
The most firm foot no more then stand.

But thou giv'st leave (dread Lord) that we
Take shelter from thy self, in thee;
And with the wings of thine own dove
Fly to thy scepter of soft love.

Dear, remember in that Day
Who was the cause thou cam'st this way.
Thy sheep was stray'd; And thou wouldst be
Even lost thy self in seeking me.

Shall all that labour, all that cost
Of love, and ev'n that losse, be lost?
And this lov'd soul, judg'd worth no lesse
Then all that way, and wearynesse?

Just mercy then, thy Reckning be
With my price, and not with me
'Twas pay'd at first with too much pain,
To be pay'd twice; or once, in vain.

Mercy (my judge) mercy I cry
With blushing Cheek and bleeding ey,
The conscious colors of my sin
Are red without and pale within.

O let thine own soft bowells pay
Thy self; And so discharge that day.
If sin can sigh, love can forgive.
O say the word my Soul shall live.

Those mercyes which thy MARY found
Or who thy crosse confes't and crown'd,
Hope tells my heart, the same loves be
Still alive; and still for me.

Though both my Prayres and teares combine,
Both worthlesse are; For they are mine.
But thou thy bounteous self still be;
And show thou art, by saving me.

O when thy last Frown shall proclaim
The flocks of goates to folds of flame,
And all thy lost sheep found shall be,
Let come ye blessed then call me.

When the dread ITE shall divide
Those Limbs of death from thy left side,
Let those life-speaking lipps command
That I inheritt thy right hand.

O hear a suppliant heart; all crush't
And crumbled into contrite dust.
My hope, my fear! my Judge, my Freind!
Take charge of me, and of my END.

FROM THE ITALIAN OF GIOVAN BATTISTA MARINO

## The Massacre of the Innocents

181       *'The Devil's Doubts'*

Yet on the other side, faine would he start
Above his feares, and thinke it cannot be.
Hee studies Scripture, strives to sound the heart,
And feele the pulse of every Prophecy.
Hee knowes (but knowes not how, or by what Art)
The Heav'n expecting Ages, hope to see
    A mighty Babe, whose pure, unspotted Birth,
    From a chast Virgin wombe, should blesse the Earth.

But these vast Mysteries his senses smother,
And Reason (for what's Faith to him?) devoure.
How she that is a maid should prove a Mother,
Yet keepe inviolate her virgin flower;
How Gods eternall Sonne should be mans Brother,
Poseth his proudest Intellectuall power.
    How a pure Spirit should incarnate bee,
    And life it selfe weare Deaths fraile Livery.

That the Great Angell-blinding light should shrinke
His blaze, to shine in a poore Shepheards eye.
That the unmeasur'd God so low should sinke,
As Pris'ner in a few poore Rags to lye.
That from his Mothers Brest hee milke should drinke,
Who feeds with Nectar Heav'ns faire family.
    That a vile Manger his low Bed should prove,
    Who in a Throne of stars Thunders above.

That hee whom the Sun serves, should fairly peepe
Through clouds of Infant flesh: that hee the old
Eternall Word should bee a Child, and weepe.
That hee who made the fire, should feare the cold;
That Heav'ns high Majesty his Court should keepe
In a clay-cottage, by each blast control'd.
    That Glories selfe should serve our Griefs, and feares:
    And free Eternity, submit to yeares.

And further, that the Lawes eternall Giver,
Should bleed in his owne lawes obedience:
And to the circumcising Knife deliver
Himselfe, the forfeit of his slaves offence.
That the unblemisht Lambe, blessed for ever,
Should take the marke of sin, and paine of sence.
    These are the knotty Riddles, whose darke doubt
    Intangles his lost Thoughts, past getting out.

182                 *Madrigal* XI

Love now no fire hath left him,
   We two betwixt us have divided it.
   Your Eyes the Light hath reft him.
The heat commanding in my Heart doth sit,
   O! that poore Love be not for ever spoyled,
   Let my Heat to your Light be reconciled.
     So shall these flames, whose worth
      Now all obscured lyes
     (Drest in those Beames) start forth
      And dance before your eyes.
     Or else partake my flames
      (I care not whither)
     And so in mutuall Names
      Of Love, burne both together.

# SIR JOHN DENHAM

## 1615–1669

### FROM THE GREEK OF HOMER

## The Iliad, Book XII

*Sarpedon's Speech to Glaucus*

Cp.
Pope

Thus to Glaucus spake
Divine Sarpedon, since he did not find
Others as great in Place, as great in Mind.
Above the rest, why is our Pomp, our Power?
Our flocks, our herds, and our possessions more?
Why all the Tributes Land and Sea affords
Heap'd in great Chargers, load our sumptuous boards?
Our chearful Guests carowse the sparkling tears
Of the rich Grape, whilst Musick charms their ears.
Why as we pass, do those on Xanthus shore,
As Gods behold us, and as Gods adore?
But that as well in danger, as degree,
We stand the first; that when our Lycians see
Our brave examples, they admiring say,
Behold our Gallant Leaders! These are They
Deserve the Greatness; and un-envied stand:
Since what they act, transcends what they command.
Could the declining of this Fate (oh friend)
Our Date to Immortality extend?
Or if Death sought not them, who seek not Death,
Would I advance? Or should my vainer breath
With such a Glorious Folly thee inspire?
But since with Fortune Nature doth conspire,
Since Age, Disease, or some less noble End,
Though not less certain, doth our days attend;
Since 'tis decreed, and to this period lead,
A thousand ways the noblest path we'll tread;
And bravely on, till they, or we, or all,
A common Sacrifice to Honour fall.

**FROM THE LATIN OF VIRGIL**

## The Aeneid

184        from *The Destruction of Troy:*
*the Death of Priam*

Thus fell the King, who yet surviv'd the State,
With such a signal and peculiar Fate.
Under so vast a ruine not a Grave,
Nor in such flames a funeral fire to have:
He, whom such Titles swell'd, such Power made proud
To whom the Scepters of all Asia bow'd,
On the cold earth lies th' unregarded King.
A headless Carkass, and a nameless Thing.*

185      *The Passion of Dido for Aeneas:*
*Dido sends her Sister Anne to ask Aeneas 'a short Reprieve'*

Cp.
Surrey

Dear Sister, my resentment had not been
So moving, if this Fate I had fore-seen;
Therefore to me this last kind office do,
Thou hast some interest in our scornful Foe,
He trusts to thee the Counsels of his mind,
Thou his soft hours, and free access canst find;
Tell him I sent not to the Ilian Coast
My Fleet to aid the Greeks; his Fathers Ghost
I never did disturb; ask him to lend
To this the last request that I shall send,
A gentle Ear; I wish that he may find
A happy passage, and a prosp'rous wind.
That contract I not plead, which he betray'd,
Nor that his promis'd Conquest be delay'd;

---

\* Thus Priam fell, and shared one common fate
  With Troy in ashes, and his ruined state—
  He, who the Sceptre of all Asia swayed,
  Whom monarchs like domestic slaves obeyed.
  On the bleak shore now lies the abandoned king,
  A headless carcase, and a nameless thing.
                Dryden, *Aeneid*, ll. 757–63.

All that I ask, is but a short Reprieve,
Till I forget to love, and learn to grieve;
Some pause and respite only I require,
Till with my tears I shall have quencht my fire.
If thy address can but obtain one day
Or two, my Death that service shall repay.
Thus she intreats; such messages with tears
Condoling Anne to him, and from him bears;
But him no Prayers, no Arguments can move,
The Fates resist, his Ears are stopt by Jove:
As when fierce Northern blasts from th' Alpes descend,
From his firm roots with struggling gusts to rend
An aged sturdy Oak, the ratling sound
Grows loud, with leaves and scatter'd arms the ground
Is over-layd; yet he stands fixt, as high
As his proud head is raised towards the Sky,
So low towards Hell his roots descend. With Pray'rs
And Tears the Hero thus assail'd, great cares
He smothers in his Breast, yet keeps his Post,
All their addresses and their labour lost.

### FROM THE LATIN OF MARTIAL

186         *Epigrams*, Book XI, 104

Prithee die and set me free,
   Or else be
Kind and brisk, and gay like me;
I pretend not to the wise ones,
   To the grave, to the grave,
Or the precise ones.

'Tis not Cheeks, nor Lips nor Eyes,
   That I prize,
Quick Conceits, or sharp Replies,
If wise thou wilt appear, and knowing,
   Repartie, Repartie
To what I'm doing.

Prithee why the Room so dark?
  Not a Spark
Left to light me to the mark;
I love day-light and a candle,
  And to see, and to see,
As well as handle.

Why so many Bolts and Locks,
  Coats and Smocks,
And those Drawers with a Pox?
I could wish, could Nature make it,
  Nakedness, Nakedness
It self were naked.

But if a Mistress I must have,
  Wise and grave,
Let her so her self behave
All the day long Susan Civil,
  Pap by night, pap by night
Or such a Divel.

# SIR EDWARD SHERBURNE

## 1616–1702

### FROM THE LATIN OF MARTIAL

187       Epigrams, Book XII, 17

*On Lentinus, being troubled with an Ague*

Lentinus! thou dost nought but fume, and fret,
To think thy Ague will not leave thee yet.
Why? it goes with thee; bathes as thou dost do,
Eats Mushromes, Oysters, Sweet-breads, wild Boar too,
Oft drunk by thee with Falern Wine is made,
Nor Cæcub drinks unless with snow allay'd:
Tumbles in Roses dawb'd with unctuous sweets,
Sleeps upon Down between pure Cambrick sheets,
And when thus well it fares with thee, wouldst thou
Have it to go unto poor Damma now?

# RICHARD LOVELACE

1618–1658

## FROM THE LATIN OF CATULLUS

## *Carmina*, XIII

Fabullus I will treat you handsomely
Shortly, if the kind gods will favour thee.
If thou dost bring with thee a del'cate messe,
An Olio or so, a pretty Lass,
Brisk wine, sharp tales, all sorts of Drollery,
These if thou bringst (I say) along with thee
You shall feed highly friend, for know the ebbs
Of my lank purse are full of Spiders webs,
But then again you shall recieve clear love
Or what more grateful or more sweet may prove,
For with an ointment I will favour thee,
My Venus's and Cupids gave to me,
Of which once smelt, the gods thou wilt implore
Fabullus that they'd make thee nose all ore.


## *Carmina*, LXIX

### *To Rufus*

That no fair woman will, wonder not why,
Clap (Rufus) under thine her tender thigh;
Not a silk gown shall once melt one of them,
Nor the delights of a transparent gemme.
A scurvy story kills thee, which doth tell
That in thine armpits a fierce goat doth dwell.
Him they all fear full of an ugly stinch,
Nor's 't fit he should lye with a handsome wench;
Wherefore this Noses cursed plague first crush,
Or cease to wonder why they fly you thus.

190 *Carmina*, LXX

*Female Inconstancy.*

Cp.
Sidney

My Mistresse sayes she'll marry none but me,
No not if Jove himself a Suitor be:
She sayes so; but what women say to kind
Lovers, we write in rapid streams and wind.

191 *Carmina*, LXXII

Cp.
Walsh

That me alone you lov'd, you once did say,
Nor should I to the King of gods give way,
Then I lov'd thee not as a common dear,
But as a Father doth his children chear;
Now thee I know, more bitterly I smart,
Yet thou to me more light and cheaper art.
What pow'r is this? that such a wrong should press
Me to love more, yet wish thee well much lesse.

192 *Carmina*, LXXXV

Cp.
Landor
Pound

I hate and love, wouldst thou the reason know?
I know not, but I burn and feel it so.

FROM THE LATIN OF AUSONIUS

193

On the Sicilian strand a Hare well wrought
Before the Hounds was by a Dog-fish caught;
Quoth she; all rape of Sea and Earth's on me,
Perhaps of Heav'n, if there a Dog-star be.

# ABRAHAM COWLEY

## 1618–1667

**TRANSLATED PARAPHRASTICALLY FROM THE GREEK**

### Anacreontea

194                                 *Love*

I'll sing of Heroes, and of Kings;
In mighty Numbers, mighty things,
Begin, my Muse; but lo the strings
To my great Song rebellious prove;
The strings will sound of nought but Love.
I broke them all, and put on new;
'Tis this or nothing sure will do.
These sure (said I) will me obey;
These sure Heroick Notes will play.
Straight I began with thundering Jove,
And all th' immortal Powers but Love.
Love smil'd, and from my'enfeebled Lyre
Came gentle Ayres, such as inspire
Melting Love, soft desire.
Farewel then Heroes, farewel Kings,
And mighty Numbers, mighty Things.
Love tunes my Heart just to my strings.

195                              *Drinking*

The thirsty Earth soaks up the Rain,
And drinks, and gapes for drink again.
The Plants suck in the Earth, and are
With constant drinking fresh and fair.
The Sea it self, which one would think
Should have but little need of Drink,
Drinks ten thousand Rivers up,
So fill'd that they o'rflow the Cup.
The busie Sun (and one would guess
By's drunken fiery face no less)
Drinks up the Sea, and when h'as done,

The Moon and Stars drink up the Sun.
They drink and dance by their own light,
They drink and revel all the night.
Nothing in Nature's Sober found,
But an eternal Health goes round.
Fill up the Bowl then, fill it high,
Fill all the Glasses there, for why
Should every Creature drink but I,
Why, Men of Morals, tell me why?

196                    *The Grasshopper*

Cp.
Stanley
for a measure
of Cowley's
expansion

Happy Insect, what can be
In happiness compar'd to Thee?
Fed with nourishment Divine.
The dewy Mornings gentle Wine!
Nature waits upon thee still,
And thy verdant Cup does fill;
'Tis fill'd where-ever thou dost tread,
Natures self's thy Ganymed.
Thou dost drink, and dance, and sing;
Happier than the happiest King!
All the Fields which thou dost see,
All the Plants belong to Thee,
All that Summer Hours produce,
Fertile made with early juice.
Man for thee does sow and plow;
Farmer He, and Landlord Thou!
Thou dost innocently joy;
Nor does thy Luxury destroy;
The Shepherd gladly heareth thee,
More Harmonious than He.
Thee Country Hinds with gladness hear,
Prophet of the ripened Year!
Thee Phœbus loves, and does inspire;
Phœbus is himself thy Sire.
To thee of all things upon Earth,
Life is no longer than thy Mirth.
Happy Insect, happy Thou,
Dost neither Age, nor Winter know.

But when thou'st drunk, and danc'd, and sung
Thy fill, the flowry Leaves among,
(Voluptuous, and Wise withal,
Epicurean Animal!)
Satiated with thy Summer Feast,
Thou retir'st to endless Rest.

197                    from *The Epicure*

Crown me with Roses whilest I Live,
Now your Wines and Oyntments give.
After Death I nothing crave,
Let me Alive my pleasures have,
All are Stoicks in the Grave.

IMITATED FROM THE LATIN OF CATULLUS

198              *Ode: Acme and Septimius*

Whil'st on Septimius panting Brest,
(Meaning nothing less than rest)
Acme lean'd her loving Head,
Thus the pleas'd Septimius said.

My dearest Acme, if I be
Once alive and love not thee
With a Passion far above
All that e're was called Love,
In Lybian Desart may
I become some Lions Prey,
Let him, Acme, let him tear
My Breast, when Acme is not there.

The God of Love who stood to hear him,
(The God of Love was always near him)
Pleas'd and tickl'd with the sound,
Sneez'd aloud, and all around
The little Loves that waited by,
Bow'd and blest the Augury.
Acme inflam'd with what he said,

Rear'd her gentle-bending head,
And her Purple Mouth with joy
Stretching to the delicious Boy
Twice (and twice could scarce suffice)
She kist his drunken rowling Eyes.

My little Life, my All (said she)
So may we ever Servents be
To this best God, and ne'er retain
Our hated Liberty again:
So may thy passion last for me,
As I a passion have for thee,
Greater and fiercer much than can
Be conceiv'd by thee a Man.
Into my Marrow it is gone,
Fixt and setled in the bone,
It reigns not only in my heart
But runs lik Life through ev'ry part.

She spoke; the God of Love aloud,
Sneez'd again, and all the croud
Of little Loves that waited by,
Bow'd and blest the Augury.

This good Omen thus from Heaven
Like a happy signal given,
Their Loves and Lives (all four) embrace,
And hand in hand run all the race,
To poor Septimius (who did now
Nothing else but Acme grow)
Acme's bosom was alone,
The whole Worlds Imperial Throne,
And to faithful Acme's mind
Septimius was all Human kind.

If the Gods would please to be
But advis'd for once by me,
I'd advise 'em when they spy
Any illustrious Piety,
To reward Her, if it be She;
To reward Him, if it be He;
With such a Husband, such a Wife,
With Acme's and Septimius's life.

## IMITATED FROM THE LATIN OF HORACE

**199**          *Odes*, Book 1, 5

Cp.
Milton
Fanshawe
Cowley
Horneck
Smart

To whom now Pyrrha, art thou kind?
   To what heart-ravisht Lover
Dost thou thy golden Locks unbind,
   Thy hidden sweets discover,
   And with large bounty open set
All the bright stores of thy rich Cabinet?

Ah simple Youth, how oft will he
   Of thy chang'd Faith complain?
And his own Fortunes find to be
   So airy and so vain,
   Of so Chamelion-like an hew,
That still their colour changes with it too?

How oft, alas, will he admire
   The blackness of the Skies?
Trembling to hear the Winds sound higher
   And see the Billows rise;
   Poor unexperienc'd He
Who ne'r, alas, before had been at Sea!

He enjoys thy calmy Sun-shine now,
   And no breath stirring hears;
In the clear Heaven of thy brow
   No smallest Cloud appears.
   He sees thee gentle, fair, and gay,
And trusts the faithless April of thy May.

Unhappy, thrice unhappy He,
   T' whom Thou untry'd dost shine!
But there's no danger now for Me,
   Since o'r Loretto's Shrine
   In witness of the Shipwrack past
My consecrated Vessel hangs at last.

200

## from *Odes*, Book III, 1

Cp.
Hopkins

Hence ye Prophane; I hate ye all;
　　Both the Great, Vulgar, and the small
To Virgin-Minds, which yet their Native whitness hold,
　　Not yet Discolour'd with the love of Gold,
　　　　(That Jaundice of the Soul,
　　Which makes it look so Gilded and so Foul)
　　To you, ye very few, these truths I tell,
The Muse inspires my Song, Hark, and observe it well.

We look on Men, and wonder at such odds
　　'Twixt things that were the same by Birth:
We look on Kings as Giants of the Earth,
These Giants are but Pigmeys to the Gods.
　　The humblest and the proudest Oak,
Are but of equal proof against the Thunder-stroke.
　　Beauty, and Strength, and Wit, and Wealth and Power
　　　　Have their short flourishing Hour;
　　　　And love to see themselves, and smile,
　　And joy in their Pre-eminence a while;
　　　　Even so in the same Land,
Poor Weeds, Rich Corn, gay Flowers, together stand;
Alas! Death mows down all with an impartial Hand.

201

## *The Country-Mouse*

A Paraphrase upon *Satires*, Book II, 6.

At the large foot of a fair hollow Tree,
Close to plow'd ground, seated commodiously,
His antient and Hereditary House,
There dwelt a good substantial Country-Mouse:
Frugal, and grave, and careful of the main,
Yet one, who once did nobly entertain
A City-Mouse well coated, sleek and gay,
A Mouse of high degree, which lost his way,
Wantonly walking forth to take the Air,
And arriv'd early, and belighted there,
For a days Lodging: the good hearty Host,
(The antient plenty of his Hall to boast)

Did all the store produce, that might excite
With various tastes, the Courtiers appetite.
Fitches, and Beans, Peason, Oats and Wheat,
And a large Chesnut the delicious Meat
Which Jove himself, were he a Mouse, would eat.
And for a Hautgoust there was mixt with these
The Swerd of Bacon, and the Coat of Cheese,
The precious Reliques; which at Harvest, he
Had gathered from the Reapers Luxurie.
Freely (said he) fall on and never spare,
The bounteous gods will for to morrow care.
And thus at ease on beds of Straw they lay,
And to their Genius they sacrific'd the day.
Yet the nice Guest's Epicurean mind,
(Though breeding made him civil seem, and kind)
Despis'd this Country Feast, and still his thought
Upon the Cakes and Pies of London wrought.
Your Bounty and Civility (said he)
Which I'm surpriz'd in these rude parts to see,
Shews that the gods have given you a mind
Too noble for the Fate which here you find.
Why should a Soul, so virt'ous, and so great,
Lose it self thus in an obscure retreat?
Let savage Beasts lodge in a Country Den,
You should see Towns, and Manners know, and Men;
And taste the gen'rous Luxury of the Court,
Where all the Mice of Quality resort;
Where thousand beaut'ous She's about you move,
And by high Fare, are plyant made to Love.
We all e'r long must render up our breath,
No cave or hole can shelter us from death.
   Since Life is so uncertain and so short,
Let's spend it all in Feasting and in Sport.
Come, worthy Sir, come with me, and partake
All the great things that Mortals happy make.
   Alas, what virtue hath sufficient Arms,
T' oppose bright Honour, and soft Pleasures charms?
What Wisdom can their Magick force repel?
It draws this rev'rend Hermit from his Cell.
It was the time when witty Poets tell,
*That Phœbus into Thetis bosome fell:*

*She blusht at first, and then put out the Light,*
*And drew the modest Curtains of the Night.*
Plainly, the troth to tell, the Sun was set,
When to the Town our wearied Trav'llers get,
To a Lords House as Lordly as can be
Made for the use of Pride and Luxurie,
They come; the gentle Courtier at the door
Stops, and will hardly enter in before.
But 'tis, Sir, your Command, and being so,
I'm sworn t'obedience, and so in they go,
Behind a Hanging in a spacious Room,
(The richest Work of Mortlackes Noble Loom)
They wait a while their wearied Limbs to rest,
Till silence should invite them to their Feast.
*About the hour that Cynthia's Silver Light*
*Had touch'd the pale Meridies of the Night;*
At last the various Supper being done
It happened that the Company was gone
Into a Room remote, Servants and all,
To please their noble Fancies with a Ball.
Our Host leads forth his Stranger, and does find
All fitted to the bounties of his mind.
Still on the Table half-fill'd dishes stood,
And with delicious bits the floor was strow'd.
The court'ous Mouse presents him with the best,
And both with fat varieties are blest.
Th' industrious Peasant every where does range,
And thanks the gods for his Life's happy change.
Loe, in the midst of a well-fraighted Pye,
They both at last glutted and wanton lye.
When see the sad Reverse of prosp'rous Fate,
And what fierce storms on mortal glories wait,
With hid'ous noise down the rude Servants come,
Six Dogs before run barking into th' room;
The wretched gluttons fly with wild affright,
And hate the fulness which retards their flight.
Our trembling Peasant wishes now in vain,
That Rocks and Mountains cover'd him again.
Oh how the change of his poor Life he curst!
This, of all lives (said he) is sure the worst.
Give me again, ye Gods, my Cave and Wood;
With Peace, let Tares and Acorns be my food.

ABRAHAM COWLEY

FROM THE LATIN OF SENECA

202    Chorus from *Thyestes*, Act II

Cp.
Wyatt
Heywood
Hale
Marvell

Upon the slippery tops of humane State,
   The guilded Pinnacles of Fate,
Let others proudly stand, and for a while
   The giddy danger to beguile,
With Joy and with disdain look down on all,
   Till their Heads turn, and they fall.
Me, O ye Gods, on Earth, or else so near
   That I no fall to Earth may fear,
And, O ye Gods, at a good distance seat
   From the long Ruins of the Great,
Here wrapt in th' Arms of Quiet let me lye;
   Quiet, Companion of Obscurity.
Here let my life, with as much silence slide,
   As time that measures it does glide.
Nor let the breath of Infamy or Fame,
From Town to Town echo about my Name.
Nor let my homely Death embroidered be
   With Scutcheon or with Elogie.
   An old Plebeian let me die,
Alas, all then are such as well as I.
   To him, alas, to him, I fear,
The face of Death will terrible appear,
Who in his life flattering his Senseless pride
By being known to all the World beside,
Does not himself, when he is Dying know
Nor what he is, nor whither he's to go.

IMITATED FROM THE LATIN OF MARTIAL

203    *Epigrams*, Book V, 59

To morrow you will Live, you always cry;
In what far Country does this Morrow lye,
That 'tis so mighty long e'r it arrive?
Beyond the Indies does this Morrow live?

171

'Tis so far fetcht this Morrow, that I fear
'Twill be both very Old and very Dear.
To morrow I will live, the Fool does say;
To Day it self's too late, the Wise liv'd Yesterday.


FROM THE LATIN OF CLAUDIAN

204        *The Old Man of Verona*

Happy the Man who his whole time doth bound
Within th'inclosure of his little ground.
Happy the Man whom the same humble place,
(Th'hereditary Cottage of his Race)
From his first rising infancy has known.
And by degrees sees gentle bending down,
With natural propension to that Earth
Which both preserv'd his Life, and gave him Birth.
Him no false distant lights by Fortune set,
Could ever into foolish wandrings get.
He never dangers either saw or fear'd:
The dreadful storms at Sea he never heard.
He never heard the shril alarms of War,
Or the worse noises of the Lawyers Bar.
No change of Consuls marks to him the year,
The change of seasons is his Calendar.
The Cold and Heat, Winter and Summer shows,
Autumn by Fruits, and Spring by Flow'rs he knows.
He measures time by Land-marks, and has found
For the whole day the Dial of his ground.
A neighbouring Wood born with himself he sees,
And loves his old contemporary trees.
H'as only heard of near Verona's Name,
And knows it like the Indies, but by Fame.
Does with the like concernment notice take
Of the Red Sea, and of Benacus Lake.
Thus Health and Strength he t'a third age enjoys,
And sees a long Posterity of Boys.
About the spacious World let others Roam,
The Voyage Life is longest made at home.

# ANDREW MARVELL

## 1621–1678

### FROM THE LATIN OF SENECA

205        Chorus from *Thyestes*, Act II

Cp.
Wyatt
Heywood
Hale
Cowley

Climb at Court for me that will
Tottering favors Pinacle;
All I seek is to lye still.
Settled in some secret Nest
In calm Leisure let me rest;
And far off the publick Stage
Pass away my silent Age.
Thus when without noise, unknown,
I have liv'd out all my span,
I shall dye, without a groan,
An old honest Country man.
Who expos'd to others Ey's,
Into his own Heart ne'r pry's,
Death to him's a Strange surprise.

# HENRY VAUGHAN

## 1622–1695

### FROM THE LATIN OF OVID

206        from *Tristium*, Book V, Elegy 3

And on this day, which Poets unto thee
Crown with full bowles, ask, What's become of me?
  Help bucksome God then! so may thy lov'd Vine
Swarm with the num'rous grape, and big with Wine
Load the kind Elm, and so thy Orgyes be
With priests lowd showtes, and Satyrs kept to thee!
So may in death Lycurgus ne'r be blest,
Nor Pentheus wandring ghost find any rest!

And so for ever bright (thy Chiefe desires,)
May thy Wifes Crown outshine the lesser fires!
If but now, mindfull of my love to thee,
Thou wilt, in what thou canst, my helper be.
You Gods have Commerce with your selves, try then
If Cæsar will restore me Rome agen.
   And you my trusty friends (the Jollie Crew
Of careless Poets!) when, without me, you
Perform this dayes glad Myst'ries, let it be
Your first Appeal unto his Deitie,
And let one of you (touch'd with my sad name)
Mixing his wine with tears, lay down the same,
And (sighing) to the rest this thought Commend,
O! Where is Ovid now our banish'd friend?
This doe, if in your brests I e'r deserv'd
So large a share, nor spitefully reserv'd,
Nor basely sold applause, or with a brow
Condemning others, did my selfe allow.
And may your happier wits grow lowd with fame
As you (my best of friends!) preserve my name.

207         De Ponto, Book III, Elegy 7

*To his friends (after his many sollicitations) refusing to
petition Caesar for his releasement.*

You have Consum'd my language, and my pen
Incens'd with begging scorns to write agen.
You grant, you knew my sute: My Muse, and I
Had taught it you in frequent Elegie,
That I believe (yet seal'd) you have divin'd
Our Repetitions, and forestal'd my mind,
So that my thronging Elegies, and I
Have made you (more then Poets) prophesie.
   But I am now awak'd; forgive my dream
Which made me Crosse the Proverb and the Stream,
And pardon, friends, that I so long have had
Such good thoughts of you, I am not so mad
As to continue them. You shall no more
Complain of troublesome Verse, or write o're
How I endanger you, and vex my Wife
With the sad legends of a banish'd life.

I'le bear these plagues my selfe: for I have past
Through greater ones, and can as well at last
These pettie Crosses. 'Tis for some young beast
To kick his bands, or wish his neck releast
From the sad Yoke. Know then, That as for me
Whom Fate hath us'd to such calamitie,
I scorn her spite and yours, and freely dare
The highest ills your malice can prepare.
   'Twas Fortune threw me hither, where I now
Rude Getes and Thrace see, with the snowie brow
Of Cloudie Æmus, and if she decree
Her sportive pilgrims last bed here must be
I am content; nay more, she cannot doe
That Act which I would not consent unto.
I can delight in vain hopes, and desire
That state more then her Change and Smiles, then high'r
I hugge a strong despaire, and think it brave
To baffle faith, and give those hopes a grave.
Have you not seen cur'd wounds enlarg'd, and he
That with the first wave sinks, yielding to th'free
Waters, without th'Expence of armes or breath
Hath still the easiest, and the quickest death.
Why nurse I sorrows then? why these desires
Of Changing Scythia for the Sun and fires
Of some calm kinder aire? what did bewitch
My frantick hopes to flye so vain a pitch,
And thus out-run my self? Mad-man! could I
Suspect fate had for me a Courtesie?
These errours grieve: And now I must forget
Those pleas'd Idœa's I did frame and set
Unto my selfe, with many fancyed Springs
And Groves, whose only losse new sorrow brings.
And yet I would the worst of fate endure,
E're you should be repuls'd, or lesse secure,
But (base, low soules!) you left me not for this,
But 'cause you durst not. Cæsar could not misse
Of such a trifle, for I know that he
Scorns the Cheap triumphs of my miserie.
   Then since (degen'rate friends) not he, but you
Cancell my hopes, and make afflictions new,
You shall Confesse, and fame shall tell you, I
At Ister dare as well as Tyber dye.

208     *from* De Ponto, Book IV, Elegy 3a

*To his Inconstant friend, translated for the use of all Judases
of this touch-stone-Age*

Shall I complain, or not? Or shall I mask
Thy hatefull name, and in this bitter task
Master my just Impatience, and write down
Thy crime alone, and leave the rest unknown?
Or wilt thou the succeeding years should see
And teach thy person to posteritie?
No, hope it not; for know, most wretched man,
'Tis not thy base and weak detraction can
Buy thee a Poem, nor move me to give
Thy name the honour in my Verse to live.
   Whilst yet my Ship did with no stormes dispute
And temp'rate winds fed with a calme salute
My prosp'rous sailes, thou wert the only man
That with me then an equall fortune ran,
But now since angry heav'n with Clouds and night
Stifled those Sun-beams, thou hast ta'ne thy flight,
Thou know'st I want thee, and art meerly gone
To shun that rescue, I rely'd upon;
Nay, thou dissemblest too, and doest disclame
Not only my Acquaintance, but my name;
Yet know (though deafe to this) that I am he
Whose years and love had the same Infancie
With thine, Thy deep familiar, that did share
Soules with thee, and partake thy Joyes or Care,
Whom the same Roofe lodg'd, and my Muse those nights
So solemnly endear'd to her delights;
But now, perfidious traitour, I am grown
The Abject of thy brest, not to be known
In that false Closet more; Nay, thou wilt not
So much as let me know, I am forgot.
If thou wilt say, thou didst not love me, then
Thou didst dissemble: or, if love agen,
Why now Inconstant? came the Crime from me
That wrought this Change? Sure, if no Justice be

Of my side, thine must have it. Why dost hide
Thy reasons then? for me, I did so guide
My selfe and actions, that I cannot see
What could offend thee, but my miserie.


209        *from* Tristium, Book III, Elegy 3a

    *To his Wife at Rome, when he was sick*
            '*Ovid's Epitaph*'

And here I wish my Soul died with my breath
And that no part of me were free from death,
For, if it be Immortall, and outlives
The body, as Pythagoras believes,
Betwixt these Sarmates ghosts, a Roman I
Shall wander, vext to all Eternitie.
   But thou (for after death I shall be free,)
Fetch home these bones, and what is left of me,
A few Flowers give them, with some Balme, and lay
Them in some Suburb-grave hard by the way,
And to Informe posterity, who's there,
This sad Inscription let my marble weare,
     '*Here lyes the soft-soul'd Lecturer of Love,*
        *Whose envy'd wit did his own ruine prove.*'
But thou, (who e'r thou beest, that passing by
Lendst to this sudden stone a hastie Eye,)
If e'r thou knew'st of Love the sweet disease,
Grudge not to say, May Ovid rest in peace!
This for my tombe: but in my books they'l see
More strong and lasting Monuments of mee,
Which I believe (though fatall) will afford
An Endless name unto their ruin'd Lord.

## FROM THE LATIN OF JUVENAL

210                    *from* Satires, X

'*Hannibal*'

Cp.
Gifford
Lowell                    ... Put Hannibal i'th' scale,
What weight affords the mighty Generall?
This is the man, whom Africks spacious Land
Bounded by th' Indian Sea, and Niles hot sand,
Could not containe; (Ye gods! that give to men
Such boundles appetites, why state you them
So short a time? either the one deny,
Or give their acts, and them Eternitie)
All Æthiopia, to the utmost bound
Of Titans course, (then which no Land is found
Lesse distant from the Sun) with him that ploughs
That fertile soile where fam'd Iberus flowes,
Are not enough to conquer; past now o're
The Pyrene hills, The Alps with all its store
Of Ice, and Rocks clad in eternall snow
(As if that Nature meant to give the blow)
Denyes him passage; straight on ev'ry side
He wounds the Hill, and by strong hand divides
The monstrous pile, nought can ambition stay,
The world, and nature yeeld to give him way:
And now past o're the Alps, that mighty bar
'Twixt France, and Rome, feare of the future war
Strikes Italy; successe, and hope doth fire
His lofty spirits with a fresh desire.
All is undone as yet (saith he) unlesse
Our Pænish forces we advance, and presse
Upon Rome's selfe; break downe her gates, and wall,
And plant our Colours in Suburra's Vale.
O the rare sight! if this great souldier wee
Arm'd on his Getick Elephant might see!
But what's the event? O glory! how the itch
Of thy short wonders doth mankinde bewitch!
He that but now all Italy, and Spaine,
Had conquer'd o're, is beaten out againe;

And in the heart of Africk, and the sight
Of his owne Carthage, forc'd to open flight.
Banish'd from thence, a fugitive he posts
To Syria first, then to Bythinia's Coasts;
Both places by his sword secur'd; though he
In this distresse must not acknowledg'd be;
Where once a Generall he triumphed, now
To shew what Fortune can, he begs as low.

    And thus that soule, which through all nations hurl'd
Conquest, and warre, and did amaze the world;
Of all those glories rob'd at his last breath,
Fortune would not vouchsafe a souldiers death,
For all that bloud the field of Cannæ boasts,
And sad Apulia fill'd with Roman ghoasts:
No other end (freed from the pile, and sword)
Then a poore Ring would Fortune him afford.

    Goe now ambitious man! new plots designe,
March o're the snowie Alps, and Apennine;
That after all, at best thou mayst but be
A pleasing story to posteritie!


## FROM THE LATIN OF BOETHIUS

211      from *The Consolation of Philosophy*

Happy that first white age! when wee
Lived by the Earths meere Charitie,
No soft luxurious Diet then
Had Effeminated men,
No other meat, nor wine had any
Than the Course Mast, or simple honey,
And by the Parents care layd up
Cheap Berries did the Children sup.
No pompous weare was in those dayes
Of gummie Silks, or Skarlet bayes,
Their beds were on some flowrie brink
And clear Spring-water was their drink.
The shadie Pine in the Suns heat
Was their Coole and known Retreat,
For then 'twas not cut down, but stood
The youth and glory of the wood.

The daring Sailer with his slaves
Then had not cut the swelling waves,
Nor for desire of forraign store
Seen any but his native shore.
No stirring Drum had scarr'd that age,
Nor the shrill Trumpets active rage,
No wounds by bitter hatred made
With warm bloud soil'd the shining blade;
For how could hostile madness arm
An age of love to publick harm?
When Common Justice none withstood,
Nor sought rewards for spilling bloud.
   O that at length our age would raise
Into the temper of those dayes!
But (worse then Ætna's fires!) debate
And Avarice inflame our state.
Alas! who was it that first found
Gold hid of purpose under ground,
That sought out Pearles, and div'd to find
Such pretious perils for mankind!

# THOMAS STANLEY

## 1626–1678

### FROM THE GREEK

### Anacreontea

212        *Beauty*

Hornes to Buls wise Nature lends:
Horses she with hoofs defends:
Hares with nimble feet relieves:
Dreadful teeth to Lions gives:
Fishes learns through streams to slide:
Birds through yeelding air to glide:
Men with courage she supplies:
But to Women these denies.

What then gives she? Beauty, this
Both their arms and armour is:
She, that can this weapon use,
Fire and sword with ease subdues.

213            *The Grasshopper*

Cp.
Cowley

Grasshopper thrice-happy! who
Sipping the cool morning dew,
Queen-like chirpest all the day
Seated on some verdant spray;
Thine is all what ere earth brings,
Or the howrs with laden wings;
Thee, the Ploughman calls his Joy,
'Cause thou nothing dost destroy:
Thou by all art honour'd; All
Thee the Springs sweet Prophet call;
By the Muses thou admir'd,
By Apollo art inspir'd,
Agelesse, ever singing, good,
Without passion, flesh or blood;
Oh how near thy happy state
Comes the Gods to imitate!

214           '*Young Men Dancing*'

Young Men dancing, and the old
Sporting I with joy behold;
But an old Man gay and free
Dancing most I love to see:
Age and youth alike he shares,
For his Heart belies his Haires.

FROM THE LATIN (ANONYMOUS)

215          from *Venus Vigils*

*Love he to morrow, who lov'd never;*
*To morrow, who hath lov'd, persever.*
The Spring appears, in which the Earth

Receives a new harmonious Birth;
When all things mutual Love unites;
When Birds perform their nuptial rites;
And fruitful by her watry Lover,
Each grove its tresses doth recover;
Loves Queen to morrow, in the shade
Which by these verdant trees is made,
Their sprouting tops in wreaths shall bind,
And Myrtles into Arbours wind;
To morrow rais'd on a high throne,
Dione shall her Laws make known.
*Love he to morrow, who lov'd never;*
*To morrow, who hath lov'd, persever.*
Then the round Oceans foaming flood,
Immingled with Celestial blood,
'Mongst the blew People of the Main,
And Horses whom two feet sustain,
Rising Dione did beget,
With fruitful waters dropping wet.
*Love he to morrow, who lov'd never;*
*To morrow, who hath lov'd, persever.*

\*

The Goddesse bade the Nymphs remove
Unto the shady Myrtle grove;
The boy goes with the maids, yet none
Will trust, or think love tame is grown,
If they perceive that any where
He Arrows doth about him bear.
Go fearlesse Nymphs, for love hath laid
Aside his Armes, and tame is made.
His weapons by command resign'd,
Naked to go he is enjoyn'd:
Lest he hurt any by his craft,
Either with flame, or bow, or shaft.
But yet take heed young Nymphs, beware
You trust him not, for Cupid's fair,
Lest by his beauty you be harm'd;
Love naked is compleatly arm'd.
*Love he to morrow, who lov'd never;*
*To morrow, who hath lov'd, persever.*

FROM THE LATIN OF JOHANNES SECUNDUS

216 *Basia*, VIII

Not alwayes give a melting Kiss,
    And Smiles with pleasing Whispers joyn'd;
Nor alwayes extasi'd with Bliss
    About my Neck thy fair Arms wind.

The wary Lover learns by measure
    To circumscribe his greatest joy;
Lest, what well-husbanded yeilds pleasure,
    Might by the Repetition cloy.

When thrice three Kisses I require,
    Give me but two, withhold the other;
Such as cold Virgins to their Sire,
    Or chaste Diana gives her Brother.

Then wantonly snatch back thy Lip,
    And smoothly, as sly Fishes glide
Through Water giving me the slip,
    Thy self in some dark Corner hide.

I'le follow Thee with eager haste
    And having caught (as Hawks their Pray)
In my victorious Arm held fast
    Panting for Breath, bear thee away.

Then thy soft Arms about me twin'd
    Thou shalt use all thy skill to please me,
And offer all that was behind,
    The poor Seven Kisses, to appease me.

How much mistaken wilt thou be!
    For seven times seven shalt thou pay,
Whilst in my Arms I fetter Thee
    Lest thou once more should'st get away.

'Till I at last have made thee swear
  By all thy Beauty and my Love,
That thou again the same severe
  Revenge for the same Crime would'st prove.


## FROM THE ITALIAN OF GIROLAMO CASONE

217                    *Time Recover'd*

Come (my dear) whilst youth conspires
With the warmth of our desires;
Envious Time about thee watches,
And some Grace each minute snatches:
Now a spirit, now a Ray
From thy Eye he steals away,
Now he blasts some blooming Rose
Which upon thy fresh Cheek grows;
Gold now plunders in a Hair;
Now the Rubies doth impair
Of thy lips; and with sure hast
All thy wealth will take at last;
Onely that of which Thou mak'st
Use in time, from time Thou tak'st.


## FROM THE SPANISH OF JUAN PEREZ DE MONTALVAN

218                    *The Self-Deceaver*

Deceav'd and undeceav'd to be
  At once I seek with equal care,
Wretched in the discovery,
  Happy if cozen'd still I were:
Yet certain ill of ill hath lesse
Then the mistrust of happinesse.

But if when I have reach'd my Aime,
  (That which I seek less worthy prove,)
Yet still my Love remains the same,
  The subject not deserving Love;
I can no longer be excus'd,
Now more in fault as less abus'd.

Then let me flatter my Desires,
    And doubt what I might know too sure,
He that to cheat himself conspires,
    From falsehood doth his Faith secure;
In Love uncertain to believe
I am deceiv'd, doth undeceive.

For if my Life on Doubt depend,
    And in distrust inconstant steer,
If I essay the strife to end
    (When Ignorance were Wisdom here;)
All thy attempts how can I blame
To work my Death? I seek the same.


# JOHN DRYDEN

### 1631–1700

#### FROM THE GREEK OF HOMER

## The Iliad

219                     '*The Invocation*'

The wrath of Peleus Son, O Muse, resound;
Whose dire Effects the Grecian Army found:
And many a Heroe, King, and hardy Knight,
Were sent, in early Youth, to Shades of Night:
Their Limbs a Prey to Dogs and Vulturs made;
So was the Sov'reign Will of Jove obey'd:
From that ill-omen'd Hour when Strife begun,
Betwixt Atrides Great, and Thetis God-like Son.


220          '*Achilles, threatened by Agamemnon*'

  At this th' Impatient Hero sowrly smil'd:
His Heart, impetuous in his Bosom boil'd,
And justled by two Tides of equal sway,
Stood, for a while, suspended in his way.

Betwixt his Reason, and his Rage untam'd;
One whisper'd soft, and one aloud reclaim'd:
That only counsell'd to the safer side;
This to the Sword, his ready Hand apply'd.
Unpunish'd to support th' Affront was hard:
Nor easy was th' Attempt to force the Guard.
But soon the thirst of Vengeance fir'd his Blood:
Half shone his Faulchion, and half sheath'd it stood.
   In that nice moment, Pallas, from above,
Commission'd by th' Imperial Wife of Jove,
Descended swift: (the white arm'd Queen was loath
The Fight shou'd follow; for she favour'd both:)
Just as in Act he stood, in Clouds inshrin'd,
Her Hand she fasten'd on his Hair behind;
Then backward by his yellow Curls she drew:
To him, and him alone confess'd in view.
Tam'd by superiour Force he turn'd his Eyes
Aghast at first, and stupid with Surprize.

221          *'Achilles' Wrath'*

   At her departure his Disdain return'd:
The Fire she fan'd, with greater Fury burn'd;
Rumbling within till thus it found a vent:
Dastard, and Drunkard, Mean and Insolent:
Tongue-valiant Hero, Vaunter of thy Might,
In Threats the foremost, but the lag in Fight;
When did'st thou thrust amid the mingled Preace,
Content to bid the War aloof in Peace?
Arms are the Trade of each Plebeyan Soul;
'Tis Death to fight; but Kingly to controul.
Lord-like at ease, with arbitrary Pow'r,
To peel the Chiefs, the People to devour.
These, Traitor, are thy Tallents; safer far
Than to contend in Fields, and Toils of War.
Nor coud'st thou thus have dar'd the common Hate,
Were not their Souls as abject as their State.
But, by this Scepter, solemnly I swear,
(Which never more green Leaf or growing Branch shall bear:
Torn from the Tree, and giv'n by Jove to those
Who Laws dispence and mighty Wrongs oppose)
That when the Grecians want my wonted Aid,
No Gift shall bribe it, and no Pray'r persuade.

222      *'The Sacrifice to Apollo'*

Now when the solemn Rites of Pray'r were past,
Their salted Cakes on crackling Flames they cast.
Then, turning back, the Sacrifice they sped:
The fatted Oxen slew, and flea'd the Dead.
Chop'd off their nervous Thighs, and next prepar'd
T' involve the lean in Cauls, and mend with Lard.
Sweet-breads and Collops, were with Skewers prick'd
About the Sides; inbibing what they deck'd.
The Priest with holy Hands was seen to tine
The cloven Wood, and pour the ruddy Wine.
The Youth approach'd the Fire and as it burn'd
On five sharp Broachers rank'd, the Roast they turn'd:
These Morsels stay'd their Stomachs; then the rest
They cut in Legs and Fillets for the Feast;
Which drawn and serv'd, their Hunger they appease
With sav'ry Meat, and set their Minds at ease.
Now when the rage of Eating was repell'd,
The Boys with generous Wine the Goblets fill'd.
The first Libations to the Gods they pour:
And then with Songs indulge the Genial Hour.
Holy Debauch! Till Day to Night they bring,
With Hymns and Pæans to the Bowyer King.
At Sun-set to their Ship they make return,
And snore secure on Decks, till rosy Morn.

223      *'Thetis asks Jove to revenge her Son Achilles'*

Now, when twelve Days compleat had run their Race,
The Gods bethought them of the Cares belonging to their place.
Jove at their Head ascending from the Sea,
A shoal of puny Pow'rs attend his way.
Then Thetis not unmindful of her Son
Emerging from the Deep, to beg her Boon,
Pursu'd their Track; and waken'd from his rest,
Before the Soveraign stood a Morning Guest.
Him in the Circle but apart, she found:
The rest at awful distance stood around.
She bow'd, and e'er she durst her Sute begin,
One Hand embrac'd his Knees, one prop'd his Chin.

Then thus. If I, Celestial Sire, in aught
Have serv'd thy Will, or gratify'd thy Thought,
One glimpse of Glory to my Issue give;
Grac'd for the little time he has to live.
Dishonour'd by the King of Men he stands:
His rightful Prize is ravish'd from his Hands.
But thou, O Father, in my Son's Defence,
Assume thy Pow'r, assert thy Providence.
Let Troy prevail, till Greece th' Affront has paid,
With doubled Honours; and redeem'd his Aid.
　　She ceas'd, but the consid'ring God was mute:
'Till she resolv'd to win, renew'd her Sute:
Nor loos'd her Hold, but forc'd him to reply,
Or grant me my Petition, or deny:
Jove cannot fear: Then tell me to my Face
That I, of all the Gods am least in grace.
This I can bear: The Cloud-Compeller mourn'd,
And sighing, first, this Answer he return'd.
　　Know'st thou what Clamors will disturb my Reign,
What my stun'd Ears from Juno must sustain?
In Council she gives Licence to her Tongue,
Loquacious, Brawling, ever in the wrong.
And now she will my partial Pow'r upbraid,
If alienate from Greece, I give the Trojans Aid.
But thou depart, and shun her jealous Sight,
The Care be mine, to do Pelides right.
Go then, and on the Faith of Jove rely;
When nodding to thy Sute, he bows the Sky.
This ratifies th' irrevocable Doom:
The Sign ordain'd, that what I will shall come:
The Stamp of Heav'n, and Seal of Fate: He said,
And shook the sacred Honours of his Head.
With Terror trembled Heav'ns subsiding Hill:
And from his shaken Curls Ambrosial Dews distil.
The Goddess goes exulting from his Sight,
And seeks the Seas profound; and leaves the Realms of Light.
　　He moves into his Hall: The Pow'rs resort,
Each from his House to fill the Soveraign's Court.
Nor waiting Summons, nor expecting stood;
But met with Reverence, and receiv'd the God.
He mounts the Throne; and Juno took her place:
But sullen Discontent sate lowring on her Face.

With jealous Eyes, at distance she had seen,
Whisp'ring with Jove the Silver-footed Queen;
Then, impotent of Tongue (her Silence broke)
Thus turbulent in rattling Tone she spoke.

   Author of Ills, and close Contriver Jove,
Which of thy Dames, what Prostitute of Love,
Has held thy Ear so long and begg'd so hard
For some old Service done, some new Reward?
Apart you talk'd, for that's your special care
The Consort never must the Council share.
One gracious Word is for a Wife too much:
Such is a Marriage-Vow, and Jove's own Faith is such.

   Then thus the Sire of Gods, and Men below,
What I have hidden, hope not thou to know.
Ev'n Goddesses are Women: And no Wife
Has Pow'r to regulate her Husband's Life:
Counsel she may; and I will give thy Ear
The Knowledge first, of what is fit to hear.
What I transact with others, or alone,
Beware to learn; nor press too near the Throne.

   To whom the Goddess with the charming Eyes,
What hast thou said, O Tyrant of the Skies,
When did I search the Secrets of thy Reign,
Though priviledg'd to know, but priviledg'd in vain?
But well thou dost, to hide from common Sight
Thy close Intrigues, too bad to bear the Light.
Nor doubt I, but the Silver-footed Dame,
Tripping from Sea, on such an Errand came,
To grace her Issue, at the Grecians Cost,
And for one peevish Man destroy an Host.

   To whom the Thund'rer made this stern Reply;
My Household Curse, my lawful Plague, the Spy
Of Jove's Designs, his other squinting Eye;
Why this vain prying, and for what avail?
Jove will be Master still and Juno fail.
Shou'd thy suspicious Thoughts divine aright,
Thou but becom'st more odious to my Sight,
For this Attempt: uneasy Life to me
Still watch'd, and importun'd, but worse for thee.
Curb that impetuous Tongue, before too late
The Gods behold, and tremble at thy Fate.

Pitying, but daring not in thy Defence,
To lift a Hand against Omnipotence.
    This heard, the Imperious Queen sate mute with Fear;
Nor further durst incense the gloomy Thunderer.
Silence was in the Court at this Rebuke:
Nor cou'd the Gods abash'd, sustain their Sov'reigns Look.
    The Limping Smith, observ'd the sadden'd Feast;
And hopping here and there (himself a Jest)
Put in his Word, that neither might offend;
To Jove obsequious, yet his Mother's Friend.
What end in Heav'n will be of civil War,
If Gods of Pleasure will for Mortals jar?
Such Discord but disturbs our Jovial Feast;
One Grain of Bad, embitters all the best.
Mother, tho' wise your self, my Counsel weigh;
'Tis much unsafe my Sire to disobey.
Not only you provoke him to your Cost,
But Mirth is marr'd, and the good Chear is lost.
Tempt not his heavy Hand; for he has Pow'r
To throw you Headlong, from his Heav'nly Tow'r.
But one submissive Word, which you let fall,
Will make him in good Humour with us All.
    He said no more but crown'd a Bowl, unbid:
The laughing Nectar overlook'd the Lid:
Then put it to her Hand; and thus pursu'd,
This cursed Quarrel be no more renew'd.
Be, as becomes a Wife, obedient still;
Though griev'd, yet subject to her Husband's Will.
I wou'd not see you beaten; yet affraid
Of Jove's superior Force, I dare not aid.
Too well I know him, since that hapless Hour
When I, and all the Gods employ'd our Pow'r
To break your Bonds: Me by the Heel he drew;
And o'er Heav'n's Battlements with Fury threw.
All Day I fell; My Flight at Morn begun,
And ended not but with the setting Sun.
Pitch'd on my Head, at length the Lemnian-ground
Receiv'd my batter'd Skull, the Sinthians heal'd my Wound.
    At Vulcan's homely Mirth his Mother smil'd,
And smiling took the Cup the Clown had fill'd.
The Reconciler Bowl, went round the Board,
Which empty'd, the rude Skinker still restor'd.

Loud Fits of Laughter seiz'd the Guests, to see
The limping God so deft at his new Ministry.
The Feast continu'd till declining Light:
They drank, they laugh'd, they lov'd, and then 'twas Night.
Nor wanted tuneful Harp, nor vocal Quire;
The Muses sung; Apollo touch'd the Lyre.
Drunken at last, and drowsy they depart,
Each to his House; Adorn'd with labour'd Art
Of the lame Architect: The thund'ring God
Ev'n he withdrew to rest, and had his Load.
His swimming Head to needful Sleep apply'd;
And Juno lay unheeded by his Side.

FROM THE GREEK OF THEOCRITUS

**224**                    *Idylls*, XXVII

| | |
|---|---|
| *Daphnis* | The Shepheard Paris bore the Spartan Bride |
| | By force away, and then by force enjoy'd; |
| | But I by free consent can boast a Bliss, |
| | A fairer Helen, and a sweeter kiss. |
| *Chloris* | Kisses are empty joyes and soon are o're. |
| *Daphnis* | A Kiss betwixt the lips is something more. |
| *Chloris* | I wipe my mouth, and where's your kissing then? |
| *Daphnis* | I swear you wipe it to be kiss'd agen. |
| *Chloris* | Go tend your Herd, and kiss your Cows at home; |
| | I am a Maid, and in my Beauties bloom. |
| *Daphnis* | 'Tis well remember'd, do not waste your time; |
| | But wisely use it e're you pass your prime. |
| *Chloris* | Blown Roses hold their sweetness to the last, |
| | And Raisins keep their luscious native taste. |
| *Daphnis* | The Sun's too hot; those Olive shades are near; |
| | I fain wou'd whisper something in your ear. |
| *Chloris* | 'Tis honest talking where we may be seen, |
| | God knows what secret mischief you may mean; |
| | I doubt you'l play the Wag and kiss agen. |
| *Daphnis* | At least beneath yon' Elm you need not fear; |
| | My Pipe's in tune, if you'r dispos'd to hear. |
| *Chloris* | Play by your self, I dare not venture thither: |
| | You, and your naughty Pipe go hang together. |

| | |
|---|---|
| *Daphnis* | Coy Nymph beware, lest Venus you offend: |
| *Chloris* | I shall have chaste Diana still to friend. |
| *Daphnis* | You have a Soul, and Cupid has a Dart; |
| *Chloris* | Diana will defend, or heal my heart. |
| | Nay, fie what mean you in this open place; |
| | Unhand me, or, I sware, I'le scratch your face. |
| | Let go for shame; you make me mad for spight; |
| | My mouth's my own; and if you kiss I'le bite. |
| *Daphnis* | Away with your dissembling Female tricks: |
| | What, wou'd you 'scape the fate of all your Sex? |
| *Chloris* | I swear I'le keep my Maidenhead till death, |
| | And die as pure as Queen Elizabeth. |
| *Daphnis* | Nay mum for that; but let me lay thee down; |
| | Better with me, than with some nauseous Clown. |
| *Chloris* | I'de have you know, if I were so inclin'd, |
| | I have bin wo'd by many a wealthy Hind; |
| | But never found a Husband to my mind. |
| *Daphnis* | But they are absent all; and I am here; |
| *Chloris* | The matrimonial Yoke is hard to bear; |
| | And Marriage is a woful word to hear. |
| *Daphnis* | A scar Crow, set to frighten fools away; |
| | Marriage has joys; and you shall have a say. |
| *Chloris* | Sour sawce is often mix'd with our delight, |
| | You kick by day more than you kiss by night. |
| *Daphnis* | Sham stories all; but say the worst you can, |
| | A very Wife fears neither God nor Man. |
| *Chloris* | But Child-birth is they say, a deadly pain; |
| | It costs at least a Month to knit again. |
| *Daphnis* | Diana cures the wounds Lucina made; |
| | Your Goddess is a Midwife by her Trade. |
| *Chloris* | But I shall spoil my Beauty if I bear. |
| *Daphnis* | But Mam and Dad are pretty names to hear. |
| *Chloris* | But there's a Civil question us'd of late; |
| | Where lies my jointure, where your own Estate? |
| *Daphnis* | My Flocks, my Fields, my Wood, my Pastures take, |
| | With settlement as good as Law can make. |
| *Chloris* | Swear then you will not leave me on the common, |
| | But marry me, and make an honest Woman. |
| *Daphnis* | I swear by Pan (tho' he wears horns you'll say) |
| | Cudgell'd and kick'd, I'le not be forc'd away. |
| *Chloris* | I bargain for a wedding Bed at least, |
| | A house, and handsome Lodging for a guest. |

*Daphnis*     A house well furnish'd shall be thine to keep;
            And for a flock-bed I can sheer my Sheep.
*Chloris*      What Tale shall I to my old Father tell?
*Daphnis*    'T will make him Chuckle thou'rt bestow'd so well.
*Chloris*      But after all, in troth I am to blame
            To be so loving, e're I know your Name.
            A pleasant sounding name's a pretty thing:
*Daphnis*    Faith, mine's a very pretty name to sing;
            They call me Daphnis: Lycidas my Syre,
            Both sound as well as Woman can desire.
            Nomæa bore me; Farmers in degree,
            He a good Husband, a good Housewife she.
*Chloris*      Your kindred is not much amiss, 'tis true,
            Yet I am somewhat better born than you.
*Daphnis*    I know your Father, and his Family;
            And without boasting am as good as he
            Menalcas; and no Master goes before.
*Chloris*      Hang both our Pedigrees; not one word more;
            But if you love me let me see your Living,
            Your House and Home; for seeing is believing.
*Daphnis*    See first yon Cypress Grove, (a shade from noon;)
*Chloris*      Browze on my goats; for I'le be with you soon.
*Daphnis*    Feed well my Bulls, to whet your appetite;
            That each may take a lusty Leap at Night.
*Chloris*      What do you mean (uncivil as you are,)
            To touch my breasts, and leave my bosome bare?
*Daphnis*    These pretty bubbies first I make my own.
*Chloris*      Pull out your hand, I swear, or I shall swoon.
*Daphnis*    Why does thy ebbing blood forsake thy face?
*Chloris*      Throw me at least upon a cleaner place:
            My Linnen ruffled, and my Wastcoat soyling,
            What, do you think new Cloaths, were made for spoyling?
*Daphnis*    I'le lay my Lambskins underneath thy back:
*Chloris*      My Head Geer's off; what filthy work you make!
*Daphnis*    To Venus first, I lay these off'rings by;
*Chloris*      Nay first look round, that no body be nigh:
            Methinks I hear a whisp'ring in the Grove.
*Daphnis*    The Cypress Trees are telling Tales of love.
*Chloris*      You tear off all behind me, and before me;
            And I'm as naked as my Mother bore me.
*Daphnis*    I'le buy thee better Cloaths than these I tear,
            And lie so close, I'le cover thee from Air.

| | |
|---|---|
| *Chloris* | Y'are liberal now; but when your turn is sped, |
| | You'l wish me choak'd with every crust of Bread. |
| *Daphnis* | I'le give thee more, much more than I have told; |
| | Wou'd I cou'd coyn my very heart to Gold. |
| *Chloris* | Forgive thy handmaid (Huntress of the wood,) |
| | I see there's no resisting flesh and blood! |
| *Daphnis* | The noble deed is done; my Herds I'le cull; |
| | Cupid, be thine a Calf; and Venus, thine a Bull. |
| *Chloris* | A Maid I came, in an unlucky hour, |
| | But hence return, without my Virgin flour. |
| *Daphnis* | A Maid is but a barren Name at best; |
| | If thou canst hold, I bid for twins at least. |

Thus did this happy Pair their love dispence
With mutual joys, and gratifi'd their sense;
The God of Love was there a bidden Guest;
And present at his own Mysterious Feast.
His azure Mantle underneath he spred,
And scatter'd Roses on the Nuptial Bed;
While folded in each others arms they lay,
He blew the flames, and furnish'd out the play,
And from their Foreheads wip'd the balmy sweat away.
First rose the Maid, and with a glowing Face,
Her down cast eyes beheld her print upon the grass;
Thence to her Herd she sped her self in haste:
The Bridegroom started from his Trance at last,
And pipeing homeward jocoundly he past.


### FROM THE LATIN OF LUCRETIUS

## from *De Rerum Natura*

225    Delight of Humane kind, and Gods above;
Parent of Rome; Propitious Queen of Love;
Whose vital pow'r, Air, Earth, and Sea supplies;
And breeds what e'r is born beneath the rowling Skies:
For every kind, by thy prolifique might,
Springs, and beholds the Regions of the light:
Thee, Goddess thee, the clouds and tempests fear,
And at thy pleasing presence disappear:

For thee the Land in fragrant Flow'rs is drest,
For thee the Ocean smiles, and smooths her wavy breast;
And Heav'n it self with more serene, and purer light is blest.
For when the rising Spring adorns the Mead,
And a new Scene of Nature stands display'd,
When teeming Budds, and chearful greens appear,
And Western gales unlock the lazy year,
The joyous Birds thy welcome first express,
Whose native Songs thy genial fire confess:
Then salvage Beasts bound o're their slighted food,
Strook with thy darts, and tempt the raging floud:
All Nature is thy Gift; Earth, Air, and Sea:
Of all that breaths, the various progeny,
Stung with delight, is goaded on by thee.
O're barren Mountains, o're the flow'ry Plain,
The leavy Forest, and the liquid Main
Extends thy uncontroul'd and boundless reign.
Through all the living Regions dost thou move,
And scatter'st, where thou goest, the kindly seeds of Love:
Since then the race of every living thing,
Obeys thy pow'r; since nothing new can spring
Without thy warmth, without thy influence bear,
Or beautiful, or lovesome can appear,
Be thou my ayd: My tuneful Song inspire,
And kindle with thy own productive fire.

226        *Against the Fear of Death*

What has this Bugbear death to frighten Man,
If Souls can die, as well as Bodies can?
For, as before our Birth we felt no pain
When Punique arms infested Land and Mayn,
When Heav'n and Earth were in confusion hurl'd
For the debated Empire of the World,
Which aw'd with dreadful expectation lay,
Sure to be Slaves, uncertain who shou'd sway:
So, when our mortal frame shall be disjoyn'd,
The lifeless Lump, uncoupled from the mind,
From sense of grief and pain we shall be free;
We shall not feel, because we shall not Be.
Though Earth in Seas, and Seas in Heav'n were lost,
We shou'd not move, we only shou'd be tost.

Nay, ev'n suppose when we have suffer'd Fate,
The Soul cou'd feel in her divided state,
What's that to us, for we are only we
While Souls and bodies in one frame agree?
Nay, tho' our Atoms shou'd revolve by chance,
And matter leape into the former dance;
Tho' time our Life and motion cou'd restore,
And make our Bodies what they were before,
What gain to us wou'd all this bustle bring,
The new made man wou'd be another thing;
When once an interrupting pause is made,
That individual Being is decay'd.

*

And therefore if a Man bemoan his lot,
That after death his mouldring limbs shall rot,
Or flames, or jaws of Beasts devour his Mass,
Know he's an unsincere, unthinking Ass.
A secret Sting remains within his mind,
The fool is to his own cast offals kind;
He boasts no sense can after death remain,
Yet makes himself a part of life again:
As if some other He could feel the pain.
If, while he live, this thought molest his head,
What Wolf or Vulture shall devour me dead,
He wasts his days in idle grief, nor can
Distinguish 'twixt the Body and the Man:
But thinks himself can still himself survive;
And what when dead he feels not, feels alive.
Then he repines that he was born to die,
Nor knows in death there is no other He,
No living He remains his grief to vent,
And o're his senseless Carcass to lament.
If after death 'tis painful to be torn
By Birds and Beasts, then why not so to burn,
Or drench'd in floods of honey to be soak'd,
Imbalm'd to be at once preserv'd and choak'd;
Or on an ayery Mountains top to lie
Expos'd to cold and Heav'ns inclemency,
Or crowded in a Tomb to be opprest
With Monumental Marble on thy breast?

But to be snatch'd from all thy household joys,
From thy Chast Wife, and thy dear prattling boys,
Whose little arms about thy Legs are cast
And climbing for a Kiss prevent their Mothers hast,
Inspiring secret pleasure thro' thy Breast,
All these shall be no more: thy Friends opprest,
Thy Care and Courage now no more shall free:
Ah Wretch, thou cry'st, ah! miserable me,
One woful day sweeps children, friends, and wife,
And all the brittle blessings of my life!
Add one thing more, and all thou say'st is true;
Thy want and wish of them is vanish'd too,
Which well consider'd were a quick relief,
To all thy vain imaginary grief.
For thou shalt sleep and never wake again,
And quitting life, shall quit thy living pain.
But we thy friends shall all those sorrows find,
Which in forgetful death thou leav'st behind,
No time shall dry our tears, nor drive thee from our mind.

\*

All things, like thee, have time to rise and rot;
And from each others ruin are begot;
For life is not confin'd to him or thee;
'Tis giv'n to all for use; to none for Property.
Consider former Ages past and gone,
Whose Circles ended long e're thine begun,
Then tell me Fool, what part in them thou hast?
Thus may'st thou judge the future by the past.
What horrour seest thou in that quiet state,
What Bugbear dreams to fright thee after Fate?
No Ghost, no Gobblins, that still passage keep,
But all is there serene, in that eternal sleep.
For all the dismal Tales that Poets tell,
Are verify'd on Earth, and not in Hell.
No Tantalus looks up with fearful eye,
Or dreads th' impending Rock to crush him from on high:
But fear of Chance on earth disturbs our easie hours:
Or vain imagin'd wrath, of vain imagin'd Pow'rs.
No Tityus torn by Vultures lies in Hell;
Nor cou'd the Lobes of his rank liver swell
To that prodigious Mass for their eternal meal.

Not tho' his monstrous bulk had cover'd o're
Nine spreading Acres, or nine thousand more;
Not tho' the Globe of earth had been the Gyants floor.
Nor in eternal torments cou'd he lie;
Nor cou'd his Corps sufficient food supply.
But he's the Tityus, who by Love opprest,
Or Tyrant Passion preying on his breast,
And ever anxious thoughts, is robb'd of rest.
The Sisiphus is he, whom noise and strife
Seduce from all the soft retreats of life,
To vex the Government, disturb the Laws;
Drunk with the Fumes of popular applause,
He courts the giddy Crowd to make him great,
And sweats and toils in vain, to mount the sovereign Seat.
For still to aim at pow'r, and still to fail,
Ever to strive and never to prevail,
What is it, but in reasons true account
To heave the Stone against the rising Mount;
Which urg'd, and labour'd, and forc'd up with pain,
Recoils and rowls impetuous down, and smoaks along the plain.

\*

Mean time, when thoughts of death disturb thy head;
Consider, Ancus great and good is dead;
Ancus thy better far, was born to die,
And thou, dost thou bewail mortality?
So many Monarchs with their mighty State,
Who rul'd the World, were overrul'd by fate.
That haughty King, who Lorded o're the Main,
And whose stupendous Bridge did the wild Waves restrain,
(In vain they foam'd, in vain they threatned wreck,
While his proud Legions march'd upon their back:)
Him death, a greater Monarch, overcame;
Nor spared his guards the more, for their immortal name.
The Roman chief, the Carthaginian dread,
Scipio the Thunder Bolt of War is dead,
And like a common Slave, by fate in triumph led.
The Founders of invented Arts are lost;
And Wits who made Eternity their boast;
Where now is Homer who possest the Throne?
Th' immortal Work remains, the mortal Author's gone.

# JOHN DRYDEN

Democritus perceiving age invade,
His Body weakn'd, and his mind decay'd,
Obey'd the summons with a chearful face;
Made hast to welcome death, and met him half the race.
That stroke, ev'n Epicurus cou'd not bar,
Though he in Wit surpass'd Mankind, as far
As does the midday Sun, the midnight Star.
And thou, dost thou disdain to yield thy breath,
Whose very life is little more than death?
More than one half by Lazy sleep possest;
And when awake, thy Soul but nods at best,
Day-Dreams and sickly thoughts revolving in thy breast.
Eternal troubles haunt thy anxious mind,
Whose cause and cure thou never hop'st to find;
But still uncertain, with thy self at strife,
Thou wander'st in the Labyrinth of Life.


## FROM THE LATIN OF VIRGIL

## from *The Aeneid*

**227**

Cp.
Douglas
Stanyhurst

Arms, and the Man I sing, who, forc'd by Fate,
And haughty Juno's unrelenting Hate;
Expell'd and exil'd, left the Trojan Shoar:
Long Labours, both by Sea and Land he bore;
And in the doubtful War, before he won
The Latian Realm, and built the destin'd Town:
His banish'd Gods restor'd to Rites Divine,
And setl'd sure Succession in his Line:
From whence the Race of Alban Fathers come,
And the long Glories of Majestick Rome.
      O Muse! the Causes and the Crimes relate,
What Goddess was provok'd, and whence her hate:
For what Offence the Queen of Heav'n began
To persecute so brave, so just a Man!
Involv'd his anxious Life in endless Cares,
Expos'd to Wants, and hurry'd into Wars!
Can Heav'nly Minds such high resentment show;
Or exercise their Spight in Human Woe?

228        *'The Building of Carthage'*

Cp.        The Prince, with Wonder, sees the stately Tow'rs,
Douglas    Which late were Huts, and Shepherds homely Bow'rs;
           The Gates and Streets; and hears, from ev'ry part,
           The Noise, and buisy Concourse of the Mart.
           The toiling Tyrians on each other call,
           To ply their Labour. Some extend the Wall,
           Some build the Citadel; the brawny Throng,
           Or dig, or push unweildy Stones along.
           Some for their Dwelling chuse a Spot of Ground,
           Which, first design'd, with Ditches they surround.
           Some Laws ordain, and some attend the Choice
           Of holy Senates, and elect by Voice.
           Here some design a Mole, while others there
           Lay deep Foundations for a Theatre:
           From Marble Quarries mighty Columns hew,
           For Ornaments of Scenes, and future view.
           Such is their Toyl, and such their buisy Pains,
           As exercise the Bees in flow'ry Plains;
           When Winter past, and Summer scarce begun,
           Invites them forth to labour in the Sun:
           Some lead their Youth abroad, while some condense
           Their liquid Store, and some in Cells dispence.
           Some at the Gate stand ready to receive
           The Golden Burthen, and their Friends relieve.
           All, with united Force, combine to drive
           The lazy Drones from the laborious Hive;
           With Envy stung, they view each others Deeds;
           The fragrant Work with Diligence proceeds.


229                    *'Fame'*

           The loud Report through Lybian Cities goes;
           Fame, the great Ill, from small beginnings grows.
           Swift from the first; and ev'ry Moment brings
           New Vigour to her flights, new Pinions to her wings.
           Soon grows the Pygmee to Gygantic size;
           Her Feet on Earth, her Forehead in the Skies:

Inrag'd against the Gods, revengeful Earth
Produc'd her last of the Titanian birth.
Swift is her walk, more swift her winged hast:
A monstrous Fantom, horrible and vast;
As many Plumes as raise her lofty flight,
So many piercing Eyes inlarge her sight:
Millions of opening Mouths to Fame belong;
And ev'ry Mouth is furnish'd with a Tongue:
And round with listning Ears the flying Plague is hung.
She fills the peaceful Universe with Cries;
No Slumbers ever close her wakeful Eyes.
By Day from lofty Tow'rs her Head she shews;
And spreads through trembling Crowds disastrous News.
With Court Informers haunts, and Royal Spies,
Things done relates, not done she feigns; and mingles Truth
    with Lyes.
Talk is her business; and her chief delight
To tell of Prodigies, and cause affright.

230               *'Charon'*

Cp.
Douglas

There Charon stands, who rules the dreary Coast:
A sordid God; down from his hoary Chin
A length of Beard descends; uncomb'd, unclean:
His Eyes, like hollow Furnaces on Fire:
A Girdle, foul with grease, binds his obscene Attire.
He spreads his Canvas, with his Pole he steers;
The Freights of flitting Ghosts in his thin Bottom bears.
He look'd in Years; yet in his Years were seen
A youthful Vigour, and Autumnal green.
An Airy Crowd came rushing where he stood;
Which fill'd the Margin of the fatal Flood.
Husbands and Wives, Boys and unmarry'd Maids;
And mighty Heroes more Majestick Shades.
And Youths, intomb'd before their Fathers Eyes,
With hollow Groans, and Shrieks, and feeble Cries:
Thick as the Leaves in Autumn strow the Woods:
Or Fowls, by Winter forc'd, forsake the Floods,
And wing their hasty flight to happier Lands:
Such, and so thick, the shiv'ring Army stands:
And press for passage with extended hands.

231 *Diomede mourns his Fate and that of his Friends*
*to the Latian Ambassador who seeks his Alliance against*
*Aeneas'*

Attentively he heard us, while we spoke;
Then, with soft Accents, and a pleasing Look,
Made this return. Ausonian Race, of old
Renown'd for Peace, and for an Age of Gold,
What Madness has your alter'd Minds possess'd,
To change for War hereditary Rest?
Sollicite Arms unknown, and tempt the Sword,
(A needless Ill your Ancestors abhorr'd?)
We (for my self I speak, and all the Name
Of Grecians, who to Troy's Destruction came;)
Omitting those who were in Battel slain,
Or born by rowling Simois to the Main:
Not one but suffer'd, and too dearly bought
The Prize of Honour which in Arms he sought.
Some doom'd to Death, and some in Exile driv'n,
Out-casts, abandon'd by the Care of Heav'n:
So worn, so wretched, so despis'd a Crew,
As ev'n old Priam might with Pity view.
Witness the Vessels by Minerva toss'd
In Storms, the vengeful Capharæan Coast;
Th' Eubæan Rocks! The Prince, whose Brother led
Our Armies to revenge his injur'd Bed,
In Egypt lost; Ulysses, with his Men,
Have seen Charybdis, and the Cyclops Den:
Why shou'd I name Idomeneus, in vain
Restor'd to Scepters, and expell'd again?
Or young Achilles by his Rival slain?
Ev'n he, the King of Men, the foremost Name
Of all the Greeks, and most renown'd by Fame,
The proud Revenger of another's Wife,
Yet by his own Adult'ress lost his Life:
Fell at his Threshold, and the Spoils of Troy,
The foul Polluters of his Bed enjoy.
The Gods have envy'd me the sweets of Life,
My much lov'd Country, and my more lov'd Wife:

Banish'd from both, I mourn; while in the Sky
Transform'd to Birds, my lost Companions fly:
Hov'ring about the Coasts they make their Moan;
And cuff the cliffs with Pinions not their own.


232      *'Turnus and the wanton Courser'*

Cp.
Pope's
Paris

Exulting in his Strength, he seems to dare
His absent Rival, and to promise War.
 Freed from his Keepers, thus with broken Reins,
The wanton Courser prances o're the Plains:
Or in the Pride of Youth o'releaps the Mounds;
And snuffs the Females in forbidden Grounds.
Or seeks his wat'ring in the well known Flood,
To quench his Thirst, and cool his fiery Blood:
He swims luxuriant, in the liquid Plain,
And o're his Shoulder flows his waving Mane:
He neighs, he snorts, he bears his Head on high;
Before his ample Chest the frothy Waters fly.


233      *'Turnus and the Stone'*

Cp.
Pope's
Hector

As when a Fragment, from a Mountain torn
By raging Tempests, or by Torrents born,
Or sapp'd by time, or loosen'd from the Roots,
Prone thro' the Void the Rocky Ruine shoots,
Rowling from Crag to Crag, from Steep to Steep;
Down sink, at once the Shepherds and their Sheep,
Involv'd alike, they rush to neather Ground,
Stun'd with the shock they fall, and stun'd from Earth rebound:
So Turnus, hasting headlong to the Town,
Should'ring and shoving, bore the Squadrons down.

FROM THE LATIN OF HORACE

234 *Odes*, Book I, 9

Cp.
Fanshawe

Behold yon' Mountains hoary height
   Made higher with new Mounts of Snow;
Again behold the Winters weight
   Oppress the lab'ring Woods below:
And streams with Icy fetters bound,
Benum'd and crampt to solid ground.

With well heap'd Logs dissolve the cold,
   And feed the genial hearth with fires;
Produce the Wine, that makes us bold,
   And sprightly Wit and Love inspires:
For what hereafter shall betide,
God, if 'tis worth his care, provide.

Let him alone with what he made,
   To toss and turn the World below;
At his command the storms invade;
   The winds by his Commission blow
Till with a Nod he bids 'em cease,
And then the Calm returns, and all is peace.

To morrow and her works defie,
   Lay hold upon the present hour,
And snatch the pleasures passing by,
   To put them out of Fortunes pow'r:
Nor love, nor love's delights disdain,
What e're thou get'st to day is gain.

Secure those golden early joyes,
   That Youth unsowr'd with sorrow bears,
E're with'ring time the taste destroyes,
   With sickness and unwieldy years!
For active sports, for pleasing rest,
This is the time to be possest;
The best is but in season best.

The pointed hour of promis'd bliss,
  The pleasing whisper in the dark,
The half unwilling willing kiss,
  The laugh that guides thee to the mark,
When the kind Nymph wou'd coyness feign,
And hides but to be found again,
These, these are joyes the Gods for Youth ordain.

235        *Odes*, Book III, 29

Paraphras'd in Pindarique Verse; and Inscrib'd to the Right Honourable
Lawrence Earl of Rochester

### I

Descended of an ancient Line,
  That long the Tuscan Scepter sway'd,
Make haste to meet the generous wine,
  Whose piercing is for thee delay'd:
The rosie wreath is ready made;
  And artful hands prepare
The fragrant Syrian Oyl, that shall perfume thy hair.

### II

When the Wine sparkles from a far,
  And the well-natur'd Friend cries, come away;
Make haste, and leave thy business and thy care,
  No mortal int'rest can be worth thy stay.

### III

Leave for a while thy costly Country Seat;
  And, to be Great indeed, forget
The nauseous pleasures of the Great:
    Make haste and come:
Come and forsake thy cloying store;
  Thy Turret that surveys, from high,
The smoke, and wealth, and noise of Rome;
  And all the busie pageantry
That wise men scorn, and fools adore:
Come, give thy Soul a loose, and taste the pleasures of the poor.

## IV

Sometimes 'tis grateful to the Rich, to try
A short vicissitude, and fit of Poverty:
    A savoury Dish, a homely Treat,
    Where all is plain, where all is neat,
    Without the stately spacious Room,
The Persian Carpet, or the Tyrian Loom,
Clear up the cloudy foreheads of the Great.

## V

The Sun is in the Lion mounted high;
      The Syrian Star
      Barks from a far;
And with his sultry breath infects the Sky;
The ground below is parch'd, the heav'ns above us fry.
    The Shepheard drives his fainting Flock,
    Beneath the covert of a Rock;
    And seeks refreshing Rivulets nigh:
    The Sylvans to their shades retire,
Those very shades and streams, new shades and streams require;
And want a cooling breeze of wind to fan the rageing fire.

## VI

Thou, what befits the new Lord May'r,
And what the City Faction dare,
And what the Gallique Arms will do,
And what the Quiver bearing Foe,
Art anxiously inquisitive to know:
But God has, wisely, hid from humane sight
    The dark decrees of future fate;
    And sown their seeds in depth of night;
He laughs at all the giddy turns of State;
When Mortals search too soon, and fear too late.

## VII

Enjoy the present smiling hour;
And put it out of Fortunes pow'r:
The tide of bus'ness, like the running stream,
    Is sometimes high, and sometimes low,
A quiet ebb, or a tempestuous flow,
      And alwayes in extream.
Now with a noiseless gentle course

It keeps within the middle Bed;
Anon it lifts aloft the head,
And bears down all before it, with impetuous force:
And trunks of Trees come rowling down,
Sheep and their Folds together drown:
Both House and Homested into Seas are borne,
And Rocks are from their old foundations torn,
And woods made thin with winds, their scatter'd honours mourn.

### VIII

Happy the Man, and happy he alone,
He, who can call to day his own:
He, who secure within, can say
To morrow do thy worst, for I have liv'd to day.
Be fair, or foul, or rain, or shine,
The joys I have possest, in spight of fate are mine.
Not Heav'n it self upon the past has pow'r;
But what has been, has been, and I have had my hour.

### IX

Fortune, that with malicious joy,
Does Man her slave oppress,
Proud of her Office to destroy,
Is seldome pleas'd to bless.
Still various and unconstant still;
But with an inclination to be ill;
Promotes, degrades, delights in strife,
And makes a Lottery of life.
I can enjoy her while she's kind;
But when she dances in the wind,
And shakes her wings, and will not stay,
I puff the Prostitute away:
The little or the much she gave, is quietly resign'd:
Content with poverty, my Soul, I arm;
And Vertue, tho' in rags, will keep me warm.

### X

What is't to me,
Who never sail in her unfaithful Sea,
If Storms arise, and Clouds grow black;
If the Mast split and threaten wreck,

Then let the greedy Merchant fear
For his ill gotten gain;
And pray to Gods that will not hear,
While the debating winds and billows bear
His Wealth into the Main.
For me secure from Fortunes blows,
(Secure of what I cannot lose,)
In my small Pinnace I can sail,
Contemning all the blustring roar;
And running with a merry gale,
With friendly Stars my safety seek
Within some little winding Creek;
And see the storm a shore.


FROM THE LATIN OF OVID

## Metamorphoses

### 236 'Jove looses the South Wind and Neptune the Floods'

The Northern breath, that freezes Floods, he binds;
With all the race of Cloud-dispelling Winds:
The South he loos'd, who Night and Horror brings;
And Foggs are shaken from his flaggy Wings.
From his divided Beard, two Streams he pours,
His head and rhumy eyes, distill in showers.
With Rain his Robe and heavy Mantle flow;
And lazy mists, are lowring on his brow:
Still as he swept along, with his clench't fist
He squeez'd the Clouds, th' imprison'd Clouds resist:
The Skies from Pole to Pole, with peals resound;
And show'rs inlarg'd, come pouring on the ground.
Then, clad in Colours of a various dye,
Junonian Iris, breeds a new supply;
To feed the Clouds: Impetuous Rain descends;
The bearded Corn, beneath the Burden bends:
Defrauded Clowns, deplore their perish'd grain;
And the long labours of the Year are vain.

*

The Floods, by Nature Enemies to Land,
And proudly swelling with their new Command,
Remove the living Stones, that stopt their way,
And gushing from their Source, augment the Sea.
Then, with his Mace, their Monarch struck the Ground:
With inward trembling, Earth receiv'd the wound;
And rising streams a ready passage found.
Th' expanded Waters gather on the Plain:
They flote the Fields, and over-top the Grain;
Then rushing onwards, with a sweepy sway,
Bear Flocks and Folds, and lab'ring Hinds away.
Nor safe their Dwelling were, for, sap'd by Floods,
Their Houses fell upon their Household Gods.
The solid Piles, too strongly built to fall,
High o're their Heads, behold a watry Wall:
Now Seas and Earth were in confusion lost;
A World of Waters, and without a Coast.
    One climbs a Cliff; one in his Boat is born;
And Ploughs above, where late he sow'd his Corn.
Others o're Chimney tops and Turrets row,
And drop their Anchors, on the Meads below:
Or downward driv'n, they bruise the tender Vine,
Or tost aloft, are knock't against a Pine.
And where of late, the Kids had cropt the Grass,
The Monsters of the deep, now take their place.
Insulting Nereids on the Cities ride,
And wondring Dolphins o're the Palace glide.
On leaves and masts of mighty Oaks they brouze;
And their broad Finns, entangle in the Boughs,
The frighted Wolf, now swims amongst the Sheep;
The yellow Lyon wanders in the deep:
His rapid force, no longer helps the Boar:
The Stag swims faster, than he ran before.
The Fowls, long beating on their Wings in vain,
Despair of Land, and drop into the Main.
Now Hills and Vales, no more distinction know;
And levell'd Nature, lies oppress'd below.
The most of Mortals perish in the Flood:
The small remainder dies for want of Food.

237     *'Deucalion and Pyrrha renew Creation*
*by casting stones behind them'*

The Stones (a Miracle to Mortal View,
But long Tradition makes it pass for true)
Did first the Rigour of their Kind expell,
And, suppl'd into softness, as they fell,
Then swell'd, and swelling, by degrees grew warm;
And took the Rudiments of Humane Form.
Imperfect shapes: in Marble such are seen
When the rude Chizzel does the Man begin;
While yet the roughness of the Stone remains,
Without the rising Muscles, and the Veins.
The sappy parts, and next resembling juice,
Were turn'd to moisture, for the Bodies use:
Supplying humours, blood, and nourishment;
The rest, (too solid to receive a bent;)
Converts to bones; and what was once a vein
Its former Name, and Nature did retain.
By help of Pow'r Divine, in little space
What the Man threw, assum'd a Manly face;
And what the Wife, renew'd the Female Race.
Hence we derive our Nature; born to bear
Laborious life; and harden'd into care.
    The rest of Animals, from teeming Earth
Produc'd, in various forms receiv'd their birth.
The native moisture, in its close retreat,
Digested by the Sun's Ætherial heat,
As in a kindly Womb, began to breed:
Then swell'd, and quicken'd by the vital seed.
And some in less, and some in longer space,
Were ripen'd into form, and took a several face.
Thus when the Nile from Pharian Fields is fled,
And seeks with Ebbing Tides, his ancient Bed,
The fat Manure, with Heav'nly Fire is warm'd;
And crusted Creatures, as in Wombs are form'd;
These, when they turn the Glebe, the Peasants find;
Some rude; and yet unfinish'd in their Kind:
Short of their Limbs, a lame imperfect Birth;
One half alive; and one of lifeless Earth.

For heat and moisture, when in Bodies joyn'd,
The temper that results from either Kind
Conception makes; and fighting till they mix,
Their mingl'd Atoms in each other fix.
Thus Nature's hand, the Genial Bed prepares,
With Friendly Discord, and with fruitful Wars.
    From hence the surface of the Ground, with Mud
And Slime besmear'd, (the faeces of the Flood)
Receiv'd the Rays of Heav'n; and sucking in
The Seeds of Heat, new Creatures did begin:
Some were of sev'ral sorts produc'd before,
But of new Monsters, Earth created more.

238          *Baucis and Philemon*

Then Lelex rose, an old experienc'd Man,
And thus with sober Gravity began:
Heav'ns Pow'r is Infinite: Earth, Air, and Sea,
The Manufacture Mass, the making Pow'r obey:
By Proof to clear your Doubt; In Phrygian Ground
Two neighb'ring Trees, with Walls encompass'd round,
Stand on a mod'rate Rise, with wonder shown,
One a hard Oak, a softer Linden one:
I saw the Place and them, by Pittheus sent
To Phrygian Realms, my Grandsire's Government.
Not far from thence is seen a Lake, the Haunt
Of Coots, and of the fishing Cormorant:
Here Jove with Hermes came; but in Disguise
Of mortal Men conceal'd their Deities;
One laid aside his Thunder, one his Rod;
And many toilsom Steps together trod:
For Harbour at a thousand Doors they knock'd,
Not one of all the thousand but was lock'd.
At last an hospitable House they found,
A homely Shed; the Roof, not far from Ground,
Was thatch'd with Reeds, and Straw together bound.
There Baucis and Philemon liv'd, and there
Had liv'd long marry'd, and a happy Pair:
Now old in Love, though little was their Store,
Inur'd to Want, their Poverty they bore,
Nor aim'd at Wealth, professing to be poor.

For Master or for Servant here to call,
Was all alike, where only Two were All.
Command was none, where equal Love was paid,
Or rather both commanded, both obey'd.
  From lofty Roofs the Gods repuls'd before,
Now stooping, enter'd through the little Door:
The Man (their hearty Welcome first express'd)
A common Settle drew for either Guest,
Inviting each his weary Limbs to rest.
But e'er they sat, officious Baucis lays
Two Cushions stuff'd with Straw, the Seat to raise;
Course, but the best she had; then rakes the Load
Of Ashes from the Hearth, and spreads abroad
The living Coals; and, lest they shou'd expire,
With Leaves and Barks she feeds her Infant-fire:
It smoaks; and then with trembling Breath she blows,
Till in a chearful Blaze the Flames arose.
With Brush-wood and with Chips she strengthens these,
And adds at last the Boughs of rotten Trees.
The Fire thus form'd, she sets the Kettle on,
(Like burnish'd Gold the little Seether shone)
Next took the Coleworts which her Husband got
From his own Ground, (a small well-water'd Spot;)
She stripp'd the Stalks of all their Leaves; the best
She cull'd, and then with handy-care she dress'd.
High o'er the Hearth a Chine of Bacon hung;
Good old Philemon seiz'd it with a Prong,
And from the sooty Rafter drew it down,
Then cut a Slice, but scarce enough for one;
Yet a large Portion of a little Store,
Which for their Sakes alone he wish'd were more.
This in the Pot he plung'd without delay,
To tame the Flesh, and drain the Salt away.
The Time between, before the Fire they sat,
And shorten'd the Delay by pleasing Chat.
  A Beam there was, on which a Beechen Pail
Hung by the Handle, on a driven Nail:
This fill'd with Water, gently warm'd, they set
Before their Guests; in this they bath'd their Feet,
And after with clean Towels dry'd their Sweat:
This done, the Host produc'd the genial Bed,

Sallow the Feet, the Borders, and the Sted,
Which with no costly Coverlet they spread;
But course old Garments, yet such Robes as these
They laid alone, at Feasts, on Holydays.
The good old Huswife tucking up her Gown,
The Table sets; th' invited Gods lie down.
The Trivet-Table of a Foot was lame,
A Blot which prudent Baucis overcame,
Who thrusts beneath the limping Leg, a Sherd,
So was the mended Board exactly rear'd:
Then rubb'd it o'er with newly-gather'd Mint,
A wholesom Herb, that breath'd a grateful Scent.
Pallas began the Feast, where first was seen
The party-colour'd Olive, Black, and Green:
Autumnal Cornels next in order serv'd,
In Lees of Wine well pickl'd, and preserv'd.
A Garden-Sallad was the third Supply,
Of Endive, Radishes, and Succory:
Then Curds and Cream, the Flow'r of Country-Fare,
And new-laid Eggs, which Baucis busie Care
Turn'd by a gentle Fire, and roasted rear.
All these in Earthen Ware were serv'd to Board;
And next in place, an Earthen Pitcher stor'd
With Liquor of the best the Cottage cou'd afford.
This was the Tables Ornament, and Pride,
With Figures wrought: Like Pages at his Side
Stood Beechen Bowls; and these were shining clean,
Vernish'd with Wax without, and lin'd within.
By this the boiling Kettle had prepar'd,
And to the Table sent the smoaking Lard;
On which with eager Appetite they dine,
A sav'ry Bit, that serv'd to rellish Wine;
The Wine it self was suiting to the rest,
Still working in the Must, and lately press'd.
The Second Course succeeds like that before,
Plums, Apples, Nuts, and of their Wintry Store,
Dry Figs, and Grapes, and wrinkl'd Dates were set
In Canisters, t' enlarge the little Treat:
All these a Milk-white Honey-comb surround,
Which in the midst the Country-Banquet crown'd:
But the kind Hosts their Entertainment grace
With hearty Welcom, and an open Face:

In all they did, you might discern with ease,
A willing Mind, and a Desire to please.
　Mean time the Beechen Bowls went round, and still
Though often empty'd, were observ'd to fill;
Fill'd without Hands, and of their own accord
Ran without Feet, and danc'd about the Board.
Devotion seiz'd the Pair, to see the Feast
With Wine, and of no common Grape, increas'd;
And up they held their Hands, and fell to Pray'r,
Excusing as they cou'd, their Country Fare.
　One Goose they had, ('twas all they cou'd allow)
A wakeful Cent'ry, and on Duty now,
Whom to the Gods for Sacrifice they vow:
Her, with malicious Zeal, the Couple view'd;
She ran for Life, and limping they pursu'd:
Full well the Fowl perceiv'd their bad intent,
And wou'd not make her Masters Compliment;
But persecuted, to the Pow'rs she flies,
And close between the Legs of Jove she lies:
He with a gracious Ear the Suppliant heard,
And sav'd her Life; then what he was declar'd,
And own'd the God. The Neighbourhood, said he,
Shall justly perish for Impiety:
You stand alone exempted; but obey
With speed, and follow where we lead the way:
Leave these accurs'd; and to the Mountains Height
Ascend; nor once look backward in your Flight.
　They haste, and what their tardy Feet deny'd,
The trusty Staff (their better Leg) supply'd.
An Arrows Flight they wanted to the Top,
And there secure, but spent with Travel, stop;
Then turn their now no more forbidden Eyes;
Lost in a Lake the floated Level lies:
A Watry Desart covers all the Plains,
Their Cot alone, as in an Isle, remains:
Wondring with weeping Eyes, while they deplore
Their Neighbours Fate, and Country now no more,
Their little Shed, scarce large enough for Two,
Seems, from the Ground increas'd, in Height and Bulk to grow.
A stately Temple shoots within the Skies,
The Crotches of their Cot in Columns rise:

The Pavement polish'd Marble they behold,
The Gates with Sculpture grac'd, the Spires and Tiles of Gold.
   Then thus the Sire of Gods, with Look serene,
Speak thy Desire, thou only Just of Men;
And thou, O Woman, only worthy found
To be with such a Man in Marriage bound.
   A while they whisper; then to Jove address'd,
Philemon thus prefers their joint Request.
We crave to serve before your sacred Shrine,
And offer at your Altars Rites Divine:
And since not any Action of our Life
Has been polluted with Domestick Strife,
We beg one Hour of Death; that neither she
With Widows Tears may live to bury me,
Nor weeping I, with wither'd Arms may bear
My breathless Baucis to the Sepulcher.
   The Godheads sign their Suit. They run their Race
In the same Tenor all th' appointed Space:
Then, when their Hour was come, while they relate
These past Adventures at the Temple-gate,
Old Baucis is by old Philemon seen
Sprouting with sudden Leaves of spritely Green:
Old Baucis look'd where old Philemon stood,
And saw his lengthen'd Arms a sprouting Wood:
New Roots their fasten'd Feet begin to bind,
Their Bodies stiffen in a rising Rind:
Then e'er the Bark above their Shoulders grew,
They give and take at once their last Adieu:
At once, Farewell, O faithful Spouse, they said;
At once th' incroaching Rinds their closing Lips invade.
Ev'n yet, an ancient Tyanæan shows
A spreading Oak, that near a Linden grows;
The Neighbourhood confirm the Prodigie,
Grave Men, not vain of Tongue, or like to lie.
I saw my self the Garlands on their Boughs,
And Tablets hung for Gifts of granted Vows;
And off'ring fresher up, with pious Pray'r,
The Good, said I, are God's peculiar Care,
And such as honour Heav'n, shall heav'nly Honour share.

239     *'Iris descends to the Cave of Sleep'*

Near the Cymmerians, in his dark Abode
Deep in a Cavern, dwells the drowzy God;
Whose gloomy Mansion nor the rising Sun
Nor setting, visits, nor the lightsome Noon:
But lazy Vapors round the Region fly,
Perpetual Twilight, and a doubtful Sky;
No crowing Cock does there his Wings display
Nor with his horny Bill provoke the Day;
Nor watchful Dogs, nor the more wakeful Geese,
Disturb with nightly Noise the sacred Peace:
Nor Beast of Nature, nor the Tame are nigh,
Nor Trees with Tempests rock'd, nor human Cry,
But safe Repose without an air of Breath
Dwells here, and a dumb Quiet next to Death.
   An Arm of Lethe with a gentle flow
Arising upwards from the Rock below,
The Palace moats, and o'er the Pebbles creeps
And with soft Murmurs calls the coming Sleeps:
Around its Entry nodding Poppies grow,
And all cool Simples that sweet Rest bestow;
Night from the Plants their sleepy Virtue drains,
And passing sheds it on the silent Plains:
No Door there was th' unguarded House to keep,
On creaking Hinges turn'd, to break his Sleep.
   But in the gloomy Court was rais'd a Bed
Stuff'd with black Plumes, and on an Ebon-sted:
Black was the Cov'ring too, where lay the God
And slept supine, his Limbs display'd abroad:
About his Head fantastick Visions fly,
Which various Images of Things supply,
And mock their Forms, the Leaves on Trees not more;
Nor bearded Ears in Fields, nor Sands upon the Shore.
   The Virgin entring bright indulg'd the Day
To the brown Cave, and brush'd the Dreams away:
The God disturb'd with this new glare of Light
Cast sudden on his Face, unseal'd his Sight,
And rais'd his tardy Head, which sunk agen,
And sinking on his Bosom knock'd his Chin;
At length shook off himself; and ask'd the Dame,
(And asking yawn'd) for what intent she came?

240      *'Of the Pythagorean Philosophy'*

This let me further add, that Nature knows
No stedfast Station, but, or Ebbs, or Flows:
Ever in motion; she destroys her old,
And casts new Figures in another Mold.
Ev'n Times are in perpetual Flux; and run
Like Rivers from their Fountain rowling on;
For Time no more than Streams, is at a stay:
The flying Hour is ever on her way;
And as the Fountain still supplies her store,
The Wave behind impels the Wave before;
Thus in successive Course the Minutes run,
And urge their Predecessor Minutes on,
Still moving, ever new: For former Things
Are set aside, like abdicated Kings:
And every moment alters what is done,
And innovates some Act till then unknown.

*

Perceiv'st thou not the process of the Year,
How the four Seasons in four Forms appear,
Resembling human Life in ev'ry Shape they wear?
Spring first, like Infancy, shoots out her Head,
With milky Juice requiring to be fed:
Helpless, tho' fresh, and wanting to be led.
The green Stem grows in Stature and in Size,
But only feeds with hope the Farmer's Eyes;
Then laughs the childish Year with Flourets crown'd,
And lavishly perfumes the Fields around,
But no substantial Nourishment receives,
Infirm the Stalks, unsolid are the Leaves.
Proceeding onward whence the Year began
The Summer grows adult, and ripens into Man.
This Season, as in Men, is most repleat,
With kindly Moisture, and prolifick Heat.
Autumn succeeds, a sober tepid age,
Not froze with Fear, nor boiling into Rage;
More than mature, and tending to decay,
When our brown Locks repine to mix with odious Grey.

Last Winter creeps along with tardy pace,
Sour is his Front, and furrow'd is his Face;
His Scalp if not dishonour'd quite of Hair,
The ragged Fleece is thin, and thin is worse than bare.

\*

Time was, when we were sow'd, and just began
From some few fruitful Drops, the promise of a Man;
Then Nature's Hand (fermented as it was)
Moulded to Shape the soft, coagulated Mass;
And when the little Man was fully form'd,
The breathless Embryo with a Spirit warm'd;
But when the Mothers Throws begin to come,
The Creature, pent within the narrow Room,
Breaks his blind Prison, pushing to repair
His stifled Breath, and draw the living Air;
Cast on the Margin of the World he lies,
A helpless Babe, but by Instinct he cries.
He next essays to walk, but downward press'd
On four Feet imitates his Brother Beast:
By slow degrees he gathers from the Ground
His Legs, and to the rowling Chair is bound;
Then walks alone; a Horseman now become
He rides a Stick, and travels round the Room:
In time he vaunts among his youthful Peers,
Strong-bon'd, and strung with Nerves, in pride of Years,
He runs with Mettle his first merry Stage,
Maintains the next abated of his Rage,
But manages his Strength, and spares his Age.
Heavy the third, and stiff, he sinks apace,
And tho' 'tis down-hill all, but creeps along the Race.
Now sapless on the verge of Death he stands,
Contemplating his former Feet, and Hands;
And Milo-like, his slacken'd Sinews sees,
And wither'd Arms, once fit to cope with Hercules,
Unable now to shake much less to tear the Trees.

\*

All Things are alter'd, nothing is destroy'd,
The shifted Scene, for some new Show employ'd.
Then to be born, is to begin to be
Some other Thing we were not formerly:

And what we call to Die, is not t' appear,
Or be the Thing that formerly we were.
Those very Elements which we partake,
Alive, when Dead some other Bodies make:
Translated grow, have Sense, or can Discourse,
But Death on deathless Substance has no force.
   That Forms are chang'd I grant; that nothing can
Continue in the Figure it began:
The Golden Age, to Silver was debas'd:
To Copper that; our Mettal came at last.
   The Face of Places, and their Forms decay;
And that is solid Earth, that once was Sea:
Seas in their turn retreating from the Shore,
Make solid Land, what Ocean was before;
And far from Strands are Shells of Fishes found,
And rusty Anchors fix'd on Mountain-Ground:
And what were Fields before, now wash'd and worn
By falling Floods from high, to Valleys turn,
And crumbling still descend to level Lands;
And Lakes, and trembling Bogs are barren Sands:
And the parch'd Desart floats in Streams unknown;
Wondring to drink of Waters not her own.


FROM THE LATIN OF JUVENAL

241          from *Satires, VI*

In Saturn's Reign, at Nature's Early Birth,
There was that Thing call'd Chastity on Earth;
When in a narrow Cave, their common shade,
The Sheep the Shepherds and their Gods were laid:
When Reeds and Leaves, and Hides of Beasts were spread
By Mountain Huswifes for their homely Bed,
And Mossy Pillows rais'd, for the rude Husband's head.
Unlike the Niceness of our Modern Dames
(Affected Nymphs with new Affected Names:)
The Cynthia's and the Lesbia's of our Years,
Who for a Sparrow's Death dissolve in Tears.
Those first unpolisht Matrons, Big and Bold,
Gave Suck to Infants of Gygantick Mold;

Rough as their Savage Lords who Rang'd the Wood,
And Fat with Akorns Belcht their windy Food.
For when the World was Bucksom, fresh, and young,
Her Sons were undebauch'd, and therefore strong;
And whether Born in kindly Beds of Earth,
Or strugling from the Teeming Oaks to Birth,
Or from what other Atom they begun,
No Sires they had, or if a Sire the Sun.
Some thin Remains of Chastity appear'd
Ev'n under Jove, but Jove without a Beard:
Before the servile Greeks had learnt to Swear
By Heads of Kings; while yet the Bounteous Year
Her common Fruits in open Plains expos'd,
E're Thieves were fear'd, or Gardens were enclos'd:
At length uneasie Justice upwards flew,
And both the Sisters to the Stars withdrew;
From that Old Æra Whoring did begin,
So Venerably Ancient is the Sin.
Adult'rers next invade the Nuptial State,
And Marriage-Beds creak'd with a Foreign Weight;
All other Ills did Iron times adorn;
But Whores and Silver in one Age were Born.

## 'Messalina, Wife of the Emperor Claudius'

The good old Sluggard but began to snore,
When from his side up rose th' Imperial Whore:
She who preferr'd the Pleasures of the Night
To Pomps, that are but impotent delight,
Strode from the Palace, with an eager pace,
To cope with a more Masculine Embrace:
Muffl'd she march'd, like Juno in a Clowd,
Of all her Train but one poor Wench allow'd,
One whom in Secret Service she cou'd trust;
The Rival and Companion of her Lust.
To the known Brothel-house she takes her way;
And for a nasty Room gives double pay;
That Room in which the rankest Harlot lay.
Prepar'd for fight, expectingly she lies,
With heaving Breasts, and with desiring Eyes:
Still as one drops, another takes his place,
And baffled still succeeds to like disgrace.

At length, when friendly darkness is expir'd,
And every Strumpet from her Cell retir'd,
She lags behind, and lingring at the Gate,
With a repining Sigh, submits to Fate:
All Filth without and all a Fire within,
Tir'd with the Toyl, unsated with the Sin.
Old Cæsar's Bed the modest Matron seeks;
The steam of Lamps still hanging on her Cheeks
In Ropy Smut; thus foul, and thus bedight,
She brings him back the Product of the Night.

\*

Some Faults, tho small, intolerable grow:
For what so Nauseous and Affected too,
As those that think they due Perfection want,
Who have not learnt to Lisp the Grecian Cant?\*
In Greece, their whole Accomplishments they seek:
Their Fashion, Breeding, Language, must be Greek:
But Raw, in all that does to Rome belong,
They scorn to cultivate their Mother Tongue.
In Greek they flatter, all their Fears they speak,
Tell all their Secrets, nay, they Scold in Greek:
Ev'n in the Feat of Love, they use that Tongue.
Such Affectations may become the Young:
But thou, Old Hag of Threescore Years and Three,
Is shewing of thy Parts in Greek, for thee?
Ζωὴ καί ψυχή! All those tender words
The Momentary trembling Bliss affords,
The kind soft Murmurs of the private Sheets,
Are Bawdy, while thou speak'st in publick Streets.
Those words have Fingers; and their force is such,
They raise the Dead, and mount him with a touch.
But all Provocatives from thee are vain;
No blandishment the slacken'd Nerve can strain.

\*

The Secrets of the Goddess nam'd the Good,
Are ev'n by Boys and Barbers understood:

---

\* Women then learnt Greek, as ours speak French. (*Dryden's note*)
Zoe kai psyche] My life, my soul
the Good] The Bona Dea, either the wife or daughter of Faunus.
Her rites were reserved for women.

Where the Rank Matrons, Dancing to the Pipe,
Gig with their Bums, and are for Action ripe;
With Musick rais'd, they spread abroad their Hair;
And toss their Heads like an enamour'd Mare:
Laufella lays her Garland by, and proves
The mimick Leachery of Manly Loves.
Rank'd with the Lady, the cheap Sinner lies;
For here not Blood, but Virtue gives the prize.
Nothing is feign'd, in this Venereal Strife;
'Tis downright Lust, and Acted to the Life.
So full, so fierce, so vigorous, and so strong;
That, looking on, wou'd make old Nestor Young.
Impatient of delay, a general sound,
An universal Groan of Lust goes round;
For then, and only then, the Sex sincere is found.
Now is the time of Action; now begin,
They cry, and let the lusty Lovers in.
The Whoresons are asleep; Then bring the Slaves,
And Watermen, a Race of strong-back'd Knaves.

*

There are, who in soft Eunuchs, place their Bliss;
To shun the scrubbing of a Bearded Kiss;
And scape Abortion; but their solid joy
Is when the Page, already past a Boy,
Is Capon'd late; and to the Guelder shown,
With his two Pounders, to Perfection grown.
When all the Navel-string cou'd give, appears;
All but the Beard; and that's the Barber's loss, not theirs.
Seen from afar, and famous for his ware,
He struts into the Bath, among the Fair:
Th' admiring Crew to their Devotions fall;
And, kneeling, on their new Priapus call.
Kerv'd for my Lady's use with her he lies;
And let him drudge for her, if thou art wise;
Rather than trust him with thy Fav'rite Boy;
He proffers Death in proffering to enjoy.

*

She duely, once a Month, renews her Face;
Mean time, it lies in Dawb, and hid in Grease;

Those are the Husband's Nights; she craves her due,
He takes fat Kisses, and is stuck in Glue.
But, to the Lov'd Adult'rer when she steers,
Fresh from the Bath, in brightness she appears:
For him the Rich Arabia sweats her Gum;
And precious Oyls from distant Indies come:
How Haggardly so e're she looks at home.
Th' Eclipse then vanishes; and all her Face
Is open'd, and restor'd to ev'ry Grace.
The Crust remov'd, her Cheeks as smooth as Silk,
Are polish'd with a wash of Asses Milk;
And, shou'd she to the farthest North be sent,
A Train of these attend her Banishment.
But, hadst thou seen her Plaistred up before,
'Twas so unlike a Face, it seem'd a Sore.

242                    *from* Satires, X
                         '*Sejanus*'

Cp.        Some ask for Envy'd Pow'r; which publick Hate
Gifford   Pursues, and hurries headlong to their Fate:
Lowell    Down go the Titles; and the Statue Crown'd,
Is by base Hands in the next River Drown'd.
The Guiltless Horses, and the Chariot Wheel
The same Effects of Vulgar Fury feel:
The Smith prepares his Hammer for the Stroke,
While the Lung'd Bellows hissing Fire provoke;
Sejanus almost first of Roman Names,
The great Sejanus crackles in the Flames:
Form'd in the Forge, the Pliant Brass is laid
On Anvils; and of Head and Limbs are made,
Pans, Cans, and Pispots, a whole Kitchin Trade.
    Adorn your Doors with Laurels; and a Bull
Milk white and large, lead to the Capitol;
Sejanus with a Rope, is drag'd along;
The Sport and Laughter of the giddy Throng!
Good Lord, they Cry, what Ethiop Lips he has,
How foul a Snout, and what a hanging Face:
By Heav'n I never cou'd endure his sight;
But say, how came his Monstrous Crimes to Light?

What is the Charge, and who the Evidence
(The Saviour of the Nation and the Prince?)
Nothing of this; but our Old Cæsar sent
A Noisie Letter to his Parliament:
Nay Sirs, if Cæsar writ, I ask no more:
He's Guilty; and the Question's out of Door.
How goes the Mob, (for that's a Mighty thing.)
When the King's Trump, the Mob are for the King:
They follow Fortune, and the Common Cry
Is still against the Rogue Condemn'd to Dye.

## FROM THE MIDDLE ENGLISH OF CHAUCER

243       from *The Cock and the Fox: or,*
          *The Tale of the Nun's Priest*

There liv'd, as Authors tell, in Days of Yore,
A Widow somewhat old, and very poor:
Deep in a Dell her Cottage lonely stood,
Well thatch'd, and under covert of a Wood.
     This Dowager, on whom my Tale I found,
Since last she laid her Husband in the Ground,
A simple sober Life, in patience led,
And had but just enough to buy her Bread:
But Huswifing the little Heav'n had lent,
She duly paid a Groat for Quarter-Rent;
And pinch'd her Belly with her Daughters two,
To bring the Year about with much ado.
     The Cattel in her Homestead were three Sows,
An Ewe call'd Mally; and three brinded Cows.
Her Parlor-Window stuck with Herbs around,
Of sav'ry Smell; and Rushes strew'd the Ground.
A Maple-Dresser, in her Hall she had,
On which full many a slender Meal she made:
For no delicious Morsel pass'd her Throat;
According to her Cloth she cut her Coat:
No paynant Sawce she knew, no costly Treat,
Her Hunger gave a Relish to her Meat:
A sparing Diet did her Health assure;
Or sick, a Pepper-Posset was her Cure.

Before the Day was done her Work she sped,
And never went by Candle-light to Bed:
With Exercise she sweat ill Humors out,
Her Dancing was not hinder'd by the Gout.
Her Poverty was glad; her Heart content,
Nor knew she what the Spleen or Vapors meant.
   Of Wine she never tasted through the Year,
But White and Black was all her homely Chear;
Brown Bread, and Milk, (but first she skim'd her Bowls)
And Rashers of sindg'd Bacon, on the Coals.
On Holy-Days, an Egg or two at most;
But her Ambition never reach'd to roast.
   A Yard she had with Pales enclos'd about,
Some high, some low, and a dry Ditch without.
Within this Homestead, liv'd without a Peer,
For crowing loud, the noble Chanticleer:
So hight her Cock, whose singing did surpass
The merry Notes of Organs at the Mass.
More certain was the crowing of a Cock
To number Hours, than is an Abbey-clock;
And sooner than the Mattin-Bell was rung,
He clap'd his Wings upon his Roost, and sung:
For when Degrees fifteen ascended right,
By sure Instinct he knew 'twas One at Night.
High was his Comb, and Coral-red withal,
In dents embattel'd like a Castle-Wall;
His Bill was Raven-black, and shon like Jet,
Blue were his Legs, and Orient were his Feet:
White were his Nails, like Silver to behold,
His Body glitt'ring like the burnish'd Gold.
   This gentle Cock for solace of his Life,
Six Misses had beside his lawful Wife;
Scandal that spares no King, tho' ne'er so good,
Says, they were all of his own Flesh and Blood:
His Sisters both by Sire, and Mother's side,
And sure their likeness show'd them near ally'd.
But make the worst, the Monarch did no more,
Than all the Ptolomeys had done before:
When Incest is for Int'rest of a Nation,
'Tis made no Sin by Holy Dispensation.
Some Lines have been maintain'd by this alone,
Which by their common Ugliness are known.

# WENTWORTH DILLON,
# EARL OF ROSCOMMON

?1633–1685

## FROM THE LATIN OF HORACE

244

## *Odes*, Book I, 22

Cp.
Johnson

Virtue, Dear Friend, needs no Defence,
The surest Guard is Innocence:
None knew, till Guilt created Fear,
What Darts or poyson'd Arrows were.

Integrity undaunted goes
Through Lybian Sands or Scythian Snows,
Or where Hydaspes wealthy side
Pays Tribute to the Persian Pride.

For as (by amorous Thoughts betray'd)
Careless in Sabine Woods I stray'd,
A grisly foaming Wolf, unfed,
Met me unarm'd, yet trembling fled.

No Beast of more portentous Size,
In the Hercinian Forest lies;
None fiercer, in Numidia bred,
With Carthage were in Triumph led.

Set me in the Remotest Place,
That Neptune's frozen Arms embrace,
Where angry Jove did never spare
One Breath of kind and temp'rate Air:

Set me, where on some pathless Plain
The swarthy Africans complain,
To see the Char'ot of the Sun
So near the scorching Country run:

The burning Zone, the Frozen Isles,
Shall hear me sing of Cælia's Smiles,
 All Cold but in her Breast I will despise,
 And dare all Heat but that of Cælia's Eyes.


# THOMAS FLATMAN

## 1635–1688

### FROM THE LATIN OF HORACE

245      Epodes, III

*To Maecenas*

In time to come, if such a crime should be
 As Parricide, (foul villany!)
A Clove of Garlick would revenge that evil;
 (Rare dish for Plough-men, or the Devil!)
Accursed root! how does it jounce and claw!
 It works like Rats-bane in my maw.
What Witch contriv'd this strat'gem for my breath!
 Poison'd at once, and stunk to death;
With this vile juice Medæa (sure) did noint
 Jason (her Love) in every joint;
When untam'd Bulls in yokes he led along,
 This made his manhood smell so strong;
This gave her Dragon venom to his sting,
 And set the Hagg upon the wing.
I burn, I parch, as dry as dust am I,
 Such drought on Puglia never came,
Alcides could not bear so much as I,
 He oft was wet, but never dry.
Mecænas! do but taste of your own Treat,
 And what you gave your Poet, eat;
Then go to Bed, and court your Mistris there,
 She'l never kiss you I dare swear.

# PHILIP AYRES

1638–1712

## FROM THE GREEK OF THEOCRITUS

246 *The Death of Adonis*

When VENUS her ADONIS found,
Just slain, and weltring on the Ground,
With Hair disorder'd, gastly Look,
And Cheeks their Roses had forsook;
She bad the Cupids fetch with speed,
The Boar that did this horrid Deed:
They, to revenge Adonis Blood,
As quick as Birds search'd all the Wood,
And straight the murd'rous Creature found,
Whom they, with Chains, securely bound;
And whilst his Net one o'er him flung,
To drag the Captive Boar along
Another follow'd with his Bow,
Pushing to make him faster go;
Who most unwillingly obey'd,
For he of VENUS was afraid.
    No sooner she the Boar espy'd,
But, Oh! Thou cruel Beast, she cry'd,
That hadst the Heart to wound this Thigh,
How couldst thou kill so sweet a Boy?
    Great Goddess (said the Boar, and stood
Trembling) I swear by all that's Good,
By thy Fair Self, by Him I've slain,
These pretty Hunters, and this Chain;
I did no Harm this Youth intend,
Much less had Thought to kill your Friend:
I gaz'd, and with my Passion strove,
For with his Charms I fell in Love:
At last that naked Thigh of his,
With Lovers Heat I ran to kiss;
Oh Fatal Cause of all my Woe!
'Twas then I gave the heedless Blow.

These Tusks with utmost Rigour draw,
Cut, break, or tear them from my Jaw,
'Tis just I should these Teeth remove,
Teeth that can have a Sense of Love;
Or this Revenge, if yet too small,
Cut off the Kissing Lips and all.
   When Venus heard this humble Tale,
Pitty did o'er her Rage prevail,
She bad them straight his Chains unty,
And set the Boar at Liberty;
Who ne'er to Wood return'd again,
But follow'd Venus in her Train,
And when by Chance to Fire he came,
His Am'rous Tusks sing'd in the Flame.


FROM THE SPANISH OF QUEVEDO

247

## The Fly

*Out of the Wine-Pot cry'd the Fly,*
*Whilst the Grave Frog sate croaking by,*
*Than live a Watry Life like thine,*
*I'd rather choose to dye in Wine.*


I.

I Never Water could endure,
   Though ne're so Crystalline and Pure,
Water's a Murmurer, and they
Design more Mischief than they say;
Where Rivers smoothest are and clear,
Oh there's the Danger, there's the Fear;
But I'll not grieve to dye in Wine,
That Name is sweet, that Sound's Divine.
   *Thus from the Wine-Pot, &c.*


II.

Dull Fish in Water live we know,
And such insipid Souls as thou;
While to the Wine do nimbly fly,
Many such pretty Birds as I:


229

With Wine refresh'd, as Flowers with Rain,
My Blood is clear'd, inspir'd my Brain;
That when the Tory Boys do sing,
I buz i'th' Chorus for the King.
    *Thus from the Wine-Pot, &c.*


### III.

I'm more belov'd than thou canst be,
Most Creatures shun thy Company;
I go unbid to ev'ry Feast,
Nor stay for Grace, but fall o'th' Best:
There while I quaff in Choicest Wine,
Thou dost with Puddle-water dine,
Which makes thee such a Croaking thing.
Learn to drink Wine, thou Fool, and sing;
    *Thus from the Wine-Pot, &c.*


### IV.

In Gardens I delight to stray,
And round the Plants do sing and play:
Thy Tune no Mortal does avail,
Thou art the Dutch-man's Nightingale:
Wouldst thou with Wine but wet thy Throat,
Sure thou wouldst leave that Dismal Note;
Lewd Water spoils thy Organs quite,
And Wine alone can set them right.
    *Thus from the Wine-Pot, &c.*


### V.

Thy Comerades still are Newts and Frogs,
Thy Dwelling Saw-pits, Holes, and Bogs:
In Cities I, and Courts am free,
An Insect too of Quality.
What Pleasures, Ah! didst thou but know,
This Heav'nly Liquor can bestow:
To drink, and drown thou'dst ne'er repine;
The Great Anacreon dy'd by Wine.
    *Thus from the Wine-Pot, &c.*

# ANTHONY HORNECK

1641–1697

## FROM THE LATIN OF HORACE

*Odes*, Book I, 5

Cp.
Fanshawe
Milton
Cowley
Smart

Pyrrha, what slender well-shap'd Beau,
Perfum'd with Essence haunts thee now,
And lures thee to some kind Recess,
To sport on Rose-Beds sunk in Ease?
Prithee what Youth would'st thou insnare,
Artless and clean, with flowing Hair?
How oft will he have cause to mourn
Thy broken Vows and Cupid's Scorn?
Unskill'd as yet, he'd wond'ring spy
Fresh Tempests raging in that Eye,
From whence he hop'd a Calmer Sky.
Who now poor Gull enjoys the Bliss,
Thinks you divine and solely his:
Born down the Tide with easie Sail,
Little suspects an Adverse Gale.
Thrice wretched they who feel thy Darts,
Whilst Strangers to thy coquet Arts!
My Garments in the Fane display'd,
As Trophies that my Vows are paid,
Own the Great Ruler of the Sea
Author of my Delivery.

# JOHN WILMOT, EARL OF ROCHESTER

## 1648–1680

### FROM THE LATIN OF SENECA

249     The Latter End of the Chorus from *Troas*,
Act II

After Death nothing is, and nothing Death;
The utmost Limits of a gasp of Breath.
Let the ambitious Zealot lay aside
His hopes of Heav'n; (whose Faith is but his Pride)
Let slavish Souls lay by their Fear,
Nor be concern'd which way or where,
After this life they shall be hurl'd:
Dead, we become the Lumber of the World;
And to that Mass of Matter shall be swept,
Where things destroy'd, with thing unborn are kept;
Devouring time swallows us whole,
Impartial Death confounds Body and Soul.
For Hell, and the foul Fiend that rules
    The everlasting fiery G⟨ao⟩ls,
Devis'd by Rogues, dreaded by Fools
With his grim griesly Dog that keeps the Door,
    Are senseless Stories, idle Tales,
Dreams, Whimseys, and no more.

# NAHUM TATE

## 1652–1715

### IMITATED FROM THE LATIN OF CATULLUS

250     *Carmina*, LV and LVIIIb

Now if thou hast one dram of Grace,
Save a Friends Life and shew thy Face.
From me before thou ne're wast hid.
I saw thee tho the Sun ne're did.

Come forth I say thou sculking Elf,
Save a Friends Life and shew thy self.
For thee I've searched, and search'd again
Park, Tavern, Play-house, but in vain;
All these thou long hast left i'th lurch,
I might as well have search'd a Church.
Distracted now I scour the street,
And seize all Females that I meet;
Where's my Friend aloud I cry,
Naughty Creatures, speak or die,
One, making bare her snowy Breasts,
Cry'd—Seek no further, here he rests.
I'm tired with this Herculean work,
'Tis worse than tugging for the Turk.
Y'are in intrigue you'l say—be't so!
With Quality—That may be too;
Come tell your Conquest then say I,
That's Pleasure—T'other's Drudgery.
Mischief take Thee Graceless Elf.
Where canst thou thus conceal thy self?
I think (I'll swear) should I turn Witch,
To ride upon a liquer'd Switch,
Mount Lightning, and out-fly the Wind,
This Sculker I shall never find.


# JOHN OLDHAM

1653–1683

IMITATED FROM THE LATIN OF HORACE

251              from *The Art of Poetry*

Should some ill Painter, in a wild Design,
To a Man's Head, an Horse's Shoulders join,
Or Fish's Tail, to a fair Woman's Waste,
Or draw the Limbs of many a different Beast,
Ill-match'd, and with as motly Feathers drest!
If you, by chance, were to pass by his Shop;
Could you forbear from laughing at the Fop,

And not believe him whimsical, or mad?
Credit me, Sir, that Book is quite as bad,
As worthy Laughter, which, throughout, is fill'd
With monstrous Inconsistences, more vain and wild,
Than sick Mens Dreams, whose neither Head nor Tail,
Nor any Parts, in due Proportion, fall
But 'twill be said, *None ever did deny*
*Painters, and Poets, their free Liberty*
*Of feigning any thing:* We grant it true,
And the same Privilege crave, and allow:
But to mix Natures clearly opposite,
To make the Serpent, and the Dove, unite,
Or Lambs, from savage Tigers, seek Defence,
Shocks Reason, and the Rules of common Sense.
    Some, who would have us think they meant to treat,
At first, on Arguments of greatest Weight,
Are proud, when here, and there, a glittering Line
Does, through the Mass of their coarse Rubbish, shine:
In gay Digressions they delight to rove,
Describing, here, a Temple, there, a Grove,
A Vale enamell'd o'er with pleasant Streams,
A painted Rainbow, or the gliding Thames.
But how does this relate to their Design?
Tho'good, elsewhere, 'tis here, but foisted in.
A common Dawber may, perhaps, have Skill
To paint a Tavern-Sign, or Landskip, well;
But what is this to drawing of a Fight,
A Wreck, a Storm, or the last Judgment, right?
When the fair Model, and Foundation, shews,
That you some great Escurial would produce,
How comes it dwindled to a Cottage thus?
In fine, whatever Work you mean to frame,
Be uniform, and every where, the same.

# JOHN OLDHAM

## IMITATED FROM THE FRENCH OF BOILEAU

252  from *Satires*, VIII

*The poet brings himself in, as discoursing with a Doctor of the University
upon the Subject ensuing*

Of all the Creatures, in the World, that be,
Beast, Fish, or Fowl, that go, or swim, or fly
Throughout the Globe, from London to Japan,
The arrant'st Fool, in my Opinion's Man.
    What (strait I'm taken up) an Ant, a Fly,
A tiny Mite, which we can hardly see
Without a Perspective, a silly Ass,
Or freakish Ape, Dare you affirm, that these
Have greater Sense than Man? Ay, questionless,
Doctor, I find you're shock'd at this Discourse:
Man is (you cry) Lord of the Universe;
For him was this fair Frame of Nature made,
And all the Creatures for his Use, and Aid:
To him alone, of all the living Kind,
Has bounteous Heav'n, the Reas'ning-Gift, assign'd.
True Sir, that Reason ever was his Lot,
But thence, I argue, Man the greater Sot.
    This idle Talk (you say) and rambling Stuff
May pass in Satire, and take well enough
With sceptick Fools, who are dispos'd to jeer
At serious things: but you must make't appear
By solid Proof. Believe me, Sir, I'll do't:
Take you the Desk, and let's dispute it out.
Then, by your Favour, tell me, first of all,
What 'tis, which your grave Doctors, Wisdom call;
You answer: 'Tis an Evenness of Soul,
A steddy Temper, which no Cares controul.
No Passions ruffle, nor Desires inflame,
Still constant to it self, and still the same,
That does in all its slow Resolves advance,
With graver Steps, than Benchers, when they dance.
Most true; yet is not this, I dare maintain,
Less us'd by any, than the Fool, call'd Man.

Benchers] magistrate, judge, or one of the senior members of the Inns of Court

235

The wiser Emmet, quoted just before,
In Summer time, ranges the Fallows o'er
With Pains, and Labour, to lay in his Store;
But when the blust'ring North, with ruffling Blasts,
Saddens the Year, and Nature overcasts;
The prudent Insect, hid in Privacy,
Enjoys the Fruits of his past Industry.
No Ant, of Sense, was e'er so aukward seen,
To drudge in Winter, loiter in the Spring.
    But silier Man, in his mistaken way,
By Reason, his false Guide, is led astray:
Tost by a thousand Gusts of wav'ring Doubt,
His restless Mind still rolls from Thought to Thought:
In each Resolve, unsteddy, and unfixt,
And what he one Day loaths, desires the next.
    'Shall I, so fam'd for many a truant Jest
On wiving, now go take a Jilt at last?
Shall I turn Husband, and my Station chuse,
Amongst the rev'rend Martyrs of the Noose!
No, there are Fools enough besides, in Town,
To furnish Work for Satire, and Lampoon:'
Few Months before, cry'd the unthinking Sot;
Who quickly after, hamper'd in the Knot,
Was quoted for an Instance by the rest,
And bore his Fate, as tamely as the best,
And thought, that Heav'n from some mirac'lous side,
For him, alone, had drawn a faithful Bride.
    This is our Image just: such is that vain,
That foolish, fickle, motly-Creature, Man:
More changing than a Weather-cock, his Head
Ne'er wakes, with the same Thoughts, he went to Bed,
Irksome to all beside, and ill at Ease,
He neither others, nor himself, can please:
Each Minute round his whirling Humours run,
Now he's a Trooper, and a Priest anon,
To Day, in Buff, to morrow, in a Gown.
    Yet pleas'd with idle Whimsies of his Brain,
And puft with Pride, this haughty thing would fain
Be thought himself the only Stay, and Prop,
That holds the mighty Frame of Nature up:
The Skies, and Stars, his Properties must seem,
And turn-spit Angels, tread the Spheres for him.

# THOMAS CREECH

## 1659–1700

### FROM THE GREEK OF THEOCRITUS

253            *from* Idylls, II

### *The Enchantment*

Samœtha being forsaken by Delphis resolves to try the force of Charms to recover his affection; applyes herself to the Moon as a powerful Goddess in both those matters, and after she hath sent away her maid, tells the story of her misfortune.

Maid, where's my Lawrel? Oh my rageing Soul!
Maid, where's the Potion? fill the Bason full,
And crown the narrow brim with Purple wool:
That I might charm my false, my perjur'd Swain,
And force him back into my arms again:
For Cruel he these Twelve long days hath fled,
And knows not whether I'me alive or dead:
He hath not broke my Doors these Twelve long days,
Ah me! perhaps his varying Love decays,
Or else he dotes upon another face.
I'le run to morrow to the Fencing house,
And ask him what he means to use me thus:
But now I'le charm him, Moon, shine bright and clear,
To thee I will direct my secret prayer;
To Thee, and Hecate, whom Dogs do dread
When stain'd with gore, she stalks amidst the dead:
Hail frightful Hecate, assist me still
Make mine as great as fam'd Medea's skill:
    *Jynx restore my false, my perjur'd Swain*
    *And force him back into my Arms again.*
First burn the Flowr, then strew the other on,
Strew it. How? where's your sense and duty gone?
Base Thestylis! and am I so forlorn,
And grown so low that I'me become your scorn!

Jynx] a Bird sacred to Venus much used in Love Charms
                               (*Creech's note*)
        Thestylis] the maid

But strew the Salt, and say in angry tones
I scatter Delphids, perjur'd Delphids bones,
*Jynx restore my false, my perjur'd Swain*
*And force him back into my Arms again.*

\*

*Tell sacred Moon what first did raise my flame*
*And whence my Pain, and whence my Passion came.*
Near Lyco's House break thro the yielding throng,
I saw my Delphis, vigorous, stout, and young,
A Golden Down spread o're his youthful Chin,
His breast, bright Moon, was brighter far than thine:
For spread with glorious Oyl he lately came
From noble Fenceing, and from winning Fame:
*Tell sacred Moon what first did raise my flame*
*And whence my Pain, and whence my Passion came.*

\*

At last I told my Maid the naked truth,
Go Thestylis, have pitty on my youth;
Go find some cure to ease my rageing smart;
Young Delphid is the Tyrant of my Heart:
Go to the Fenceing House, ther's his delight,
For there he walks, and there he loves to sit.
*Tell sacred Moon what first did raise my flame,*
*And whence my Pain, and whence my Passion came.*
And if alone, give him a gentle Nod,
And softly tell that Samœtha wou'd
(Speak, speak, tho modest fear doth strike thee dumb)
Enjoy him here, and beg him he would come.
She went, she found, and told him what I said,
He Gladly heard, and eagerly obey'd.

\*

*Tell sacred Moon what first did raise my flame,*
*And whence my Pain, and whence my Passion came.*
Young tender Maids to unknown Madness drives,
And from warm Husbands Arms it forces Wives:
Thus He, and heedless I believ'd too soon,
He prest My hand in His, and laid me down
On the soft bed, when streight lock't Arm in Arm
In strickt embraces both grew gently warm;

238

Our breath was hot and short, we panting lay,
We look't, we murmur'd, and we dy'd away:
Our Cheeks did glow, and fainting vertue strove,
At last it yielded to the force of Love:
But what need all this talk? bright sacred Moon,
Both were well pleas'd, and some strange thing was done:
And ever since we lov'd, and liv'd at ease,
No sullen Minutes broke our Happiness;
Till soon this morning e're the Sun could rise,
And drive his Charriot thro the yielding Skies
To fetch the Rosy Morn from waves below,
I heard the fatal news, and knew my woe:
My Maids own Mother, she that lives hard by
An Honest Woman, and she scorns to ly;
She came and askt me, is your Delphid kind?
And have you firm possession of his Mind?
For I am sure, but whether Maid or Boy
I cannot tell, he courts another joy:
For he drinks Healths, and when those Healths are past,
He must be gone, and goes away in hast.
Besides with Garlands all his Rooms are drest,
And he prepares, as for a Marriage Feast;
This as she walkt last night she chanc't to view,
And told it me, and oh, I fear 'tis true!
For He was wont to come twice, thrice a day,
He saw me still as he return'd from play;
But now since he was here twelve nights are past,
Am I forgotten? am I left at last?
Whilst perjur'd he for other Beauty burns,
My Love I'me sure deserv'd more kind returns,
But now I'le Charm, but if he scorns me still
I'le force him down to Hell, by Fate, I will:
Such powerful drugs a Witch did once impart
She taught me such strange Charms, such force of Art:
But now farewel bright Moon, turn lovely Moon
To Waves below, and drive thy Charriot down,
Go lovely Moon, and wake the sleepy Morn:
I'le bear my trouble still, as I have born;
Farewel, and you attending Stars that wheel
Round Nights black Axle-tree, bright Stars, farewel.

FROM THE LATIN OF LUCRETIUS

*from* De Rerum Natura

254          '*The Elements Changeable*'

Now since the members of the World we view,
Are chang'd, consum'd and all produc'd anew;
It follows then, for which our proofs contend,
That this vast Frame began, and so must end.
   But lest you think, I poorly beg the Cause,
And that it disagrees with Nature's Laws,
That Water, Air, that Fire, and Earth should cease,
And fail; that they can die, or else increase;
Consider Earth, when parcht with busie beams,
And trodden much, flies up in dusky streams,
And little clouds of thickning dust arise,
Disperst by winds thro all the lower skies;
And gentle Rivers too, with wanton play
That kiss their rocky banks, and glide away,
Take somewhat still from the ungentle stone,
Soften the parts, and make them like their own.
   But more:
By what another Thing is fed, and grows,
That Thing some portion of its own must lose.
Now since all spring from Earth, and since we call,
And justly too, the Earth the Source of all;
Since All, when cruel Death dissolves, return
To Earth again, and She's both Womb and Urn:
The Earth is chang'd, some parts must sometimes cease,
And sometimes new come on, and she increase.
   Besides, that Seas, that Rivers wast, and die,
And still increase by constant new supply,
What need of proofs? This streams themselves do show,
And in soft murmurs babble as they flow.
But lest the Mass of Water prove too great,
The Sun drinks some, to quench his natural heat;
And some the Winds brush off, with wanton play
They dip their wings, and bear some parts away:
Some passes thro the Earth, diffus'd all o're,
And leaves its salt behind in every Pore;

For all returns thro narrow channels spread,
And joyns where e're the fountain shews her head:
And thence sweet streams in fair Meanders play,
And thro the Vallies cut their liquid way;
And Herbs, and Flowers on every side bestow,
The Fields all smile with flowers where e're they flow.
 But more, the Air thro all the mighty Frame
Is chang'd each hour, we breath not twice the same:
Because as all things wast, the parts must flie
To the vast Sea of Air; they mount on high,
And softly wander in the lower sky.
Now did not this the wasting things repair,
All had been long ago dissolv'd, all Air.
Well then, since all things wast, their vital chain
Dissolv'd, how can the frame of Air remain?
It rises from, and makes up things again.


# TOM BROWN

## 1663–1704

### FROM THE LATIN OF CATULLUS

**255**

### *Carmina*, XCII

I

Cp.
Swift
Landor

Each Moment of the long-liv'd Day,
Lesbia for me does backward pray,
 And rails at me sincerely;
Yet I dare pawn my Life, my Eyes,
 My Soul, and all that Mortals prize,
That Lesbia loves me dearly.


II

Why shou'd you thus conclude, you'll say,
Faith 'tis my own beloved Way,
 And thus I hourly prove her;
Yet let me all those Curses share
That Heav'n can give, or Man can bear,
 If I don't strangely love her.

241

### FROM THE LATIN OF MARTIAL

256          *Epigrams*, Book I, 32

> I do not love thee, Dr Fell,
> The reason why I cannot tell.


# GEORGE STEPNEY

## 1663–1707

### IMITATED FROM THE LATIN OF HORACE

257          *Odes*, Book III, 7

I.

Dear Molly, why so oft in Tears?
Why all these Jealousies and Fears,
   For thy bold Son of Thunder?
Have Patience till we've conquer'd France,
Thy Closet shall be stor'd with Nants;
   Ye Ladies like such Plunder.


II.

Before Toulon thy Yoke-mate lies,
Where all the live-long Night he sighs
   For thee in lowsy Cabbin:
And tho' the Captain's Chloe cries,
*'Tis I, dear Bully, prithee rise*—
   He will not let the Drab in.


III.

But she, the Cunning'st Jade alive,
Says, 'Tis the ready way to thrive,
   By sharing Female Bounties:
And, if he'll be but kind one Night,
She Vows, He shall be dubb'd a Knight,
   When she is made a Countess.

### IV.

Then tells of smooth young Pages whipp'd,
Cashier'd, and of their Liv'ries stripp'd,
  Who late to Peers belonging;
Are nightly now compell'd to trudge
With Links, because they would not drudge
  To save their Ladies Longing.

### V.

But Vol the Eunuch cannot be
A Colder Cavalier than he,
  In all such Love-Adventures:
Then pray do you, dear Molly, take
Some Christian Care, and do not break
  Your Conjugal Indentures.

### VI.

Bellair! Who does not Bellair know?
The Wit, the Beauty, and the Beau,
  Gives out, He loves you dearly:
And many a Nymph attack'd with Sighs,
And soft Impertinence and Noise,
  Full oft has beat a Parley.

### VII.

But, pretty Turtle, when the Blade
Shall come with am'rous Serenade,
  Soon from the Window rate him:
But if Reproof will not prevail,
And he perchance attempt to scale,
  Discharge the Jordan at him.

# WILLIAM WALSH

## 1663–1708

### FROM THE LATIN OF CATULLUS

258                    *Carmina*, LXXII

Cp.
Lovelace

Thou saidst that I alone thy Heart cou'd move,
And that for me thou wou'dst abandon Jove.
I lov'd thee then, not with a Love defil'd,
But as a Father loves his only Child.
I know thee now, and tho' I fiercelier burn,
Thou art become the Object of my Scorn.
See what thy Falshood gets; I must confess
I love thee more, but I esteem thee less.


# MATTHEW PRIOR

## 1664–1721

### FROM THE GREEK OF MOSCHUS

259                    *Cupid a Plowman*

His Lamp his Bow and Quiver laid aside,
A rustic Wallet o'er his Shoulders ty'd
Sly Cupid always on new Mischief bent
To the Rich Field and furrow'd Tillage went.
Like any Plowman toil'd the little God,
His Tune he whistl'd, and his Wheat he sow'd
Then sat and laugh'd, and to the Skys above
Raising his Eye He thus insulted Jove:
Lay by your Hail your hurtful Storms restrain,
And as I bid You let it Shine or rain
Else you again beneath my Yoke shal bow
Feel the sharp Goad, and draw the Servile plough;
What once Europa was Nanet is now.

## FROM THE LATIN OF CATULLUS

260                    *Carmina*, XXII

Suffenus whom you know, the Witty,
The Gay, the Talkative, and Pretty;
And, all his Wonders to rehearse,
The THING which makes a World of Verse,
I'm certain I shou'd not bely him,
To say he has several thousands by him,
Yet none deform'd with Critick blot,
Or wrote on Vellom to rub out.
Royal Paper! Scarlet Strings!
Gilded Backs; and such fine things!
But—When you read 'em, then the Witty,
The Gay Suffenus, and the Pretty:
Is the dullest, heaviest Clown,
So alter'd, he can scarce be known.
This is strange! that he who now
Cou'd so flatter, laugh, and bow,
So much Wit, such breeding show,
Shou'd be so ungenteel a Wight,
Whenever he attempts to write,
And yet the Wretch is ne're so pleas'd,
As when he's with this madness seiz'd.

Faith, Sir, w'are all deceiv'd alike,
All Labour in the same mistake,
Nor is the best of Men so clear
From every Folly, but somewhere
Still the Suffenus will appear.
Quickly we others Errors find,
But see not our own Load behind.

## FROM THE LATIN OF THE EMPEROR HADRIAN

261      *Adriani Morientis ad Animam Suam.*
          *Imitated*

Cp.
Byron
Stevie Smith
Cunningham

Poor little, pretty, flutt'ring Thing,
    Must We no longer live together?
And dost Thou prune thy trembling Wing,
    To take thy Flight Thou know'st not whither?

Thy humorous Vein, thy pleasing Folly
    Lyes all neglected, all forgot:
And pensive, wav'ring, melancholy,
    Thou dread'st and hop'st Thou know'st not what.

## FROM THE FRENCH OF DE GOMBAULD

262              *Epigram*

To John I ow'd great Obligation;
    But John, unhappily, thought fit
To publish it to all the Nation:
    Sure John and I are more than Quit.

# JONATHAN SWIFT

### 1667–1745

## FROM THE LATIN OF CATULLUS

263             *Carmina*, XCII

Cp.
Brown
Landor

Lesbia for ever on me rails;
    To talk on me she never fails:
Yet, hang me, but for all her Art;
    I find that I have gain'd her Heart:
My proof is thus: I plainly see
    The Case is just the same with me:
I curse her ev'ry hour sincerely;
    Yet, hang me, but I love her dearly.

## FROM THE LATIN OF HORACE

264              *from* Odes, Book III, 2

*To The Earl of Oxford, Late Lord Treasurer.*
*Sent to him when he was in the Tower, before his Tryal.*

How blest is he, who for his Country dies;
Since Death pursues the Coward as he flies.
The Youth, in vain, would fly from Fate's Attack,
With trembling Knees, and Terror at his Back;
Though Fear should lend him Pinions like the Wind,
Yet swifter Fate will seize him from behind.

Virtue repuls't, yet knows not to repine;
But shall with unattainted Honour shine;
Nor stoops to take the Staff, nor lays it down,
Just as the Rabble please to smile or frown.

Virtue, to crown her Fav'rites, loves to try
Some new unbeaten Passage to the Sky;
Where Jove a Seat among the Gods will give
To those who die, for meriting to live.

Next, faithful Silence hath a sure Reward:
Within our Breast be ev'ry Secret barr'd:
He who betrays his Friend, shall never be
Under one Roof, or in one Ship with me.
For, who with Traytors would his Safety trust,
Lest with the Wicked, Heaven involve the Just?
And, though the Villain 'scape a while, he feels
Slow Vengeance, like a Blood-hound at his Heels.

265   *Part of the 9th Ode of the 4th Book of Horace,*
        *address'd to Doctor William King,*
        *late Lord Archbishop of Dublin.*

Virtue conceal'd within our Breast
Is Inactivity at best:
But, never shall the Muse endure
To let your Virtues lye obscure,
Or suffer Envy to conceal
Your Labours for the Publick Weal.
Within your Breast all Wisdom lyes,
Either to govern or advise;
Your steady Soul preserves her Frame
In good and evil Times the same.
Pale Avarice and lurking Fraud
Stand in your sacred Presence aw'd;
Your Hand alone from Gold abstains,
Which drags the slavish World in Chains.

Him for an happy Man I own,
Whose Fortune is not overgrown;
And, happy he, who wisely knows
To use the Gifts, that Heav'n bestows;
Or, if it please the Powers Divine,
Can suffer Want, and not repine.
The Man, who Infamy to shun,
Into the Arms of Death would run,
That Man is ready to defend
With Life his Country, or his Friend.

FROM THE IRISH OF HUGH MACGOWRAN

266        *The Description of an Irish-Feast*

O Rourk's noble Fare
    Will ne'er be forgot,
By those who were there,
    Or those who were not.

His Revels to keep,
   We sup and we dine,
On seven Score Sheep,
   Fat Bullocks and Swine.
Usquebagh to our Feast
   In Pails was brought up,
An Hundred at least,
   And a Madder our Cup.
O there is the Sport,
   We rise with the Light,
In disorderly Sort,
   From snoring all Night.
O how was I trick't,
   My Pipe it was broke,
My Pocket was pick't,
   I lost my new Cloak.
I'm rifled, quoth Nell,
   Of Mantle and Kercher,
Why then fare them well,
   The De'el take the Searcher.
Come, Harper, strike up,
   But first by your Favour,
Boy, give us a Cup;
   Ay, this has some Savour:
O Rourk's jolly Boys
   Ne'er dream't of the Matter,
Till rowz'd by the Noise,
   And musical Clatter,
They bounce from their Nest,
   No longer will tarry,
They rise ready drest,
   Without one Ave Mary.
They dance in a Round,
   Cutting Capers and Ramping,
A Mercy the Ground
   Did not burst with their stamping.
The Floor is all wet
   With Leaps and with Jumps,
While the Water and Sweat,
   Splish, splash in their Pumps.

Madder] wooden vessel

Bless you late and early,
　　Laughlin O Enagin,
By my Hand, you dance rarely,
　　Margery Grinagin.
Bring Straw for our Bed,
　　Shake it down to the Feet,
Then over us spread,
　　The winnowing Sheet.
To show, I don't flinch,
　　Fill the Bowl up again,
Then give us a Pinch
　　Of your Sneezing; a Yean.
Good Lord, what a Sight,
　　After all their good Cheer,
For People to fight
　　In the Midst of their Beer:
They rise from their Feast,
　　And hot are their Brains,
A Cubit at least
　　The Length of their Skeans.
What Stabs and what Cuts,
　　What clatt'ring of Sticks,
What Strokes on Guts,
　　What Bastings and Kicks!
With Cudgels of Oak,
　　Well harden'd in Flame,
An hundred Heads broke,
　　An hundred struck lame.
You Churle, I'll maintain
　　My Father built Lusk,
The Castle of Slain,
　　And Carrickdrumrusk:
The Earl of Kildare,
　　And Moynalta, his Brother,
As great as they are,
　　I was nurs'd by their Mother.
Ask that of old Madam,
　　She'll tell you who's who,
As far up as Adam,
　　She knows it is true,

Skeans] daggers or short swords.

Come down with that Beam,
   If Cudgels are scarce,
A Blow on the Weam,
   Or a Kick on the A—se.

## FROM THE FRENCH (ANONYMOUS)

267       *Epigram on Fasting*

Who can believe with common Sense,
A Bacon-slice gives God Offence?
Or, how a Herring hath a Charm
Almighty Anger to disarm?
Wrapt up in Majesty divine,
Does he regard on what we dine?

# WILLIAM CONGREVE

### 1670–1729

## FROM THE GREEK OF HOMER

## The Iliad

268      *Andromache's Lamentation*

O my lost Husband! let me ever mourn
Thy early Fate, and too untimely Urn:
In the full Pride of Youth thy Glories fade,
And thou in ashes must with them be laid.
  Why is my Heart thus miserably torn!
Why am I thus distress'd! why thus forlorn!
Am I that wretched Thing, a Widow left?
Why do I live, who am of Life bereft!
Yet I were blest, were I alone undone;
Alas, my Child! where can an Infant run?

Unhappy Orphan! thou in Woes art nurst;
Why were you born?—I am with Blessings curst!
For long e're thou shalt be to Manhood grown,
Wide Desolation will lay waste this Town:
Who is there now that can Protection give,
Since He, who was her strength, no more doth live?
Who of her Rev'rend Matrons, will have Care?
Who save her Children from the Rage of War?
For He to All Father and Husband was,
And all are Orphans now, and Widows by his Loss.
Soon will the Grecians, now, insulting come,
And bear us Captives to their distant Home;
I, with my Child, must the same Fortune share,
And all alike, be Pris'ners of the War:
'Mongst base-born Wretches he, his Lot must have,
And be to some inhuman Lord, a Slave.
Else some avenging Greek, with Fury fill'd,
Or for an only Son, or Father kill'd
By Hector's hand, on him will vent his Rage,
And with his Blood his thirsty grief asswage;
For many fell by his relentless Hand,
Biting that Ground, which with their Blood was stain'd.
  Fierce was thy Father (O my Child) in War,
And never did his Foe in Battel spare;
Thence come these suff'rings, which, so much have cost,
Much Woe to all, but sure to me the most.
I saw him not, when in the pangs of Death,
Nor did my Lips receive his latest Breath;
Why held he not to me his dying hand?
And why receiv'd not I his last Command?
Something he wou'd have said, had I been there,
Which I should still in sad remembrance bear;
For I could never, never Words forget,
Which Night and Day, I wou'd with Tears repeat.


269                    *Helen's Lamentation*

       O Hector, thou wert rooted in my Heart,
       No Brother there had half so large a Part!
       Scarce my own Lord, to whom such Love I bore,
       That I forsook my Home; scarce he had more!

O would I ne're had seen that fatal day,
Would I had perish'd, when I came away.
Now, twenty Years are past, since that sad hour,
When first I landed on this ruin'd Shoar.
For Ruin (sure) and I, together came!
Yet all this time, from thee I ne're had blame,
Not one ungentle word, or look of Scorn,
Which I too often have from others born.
When you from their Reproach have set me free,
And kindly have reprov'd their Cruelty;
If by my Sisters, and the Queen revil'd
(For the good King, like you, was ever mild)
Your kindness still has all my grief beguil'd.
Even in tears let me your loss bemoan,
Who had no Friend alive, but you alone:
All will reproach me now, where ere I pass,
And fly with Horrour from my hated Face.
This said; she wept, and the vast Throng was mov'd,
And with a general Sigh her Grief approv'd.

## The Hymn to Venus
(*formerly ascribed to Homer*)

270     *'Venus goes after Anchises'*

Among the Springs which flow from Ida's Head
His lowing Herds the young Anchises fed:
Whose Godlike Form and Face the smiling Queen
Beheld, and lov'd to Madness soon as seen.
To Cyprus straight the wounded Goddess flies,
Where Paphian Temples in her Honour rise,
And Altars smoke with daily Sacrifice.
Soon as arriv'd, she to her Shrine repair'd,
Where entring quick, the shining Gates she barr'd.
The ready Graces wait, her Baths prepare,
And oint with fragrant Oils her flowing Hair;
Her flowing Hair around her Shoulders spreads,
And all adown Ambrosial Odour sheds.
Last, in transparent Robes her Limbs they fold,
Enrich'd with Ornaments of purest Gold,
And thus attir'd, her Chariot she ascends,
And Cyprus left, her Flight to Troy she bends.

On Ida she alights, then seeks the Seat
Which lov'd Anchises chose for his Retreat:
And ever as she walk'd thro' Lawn or Wood,
Promiscuous Herds of Beasts admiring stood.
Some humbly follow, while some fawning meet,
And lick the Ground, and crouch beneath her Feet.
Dogs, Lions, Wolves and Bears their Eyes unite,
And the swift Panther stops to gaze with fix'd Delight.
For, ev'ry Glance she gives, soft Fire imparts,
Enkindling sweet Desire in Savage Hearts.
Inflam'd with Love, all single out their Mates,
And to their shady Dens each Pair retreats.

271 *'Venus tells Anchises the Story of Aurora and Tithonus'*

But when the Golden-thron'd Aurora made
Tithonus Partner of her rosy Bed,
(Tithonus too was of the Trojan Line,
Resembling Gods in Face and Form Divine)
For him she straight the Thunderer address'd,
That with perpetual Life he might be bless'd:
Jove heard her Pray'r, and granted her Request.
But ah! how rash was she, how indiscreet!
The most material Blessing to omit;
Neglecting, or not thinking to provide,
That Length of Days might be with Strength supply'd;
And to her Lover's endless Life, engage
An endless Youth, incapable of Age.
But hear what Fate befell this heav'nly Fair,
In Gold inthron'd, the brightest Child of Air,
Tithonus, while of pleasing Youth possess'd,
Is by Aurora with Delight caress'd;
Dear to her Arms, he in her Court resides,
Beyond the Verge of Earth, and Ocean's utmost Tides.
But, when he saw gray Hairs begin to spread,
Deform his Beard, and disadorn his Head,
The Goddess cold in her Embraces grew,
His Arms declin'd, and from his Bed withdrew;
Yet still a kind of nursing Care she show'd,
And Food ambrosial, and rich clothes bestow'd:

But when of Age he felt the sad Extreme,
And ev'ry Nerve was shrunk, and Limb was lame,
Lock'd in a Room her useless Spouse she left,
Of Youth, of Vigour, and of Voice bereft.
On Terms like these, I never can desire
Thou shouldst to Immortality aspire.

# JOSEPH ADDISON

## 1672–1719

### FROM THE LATIN OF OVID

## Metamorphoses

272    *'Apollo, Phaeton and the Chariot of the Sun'*

Soon as the Father saw the rosy Morn,
And the Moon shining with a blunter Horn,
He bid the nimble Hours, without Delay,
Bring forth the Steeds; the nimble Hours obey:
From their full Racks the gen'rous Steeds retire,
Dropping ambrosial Foams, and snorting Fire.
Still anxious for his Son, the God of Day,
To make him Proof against the burning Ray,
His Temples with Celestial Ointment wet,
Of sov'raign Virtue to repel the Heat;
Then fix'd the beamy Circle on his Head,
And fetch'd a deep foreboding Sigh, and said,
   'Take this at least, this last Advice, my Son,
Keep a stiff Rein, and move but gently on:
The Coursers of themselves will run too fast,
Your Art must be to Moderate their Haste.
Drive 'em not on Directly through the Skies,
But where the Zodiac's Winding Circle lies,
Along the midmost Zone; but sally forth
Nor to the distant South, nor stormy North.
The Horses Hoofs a beaten Track will show,
But neither mount too high, nor sink too low.

That no new Fires, or Heav'n, or Earth infest;
Keep the mid Way, the middle Way is best.
Nor, where in radiant Folds the Serpent twines,
Direct your Course, nor where the Altar shines.
Shun both Extreams; the rest let Fortune guide,
And better for thee than thy self provide!
See, while I speak, the Shades disperse away,
Aurora gives the Promise of a Day;
I'm call'd, nor can I make a longer Stay.
Snatch up the Reins; or still th' Attempt forsake,
And not my Chariot, but my Counsel take,
While yet securely on the Earth you stand;
Nor touch the Horses with too rash a Hand.
Let Me alone to light the World, while You
Enjoy those Beams which you may safely view.'
He spoke in vain; the Youth with active Heat
And sprightly Vigour vaults into the Seat;
And joys to hold the Reins, and fondly gives
Those Thanks his Father with Remorse receives.

    Mean while the restless Horses neigh'd aloud,
Breathing out Fire, and pawing where they stood.
Tethys, not knowing what had past, gave way,
And all the Waste of Heav'n before 'em lay.
They spring together out, and swiftly bear
The flying Youth through Clouds and yielding Air;
With wingy Speed outstrip the Eastern Wind,
And leave the Breezes of the Morn behind.
The Youth was light, nor could he fill the Seat,
Or poise the Chariot with its wonted Weight:
But as at Sea th'unballass'd Vessel rides,
Cast to and fro, the Sport of Winds and Tides;
So in the bounding Chariot toss'd on high,
The Youth is hurry'd headlong through the Sky.
Soon as the Steeds perceive it, they forsake
Their stated Course, and leave the beaten Track.
The Youth was in a Maze, nor did he know
Which way to turn the Reins, or where to go;
Nor wou'd the Horses, had he known, obey.
Then the Sev'n Stars first felt Apollo's Ray,
And wish'd to dip in the forbidden Sea.

    Tethys] daughter of Uranus (Heaven)

The folded Serpent next the frozen Pole,
Stiff and benum'd before, began to roll,
And rag'd with inward Heat, and threaten'd War,
And shot a redder Light from ev'ry Star;
Nay, and 'tis said Bootes too, that fain
Thou wou'd'st have fled, tho' cumber'd with thy Wane.
    Th'unhappy Youth then, bending down his Head,
Saw Earth and Ocean far beneath him spread.
His Colour chang'd, he startled at the Sight,
And his Eyes Darken'd by too great a Light.
Now cou'd he wish the fiery Steeds untry'd,
His Birth obscure, and his Request deny'd:
Now wou'd he Merops for his Father own,
And quit his boasted Kindred to the Sun.
    So fares the Pilot, when his Ship is tost
In troubled Seas, and all its Steerage lost,
He gives her to the Winds, and in Despair
Seeks his last Refuge in the Gods and Pray'r.
    What cou'd he do? his Eyes, if backward cast,
Find a long Path he had already past;
If forward, still a longer Path they find:
Both he compares, and measures in his Mind;
And sometimes casts an Eye upon the East,
And sometimes looks on the forbidden West.
The Horses Names he knew not in the Fright,
Nor wou'd he loose the Reins, nor cou'd he hold 'em right.
    Now all the Horrors of the Heav'ns he spies,
And monstrous Shadows of prodigious Size,
That, deck'd with Stars, lye scatter'd o're the Skies.
There is a Place above, where Scorpio bent
In Tail and Arms surrounds a vast Extent;
In a wide Circuit of the Heav'ns he shines,
And fills the Space of Two Cœlestial Signs.
Soon as the Youth beheld him, vex'd with Heat,
Brandish his Sting, and in his Poison sweat,
Half dead with sudden Fear he dropt the Reins;
The Horses felt 'em loose upon their Mains,
And, flying out through all the Plains above,
Ran uncontroul'd where-e'er their Fury drove;

Bootes] a constellation, the Wagoner, at the tail of the Great Bear

Rush'd on the Stars, and through a pathless Way
Of unknown Regions hurry'd on the Day.
And now above, and now below they flew,
And near the Earth the burning Chariot drew.

    The Clouds disperse in Fumes, the wond'ring Moon
Beholds her Brother's Steeds beneath her own;
The Highlands smoak, cleft by the piercing Rays,
Or, clad with Woods, in their own Fewel blaze.
Next o'er the Plains, where ripen'd Harvests grow,
The running Conflagration spreads Below.
But these are trivial Ills: whole Cities burn,
And peopled Kingdoms into Ashes turn.

    The Mountains kindle as the Car draws near,
Athos and Tinolus red with Fires appear;
Œagrian Hæmus (then a single Name)
And Virgin Helicon increase the Flame;
Taurus and Oetè glare amid the Sky,
And Ida, spight of all her Fountains, Dry.
Eryx, and Othrys, and Cithæron, glow,
And Rhodopè, no longer cloath'd in Snow;
High Pindus, Mimas, and Parnassus, sweat,
And Ætna rages with redoubled Heat.
Ev'n Scythia, through her hoary Regions warm'd,
In vain with all her native Frost was arm'd.
Cover'd with Flames, the tow'ring Appennine,
And Caucasus, and proud Olympus, shines
And, where the long-extended Alpes aspire,
Now stands a huge continu'd Range of Fire.

    Th' astonisht Youth, where-e'er his Eyes cou'd turn,
Beheld the Universe around him burn:
The World was in a Blaze; nor cou'd he bear
The sultry Vapours and the scorching Air,
Which from below, as from a Furnace, flow'd;
And now the Axle-tree beneath him glow'd:
Lost in the whirling Clouds, that round him broke,
And white with Ashes, hov'ring in the Smoke,
He flew where-e'er the Horses drove, nor knew
Whither the Horses drove, or where he flew.

    'Twas then, they say, the swarthy Moor begun
To change his Hue, and Blacken in the Sun.
Then Libya first, of all her Moisture drain'd,
Became a barren Waste, a Wild of Sand.

The Water-Nymphs lament their empty Urns,
Bœotia, robb'd of Silver Dirce, mourns,
Corinth Pyrene's wasted Spring bewails,
And Argos grieves whilst Amymonè fails.
    The Floods are drain'd from ev'ry distant Coast,
Ev'n Tanaïs, tho' fix'd in Ice, was lost.
Enrag'd Caïcus and Lycormas roar,
And Xanthus, fated to be burnt once more.
The fam'd Mæander, that unweary'd strays
Through mazy Windings, smoaks in ev'ry Maze.
From his lov'd Babylon Euphrates flies;
The big-swoln Ganges and the Danube rise
In thick'ning Fumes, and darken half the Skies.
In Flames Ismenos and the Phasis roul'd,
And Tagus floating in his melted Gold.
The Swans, that on Caÿster often try'd
Their tuneful Songs, now sung their last and dy'd.
The frighted Nile ran off, and under Ground
Conceal'd his Head, nor can it yet be found:
His sev'n divided Currents all are dry,
And where they roul'd, sev'n Gaping Trenches lye.
No more the Rhine or Rhone their Course maintain,
Nor Tiber, of his promis'd Empire vain.
    The Gound, deep-cleft, admits the dazling Ray,
And startles Pluto with the Flash of Day.
The Seas shrink in, and to the Sight disclose
Wide naked Plains, where once their Billows rose;
Their Rocks are all discovered, and increase
The Number of the scatter'd Cyclades.
The Fish in Sholes about the Bottom creep,
Nor longer dares the crooked Dolphin leap.
Gasping for Breath, th'unshapen Phocæ die,
And on the boiling Wave extended lye.
Nereus, and Doris with her Virgin Train,
Seek out the last Recesses of the Main;
Beneath unfathomable Depths they faint,
And secret in their gloomy Caverns pant.
Stern Neptune thrice above the Waves upheld
His Face, and thrice was by the Flames repell'd.
    The Earth at length, on ev'ry Side embrac'd
With scalding Seas, that floated round her Waste,

When now she felt the Springs and Rivers come,
And crowd within the Hollow of her Womb,
Up-lifted to the Heav'ns her blasted Head,
And clapt her Hand upon her Brows, and said;
(But first, impatient of the sultry Heat,
Sunk deeper down, and sought a cooler Seat:)
  'If you, great King of Gods, my Death approve,
And I deserve it, let me die by Jove;
If I must perish by the Force of Fire,
Let me transfix'd with Thunderbolts expire.
See, whilst I speak, my Breath the Vapours choak,
(For now her Face lay wrapt in Clouds of Smoak)
See my singe'd Hair, behold my faded Eye,
And wither'd Face, where Heaps of Cinders lye!
And does the Plow for This my Body tear?
This the Reward for all the Fruits I bear,
Tortur'd with Rakes, and harrass'd all the Year?
That Herbs for Cattle daily I renew,
And Food for Man, and Frankincense for You?
But grant Me guilty; what has Neptune done?
Why are his Waters boiling in the Sun?
The wavy Empire, which by Lot was giv'n,
Why does it waste, and further shrink from Heav'n?
If I nor He your Pity can provoke,
See your own Heav'ns, the Heav'ns begin to smoke!
Shou'd once the Sparkles catch those bright Abodes,
Destruction seizes on the Heav'ns and Gods;
Atlas becomes unequal to his Freight,
And almost faints beneath the glowing Weight.
If Heav'n, and Earth, and Sea, together burn,
All must again into their Chaos turn.
Apply some speedy Cure, prevent our Fate,
And succour Nature, e'er it be too late.'
She ceas'd, for choak'd with Vapours round her spread,
Down to the deepest Shades she sunk her Head.
  Jove call'd to witness ev'ry Pow'r above,
And ev'n the God, whose Son the Chariot drove,
That what he acts he is compell'd to do,
Or universal Ruin must ensue.
Strait he ascends the high Æthereal Throne,
From whence he us'd to dart his Thunder down,

From whence his Show'rs and Storms he us'd to pour,
But now cou'd meet with neither Storm nor Show'r.
Then, aiming at the Youth, with lifted Hand,
Full at his Head he hurl'd the forky Brand,
In dreadful Thund'rings. Thus th' Almighty Sire
Suppress'd the Raging of the Fires with Fire.
    At once from Life, and from the Chariot driv'n,
Th'ambitious Boy fell Thunder-struck from Heav'n.
The Horses started with a sudden Bound,
And flung the Reins and Chariot to the Ground:
The studded Harness from their Necks they broke,
Here fell a Wheel, and here a Silver Spoke,
Here were the Beam and Axle torn away;
And, scatter'd o'er the Earth, the shining Fragments lay.
The Breathless Phaeton, with flaming Hair,
Shot from the Chariot, like a falling Star,
That in a Summer's Ev'ning from the Top
Of Heav'n drops down, or seems at least to drop;
Till on the Po his Blasted Corps was hurl'd,
Far from his Country, in the Western World.


# NICHOLAS ROWE

## 1674–1718

### FROM THE LATIN OF LUCAN

## Pharsalia

273    *'The Rivalry between Caesar and Pompey'*

    Thee Pompey thy past deeds by turns infest,
And jealous Glory burns within thy breast,
Thy fam'd pyratick lawrel seems to fade,
Beneath successful Cæsar's rising shade;
His Gallick wreaths thou view'st with anxious eyes
Above thy naval crowns triumphant rise.
Thee Cæsar thy long labours past incite,
Thy use of war, and custom of the fight;
While bold Ambition prompts thee in the race,
And bids thy courage scorn a second place.

Superior pow'r, fierce Faction's dearest care,
One could not brook, and one disdain'd to share.
Justly to name the better cause were hard,
While greatest names for either side declar'd:
Victorious Cæsar by the Gods was crown'd,
The vanquish'd party was by Cato own'd.
Nor came the Rivals equal to the field;
One to increasing years began to yield,
Old Age came creeping in the peaceful gown,
And civil functions weigh'd the Soldier down;
Disus'd to Arms, he turn'd him to the Laws,
And pleas'd himself with popular applause;
With Gifts, and lib'ral bounty sought for fame,
And lov'd to hear the vulgar shout his name;
In his own Theatre rejoyc'd to sit,
Amidst the noisie praises of the pit.
Careless of future ills that might betide,
No aid he sought to prop his failing side,
But on his former fortune much rely'd.
Still seem'd he to possess, and fill his place;
But stood the shadow of what once he was.
So in the field with Ceres' bounty spread,
Uprears some antient Oak his rev'rend head;
Chaplets and sacred gifts his boughs adorn,
And spoils of war by mighty Heroes worn.
But the first vigour of his root now gone,
He stands dependant on his weight alone;
All bare his naked branches are display'd,
And with his leafless trunk he forms a shade:
Yet tho' the winds his ruin daily threat,
As ev'ry blast wou'd heave him from his seat;
Tho' thousand fairer trees the field supplies,
That rich in youthful verdure round him rise;
Fix'd in his antient state he yields to none,
And wears the honours of the grove alone.
But Cæsar's greatness, and his strength, was more
Than past renown, and antiquated pow'r;
'Twas not the fame of what he once had been,
Of tales in old Records and Annals seen;
But 'twas a valour, restless, unconfin'd,
Which no success could sate, nor limits bind;

## NICHOLAS ROWE

'Twas shame, a Soldier's shame, untaught to yield,
That blush'd for nothing but an ill-fought field:
Fierce in his hopes he was, nor knew to stay,
Where vengeance or Ambition led the way;
Still prodigal of war whene'er withstood,
Nor spar'd to stain the guilty sword with blood:
Urging advantage he improv'd all odds,
And made the most of Fortune and the Gods;
Pleas'd to o'erturn whate'er with-held his prize,
And saw the ruin with rejoicing eyes.


# ISAAC WATTS

## 1674–1748

### IMITATED FROM THE HEBREW*
via The Authorized Version

274    *Psalm 90: 1–5: Man frail and God eternal*

Our God our help in ages past,
Our hope for years to come,
Our shelter from the stormy blast,
And our eternal home.

Under the shadow of thy throne
Thy saints have dwelt secure,
Sufficient is thine arm alone,
And our defence is sure.

Before the hills in order stood
Or earth receiv'd her frame,
From everlasting thou art God,
To endless years the same.

---

\* Watts's full title runs *The Psalms of David Imitated in the Language of the New Testament*

Thy word commands our flesh to dust,
'Return ye sons of men':
All nations rose from earth at first
And turn to earth again.

A thousand ages in thy sight
Are like an ev'ning gone,
Short as the watch that ends the night
Before the rising sun.

The busy tribes of flesh and blood
With all their lives and cares
Are carry'd downwards by thy flood
And lost in following years.

Time like an everrolling stream
Bears all its sons away,
They fly forgotten as a dream
Dies at the op'ning day.

Like flow'ry fields the nations stand
Pleas'd with the morning light,
The flow'rs beneath the mower's hand
Lie with'ring ere tis night.

Our God our help in ages past,
Our hope for years to come,
Be thou our guard while troubles last,
And our eternal home.

# THOMAS PARNELL

## 1679–1718

275    *from* The Battle of the Frogs and Mice
(*formerly ascribed to Homer*)

*'The King of the Frogs invites the King of the Mice to voyage on his Back'*

Ascend my Shoulders, firmly keep thy Seat,
And reach my marshy Court, and feast in State.
  He said, and leant his Back; with nimble Bound
Leaps the light Mouse, and clasps his Arms around,
Then wond'ring floats, and sees with glad Survey
The winding Banks dissemble Ports at Sea.
But when aloft the curling Water rides,
And wets with azure Wave his downy Sides,
His thoughts grow conscious of approaching Woe,
His idle Tears with vain Repentance flow,
His Locks he rends, his trembling Feet he rears,
Thick beats his Heart with unaccustom'd Fears;
He sighs, and chill'd with Danger, longs for Shore:
His Tail extended forms a fruitless Oar,
Half-drench'd in liquid Death his Pray'rs he spake,
And thus bemoan'd him from the dreadful Lake.
  So pass'd Europa thro' the rapid Sea,
Trembling and fainting all the vent'rous Way;
With oary Feet the Bull triumphant rode,
And safe in Crete depos'd his lovely Load.
Ah safe at last! may thus the Frog support
My trembling Limbs to reach his ample Court.
  As thus he sorrows, Death ambiguous grows,
Lo! from the deep a Water-Hydra rose;
He rolls his sanguin'd Eyes, his Bosom heaves,
And darts with active Rage along the Waves.
Confus'd, the Monarch sees his hissing Foe,
And dives to shun the sable Fates below.
Forgetful Frog! The Friend thy Shoulders bore,
Unskill'd in Swimming, floats remote from Shore.

He grasps with fruitless Hands to find Relief,
Supinely falls, and grinds his Teeth with Grief,
Plunging he sinks, and struggling mounts again,
And sinks, and strives, but strives with Fate in vain.
The weighty Moisture clogs his hairy Vest,
And thus the Prince his dying Rage exprest.
   Nor thou, that flings me flound'ring from thy Back,
As from hard Rocks rebounds the shatt'ring Wrack,
Nor thou shalt 'scape thy Due, perfidious King!
Pursu'd by Vengeance on the swiftest Wing:
At Land thy Strength could never equal mine,
At Sea to conquer, and by Craft, was thine.
But Heav'n has Gods, and Gods have searching Eyes:
Ye Mice, ye Mice, my great Avengers rise!

# ELIJAH FENTON

## 1683–1730

### FROM THE LATIN OF MARTIAL

276                        *Epigram* (ascribed)

Milo's from home; and, Milo being gone,
His lands bore nothing, but his wife a son:
Why she so fruitful, and so bare the field?
The lands lay fallow, but the wife was till'd.

277                  *Epigrams*, Book X, 47

Cp.
Surrey
Jonson
Fanshawe

Would you, my friend, in little room express
The just description of true happiness;
First set me down a competent estate,
But rais'd and left me by a parent's sweat;
('Tis pleasure to improve, but toil to get:)
Not large, but always large enough to yield
A cheerful fire, and no ungrateful field.
Averse to law-suits, let me peace enjoy,
And rarely pester'd with a town employ.
Smooth be my thoughts, my mind serene and clear,
A healthful body with such limbs I'd bear

As should be graceful, well-proportion'd, just,
And neither weak nor boorishly robust.
Nor fool, nor knave, but innocently wise;
Some friends indulge me, let a few suffice:
But suited to my humour and degree,
Not nice, but easily pleas'd, and fit for me;
So let my board and entertainments be.
With wholesome homely food, not serv'd in state,
What tastes as well in pewter as in plate,
Mirth and a glass my cheerful evenings share,
At equal distance from debauch and care.
To bed retiring, let me find it blest
With a kind modest spouse and downy rest:
Pleas'd always with the lot my fates assign,
Let me no change desire, no change decline;
With every turn of Providence comply,
Not tir'd with life, nor yet afraid to die.

# JOHN GAY

1685–1732

## FROM THE LATIN OF OVID

278          *Metamorphoses*

[Arachne, famed for weaving, challenges Pallas Athene to compete with her and
weaves the amours of the gods.]

Not Pallas, not ev'n Spleen it self could blame
The wond'rous Work of the Mæonian Dame;
With Grief her vast Success the Goddess bore,
And of Celestial Crimes the Story tore.
Her boxen Shuttle, now enrag'd, she took,
And thrice the proud Idmonian Artist struck:
Th' unhappy Maid, to see her Labours vain,
Grew resolute with Pride, and Shame, and Pain.
Around her Neck a fatal Noose she ty'd,
And sought by sudden Death her Guilt to hide.
Pallas with Pity saw the desp'rate deed,
And thus the Virgin's milder Fate decreed.

'Live, Impious Rival, mindful of thy Crime,
Suspended thus to waste thy future time,
Thy Punishment involves thy num'rous Race,
Who, for thy Fault, shall share in thy Disgrace:'
Her Incantation Magick Juices aid,
With sprinkling Drops she bath'd the pendent Maid,
And thus the Charm its noxious Pow'r display'd.
Live Leaves in Autumn drop her falling Hairs,
With these, her Nose, and next her rising Ears,
Her Head to the minutest Substance shrunk,
The potent Juice contracts her changing Trunk;
Close to her Sides, her slender Fingers clung,
There chang'd to nimble Feet, in order hung;
Her bloated Belly swells to larger size,
Which now with smallest Threads her Work supplies;
The Virgin in the Spider still remains,
And in that Shape her former Art retains.

# WILLIAM DIAPER

### ?1686–1717

#### FROM THE GREEK OF OPPIAN

## Halieutica

279 *'Eels'*

Strange the Formation of the Eely Race,
That know no Sex, yet love the close Embrace.
Their folded Lengths they round each other twine,
Twist am'rous Knots, and slimy Bodies joyn;
Till the close Strife brings off a frothy Juice,
The Seed that must the wriggling Kind produce.
Regardless they their future Offspring leave,
But porous Sands the spumy Drops receive.
That genial Bed impregnates all the Heap,
And little Eelets soon begin to creep.
Half-Fish, Half-Slime they try their doubtful strength,
And slowly trail along their wormy Length.

What great Effects from slender Causes flow!
Congers their Bulk to these Productions owe:
The Forms which from the frothy Drop began,
Stretch out immense, and eddy all the Main.

280                        *'The Lampreys'*

The Lamprey, glowing with uncommon Fires,
The Earth-bred Serpents purfled Curls admires.
He no less kind makes amorous Returns,
With equal Love the grateful Serpent burns.
Fixt on the Joy he bounding shoots along,
Erects his azure Crest, and darts his forky Tongue.
Now his red Eye-balls glow with doubled Fires;
Proudly he mounts upon his folded Spires,
Displays his glossy Coat, and speckled Side,
And meets in all his Charms the wat'ry Bride.
But lest he cautless might his Consort harm,
The gentle Lover will himself disarm,
Spit out the venom'd Mass, and careful hide
In cranny'd Rocks, far from the washing Tide;
There leaves the Furies of his noxious Teeth,
And putrid Bags, the pois'nous Fund of Death.
His Mate he calls with softly hissing Sounds;
She joyful hears, and from the Ocean bounds.
Swift as the bearded Arrow'd Hast she flies,
To own her Love, and meet the Serpent's Joys.
At her approach, no more the Lover bears
Odious Delay, nor sounding Waters fears.
Onward he moves on shining Volumes roll'd,
The Foam all burning seems with wavy Gold.
At length with equal Hast the Lovers meet,
And strange Enjoyments slake their mutual Heat.
She with wide-gaping Mouth the Spouse invites,
Sucks in his Head, and feels unknown Delights.
When full Fruition has asswag'd Desire,
Well-pleas'd the Bride will to her Home retire.
Tir'd with the Strife the Serpent hies to Land,
And leaves his Prints on all the furrow'd Sand;
With anxious Fear seeks the close private Cleft,
Where he in Trust th'important Secret left.

From the stain'd Rock he sucks the pois'nous Heaps,
Feels his returning Strength, and hissing leaps;
With brandish'd Tongue the distant Foe defies,
And darts new Light'nings from his Blood-shot Eyes.
But if some Swain mean while observing spies
Where odious Spume, and venom'd Spittle lies,
And while the Serpent wooes, from neighb'ring Seas
The cleansing Waters to the Rock conveys;
The Serpent comes, and finds his Treasure gone,
Looks sorrowing round, and blames the faithless Stone;
Disarm'd no more his wonted Pleasure takes,
Curls in the Grass, or hisses in the Brakes.
He creeps with Shame a tawdry speckled Worm,
And prides no longer in his beauteous Form.
On the same Rock with Head reclin'd he lies,
And, where he lost his Arms, despairing dies.

281   *'The Slime-Fish'*

When they in Throngs a safe Retirement seek,
Where pointed Rocks the rising Surges break,
Or where calm Waters in their Bason sleep,
While chalky Cliffs o'erlook the shaded Deep,
The Seas all gilded o'er the Shoal betray,
And shining Tracks inform their wand'ring Way.
  As when soft Snows, brought down by Western Gales,
Silent descend and spread on all the Vales;
Add to the Plains, and on the Mountains shine,
While in chang'd Fields the starving Cattle pine;
Nature bears all one Face, looks coldly bright,
And mourns her lost Variety in White,
Unlike themselves the Objects glare around,
And with false Rays the dazzled Sight confound:
So, where the Shoal appears, the changing Streams
Lose their Sky-blew, and shine with silver Gleams.

# ALLAN RAMSAY

## 1686–1758

### IMITATED FROM THE LATIN OF HORACE

## Odes, Book I, 4

### *Ode to Mr F——.*

Now gowans sprout, an' lavrocks sing,
An' welcome west winds warm the spring.
O'er hill an' dale they saftly blaw,
An' drive the winter's cauld awa.
The ships, lang gyzen'd at the pier,
Now spread their sails, an' smoothly steer;
The nags an' nowt hate wissen'd strae,
An' frisking to the fields they gae;
Nor hynds, wi' elson an' hemp lingle.
Sit soling shoon out-owre the ingle.
Now bonny haughs their verdure boast,
That late were clad wi' snaw an' frost;
Wi' her gay train the Paphian Queen,
By moon-light, dances on the green;
She leads, while Nymphs an' Graces sing,
An' trip around the fairy ring.
Meantime, poor Vulcan, hard at thrift,
Gets mony a sair an' heavy lift,
Whilst, rinnin' down, his haff-blind lads
Blaw up the fire, an' thump the gads.
    Now leave your fitsted on the dew,
An' busk yoursell in habit new;
Be gratefu' to the guiding powers,
An' blythly spend your easy hours.
O canny F——! tutor time,
An' live as lang's ye're in your prime;
That ill-bred death has nae regard
To king, or cottar, or a laird;

gowans]daisies    lavrocks] larks    gyzen'd] shrunk with dryness
  nowt] black cattle    elson] awl    lingle] shoemaker's thread
            haughs] valleys    fitsted] footprint

As soon a castle he'll attack,
As wa's o' divots roof'd wi' thack.
Immediately we'll a' tak flight
Unto the mirk realms o' night,
As stories gang, wi' ghaists to roam,
In gloomy Pluto's gousty dome;
Bid fair guid-day to pleasure syne
O' bonny lasses an' red wine.

    Then deem ilk little care a crime,
Daurs waste an hour o' precious time;
An' since our life's sae unco short,
Enjoy it a', ye've nae mair for't.

## 283      Odes, Book I, 31

### The Poet's Wish

Frae great Apollo, poet say,
What is thy wish, what wadst thou hae,
    When thou bows at his shrine?
Not Carse o' Gowrie's fertile field,
Nor a' the flocks the Grampians yield,
    That are baith sleek an' fine:
Not costly things brought frae afar,
    As ivory, pearl, an' gems!
Nor those fair straths that water'd are
    Wi' Tay an' Tweed's smooth streams,
    Which gentily, and daintily,
      Eat down the flowery braes,
    As greatly, an' quietly,
      They wimple to the seas.

divot] turf    thack] thatch
gousty] ghostly, desolate    daurs] dares
283 strath] riverside plain    wimple] meander

# ALLAN RAMSAY

Whaever by his canny fate
Is master o' a guid estate,
   That can ilk thing afford,
Let him enjoy't withoutten care,
An' wi' the wale o' curious fare
   Cover his ample board.
Much dawted by the gods is he,
   Wha to the Indian plain
Successfu' ploughs the wally sea,
   An' safe returns again
    Wi' riches, that hitches
     Him high aboon the rest
    O' sma' fouk, an' a' fouk
     That are wi' poortith prest.

For me, I can be weel content
To eat my bannock on the bent,
   An' kitchen't wi' fresh air;
O' lang-kail I can mak a feast,
An' cantily haud up my crest,
   An' laugh at dishes rare.
Nought frae Apollo I demand,
   But through a lengthen'd life
My outer fabric firm may stand,
   An' saul clear without strife.
    May he then but gie then
     Those blessings for my skair,
    I'll fairly an' squarely
     Quit a', an' seek nae mair.

wale] choice    dawted] favoured
wally] wide    poortith] poverty    bent] open field
kitchen] anything eaten with bread    lang-kail] greens
cantily] merrily    skair] share

# ALEXANDER POPE

## 1688–1744

### FROM THE GREEK OF HOMER

# The Iliad

### SOME SIMILES

284   *'The Greeks like the Sea, the Trojans like Flocks'*

Cp.
Chapman

As when the Winds, ascending by degrees,
First move the whitening Surface of the Seas,
The Billows float in order to the Shore,
The Wave behind rolls on the Wave before;
Till, with the growing Storm, the Deeps arise,
Foam o'er the Rocks, and thunder to the Skies.
So to the Fight the thick Battalions throng,
Shields urg'd on Shields, and Men drove Men along.
Sedate and silent move the num'rous Bands;
No Sound, no Whisper, but the Chief's Commands,
Those only heard; with Awe the rest obey,
As if some God had snatch'd their Voice away.
Not so the Trojans, from their Host ascends
A gen'ral Shout that all the Region rends.
As when the fleecy Flocks unnumber'd stand
In wealthy Folds, and wait the Milker's Hand,
The hollow Vales incessant Bleating fills,
The Lambs reply from all the neighb'ring Hills:
Such Clamours rose from various Nations round,
Mix'd was the Murmur, and confus'd the Sound.

285   *'The Greeks and th'Embattel'd Clouds'*

Cp.
Chapman

Embodied close, the lab'ring Grecian Train
The fiercest Shock of charging Hosts sustain;
Unmov'd and silent, the whole War they wait,
Serenely dreadful, and as fix'd as Fate.

274

So when th'embattel'd Clouds in dark Array
Along the Skies their gloomy Lines display,
When now the North his boist'rous Rage has spent,
And peaceful sleeps the liquid Element,
The low-hung Vapors, motionless and still,
Rest on the Summits of the shaded Hill;
'Till the Mass scatters as the Winds arise,
Dispers'd and broken thro' the ruffled Skies.

286            *'Like Leaves on Trees...'*

Cp.
Chapman
Ecclesiasticus
Johnson

Like Leaves on Trees the Race of Man is found
Now green in Youth, now with'ring on the Ground,
Another Race the following Spring supplies,
They fall successive, and successive rise;
So Generations in their Course decay,
So flourish these, when those are past away.

287            *'Paris and the wanton Courser'*

Cp.
Chapman
Dryden's
Turnus
Tennyson

But now, no longer deaf to Honour's Call,
Forth issues Paris from the Palace Wall.
In Brazen Arms that cast a gleamy Ray,
Swift thro' the Town the Warrior bends his way.
The wanton Courser thus, with Reins unbound,
Breaks from his Stall, and beats the trembling Ground;
Pamper'd and proud, he seeks the wonted Tides,
And laves, in Height of Blood, his shining Sides;
His Head now freed, he tosses to the Skies;
His Mane dishevel'd o'er his Shoulders flies;
He snuffs the Females in the distant Plain,
And springs, exulting, to his Fields again.
With equal Triumph, sprightly, bold and gay,
In Arms refulgent as the God of Day,
The Son of Priam, glorying in his Might,
Rush'd forth with Hector to the Fields of Fight.

288 *'The Watch and the Dogs'*

Th' unweary'd Watch their list'ning Leaders keep,
And crouching close, repell invading Sleep.
So faithful Dogs their fleecy Charge maintain,
With Toil protected from the prowling Train;
When the gaunt Lioness, with Hunger bold,
Springs from the Mountains tow'rd the guarded Fold:
Thro' breaking Woods her rust'ling Course they hear;
Loud, and more loud, the Clamours strike their Ear
Of Hounds and Men; they start, they gaze around;
Watch ev'ry Side, and turn to ev'ry Sound.
Thus watch'd the Grecians, cautious of Surprize,
Each Voice, each Motion, drew their Ears and Eyes;
Each Step of passing Feet increas'd th'Affright;
And hostile Troy was ever full in sight.

289 *'Stones and Snow'*

Their Ardour kindles all the Grecian Pow'rs;
And now the Stones descend in heavier Show'rs.
As when high Jove his sharp Artill'ry forms,
And opes his cloudy Magazine of Storms;
In Winter's bleak, uncomfortable Reign,
A Snowy Inundation hides the Plain;
He stills the Winds, and bids the Skies to sleep;
Then pours the silent Tempest, thick, and deep:
And first the Mountain Tops are cover'd o'er,
Then the green Fields, and then the sandy Shore;
Bent with the Weight the nodding Woods are seen,
And one bright Waste hides all the Works of Men:
The circling Seas alone absorbing all,
Drink the dissolving Fleeces as they fall.
So from each side increas'd the stony Rain,
And the white Ruin rises o'er the Plain.

### 290                 'Hector and the Stone'

Cp.
Dryden's
Turnus

Fierce they drove on, impatient to destroy;
Troy charg'd the first, and Hector first of Troy.
As from some Mountain's craggy Forehead torn,
A Rock's round fragment flies, with Fury born,
(Which from the stubborn Stone a Torrent rends)
Precipitate the pond'rous Mass descends:
From Steep to Steep the rolling Ruin bounds;
At ev'ry Shock the crackling Wood resounds;
Still gath'ring Force, it smoaks; and, urg'd amain,
Whirls, leaps, and thunders down, impetuous to the Plain:
There stops—So Hector: Their whole Force he prov'd,
Resistless when he rag'd, and when he stop'd, unmov'd.

### 291                 'Ajax and his Brother'

Cp.
Chapman
Cowper

Now side by side, with like unweary'd Care,
Each Ajax labour'd thro' the Field of War.
So when two lordly Bulls, with equal Toil,
Force the bright Plowshare thro' the fallow Soil,
Join'd to one Yoke, the stubborn Earth they tear,
And trace large Furrows with the shining Share;
O'er their huge Limbs the Foam descends in Snow,
And Streams of Sweat down their sow'r Foreheads flow.

### 292                 'The Wasps'

Cp.
Logue

Meanwhile the Troops beneath Patroclus' Care,
Invade the Trojans, and commence the War.
As Wasps, provok'd by Children in their Play,
Pour from their Mansions by the broad High-way,
In Swarms the guiltless Traveller engage,
Whet all their Stings, and call forth all their Rage;
All rise in Arms, and with a gen'ral Cry
Assert their waxen Domes, and buzzing Progeny.
Thus from the Tents the fervent Legion swarms,
So loud their Clamours, and so keen their Arms.
Their rising Rage Patroclus' Breath inspires,
Who thus inflames them with heroick Fires.

293 *'Hector flees before Achilles'*

Thus at the panting Dove a Falcon flies,
(The swiftest Racer of the liquid Skies)
Just when he holds or thinks he holds his Prey,
Obliquely wheeling thro' th' aerial Way;
With open Beak and shrilling Cries he springs,
And aims his Claws, and shoots upon his Wings:
No less fore-right the rapid Chace they held,
One urg'd by Fury, one by Fear impell'd;
Now circling round the Walls their Course maintain,
Where the high Watch-tow'r overlooks the Plain;
Now where the Fig-trees spread their Umbrage broad,
(A wider Compass) smoak along the Road.
Next by Scamander's double Source they bound,
Where two fam'd Fountains burst the parted Ground;
This hot thro' scorching Clefts is seen to rise,
With Exhalations steaming to the Skies;
That the green Banks in Summer's Heat o'erflows,
Like Crystal clear, and cold as Winter-Snows.
Each gushing Fount a marble Cistern fills,
Whose polish'd Bed receives the falling Rills;
Where Trojan Dames, (e'er yet alarm'd by Greece,)
Wash'd their fair Garments in the Days of Peace.
By these they past, one chasing, one in Flight,
(The Mighty fled, pursu'd by stronger Might)
Swift was the Course; No vulgar Prize they play,
No vulgar Victim must reward the Day,
(Such as in Races crown the speedy Strife)
The Prize contended was great Hector's Life.

OTHER INCIDENTS

294 *'Paris and Menelaus'*

Cp.
Chapman
Now Front to Front the hostile Armies stand,
Eager of Fight, and only wait Command:
When, to the Van, before the Sons of Fame
Whom Troy sent forth, the beauteous Paris came:
In Form a God! the Panther's speckled Hyde
Flow'd o'er his Armour with an easy Pride,

His bended Bow a-cross his Shoulders flung,
His Sword beside him negligently hung,
Two pointed Spears he shook with gallant Grace,
And dar'd the Bravest of the Grecian Race.
As thus with glorious Air and proud Disdain,
He boldly stalk'd, the foremost on the Plain,
Him Menelaus, lov'd of Mars, espies,
With Heart elated, and with joyful Eyes:
So joys a Lion if the branching Deer
Or Mountain Goat, his bulky Prize, appear;
Eager he seizes, and devours the slain,
Prest by bold Youths and baying Dogs in vain.
Thus fond of Vengeance, with a furious Bound,
In clanging Arms he leaps upon the Ground
From his high Chariot: Him, approaching near,
The beauteous Champion views with Marks of Fear,
Smit with a conscious Sense, retires behind,
And shuns the Fate he well deserv'd to find.
As when some Shepherd from the rustling Trees
Shot forth to View, a scaly Serpent sees;
Trembling and pale, he starts with wild Affright,
And all confus'd, precipitates his Flight.
So from the King the shining Warrior flies,
And plung'd amid the thickest Trojans lies.

**295**     *'The old Trojan Chiefs see Helen'*

Cp.
Chapman

     There sate the Seniors of the Trojan Race,
(Old Priam's Chiefs, and most in Priam's Grace)
The King the first; Thymætes at his side;
Lampus and Clytius, long in Council try'd;
Panthus, and Hicetäon, once the strong,
And next the wisest of the Rev'rend Throng,
Antenor grave, and sage Ucalegon,
Lean'd on the Walls, and bask'd before the Sun.
Chiefs, who no more in bloody Fights engage,
But Wise thro' Time, and Narrative with Age,
In Summer-Days like Grasshoppers rejoice,
A bloodless Race, that send a feeble Voice.
These, when the Spartan Queen approach'd the Tow'r,
In secret own'd resistless Beauty's Pow'r:

279

They cry'd, No wonder such Celestial Charms
For nine long Years have set the World in Arms;
What winning Graces! what majestick Mien!
She moves a Goddess, and she looks a Queen!
Yet hence oh Heav'n! convey that fatal Face,
And from Destruction save the Trojan Race.

296    *'Night Piece: the Trojans outside Troy'*

Cp.
Chapman
Cowper
Tennyson

   The Troops exulting sate in order round,
And beaming Fires illumin'd all the Ground.
As when the Moon, refulgent Lamp of Night!
O'er Heav'ns clear Azure spreads her sacred Light,
When not a Breath disturbs the deep Serene;
And not a Cloud o'ercasts the solemn Scene;
Around her Throne the vivid Planets roll,
And Stars unnumber'd gild the glowing Pole,
O'er the dark Trees a yellower Verdure shed,
And tip with Silver ev'ry Mountain's Head;
Then shine the Vales, the Rocks in Prospect rise,
A Flood of Glory bursts from all the Skies:
The conscious Swains, rejoicing in the Sight,
Eye the blue Vault, and bless the useful Light.
So many Flames before proud Ilion blaze,
And lighten glimm'ring Xanthus with their Rays.
The long Reflections of the distant Fires
Gleam on the Walls, and tremble on the Spires.
A thousand Piles the dusky Horrors gild,
And shoot a shady Lustre o'er the Field.
Full fifty Guards each flaming Pile attend,
Whose umber'd Arms, by fits, thick Flashes send.
Loud neigh the Coursers o'er their Heaps of Corn,
And ardent Warriors wait the rising Morn.

297    *'The Destruction of the Grecian Fort'*

Nor long the Trench or lofty Walls oppose;
With Gods averse th'ill-fated Works arose;
Their Pow'rs neglected and no Victim slain,
The Walls were rais'd, the Trenches sunk in vain.

Without the Gods, how short a Period stands
The proudest Monument of mortal Hands!
This stood, while Hector and Achilles rag'd,
While sacred Troy the warring Hosts engag'd;
But when her Sons were slain, her City burn'd,
And what surviv'd of Greece to Greece return'd;
Then Neptune and Apollo shook the Shore,
Then Ida's Summits pour'd their wat'ry Store;
Rhesus and Rhodius then unite their Rills,
Caresus roaring down the stony Hills,
Æsepus, Granicus, with mingled Force,
And Xanthus foaming from his fruitful Source;
And gulphy Simois, rolling to the Main
Helmets, and Shields, and God-like Heroes slain:
These, turn'd by Phœbus from their wonted ways,
Delug'd the Rampire nine continual Days;
The Weight of Waters saps the yielding Wall,
And to the Sea the floating Bulwarks fall.
Incessant Cataracts the Thund'rer pours,
And half the Skies descend in sluicy Show'rs.
The God of Ocean, marching stern before,
With his huge Trident wounds the trembling Shore,
Vast Stones and Piles from their Foundation heaves,
And whelms the smoaky Ruin in the Waves.
Now smooth'd with Sand, and levell'd by the Flood,
No Fragment tells where once the Wonder stood;
In their old Bounds the Rivers roll again,
Shine 'twixt the Hills, or wander o'er the Plain.

298        'The Speech of Sarpedon
          (*an Ally of the Trojans*) *to Glaucus*'

Cp.         Why boast we, Glaucus! our extended Reign,
Denham    Where Xanthus' Streams enrich the Lycian Plain,
          Our num'rous Herds that range the fruitful Field,
          And Hills where Vines their purple Harvest yield,
          Our foaming Bowls with purer Nectar crown'd,
          Our Feasts enhanc'd with Music's sprightly Sound?
          Why on those Shores are we with Joy survey'd,
          Admir'd as Heroes, and as Gods obey'd?

Unless great Acts superior Merit prove,
And vindicate the bount'ous Pow'rs above.
'Tis ours, the Dignity they give, to grace;
The first in Valour, as the first in Place.
That when with wond'ring Eyes our martial Bands
Behold our Deeds transcending our Commands,
Such, they may cry, deserve the sov'reign State,
Whom those that envy, dare not imitate!
Could all our Care elude the gloomy Grave,
Which claims no less the fearful than the brave,
For Lust of Fame I should not vainly dare
In fighting Fields, nor urge thy Soul to War.
But since, alas! ignoble Age must come,
Disease, and Death's inexorable Doom;
The Life which others pay, let us bestow,
And give to Fame what we to Nature owe;
Brave tho' we fall, and honour'd if we live,
Or let us Glory gain, or Glory give!

299　　　*'Hector, recovered, renews the Attack*
*and Apollo aids the Trojans'*

The Greeks dismay'd, confus'd disperse or fall,
Some seek the Trench, some skulk behind the Wall,
While these fly trembling, others pant for Breath,
And o'er the Slaughter stalks gigantic Death.
On rush'd bold Hector, gloomy as the Night,
Forbids to plunder, animates the Fight,
Points to the Fleet: For by the Gods, who flies,
Who dares but linger, by this Hand he dies:
No weeping Sister his cold Eye shall close,
No friendly Hand his fun'ral Pyre compose.
Who stops to plunder, in this signal Hour,
The Birds shall tear him, and the Dogs devour.
　　Furious he said; the smarting Scourge resounds;
The Coursers fly; the smoking Chariot bounds:
The Hosts rush on; loud Clamours shake the Shore;
The Horses thunder, Earth and Ocean roar!
Apollo, planted at the Trench's Bound,
Push'd at the Bank: Down sunk th' enormous Mound:

Roll'd in the Ditch the heapy Ruin lay;
A sudden Road! a long and ample way.
O'er the dread Fosse (a late-impervious Space)
Now Steeds, and Men, and Cars, tumultuous pass.
The wond'ring Crowds the downward Level trod;
Before them flam'd the Shield, and march'd the God.
Then with his Hand he shook the mighty Wall;
And lo! the Turrets nod, the Bulwarks fall.
Easy, as when ashore an Infant stands,
And draws imagin'd Houses in the Sands;
The sportive Wanton, pleas'd with some new Play,
Sweeps the slight Works and fashion'd Domes away.
Thus vanish'd, at thy touch, the Tow'rs and Walls;
The Toil of thousands in a Moment falls.

300     *'Vulcan forges the Shield of Achilles'*

Then first he form'd th' immense and solid Shield;
Rich, various Artifice emblaz'd the Field;
Its utmost Verge a threefold Circle bound;
A silver Chain suspends the massy Round,
Five ample Plates the broad Expanse compose,
And god-like Labours on the Surface rose.
There shone the Image of the Master Mind:
There Earth, there Heav'n, there Ocean he design'd;
Th' unweary'd Sun, the Moon compleatly round;
The starry Lights that Heav'ns high Convex crown'd;
The Pleiads, Hyads, with the Northern Team;
And great Orion's more refulgent Beam;
To which, around the Axle of the Sky,
The Bear revolving, points his golden Eye,
Still shines exalted on the' ætherial Plain,
Nor bathes his blazing Forehead in the Main.
Two Cities radiant on the Shield appear,
The Image one of Peace, and one of War.
Here sacred Pomp, and genial Feast delight,
And solemn Dance, and Hymenæal Rite;
Along the Street the new-made Brides are led,
With Torches flaming, to the nuptial Bed;
The youthful Dancers in a Circle bound
To the soft Flute, and Cittern's silver Sound:

Thro' the fair Streets, the Matrons in a Row,
Stand in their Porches, and enjoy the Show.
　　There, in the Forum swarm a num'rous Train;
The Subject of Debate, a Townsman slain:
One pleads the Fine discharg'd, which one deny'd,
And bade the Publick and the Laws decide:
The Witness is produc'd on either Hand;
For this, or that, the partial People stand:
Th' appointed Heralds still the noisy Bands,
And form a Ring, with Scepters in their Hands;
On Seats of Stone, within the sacred Place,
The rev'rend Elders nodded o'er the Case;
Alternate, each th' attesting Scepter took,
And rising solemn, each his Sentence spoke.
Two golden Talents lay amidst, in sight,
The Prize of him who best adjudg'd the Right.
　　Another Part (a Prospect differing far)
Glow'd with refulgent Arms, and horrid War.
Two mighty Hosts a leaguer'd Town embrace,
And one would pillage, one wou'd burn the Place.
Meantime the Townsmen, arm'd with silent Care,
A secret Ambush on the Foe prepare:
Their Wives, their Children, and the watchful Band,
Of trembling Parents on the Turrets stand.
They march; by Pallas and by Mars made bold;
Gold were the Gods, their radiant Garments Gold,
And Gold their Armour: These the Squadron led,
August, Divine, Superior by the Head!
A Place for Ambush fit, they found, and stood
Cover'd with Shields, beside the silver Flood.
Two Spies at distance lurk, and watchful seem
If Sheep or Oxen seek the winding Stream.
Soon the white Flocks proceeded o'er the Plains,
And Steers slow-moving, and two Shepherd Swains;
Behind them, piping on their Reeds, they go,
Nor fear an Ambush, nor suspect a Foe.
In Arms the glitt'ring Squadron rising round
Rush sudden; Hills of Slaughter heap the Ground,
Whole Flocks and Herds lye bleeding on the Plains,
And, all amidst them, dead, the Shepherd Swains!
The bellowing Oxen the Besiegers hear;
They rise, take Horse, approach, and meet the War;

They fight, they fall, beside the silver Flood;
The waving Silver seem'd to blush with Blood.
There Tumult, there Contention stood confest;
One rear'd a Dagger at a Captive's Breast,
One held a living Foe, that freshly bled
With new-made Wounds; another dragg'd a dead;
Now here, now there, the Carcasses they tore:
Fate stalk'd amidst them, grim with human Gore.
And the whole War came out, and met the Eye;
And each bold Figure seem'd to live, or die.

    A Field deep-furrow'd, next the God design'd,
The third time labour'd by the sweating Hind;
The shining Shares full many Plowmen guide,
And turn their crooked Yokes on ev'ry side.
Still as at either End they wheel around,
The Master meets 'em with his Goblet crown'd;
The hearty Draught rewards, renews their Toil;
Then back the turning Plow-shares cleave the Soil:
Behind, the rising Earth in Ridges roll'd;
And sable look'd, tho form'd of molten Gold.

    Another Field rose high with waving Grain;
With bended Sickles stand the Reaper-Train:
Here stretch'd in Ranks the level'd Swarths are found,
Sheaves heap'd on Sheaves, here thicken up the Ground.
With sweeping Stroke the Mowers strow the Lands;
The Gath'rers follow, and collect in Bands;
And last the Children, in whose Arms are born
(Too short to gripe them) the brown Sheaves of Corn.
The rustic Monarch of the Field descries
With silent Glee, the Heaps around him rise.
A ready Banquet on the Turf is laid,
Beneath the ample Oak's expanded Shade.
The Victim-Ox the sturdy Youth prepare;
The Reaper's due Repast, the Women's Care.

    Next, ripe in yellow Gold, a Vineyard shines,
Bent with the pond'rous Harvest of its Vines;
A deeper Dye the dangling Clusters show,
And curl'd on silver Props, in order glow:
A darker Metal mixt, intrench'd the Place,
And Pales of glitt'ring Tin th' Enclosure grace.
To this, one Pathway gently winding leads,
Where march a Train with Baskets on their Heads,

(Fair Maids, and blooming Youths) that smiling bear
The purple Product of th' Autumnal Year.
To these a Youth awakes the warbling Strings,
Whose tender Lay the Fate of Linus sings;
In measur'd Dance behind him move the Train,
Tune soft the Voice, and answer to the Strain.

   Here, Herds of Oxen march, erect and bold,
Rear high their Horns, and seem to lowe in Gold,
And speed to Meadows on whose sounding Shores
A rapid Torrent thro' the Rushes roars:
Four golden Herdsmen as their Guardians stand,
And nine sour Dogs compleat the rustic Band.
Two Lions rushing from the Wood appear'd;
And seiz'd a Bull, the Master of the Herd:
He roar'd: in vain the Dogs, the Men withstood,
They tore his Flesh, and drank the sable Blood.
The Dogs (oft' chear'd in vain) desert the Prey,
Dread the grim Terrors, and at distance bay.

   Next this, the Eye the Art of Vulcan leads
Deep thro' fair Forests, and a Length of Meads;
And Stalls, and Folds, and scatter'd Cotts between;
And fleecy Flocks, that whiten all the Scene.

   A figur'd Dance succeeds: Such once was seen
In lofty Gnossus, for the Cretan Queen,
Form'd by Dædalean Art. A comely Band
Of Youths and Maidens, bounding Hand in Hand:
The Maids in soft Cymarrs of Linen drest;
The Youths all graceful in the glossy Vest;
Of those the Locks with flow'ry Wreaths inroll'd,
Of these the Sides adorn'd with Swords of Gold,
That glitt'ring gay, from silver Belts depend.
Now all at once they rise, at once descend,
With well-taught Feet: Now shape, in oblique ways,
Confus'dly regular, the moving Maze:
Now forth at once, too swift for sight, they spring,
And undistinguish'd blend the flying Ring:
So whirls a Wheel, in giddy Circle tost,
And rapid as it runs, the single Spokes are lost.
The gazing Multitudes admire around;
Two active Tumblers in the Center bound;
Now high, now low, their pliant Limbs they bend,
And gen'ral Songs the sprightly Revel end.

Thus the broad Shield complete the Artist crown'd
With his last Hand, and pour'd the Ocean round:
In living Silver seem'd the Waves to roll,
And beat the Buckler's Verge, and bound the whole.

301      *'River Scamander attacks Achilles'*

Then rising in his Rage above the Shores,
From all his Deep the bellowing River roars,
Huge Heaps of Slain disgorges on the Coast,
And round the Banks the ghastly Dead are tost.
While all before, the Billows rang'd on high
(A wat'ry Bulwark) screen the Bands who fly.
Now bursting on his Head with thund'ring Sound,
The falling Deluge whelms the Hero round:
His loaded Shield bends to the rushing Tide;
His Feet, upborn, scarce the strong Flood divide,
Slidd'ring, and stagg'ring. On the Border stood
A spreading Elm, that overhung the Flood;
He seiz'd a bending Bough, his Steps to stay;
The Plant uprooted to his Weight gave way,
Heaving the Bank, and undermining all;
Loud flash the Waters to the rushing Fall
Of the thick Foliage. The large Trunk display'd
Bridg'd the rough Flood across: The Hero stay'd
On this his Weight, and rais'd upon his Hand,
Leap'd from the Chanel, and regain'd the Land.
Then blacken'd the wild Waves; the Murmur rose;
The God pursues, a huger Billow throws,
And bursts the Bank, ambitious to destroy
The Man whose Fury is the Fate of Troy.
He, like the warlike Eagle speeds his Pace,
(Swiftest and strongest of th' aerial Race)
Far as a Spear can fly, Achilles springs
At every Bound; His clanging Armour rings:
Now here, now there, he turns on ev'ry side,
And winds his Course before the following Tide;
The Waves flow after, wheresoe'er he wheels,
And gather fast, and murmur at his Heels.
So when a Peasant to his Garden brings
Soft Rills of Water from the bubbling Springs,

And calls the Floods from high, to bless his Bow'rs
And feed with pregnant Streams the Plants and Flow'rs;
Soon as he clears whate'er their passage staid,
And marks the future Current with his Spade,
Swift o'er the rolling Pebbles, down the Hills
Louder and louder purl the falling Rills,
Before him scatt'ring, they prevent his pains,
And shine in mazy Wand'rings o'er the Plains.

    Still flies Achilles, but before his eyes
Still swift Scamander rolls where'er he flies:
Not all his Speed escapes the rapid Floods;
The first of Men, but not a Match for Gods.
Oft' as he turn'd the Torrent to oppose,
And bravely try if all the Pow'rs were Foes;
So oft' the Surge, in wat'ry Mountains spread,
Beats on his Back, or bursts upon his Head.
Yet dauntless still the adverse Flood he braves,
And still indignant bounds above the Waves.
Tir'd by the Tides, his Knees relax with Toil;
Wash'd from beneath him, slides the slimy Soil;
When thus (his Eyes on Heav'ns Expansion thrown)
Forth bursts the Hero with an angry Groan.

    Is there no God Achilles to befriend,
No Pow'r t'avert his miserable End?
Prevent, oh Jove! this ignominious Date,
And make my future Life the Sport of Fate...
Like some vile Swain, whom, on a rainy Day,
Crossing a Ford, the Torrent sweeps away,
An unregarded Carcase to the Sea.

## The Odyssey

302

*'Jupiter sends Hermes to Calypso'*

Cp.
Chapman
Cowper

          The God who mounts the winged winds
Fast to his feet his golden pinions binds,
That high thro' fields of air his flight sustain
O'er the wide earth, and o'er the boundless main.
He grasps the wand that causes sleep to fly,
Or in soft slumber seals the wakeful eye:

Then shoots from heav'n to high Pieria's steep,
And stoops incumbent on the rolling deep.
So wat'ry fowl, that seek their fishy food,
With wings expanded o'er the foaming flood,
Now sailing smooth the level surface sweep,
Now dip their pinions in the briny deep.
Thus o'er the world of waters Hermes flew,
'Till now the distant Island rose in view:
Then swift ascending from the azure wave,
He took the path that winded to the cave.
Large was the Grot, in which the nymph he found,
(The fair-hair'd nymph with ev'ry beauty crown'd)
She sate and sung; the rocks resound her lays:
The cave was brighten'd with a rising blaze:
Cedar and frankincense, an od'rous pile,
Flam'd on the hearth, and wide perfum'd the Isle;
While she with work and song the time divides,
And thro' the loom the golden shuttle guides.
Without the grot, a various sylvan scene
Appear'd around, and groves of living green;
Poplars and alders ever quiv'ring play'd,
And nodding cypress form'd a fragrant shade;
On whose high branches, waving with the storm,
The birds of broadest wing their mansion form,
The chough, the sea-mew, the loquacious crow,
And scream aloft, and skim the deeps below.
Depending vines the shelving cavern screen,
With purple clusters blushing thro' the green.
Four limpid fountains from the clefts distill,
And ev'ry fountain pours a sev'ral rill,
In mazy windings wand'ring down the hill:
Where bloomy meads with vivid greens were crown'd,
And glowing violets threw odors round.
A scene, where if a God shou'd cast his sight,
A God might gaze, and wander with delight!
Joy touch'd the Messenger of heav'n: he stay'd
Entranc'd, and all the blissful haunt survey'd.

303             *'Ulysses builds his Raft'*

Cp.
Chapman

    Now toils the Heroe; trees on trees o'erthrown
Fall crackling round him, and the forests groan:
Sudden, full twenty on the plain are strow'd,
And lopp'd, and lighten'd of their branchy load.
At equal angles these dispos'd to join,
He smooth'd, and squar'd 'em, by the rule and line.
(The wimbles for the work Calypso found)
With those he pierc'd 'em, and with clinchers bound.
Long and capacious as a shipwright forms
Some bark's broad bottom to out-ride the storms,
So large he built the Raft: then ribb'd it strong
From space to space, and nail'd the planks along;
These form'd the sides: the deck he fashion'd last;
Then o'er the vessel rais'd the taper mast,
With crossing sail-yards dancing in the wind;
And to the helm the guiding rudder join'd.
(With yielding osiers fenc'd, to break the force
Of surging waves, and steer the steady course)
Thy loom, Calypso! for the future sails
Supply'd the cloth, capacious of the gales.
With stays and cordage last he rigg'd the ship,
And roll'd on leavers, launch'd her in the deep.

304             *'The Wrecking of the Raft'*

Cp.
Chapman

    A mighty wave rush'd o'er him as he spoke,
The Raft it cover'd, and the mast it broke;
Swept from the deck, and from the rudder torn,
Far on the swelling surge the chief was born:
While by the howling tempest rent in twain
Flew sail and sail-yards ratling o'er the main.
Long press'd he heav'd beneath the weighty wave,
Clogg'd by the cumbrous vest Calypso gave:
At length emerging, from his nostrils wide
And gushing mouth, effus'd the briny tyde.
Ev'n then, not mindless of his last retreat,
He seis'd the Raft, and leapt into his seat,
Strong with the fear of death. The rolling flood
Now here, now there, impell'd the floating wood.

As when a heap of gather'd thorns is cast
Now to, now fro, before th' autumnal blast;
Together clung, it rolls around the field;
So roll'd the Float, and so its texture held:
And now the south, and now the north, bear sway,
And now the east the foamy floods obey,
And now the west-wind whirls it o'er the sea.

305                    *'Ulysses in the Sea'*

While thus he thought, a monst'rous wave up-bore
The Chief, and dash'd him on the craggy shore:
Torn was his skin, nor had the ribs been whole,
But instant Pallas enter'd in his soul.
Close to the cliff with both his hands he clung,
And stuck adherent, and suspended hung:
'Till the huge surge roll'd off. Then backward sweep
The refluent tydes, and plunge him in the deep.
As when the Polypus from forth his cave
Torn with full force, reluctant beats the wave,
His ragged claws are stuck with stones and sands;
So the rough rock had shagg'd Ulysses' hands.
And now had perish'd, whelm'd beneath the main,
Th' unhappy man; ev'n Fate had been in vain:
But all-subduing Pallas lent her pow'r,
And Prudence sav'd him in the needful hour.
Beyond the beating surge his course he bore,
(A wider circle, but in sight of shore)
With longing eyes, observing, to survey
Some smooth ascent, or safe-sequester'd bay.
Between the parting rocks at length he spy'd
A falling stream with gentler waters glide;
Where to the seas the shelving shore declin'd,
And form'd a bay, impervious to the wind.
To this calm port the glad Ulysses prest,
And hail'd the river, and its God addrest.

306          *'Ulysses finds Shelter'*

There grew two Olives, closest of the grove,
With roots intwin'd, and branches interwove;
Alike their leaves, but not alike they smil'd
With sister-fruits; one fertile, one was wild.
Nor here the sun's meridian rays had pow'r,
Nor wind sharp-piercing, nor the rushing show'r;
The verdant Arch so close its texture kept:
Beneath this covert, great Ulysses crept.
Of gather'd leaves an ample bed he made,
(Thick strown by tempest thro' the bow'ry shade)
Where three at least might winter's cold defy,
Tho' Boreas rag'd along th' inclement sky.
This store, with joy the patient Heroe found,
And sunk amidst 'em heap'd the leaves around.
As some poor peasant, fated to reside
Remote from neighbours, in a forest wide,
Studious to save what human wants require,
In embers heap'd, preserves the seeds of fire:
Hid in dry foliage thus Ulysses lyes,
'Till Pallas pour'd soft slumbers on his eyes;
And golden dreams (the gift of sweet repose)
Lull'd all his cares, and banish'd all his woes.

307          *'The Garden of Alcinous'*

Cp.
Chapman      Close to the gates a spacious Garden lies,
From storms defended, and inclement skies:
Four acres was th' allotted space of ground,
Fenc'd with a green enclosure all around.
Tall thriving trees confess'd the fruitful mold;
The red'ning apple ripens here to gold,
Here the blue fig with luscious juice o'erflows,
With deeper red the full pomegranate glows,
The branch here bends beneath the weighty pear,
And verdant olives flourish round the year.
The balmy spirit of the western gale
Eternal breathes on fruits untaught to fail:
Each dropping pear a following pear supplies,
On apples apples, figs on figs arise:

The same mild season gives the blooms to blow,
The buds to harden, and the fruits to grow.
   Here order'd vines in equal ranks appear,
With all th' united labours of the year;
Some to unload the fertile branches run,
Some dry the black'ning clusters in the sun,
Others to tread the liquid harvest join,
The groaning presses foam with floods of wine.
Here are the vines in early flow'r descry'd,
Here grapes discolour'd on the sunny side,
And there in autumn's richest purple dy'd.
   Beds of all various herbs, for ever green,
In beauteous order terminate the scene.
   Two plenteous fountains the whole prospect crown'd;
This thro' the gardens leads its streams around,
Visits each plant, and waters all the ground:
While that in pipes beneath the palace flows,
And thence its current on the town bestows;
To various use their various streams they bring,
The People one, and one supplies the King.

308          *'In the Cave of Polyphemus'*

The cave we found, but vacant all within,
(His flock the Giant tended on the green)
But round the grott we gaze, and all we view
In order rang'd, our admiration drew:
The bending shelves with loads of cheeses prest,
The folded flocks each sep'rate from the rest,
(The larger here, and there the lesser lambs,
The new-fall'n young here bleating for their dams;
The kid distinguish'd from the lambkin lies:)
The cavern ecchoes with responsive cries.
Capacious chargers all around were lay'd,
Full pails, and vessels of the milking trade.
With fresh provision hence our fleet to store
My friends advise me, and to quit the shore;
Or drive a flock of sheep and goats away,
Consult our safety, and put off to sea.
Their wholsome counsel rashly I declin'd,
Curious to view the man of monstrous kind,

And try what social rites a savage lends:
Dire rites alas! and fatal to my friends!
  Then first a fire we kindle, and prepare
For his return with sacrifice and prayer.
The loaden shelves afford us full repast;
We sit expecting. Lo! he comes at last.
Near half a forest on his back he bore,
And cast the pond'rous burden at the door.
It thunder'd as it fell. We trembled then,
And sought the deep recesses of the den.
Now driv'n before him, thro' the arching rock,
Came tumbling, heaps on heaps, th' unnumber'd flock:
Big-udder'd ewes, and goats of female kind,
(The males were penn'd in outward courts behind)
Then, heav'd on high, a rock's enormous weight
To the cave's mouth he roll'd, and clos'd the gate.
(Scarce twenty four-wheel'd cars, compact and strong,
The massy load cou'd bear, or roll along)
He next betakes him to his evening cares,
And sitting down, to milk his flocks prepares;
Of half their udders eases first the dams,
Then to the mother's teats submits the lambs.
Half the white stream to hard'ning cheese he prest,
And high in wicker baskets heap'd: the rest
Reserv'd in bowls, supply'd his nightly feast.
His labour done, he fir'd the pyle that gave
A sudden blaze, and lighted all the cave:
We stand discover'd by the rising fires;
Askance the giant glares, and thus enquires.
  What are ye, guests? on what adventure, say,
Thus far ye wander thro' the wat'ry way?
Pyrates perhaps, who seek thro' seas unknown
The lives of others, and expose your own?
  His voice like thunder thro' the cavern sounds:
My bold companions thrilling fear confounds,
Appall'd at sight of more than mortal man!
At length, with heart recover'd, I began.
  From Troy's fam'd fields, sad wand'rers o'er the main,
Behold the relicks of the Grecian train!
Thro' various seas by various perils tost,
And forc'd by storms, unwilling, on your coast;

Far from our destin'd course, and native land,
Such was our fate, and such high Jove's command!
Nor what we are befits us to disclaim,
Atrides' friends, (in arms a mighty name)
Who taught proud Troy and all her sons to bow;
Victors of late, but humble suppliants now!
Low at thy knee thy succour we implore;
Respect us, human, and relieve us, poor.
At least some hospitable gift bestow;
'Tis what the happy to th' unhappy owe:
'Tis what the Gods require: Those Gods revere,
The poor and stranger are their constant care;
To Jove their cause, and their revenge belongs,
He wanders with them, and he feels their wrongs.

    Fools that ye are! (the Savage thus replies,
His inward fury blazing at his eyes)
Or strangers, distant far from our abodes,
To bid me rev'rence or regard the Gods.
Know then we Cyclops are a race above
Those air-bred people, and their goat-nurs'd Jove:
And learn our pow'r proceeds with thee and thine,
Not as He wills, but as our selves incline.
But answer, the good ship that brought ye o'er,
Where lies she anchor'd? near, or off the shore?

    Thus he. His meditated fraud I find,
(Vers'd in the turns of various humankind)
And cautious, thus. Against a dreadful rock,
Fast by your shore the gallant vessel broke.
Scarce with these few I scap'd; of all my train,
Whom angry Neptune whelm'd beneath the main;
The scatter'd wreck the winds blew back again.

    He answer'd with his deed. His bloody hand
Snatch'd two, unhappy! of my martial band;
And dash'd like dogs against the stony floor:
The pavement swims with brains and mingled gore.
Torn limb from limb, he spreads his horrid feast,
And fierce devours it like a mountain beast:
He sucks the marrow, and the blood he drains,
Nor entrails, flesh, nor solid bone remains.
We see the death from which we cannot move,
And humbled groan beneath the hand of Jove.

His ample maw with human carnage fill'd,
A milky deluge next the giant swill'd;
Then stretch'd in length o'er half the cavern'd rock,
Lay senseless, and supine, amidst the flock.
To seize the time, and with a sudden wound
To fix the slumb'ring monster to the ground,
My soul impells me; and in act I stand
To draw the sword; but Wisdom held my hand.
A deed so rash had finish'd all our fate,
No mortal forces from the lofty gate
Could roll the rock. In hopeless grief we lay,
And sigh, expecting the return of day.
Now did the rosy-finger'd morn arise,
And shed her sacred light along the skies.
He wakes, he lights the fire, he milks the dams,
And to the mother's teat submits the lambs.
The task thus finish'd of his morning hours,
Two more he snatches, murders, and devours.
Then pleas'd and whistling, drives his flock before;
Removes the rocky mountain from the door,
And shuts again; with equal ease dispos'd,
As a light quiver's lid is op'd and clos'd.
His giant voice the ecchoing region fills:
His flocks, obedient, spread o'er all the hills.
   Thus left behind, ev'n in the last despair
I thought, devis'd, and Pallas heard my prayer.
Revenge, and doubt, and caution, work'd my breast;
But this of many counsels seem'd the best:
The monster's club within the cave I spy'd,
A tree of stateliest growth, and yet undry'd,
Green from the wood; of height and bulk so vast,
The largest ship might claim it for a mast.
This shorten'd of its top, I gave my train
A fathom's length, to shape it and to plain;
The narrow'r end I sharpen'd to a spire;
Whose point we harden'd with the force of fire,
And hid it in the dust that strow'd the cave.
Then to my few companions, bold and brave,
Propos'd, who first the vent'rous deed should try?
In the broad orbit of his monstrous eye
To plunge the brand, and twirl the pointed wood;
When slumber next should tame the man of blood.

Just as I wish'd, the lots were cast on four;
My self the fifth. We stand, and wait the hour.
He comes with evening: all his fleecy flock
Before him march, and pour into the rock:
Not one, or male or female, stay'd behind;
(So fortune chanc'd, or so some God design'd)
Then heaving high the stone's unwieldy weight,
He roll'd it on the cave, and clos'd the gate.
First down he sits, to milk the woolly dams,
And then permits their udder to the lambs.
Next seiz'd two wretches more, and headlong cast,
Brain'd on the rock; his second dire repast.
I then approach'd him reeking with their gore,
And held the brimming goblet foaming o'er:
Cyclop! since human flesh has been thy feast,
Now drain this goblet, potent to digest:
Know hence what treasures in our ship we lost,
And what rich liquors other climates boast.
We to thy shore the precious freight shall bear,
If home thou send us, and vouchsafe to spare.
But oh! thus furious, thirsting thus for gore,
The sons of men shall ne'er approach thy shore,
And never shalt thou taste this Nectar more.
    He heard, he took, and pouring down his throat
Delighted swill'd the large, luxurious draught.
More! give me more, he cry'd: the boon be thine,
Whoe'er thou art that bear'st celestial wine!
Declare thy name; not mortal is this juice,
Such as th' unblest Cyclopean climes produce,
(Tho' sure our vine the largest cluster yields,
And Jove's scorn'd thunder serves to drench our fields)
But this descended from the b[l]est abodes,
A rill of Nectar, streaming from the Gods.
    He said, and greedy grasp'd the heady bowl,
Thrice drain'd, and pour'd the deluge on his soul.
His sense lay cover'd with the dozy fume;
While thus my fraudful speech I reassume.
Thy promis'd boon, O Cyclop! now I claim,
And plead my title: Noman is my name.
By that distinguish'd from my tender years,
'Tis what my parents call me, and my peers.

The Giant then. Our promis'd grace receive,
The hospitable boon we mean to give:
When all thy wretched crew have felt my pow'r,
Noman shall be the last I will devour.
　　He said; then nodding with the fumes of wine
Dropt his huge head, and snoring lay supine.
His neck obliquely o'er his shoulder hung,
Prest with the weight of sleep that tames the strong:
There belcht the mingled streams of wine and blood,
And human flesh, his indigested food.
Sudden I stir the embers, and inspire
With animating breath the seeds of fire;
Each drooping spirit with bold words repair,
And urge my train the dreadful deed to dare.
The stake now glow'd beneath the burning bed
(Green as it was) and sparkled fiery red.
Then forth the vengeful instrument I bring;
With beating hearts my fellows form a ring.
Urg'd by some present God, they swift let fall
The pointed torment on his visual ball.
My self above them from a rising ground
Guide the sharp stake, and twirl it round and round.
As when a shipwright stands his workmen o'er,
Who plye the wimble, some huge beam to bore;
Urg'd on all hands it nimbly spins about,
The grain deep-piercing till it scoops it out:
In his broad eye so whirls the fiery wood;
From the pierc'd pupil spouts the boiling blood;
Sing'd are his brows; the scorching lids grow black;
The gelly bubbles, and the fibres crack.
And as when Arm'rers temper in the ford
The keen-edg'd pole-axe, or the shining sword,
The red-hot metal hisses in the lake,
Thus in his eyeball hiss'd the plunging stake.
He sends a dreadful groan: the rocks around
Thro' all their inmost-winding caves resound.
Scar'd we receded. Forth, with frantic hand
He tore, and dash'd on earth the goary brand:
Then calls the Cyclops, all that round him dwell,
With voice like thunder, and a direful yell.
From all their dens the one-ey'd race repair,
From rifted rocks, and mountains bleak in air.

All haste assembled, at his well-known roar,
Enquire the cause, and croud the cavern door.
   What hurts thee, Polypheme? what strange affright
Thus breaks our slumbers, and disturbs the night?
Does any mortal in th' unguarded hour
Of sleep, oppress thee, or by fraud or pow'r?
Or thieves insidious thy fair flock surprize?
Thus they: the Cyclop from his den replies.
   Friends, Noman kills me; Noman in the hour
Of sleep, oppresses me with fraudful pow'r.
'If no man hurt thee, but the hand divine
Inflict disease, it fits thee to resign:
To Jove or to thy father Neptune pray.'
The brethren cry'd, and instant strode away.
   Joy touch'd my secret soul, and conscious heart,
Pleas'd with th' effect of conduct and of art.
Mean-time the Cyclop raging with his wound,
Spreads his wide arms, and searches round and round:
At last, the stone removing from the gate,
With hands extended in the midst he sate;
And search'd each passing sheep, and felt it o'er,
Secure to seize us ere we reach'd the door.
(Such as his shallow wit, he deem'd was mine)
But secret I revolv'd the deep design:
'Twas for our lives my lab'ring bosom wrought;
Each scheme I turn'd, and sharpen'd ev'ry thought:
This way and that, I cast to save my friends,
'Till one resolve my varying counsel ends.
   Strong were the Rams, with native purple fair,
Well fed, and largest of the fleecy care.
These, three and three, with osier bands we ty'd,
(The twining bands the Cyclop's bed supply'd)
The midmost bore a man; the outward two
Secur'd each side: So bound we all the crew.
One ram remain'd, the leader of the flock;
In his deep fleece my grasping hands I lock,
And fast beneath in woolly curls inwove
There cling implicite, and confide in Jove.
When rosy morning glimmer'd o'er the dales,
He drove to pasture all the lusty males:
The ewes still folded, with distended thighs
Unmilk'd, lay bleating in distressful cries.

But heedless of those cares, with anguish stung,
He felt their fleeces as they pass'd along,
(Fool that he was) and let them safely go,
All unsuspecting of their freight below.
    The master Ram at last approach'd the gate,
Charg'd with his wool, and with Ulysses' fate.
Him while he past the monster blind bespoke:
What makes my ram the lag of all the flock?
First thou wert wont to crop the flow'ry mead,
First to the field and river's bank to lead,
And first with stately step at evening hour
Thy fleecy fellows usher to their bow'r.
Now far the last, with pensive pace and slow
Thou mov'st, as conscious of thy master's woe!
Seest thou these lids that now unfold in vain?
(The deed of Noman and his wicked train)
Oh! didst thou feel for thy afflicted Lord,
And wou'd but Fate the pow'r of speech afford!
Soon might'st thou tell me, where in secret here
The dastard lurks, all trembling with his fear:
Swung round and round, and dash'd from rock to rock,
His batter'd brains shou'd on the pavement smoke.
No ease, no pleasure my sad heart receives,
While such a monster as vile Noman lives.
    The Giant spoke, and thro' the hollow rock
Dismiss'd the Ram, the father of the flock.
No sooner freed, and thro' th' enclosure past,
First I release my self, my fellows last:
Fat sheep and goats in throngs we drive before,
And reach our vessel on the winding shore.

309                *'Elpenor'*

    A youth there was, Elpenor was he nam'd,
Nor much for sense, nor much for courage fam'd;
The youngest of our band, a vulgar soul
Born but to banquet, and to drain the bowl.
He, hot and careless, on a turret's height
With sleep repair'd the long debauch of night:

The sudden tumult stirr'd him where he lay,
And down he hasten'd, but forgot the way;
Full endlong from the roof the sleeper fell,
And snapt the spinal joint, and wak'd in hell.

## 310      *'Penelope fetches Ulysses' Bow'*

Cp.
Chapman

    Now gently winding up the fair ascent,
By many an easy step, the matron went;
Then o'er the pavement glides with grace divine,
(With polish'd oak the level pavements shine)
The folding gates a dazling light display'd,
With pomp of various architrave o'erlay'd.
The bolt, obedient to the silken string,
Forsakes the staple as she pulls the ring;
The wards respondent to the key turn round;
The bars fall back; the flying valves resound;
Loud as a bull makes hill and valley ring,
So roar'd the lock when it releas'd the spring.
She moves majestic thro' the wealthy room,
Where treasur'd garments cast a rich perfume;
There from the column where aloft it hung,
Reach'd, in its splendid case, the bow unstrung:
Across her knees she lay'd the well-known bow,
And pensive sate, and tears began to flow.
To full satiety of grief she mourns,
Then silent, to the joyous hall returns,
To the proud Suitors bears in pensive state
Th' unbended bow, and arrows wing'd with Fate.

## 311      *'Ulysses (disguised) takes up the Bow'*

    And now his well-known bow the Master bore,
Turn'd on all sides, and view'd it o'er and o'er;
Lest time or worms had done the weapon wrong,
Its owner absent, and untry'd so long.
While some deriding—How he turns the bow!
Some other like it sure the man must know,
Or else wou'd copy; or in bows he deals;
Perhaps he makes them, or perhaps he steals.—

Heav'n to this wretch (another cry'd) be kind!
And bless, in all to which he stands inclin'd,
With such good fortune as he now shall find.
    Heedless he heard them; but disdain'd reply;
The bow perusing with exactest eye.
Then, as some heav'nly minstrel, taught to sing
High notes responsive to the trembling string,
To some new strain when he adapts the lyre,
Or the dumb lute refits with vocal wire,
Relaxes, strains, and draws them to and fro;
So the great Master drew the mighty bow:
And drew with ease. One hand aloft display'd
The bending horns, and one the string essay'd.
From his essaying hand the string let fly
Twang'd short and sharp, like the shrill swallow's cry.
A gen'ral horror ran thro' all the race,
Sunk was each heart, and pale was ev'ry face.

312 *'The Punishment of the Women and of Melanthius'*

    Now to dispose the dead, the care remains
To you my son, and you, my faithful swains;
Th' offending females to that task we doom,
To wash, to scent, and purify the room.
These (ev'ry table cleans'd, and ev'ry throne,
And all the melancholy labour done)
Drive to yon' court, without the Palace wall,
There the revenging sword shall smite them all;
So with the Suitors let 'em mix in dust,
Stretch'd in a long oblivion of their lust.
He said: The lamentable train appear,
Each vents a groan, and drops a tender tear;
Each heav'd her mournful burthen, and beneath
The porch, depos'd the ghastly heaps of death.
The Chief severe, compelling each to move,
Urg'd the dire task imperious from above.
With thirsty sponge they rub the tables o'er,
(The swains unite their toil) the walls, the floor
Wash'd with th' effusive wave, are purg'd of gore.
Once more the palace set in fair array,
To the base court the females take their way;

There compass'd close between the dome and wall,
(Their life's last scene) they trembling wait their fall.
    Then thus the Prince. To these shall we afford
A fate so pure, as by the martial sword?
To these, the nightly prostitutes to shame,
And base revilers of our house and name?
    Thus speaking, on the circling wall he strung
A ship's tough cable, from a column hung;
Near the high top he strain'd it strongly round,
Whence no contending foot could reach the ground.
Their heads above, connected in a row,
They beat the air with quiv'ring feet below:
Thus on some tree hung struggling in the snare,
The doves or thrushes flap their wings in air.
Soon fled the soul impure, and left behind
The empty corse to waver with the wind.
    Then forth they led Melanthius, and began
Their bloody work: They lopp'd away the man,
Morsel for dogs! then trimm'd with brazen sheers
The wretch, and shorten'd of his nose and ears;
His hands and feet last felt the cruel steel:
He roar'd, and torments gave his soul to hell—
    They wash, and to Ulysses take their way;
So ends the bloody business of the day.


313        '*The Descent of the Suitors' Shades*'

Trembling the Spectres glide, and plaintive vent
Thin, hollow screams, along the deep descent.
As in the cavern of some rifted den,
Where flock nocturnal bats, and birds obscene;
Cluster'd they hang, till at some sudden shock,
They move, and murmurs run thro' all the rock:
So cow'ring fled the sable heaps of ghosts,
And such a scream fill'd all the dismal coasts.

# SOAME JENYNS

?1703/4–1787

## FROM THE LATIN OF PETRONIUS AFRANIUS

314                    *The Snow-ball*

White as her hand fair Julia threw
  A ball of silver snow,
The frozen globe fir'd as it flew,
  My bosom felt it glow.

Strange pow'r of love! whose great command
  Can thus a snow-ball arm;
When sent, fair Julia, from thine hand,
  Ev'n ice itself can warm.

How shou'd we then secure our hearts?
  Love's pow'r we all must feel,
Who thus can, by strange magick arts,
  In ice his flames conceal.

'Tis thou alone, fair Julia, know,
  Canst quench my fierce desire,
But not with water, ice, nor snow,
  But with an equal fire.

# PHILIP FRANCIS

?1708–1773

## FROM THE LATIN OF HORACE

315                  Odes, Book I, 25

*To Lydia*

Cp.
Mr Rule's
Young
Gentlemen

The wanton Herd of Rakes profest
Thy Windows rarely now molest
With midnight Raps, or break thy Rest
                              With Riot.
Thy Door which kindly once could move
The plyant Hinge, begins to love
Its Threshold, and no more shall prove
                              Unquiet,
Now less and less assail thine Ear
These Plaints, 'Ah sleepest thou my Dear,
While I whole Nights thy True-love here
                              Am dying?
You in your Turn shall weep the Taunts
Of young and insolent Gallants,
In some dark Alley's Midnight Haunts
                              Late-plying:
While raging Tempests chill the Skies,
And burning Lust (such Lust as tries
The madding Dams of Horses) fries
                              Thy Liver,
Our Youth, regardless of thy Frown,
Their Heads with fresher Wreaths shall crown,
And fling thy wither'd Garlands down
                              The River.'

# SAMUEL JOHNSON

1709–1784

FROM THE GREEK OF HOMER

316            *The Iliad*, Book VI, 146

Cp.
Chapman
Ecclesiasticus
Pope

Frail as the leaves that quiver on the sprays,
Like them man flourishes, like them decays.

FROM THE LATIN OF HORACE

317            Odes, Book I, 22

*To Aristius Fuscus*

Cp.
Roscommon

The Man, my Friend, whose conscious Heart
   With Virtue's sacred Ardour glows,
Nor taints with Death th'envenom'd Dart,
   Nor needs the Guard of Moorish Bows.

O'er icy Caucasus he treads,
   Or torrid Afric's faithless Sands,
Or where the fam'd Hydaspes spreads
   His liquid Wealth thro' barbarous Lands.

For while in Sabine Forests, charm'd
   By Lalagé, too far I stray'd,
Me singing, careless and unarm'd,
   A furious Wolf approach'd, and fled.

No Beast more dreadful ever stain'd
   Apulia's spacious Wilds with Gore;
No Beast more fierce Numidia's Land,
   The Lion's thirsty Parent, bore.

Place me where no soft Summer Gale
   Among the quivering Branches sighs,
Where Clouds, condens'd, for ever veil
   With horrid Gloom the frowning Skies:

Place me beneath the burning Zone,
  A Clime deny'd to human Race;
My Flame for Lalagé I'll own;
  Her Voice and Smiles my Song shall grace.


318                *Odes*, Book IV, 7

Cp.
Housman

The snow dissolv'd no more is seen,
The fields, and woods, behold, are green,
The changing year renews the plain
The rivers know their banks again
The spritely Nymph and naked Grace
The mazy dance together trace.
The changing year's successive plan
Proclaims mortality to Man.
Rough Winter's blasts to Spring give way
Spring yields to Summer's sovereign ray
Then Summer sinks in Autumn's reign
And Winter chills the World again
Her losses soon the Moon supplies
But wretched Man, when once he lies
Where Priam and his Sons are laid
Is nought but Ashes and a Shade.
Who knows if Jove who counts our Score
Will toss us in a morning more?
What with your friend you nobly share
At least you rescue from your heir.
Not you, Torquatus, boast of Rome,
When Minos once has fix'd your doom,
Or Eloquence, or splendid birth
Or Virtue shall replace on earth.
Hyppolytus unjustly slain
Diana calls to life in vain,
Nor can the might of Theseus rend
The chains of hell that hold his friend.

## FROM THE LATIN OF BOETHIUS
c 470-524

# The Consolation of Philosophy

319              *Book II, 2*

Though countless as the Grains of Sand
That roll at Eurus loud Command;
Though countless as the lamps of night
That glad us with vicarious light;
Fair plenty gracious Queen shou'd pour
The blessings of a golden Show'r
Not all the gifts of Fate combin'd
Would ease the hunger of the mind,
But swallowing all the mighty Store,
Rapacity would call for more;
For still where wishes most abound
Unquench'd the thirst of gain is found
In vain the shining Gifts are sent,
For none are rich without content.


320              *Book III, 9*

O thou whose pow'r o'er moving worlds presides,
Whose voice created, and whose wisdom guides,
On darkling man in pure effulgence shine,
And chear the clouded mind with light divine.
'Tis thine alone to calm the pious breast
With silent confidence and holy rest:
From thee, great God, we spring, to thee we tend,
Path, motive, guide, original, and end.


321           from *Book III, 12*

Happy he whose Eyes have view'd
The transparent Fount of Good;
Happy whose unfetter'd Mind
Leaves the Load of Earth behind.
Tho' when Orpheus made his Moan
For his lovely Consort gone,

Tho' the Hind approach'd to hear
Where the Lyoness stood near,
And attentive to the Sound
Hares forgot the following hound,
Round him danc'd the listning Woods,
Silent Wonder stopt the Floods;
Grief and Madness unrepress'd
Rag'd within the Master's Breast
While t'asswage the Pangs of Love
Verse and Music vainly strove;
Now he sighs to heav'n, and now
Rushes on the Realms below.

\*

Tantalus astonish'd stood
Scorning now th'o'erflowing Flood,
Till at length stern Pluto cried
Conqu'ring Poet take thy Bride!
Purchas'd by thy powerful Song,
All her Charms to thee belong;
Only this Command obey
Look not on her by the way;
Tho' reluctant still refrain,
Till the Realms of Light you gain
But what Laws can Lovers awe?
Love alone to Love is Law:
Just emerging into Light,
Orpheus turn'd his eager Sight,
Fondly view'd his following Bride,
Viewing lost and losing died.

To You whose gen'rous Wishes rise
To court Communion with the Skies
    To you the Tale is told;
When grasping Bliss th'unsteady mind
Looks back on what She left behind,
    She faints and quits her hold.

# THOMAS GRAY

### 1716–1771

## FROM THE WELSH OF ANEIRIN VIA THE LATIN

322              from *The Gododdin*

> To Cattraeth's vale in glitt'ring row
> Thrice two hundred Warriors goe;
> Every Warrior's manly neck
> Chains of regal honour deck,
> Wreath'd in many a golden link:
> From the golden cup they drink
> Nectar, that the bees produce,
> Or the grape's extatic juice.
> Flush'd with mirth and hope they burn:
> But none from Cattraeth's vale return,
> Save Aeron brave, and Conan strong,
> (Bursting thro' the bloody throng)
> And I, the meanest of them all,
> That live to weep, and sing their fall.

# ANONYMOUS

### Published 1717

## FROM THE LATIN OF CATULLUS

323              *Carmina*, IV

> The Fourth Ode of Catullus. Paraphras'd
> in the manner of Cowley. Phasellus ille, &c.
> On the Boat that carried him into his own Countrey.

Cp..
Hookham
Frere

> This racer of the watry plain,
> Cou'd once outstrip the fleetest sail;
> With oary finns to swim the main,
> Or wing'd with canvass, fly before the gale!

On Pontus streams she freely rides,
Whom roots once fasten'd to the shore;
And turn'd a tenant of the tides,
Reviews the mountains where she grew before:

Where once she stood a living shade,
And (veil'd in clouds) her head did rear,
Her verdant tresses round her play'd,
Sung to the wind, and danc'd in open air.

Of old, Cytorus top she crown'd;
And, at his bottom while she moves,
Renews acquaintance with the ground,
Her kindred trees, and her coeval groves.

Here, where she tempted first the tides,
And crept on unexperienc'd oars;
On bounding billows tost she rides,
Secure on surges, as of old on shoars.

Whether when hov'ring in the sky,
The wandring winds did loosely blow;
Or sweeping from all quarters fly,
When Jove abroad on all their wings would go.

At last she left the stormy seas,
But to no gods her vows did make,
Till now her vessel, laid at ease,
Sleeps on the bosom of the gentle lake.

Here her old age its rest obtains,
Secure from all the watry war;
And consecrates its last remains,
To thee, bright Castor, and thy Brother Star!

# CHRISTOPHER SMART

## 1722–1771

### FROM THE HEBREW

via the Prayer Book, often greatly expanded and Christianized

324                      *Psalm 8*

Cp.
Coverdale

O Lord, that rul'st the human heart,
How excellent thy name and art,
    In all the world renown'd!
The glorious pillars of thy reign
No flight can reach, nor heav'ns contain,
    Nor exaltation bound!

The very babes and sucklings cry,
Almighty Father, God most high!
    Whom blasphemy profanes—
Thou hear'st and tak'st them by the hand,
Nor can the silenc'd fiend withstand
    The strength that Christ ordains.

I will my soaring thoughts exalt
To yonder heaven's cerulean vault,
    Whose height thy fingers form'd;
The moon attended at thy call,
Made marvelously fair, and all
    The stars around her swarm'd!

Lord what is man, that he should find
A place in his Creator's mind
    Or what his whole increase—
A race of rebels vain and weak,
That he should for a moment break
    Upon his Saviour's peace?

An angel quite thou mad'st him not,
A little lower is his lot,
    On earth thou set'st him down;
There his dominion and degree,
To glorify and worship thee
    For glory and a crown.

Him thou deputed to review
The scenes of nature, and subdue
    Thy creatures to his will;
Whose motley numbers own his sway,
And by his strength compell'd obey,
    Or disciplin'd by skill.

All flocks of sheep and droves of kine,
Which as his olive and his vine,
    To man their goodness yield;
And not a beast that can be nam'd,
But may be taken or be tam'd
    In woodland or in field.

In air, in ocean he controuls,
The feather'd millions, finny shoals,
    From minnows to the whale;
Whate'er beneath the waters creep,
Or glide within the yielding deep,
    Or on the surface sail.

O thou that rul'st the human heart,
Supreme of nature and of art,
    How is thy name renown'd!
How blest thy providential care,
In heav'n above, in earth and air,
    And in the vast profound!

325            *Psalm 114*

    When Israel came from Egypt's coast,
        And Goshen's marshy plains,
    And Jacob with his joyful host
        From servitude and chains;

Then was it seen how much the Jews
    Were holy in his sight,
And God did Israel's kingdom chuse
    To manifest his might.

The sea beheld it, and with dread
    Retreated to make way;
And Jordan to his fountain head
    Ran backwards in dismay.

The mountains, like the rams that bound,
    Exulted on their base;
Like lambs the little hills around
    Skipt lightly from their place.

What is the cause, thou mighty sea,
    That thou thyself shou'd shun;
And Jordan, what is come to thee,
    That thou shou'd backward run?

Ye mountains that ye leap'd so high
    From off the solid rock,
Ye hills that ye should gambols try,
    Like firstlings of the flock?

EARTH, from the centre to the sod
    His fearful presence hail,
The presence of Jeshurun's God,
    In whom our arms prevail.

Who beds of rocks in pools to stand
    Can by his word compell,
And from the veiny flint command
    The fountain and the well.

326           from *Psalm 148* (2nd version)

Hallelujah! kneel and sing
Praises to the heav'nly king;
To the God supremely great,
Hallelujah in the height!

Praise him, archangelic band,
Ye that in his presence stand;
Praise him, ye that watch and pray,
Michael's myriads in array.

Praise him, sun, at each extreme
Orient streak, and western beam,
Moon and stars of mystic dance,
Silv'ring in the blue expanse.

Praise him, O ye heights, that soar
Heav'n and heav'n for evermore;
And ye streams of living rill,
Higher yet, and purer still.

Let them praise his glorious name,
From whose fruitful word they came,
And they first began to be
As he gave the great decree.

Their constituent parts he founds
For duration without bounds,
And their covenant has seal'd,
Which shall never be repeal'd.

Praise the Lord on earth's domains,
And the mutes that sea contains,
Ye that on the surface leap,
And ye dragons of the deep.

Batt'ring hail, and fires that glow,
Steaming vapours, plumy snow,
Wind and storm his wrath incurr'd,
Wing'd and pointed at his word.

Mountains of enormous scale,
Ev'ry hill, and ev'ry vale,
Fruit-trees of a thousand dyes,
Cedars that perfume the skies.

Beasts that haunt the woodland maze,
Nibbling flocks, and droves that graze;
Reptiles of amphibious breed,
Feather'd millions form'd for speed.

FROM THE LATIN OF HORACE

327

## Odes, Book I, 5

### *To Pyrrha*

Cp.
Milton
Fanshawe
Cowley
Horneck

Say what slim youth, with moist perfumes
   Bedaub'd, now courts thy fond embrace,
There, where the frequent rose-tree blooms,
   And makes the grot so sweet a place?
Pyrrha, for whom with such an air
Do you bind back your golden hair?

So seeming in your cleanly vest,
   Whose plainness is the pink of taste—
Alas! how oft shall he protest
   Against his confidence misplac't,
And love's inconstant pow'rs deplore,
And wondrous winds, which, as they roar,

Throw black upon the alter'd scene—
   Who now so well himself deceives,
And thee all sunshine, all serene
   For want of better skill believes,
And for his pleasure has presag'd
Thee ever dear and disengag'd.

Wretched are all within thy snares,
   The inexperienc'd and the young!
For me the temple witness bears
   Where I my dropping weeds have hung,
And left my votive chart behind
To him that rules both wave and wind.

328    Odes, Book I, 38

*To His Servant*

Cp.
Cowper
Thackeray
Hopkins

Persian pomps, boy, ever I renounce them:
Scoff o' the plaited coronet's refulgence;
Seek not in fruitless vigilance the rose-tree's
    Tardier offspring.

Mere honest myrtle that alone is order'd,
Me the mere myrtle decorates, as also
Thee the prompt waiter to a jolly toper
    Hous'd in an arbour.

329    *Odes*, Book II, 18

Gold or iv'ry's not intended
    For this little house of mine,
Nor Hymettian arches, bended
    On rich Afric pillars, shine.

For a court I've no ambition,
    As not Attalus his heir,
Nor make damsels of condition
    Spin me purple for my wear.

But for truth and wit respected,
    I possess a copious vein,
So that rich men have affected
    To be number'd of my train.

With my Sabine field contented,
    Fortune shall be dunn'd no more;
Nor my gen'rous friend tormented
    To augment my little store.

One day by the next's abolish'd,
    Moons increase but to decay;
You place marbles to be polish'd
    Ev'n upon your dying day.

Death unheeding, though infirmer,
  On the sea your buildings rise,
While the Baian billows murmur,
  That the land will not suffice.

What tho' more and more incroaching,
  On new boundaries you press,
And in avarice approaching,
  Your poor neighbours dispossess;

The griev'd hind his gods displaces
  In his bosom to convey,
And with dirty ruddy faces
  Boys and wife are driven away.

Yet no palace grand and spacious
  Does more sure its lord receive,
Than the seat of death rapacious,
  Whence the rich have no reprieve.

Earth alike to all is equal,
  Whither would your views extend?
Kings and peasants in the sequel
  To the destin'd grave descend.

There, tho' brib'd, the guard infernal
  Would not shrewd Prometheus free;
There are held in chains eternal
  Tantalus, and such as he.

There the poor have consolation
  For their hard laborious lot;
Death attends each rank and station,
  Whether he is call'd or not.

# WILLIAM COWPER

1731–1800

## FROM THE GREEK OF HOMER

## The Iliad

### SOME SIMILES

330    *'The Greeks like Fire, Birds, Flies'*

As when devouring flames some forest seize
On the high mountains, splendid from afar
The blaze appears, so, moving on the plain,
The steel-clad host innum'rous flash'd to Heav'n.
And as a multitude of fowls in flocks
Assembled various, geese, or cranes, or swans
Lithe-neck'd, long hov'ring o'er Caÿster's banks
On wanton plumes, successive on the mead
Alight at last, and with a clang so loud,
That all the hollow vale of Asius rings,
In number such from ships and tents effus'd,
They cover'd the Scamandrian plain; the earth
Rebellow'd to the feet of steeds and men.
They overspread Scamander's grassy vale,
Myriads, as leaves, or as the flow'rs of spring.
As in the hovel where the peasant milks
His kine in spring-time, when his pails are fill'd,
Thick clouds of humming insects on the wing
Swarm all around him, so the Greecians swarm'd
An unsumm'd multitude o'er all the plain,
Bright-arm'd, high-crested, and athirst for war.

Caÿster] a river of Asia Minor

331 *'The two Ajaxes like Oxen'*

Cp.
Chapman
Pope

Ajax the swift swerv'd never from the side
Of Ajax son of Telamon a step;
But as in some deep fallow two black steers
Together toil, dragging the pond'rous plough,
The briny sweat around their rooted horns
Oozes profuse; they, parted, as they drudge
Along the furrow, by the yoke alone,
Cleave to its bottom sheer the stubborn glebe,
So, side by side, they, persevering fought.

332 *'As when an architect ...'*

As when an architect some palace wall
With shapely stones erects, cementing close
A barrier against all the winds of Heav'n,
So wedg'd the helmets and boss'd bucklers stood ...

## OTHER INCIDENTS

333 *'The Trojans outside Troy'*

Cp.
Pope
Tennyson

Big with great purposes and proud, they sat,
Not disarray'd, but in fair form dispos'd
Of even ranks, and watch'd their num'rous fires.
As when around the clear bright moon, the stars
Shine in full splendour, and the winds are hush'd,
The groves, the mountain-tops, the headland-heights
Stand all apparent, not a vapour streaks
The boundless blue, but ether open'd wide
All glitters, and the shepherd's heart is cheer'd;
So num'rous seem'd those fires, between the stream
Of Xanthus blazing and the fleet of Greece,
In prospect all of Troy; a thousand fires,
Each watch'd by fifty warriors seated near,
The steeds beside the chariots stood, their corn
Chewing, and waiting till the golden-thron'd
Aurora should restore the light of day.

334 *'Patroclus spears Thestor'*

The son of Enops, Thestor next he smote.
He in his chariot with his body bent
Sat cow'ring low, a fear-distracted form,
And from his palsied grasp the reins had fall'n.
Then came Patroclus nigh, and through his cheek
His teeth transpiercing, drew him by his lance
Sheer o'er the chariot-front. As when a man
On some projecting rock advanc'd, with line
And splendid hook draws forth a sea-fish huge,
So him wide-gaping from his seat he drew
At his spear-point, then shook him to the ground
Prone on his face, where gasping he expir'd.

# The Odyssey

335 *'Jove sends Hermes to Calypso'*

Cp.
Chapman
Pope

He ended, nor the Argicide refus'd,
Messenger of the skies; his sandals fair,
Ambrosial, golden, to his feet he bound,
Which o'er the moist wave, rapid as the wind,
Bear him, and o'er th' illimitable Earth,
Then took his rod, with which, at will, all eyes
He softly shuts, or opens them again.
So arm'd, forth flew the valiant Argicide.
Alighting on Pieria, down he stoop'd
To Ocean, and the billows lightly skimm'd
In form a seamew, such as, in the bays
Tremendous of the barren Deep her food
Seeking, dips oft in brine her ample wing.
In such disguise o'er many a wave he rode,
But reaching now that isle remote, forsook
The azure Deep; and, at the spacious grot,
Where dwelt the amber-tressed nymph, arriv'd,
Found her within. A fire on all the hearth
Blaz'd sprightly, and, afar-diffus'd, the scent
Of smooth-split cedar and of cypress-wood
Odorous, burning, cheer'd the happy isle.

She, busied at the loom, and plying fast
Her golden shuttle, with melodious voice
Sat chanting there; a grove on either side,
Alder and poplar, and the redolent branch
Of cypress hemm'd the dark retreat around.
There many a bird of broadest pinion built
Secure her nest, the owl, the kite, and daw,
Long-tongu'd, frequenter of the sandy shores.
A garden-vine luxuriant on all sides
Mantled the spacious cavern, cluster-hung
Profuse; four fountains of serenest lymph
Their sinuous course pursuing side by side,
Stray'd all around, and ev'ry where appear'd
Meadows of softest verdure, purpled o'er
With violets; it was a scene to fill
A God from Heav'n with wonder and delight.

## 336                    *'Scylla and Charybdis'*

Just then, forgetful of the strict command
Of Circe to forbear, I cloth'd my limbs
In radiant armour, grasp'd two quiv'ring spears,
And to the deck ascended at the prow,
Expecting earliest notice there, what time
The rock-bred Scylla should annoy my friends.
But I discern'd her not, nor could, although
To weariness of sight the dusky rock
I vigilant explor'd. Thus, many a groan
Heaving, we navigated sad the strait,
For here stood Scylla, while Charybdis there
With hoarse throat deep absorb'd the briny flood.
Oft as she vomited the deluge forth,
Like water caldron'd o'er a furious fire
The whirling Deep all murmur'd, and the spray
On both those rocky summits fell in show'rs.
But when she suck'd the salt wave down again,
Then all the pool appear'd wheeling about
Within, the rock rebellow'd, and the sea,
Drawn off into that gulf, disclos'd to view
The oozy bottom. Us pale horrour seiz'd.

Thus, dreading death, with fast-set eyes we watch'd
Charybdis; mean-time Scylla from the bark
Caught six away, the bravest of my friends;
And, as I watching stood the galley's course
And them within, uplifted high in air
Their legs and arms I saw. My name aloud
Pronouncing in their agony, they went,
My name, and never to pronounce it more.
As when from some bold point among the rocks
The angler, with his taper rod in hand,
Casts forth his bait, to snare the smaller fry,
He swings away remote his guarded line,
Then jerks aground at once the struggling prey,
So Scylla them rais'd struggling to the rock,
And at her cavern's mouth devour'd them all,
Shrieking and stretching forth to me their arms
In sign of hopeless mis'ry.


### FROM THE GREEK ANTHOLOGY

337

## An Epitaph

My name—my country—what are they to thee?
What—whether base or proud, my pedigree?
Perhaps I far surpass'd all other men—
Perhaps I fell below them all—what then?
Suffice it, stranger! that thou seest a tomb—
Thou know'st its use—it hides—no matter whom.


338

## By Heraclides

In Cnidus born, the consort I became
Of Euphron. Aretimias was my name.
His bed I shar'd, nor prov'd a barren bride,
But bore two children at a birth, and died.
One child I leave to solace and uphold
Euphron hereafter, when infirm and old;
And one, for his remembrance sake, I bear
To Pluto's realm, till he shall join me there.

### 339 *To the Swallow*

Cp.
Bishop

Attic maid! with honey fed,
 Bear'st thou to thy callow brood
Yonder locust from the mead,
 Destin'd their delicious food?

Ye have kindred voices clear,
 Ye alike unfold the wing,
Migrate hither, sojourn here,
 Both attendant on the spring.

Ah for pity drop the prize;
 Let it not, with truth, be said
That a songster gasps and dies,
 That a songster may be fed.

### 340 *On Late-Acquired Wealth*

Poor in my youth, and in life's later scenes
 Rich to no end, I curse my natal hour;
Who nought enjoy'd, while young, denied the means;
 And nought, when old, enjoy'd, denied the pow'r.

## FROM THE LATIN OF HORACE

### 341 *Odes*, Book I, 38

Cp.
Smart
Thackeray
Hopkins

Boy, I hate their empty shows,
 Persian garlands I detest,
Bring not me the late-blown rose
 Ling' ring after all the rest:

Plainer myrtle pleases me
 Thus out-stretched beneath my vine,
Myrtle more becoming thee,
 Waiting with thy master's wine.

342

Cp.
Surrey
Sidney

### *Odes*, Book II, 10

Receive, dear friend, the truths I teach,
So shalt thou live beyond the reach
   Of adverse Fortune's pow'r;
Not always tempt the distant deep,
Nor always timorously creep
   Along the treach'rous shore.

He, that holds fast the golden mean,
And lives contentedly between
   The little and the great,
Feels not the wants that pinch the poor,
Nor plagues that haunt the rich man's door,
   Imbitt'ring all his state.

The tallest pines feel most the pow'r
Of wintry blasts; the loftiest tow'r
   Comes heaviest to the ground;
The bolts, that spare the mountain's side,
His cloud-capt eminence divide,
   And spread the ruin round.

The well-inform'd philosopher
Rejoices with an wholesome fear,
   And hopes, in spite of pain;
If winter bellow from the north,
Soon the sweet spring comes dancing forth,
   And nature laughs again.

What if thine heav'n be overcast,
The dark appearance will not last;
   Expect a brighter sky;
The God that strings the silver bow
Awakes sometimes the muses too,
   And lays his arrows by.

If hindrances obstruct thy way,
Thy magnanimity display,
   And let thy strength be seen;
But oh! if Fortune fill thy sail
With more than a propitious gale,
   Take half thy canvass in.

Cowper also wrote: *A Reflection on the Foregoing Ode*

And is this all? Can reason do no more
Than bid me shun the deep and dread the shore?
Sweet moralist! afloat on life's rough sea,
The Christian has an art unknown to thee:
He holds no parley with unmanly fears;
Where duty bids, he confidently steers,
Faces a thousand dangers at her call,
And, trusting in his God, surmounts them all.

### FROM THE LATIN OF VINCENT BOURNE

343                  *The Snail*

To grass, or leaf, or fruit, or wall,
The snail sticks close, nor fears to fall,
As if he grew there, house and all
                Together.

Within that house secure he hides,
When danger imminent betides
Of storm, or other harm besides
                Of weather.

Give but his horns the slightest touch,
His self-collecting power is such,
He shrinks into his house, with much
                Displeasure.

Where'er he dwells, he dwells alone,
Except himself has chattels none,
Well satisfied to be his own
                Whole treasure.

Thus, hermit-like, his life he leads,
Nor partner of his banquet needs,
And if he meets one, only feeds
        The faster.

Who seeks him must be worse than blind,
(He and his house are so combin'd)
If, finding it, he fails to find
        Its master.

# THE YOUNG GENTLEMEN OF
# MR RULE'S ACADEMY AT ISLINGTON

Published 1766

### FROM THE LATIN OF HORACE

**344**

*Odes*, Book I, 25

Cp.
Francis

The bloods and bucks of this lewd town
   No longer shake your windows down
      With knocking;
Your door stands still, no more you hear
'I die for you, O Lydia dear',
      Love's God your slumbers rocking.

Forsaken, in some narrow lane
   You in your turn will loud complain,
      Gallants no more engaging:
Whilst north-winds roar, and lust, whose pow'r
Makes madding mares the meadows scour,
      Is in your bosom raging.

You're griev'd, and quite eat up with spleen,
   That ivy and sweet myrtle green
      Young men alone long after;
And that away they dri'd leaves throw,
And let them down the river go
      With laughter.

# WILLIAM GIFFORD

1756–1826

## FROM THE LATIN OF JUVENAL

## *from* Satires, IV

### *'The Mighty Turbot'*

When the last Flavius, drunk with fury, tore
The prostrate world, that bled at every pore,
And Rome beheld, in body as in mind,
A bald-pate Nero rise, to curse mankind;
It chanced, that where the fane of Venus stands,
Rear'd on Ancona's coast by Grecian hands,
A turbot, rushing from the Illyrian main,
Fill'd the wide bosom of the bursting seine.
Monsters so bulky, from its frozen stream,
Mæotis renders to the solar beam,
And pours them, fat with a whole winter's ease,
Through the dull Euxine's mouth, to warmer seas.
    The mighty draught the wondering fisher eyes,
And to the Pontiff's board allots his prize;
For who would dare to sell it, who to buy?
When the coast swarm'd with many a practis'd spy;
Mud-rakers! leagued to swear the fish had fled
From Cæsar's ponds, where many a year it fed,
And ought, recaptur'd now, to be restor'd
To the dominion of its ancient lord.
Nay, if Palphurius may our credit gain,
Whatever rare, or precious, swims the main,
Is forfeit to the crown, and you may seize
The obnoxious dainty, when and where you please.
This point allow'd, our wary boatman chose
To give the prize he else was sure to lose.
    Now were the dog-star's sickly fervours o'er,
Earth, pinch'd with cold, her frozen livery wore;

the last Flavius] Domitian, both emperor and pontiff
Palphurius] lawyer to Domitian

328

The old began their quartan fits to fear,
And wintry blasts deform'd the beauteous year,
And kept the turbot sweet: yet on he flew
As if the sultry south corruption blew.—
And now the lake, and now the hill he gains,
Where Alba, though in ruins, still maintains
The Trojan fire, that but for her were lost,
And worships Vesta, though with less of cost.
The wondering crowd, that gather'd to survey
Th' enormous fish, and choak'd the fisher's way,
Satiate at length, retires; then wide unfold
The gates; the senators, shut out, behold
The luscious dainty enter: on the man
To great Atrides press'd, and thus began.

'This, which no subject's kitchen can contain,
This fish, reserv'd for your auspicious reign,
O, chief, accept:—to free your stomach haste,
And here at large indulge your princely taste;
I sought him not,—he long'd his lord to treat,
And rush'd, a willing victim, to the net.'

Was flattery e'er so rank? yet he grows vain,
And his crest rises at the fulsome strain.
When to divine a mortal power we raise,
He looks for no hyperboles in praise!

But when was joy unmix'd? no pot is found
Capacious of the turbot's ample round:
In this distress, he calls the chiefs of state,
At once the objects of his scorn and hate,
In whose wan cheeks distrust and doubt appear,
And all a tyrant's friendship brings of fear.

\*

The Emperor now the important question put:
'How say ye, fathers? SHALL THE FISH BE CUT?'
'O! far be that disgrace,' Montanus cries,
'No, let us form a pot of amplest size,
Within whose slender rim, the fish, dread Sire!
May spread its vast circumference entire.
Bring, bring the temper'd clay, and let it feel
The quick gyrations of the plastic wheel;
But Cæsar, thus fore-warn'd, have special care,
And bid your potters follow you to war.'

329

He spoke: a murmur through the assembly ran,
Applausive of the speech, so worthy of the man.
Vers'd in the old court-luxury, he knew
The feasts of Nero, and his midnight crew;
And how, when potent draughts had fir'd the brain,
The jaded taste was spurr'd to gorge again.
And, in our days, none understood so well
The science of good eating; he could tell,
At the first smack, whether his oysters fed
On the Rutupian, or the Lucrine bed,
And from a crab, or lobster's colour, name
The country, nay the spot, from whence it came.

　　Here closed the solemn farce. The fathers rise,
And each, submissive, from the presence hies:—
Pale, trembling wretches, whom the chief, in sport,
Had dragg'd, astonished, to the Alban court,
As if the stern Sicambri were in arms,
Or the fierce Catti threaten'd new alarms;
As if ill news, by flying posts, had come,
And gathering nations sought the fall of Rome.

346　　　　　　　*from* Satires, X

*'Sejanus'*

Cp.
Dryden
Lowell

　　What crowds by envied POWER, the wish of all,
Are hurl'd from high; press'd, in their rapid fall,
By cumbrous names!—the statues tumbled down,
And dragg'd by hooting thousands through the town;
The cars upturn'd, the wheels to shivers broke,
And the steeds fractur'd by the axe's stroke!—
Then roar the fires; the sooty artist blows,
And all Sejanus in the furnace glows;
Sejanus once so honour'd, so ador'd,
And only second to the world's great lord,
Runs glittering from the mould, in cups and cans,
And such mean things, in pitchers, pots, and pans.

　　'Hang out your laurels, and of triumph full,
Lead to the Capitol a milk-white bull;
For lo! where great Sejanus by the throng,
A joyful spectacle, is dragg'd along.

What an ill-favour'd wretch! well, for my part,
I never lov'd him—that is, in my heart.
But tell me; why was he adjudg'd to bleed?
And who discover'd, and who prov'd the deed?'
'Prov'd? tush! a huge epistle came, they say,
From Capreæ.' 'Good! I'm satisfied: but pray,
What think the people of their favourite's fate?'—
'They follow fortune as of old, and hate
With their whole souls the victim of the state.'
Yet would the herd, thus zealous, thus on fire,
Had Nurscia met the Tuscan's fond desire,
And crush'd th' unwary prince, have all combin'd,
And hail'd Sejanus Master of mankind.
For since their votes have been no longer bought,
All public care has vanish'd from their thought;
And they who once, with unresisted sway,
Gave armies, empire, every thing, away,
For two poor claims have long resign'd the whole,
And only ask,—the Circus and the Dole.

## 'Hannibal'

Cp.
Vaughan
Lowell      Produce the urn that Hannibal contains,
And weigh the mighty dust which yet remains:
And is this all! Yet THIS was once the bold,
The aspiring chief, whom Afric could not hold,
Afric, outstretch'd from where the Atlantic roars,
To Nilus; from the Line, to Lybia's shores!
Spain conquer'd, o'er the Pyrenees he bounds;
Nature oppos'd her everlasting mounds,
Her Alps, and snows: through these he bursts his way,
And Italy already owns his sway—
Still thundering on,—'think nothing done,' he cries,
'Till low in dust our haughty rival lies;
Till through her smoking streets I lead my powers,
And plant my standard on her hated towers.'
Big words! but view his figure, view his face:
O, for some master-hand the chief to trace,
As through the Etrurian swamps, by rains increas'd,
Spoil'd of an eye he flounc'd, on his Getulian beast!

346 Nurscia] Fortuna was so called by the Tuscans

But what ensued, illusive glory! say?—
Subdued on Zama's memorable day,
He flies in exile to a foreign state,
With headlong haste; and, at a despot's gate
Sits, wond'rous suppliant! of his fate in doubt,
'Till the Bithynian's morning nap be out.
    Just to his fame, what death has Heaven assign'd
The great controller of all human kind?
Did hostile armies give the fatal wound,
Or mountains press him, struggling, to the ground?
No; three small drops, within a ring conceal'd,
Aveng'd the blood he pour'd on Cannæ's field!
Go madman, go! the paths of fame pursue,
Climb other Alps, and other realms subdue,
To please the rhetoricians, and become,
A DECLAMATION for the boys of Rome!


### 'Old Age'

'Life! length of life!' for this, with earnest cries,
Or sick or well, we supplicate the skies.
Pernicious prayer! for mark, what ills attend
Still on the old, as to the grave they bend:
A ghastly visage to themselves unknown,
For a smooth skin, a hide with scurf o'ergrown,
And such a flabby cheek as an old ape,
In Tabraca's thick woods, might haply scrape.
In youth a thousand different features strike;
All have their charms, but have not charms alike:
While age presents one universal face—
A faultering voice, a weak and trembling pace,
An ever-dropping nose, a forehead bare,
And toothless gums to mump his wretched fare.
He grows, poor wretch (now, in the dregs of life,)
So loathsome to himself, his child, his wife,
That those who hop'd the legacy to share,
And flatter'd long, disgusted disappear.
The sluggish palate dull'd, the feast no more
Excites the same sensations as of yore;
Taste, feeling, all, a universal blot,
And e'en the rites of love remember'd not:

Or if—through the long night he feebly strives,
To raise a flame where not a spark survives;
While Venus marks the effort with distrust,
And hates the gray decreptitude of lust.

# WILLIAM LISLE BOWLES

### 1762–1850

## FROM THE GREEK OF SIMONIDES

**347** *Thermopylae*

Cp.
Rexroth

Go tell the Spartans, thou that passest by,
That here, obedient to their laws, we lie.

# JOHN HOOKHAM FRERE

### 1769–1846

## FROM THE LATIN OF CATULLUS

**348** Carmina, IV

*The Yacht*

Cp.
Anon. no. 323

Stranger, the bark you see before you says
That in old times and in her early days
She was a lively vessel that could make
The quickest voyages, and overtake
All her competitors with sail or oar;
And she defies the rude Illyrian shore,
And Rhodes, with her proud harbour, and the seas
That intersect the scatter'd Cyclades,
And the Propontic and the Thracian coast,
(Bold as it is) to contradict her boast.
She calls to witness the dark Euxine sea,
And mountains that had known her as a tree,
Before her transformation, when she stood
A native of the deep Cytorian wood,

333

Where all her ancestors had flourish'd long,
And, with their old traditionary song,
Had whisper'd her responses to the breeze,
And waked the chorus of her sister trees.
Amastris, from your haven forth she went,
You witness'd her first outset and descent,
Adventuring on an unknown element.
From thence she bore her master safe and free
From danger and alarm, through many a sea;
Nor ever once was known to lag behind,
Foremost on every tack, with every wind.
At last, to this fair inland lake, she says,
She came to pass the remnant of her days,
Leaving no debt due to the Deities
For vows preferr'd in danger on the seas:
Clear of incumbrance, therefore, and all other
Contentious claims, to Castor or his brother,
As a free gift and offering she devotes
Herself, as long as she survives and floats.

349 *Carmina*, X

Varus, whom I chanced to meet
The other evening in the street,
Engaged me there, upon the spot,
To see a mistress he had got.
She seem'd, as far as I can gather,
Lively and smart, and handsome rather.
There, as we rested from our walk,
We enter'd into different talk—
As, how much might Bithynia bring?
And had I found it a good thing?
I answer'd, as it was the fact,
The province had been stript and sack'd;
That there was nothing for the prætors,
And still less for us wretched creatures,
His poor companions and toad-eaters.
'At least,' says she, 'you bought some fellows
To bear your litter; for they tell us,
Our only good ones come from there.'
I chose to give myself an air;

'Why, truly, with my poor estate,
The difference wasn't quite so great
Betwixt a province, good or bad,
That where a purchase could be had,
Eight lusty fellows, straight and tall,
I shouldn't find the wherewithal
To buy them.' But it was a lie;
For not a single wretch had I—
No single cripple fit to bear
A broken bedstead or a chair.
She, like a strumpet, pert and knowing,
Said— 'Dear Catullus, I am going
To worship at Serapis' shrine—
Do lend me, pray, those slaves of thine.'
I answered— 'It was idly said,—
They were a purchase Cinna made
(Caius Cinna, my good friend)—
It was the same thing in the end,
Whether a purchase or a loan—
I always used them as my own;
Only the phrase was inexact—
He bought them for himself in fact.
But you have caught the general vice
Of being too correct and nice,
Over curious and precise;
And seizing with precipitation
The slight neglects of conversation.'


FROM THE FRENCH OF JEAN DE LA FONTAINE

350       *'Aesop's Fable of the Frogs'*

The Frogs time out of mind
        Lived uncontroll'd.
    Their form of government was undefined,
        But reasons, strong and manifold,
    Which then were given,
Induced them to demand a King from Heaven.
        Jove heard the prayer, and to fulfil it,
        Threw them down a Log or Billet:

The Prince arrived with such a dash,
    Coming down to take possession;
Frogs are easy to abash,
    Their valour is diluted with discretion,—
In a word, their hearts forsook them:
    That instant they dissolved the Session,
Choosing the shortest way that took them
    Down to the bottom of the Bog,—
Not one remained to cry, 'God save King Log.'
There was an ancient flap-chapp'd Peer,
        Nobly born
        Of the best spawn;
    At first he kept aloof from fear,
    Waiting the close of all this storm,
    Till things should take some settled form—
        Like a great vassal
        In his castle,
        With full-blown bags,
Intrench'd with lofty bulrushes and flags.
A wish to gain the sovereign's ear
    Made him draw near;
He saw him where he lay in state
    With a solidity and weight
    That bespoke him truly great.
Then came a shoal in quest of posts and charges,
Much like our ancient courtiers with their barges,
    They ventured barely within reach—
    The Chancellor discharged a speech:
They waited for his majesty's reply,—
They waited a long, tedious, awkward space,
    Then stared each other in the face,
        And drew more nigh,—
        Till growing bolder,
    They leap'd upon the back and shoulder
        Of their Stadholder.
The worthy monarch all that while
Was never seen to frown or smile,
He never look'd, he never stirr'd,—
He never spoke a single word,
        Bad or good.
    It seem'd as if he never heard
        Nor understood.

The Frogs, like Russian nobles in such cases,
Reading each others' meaning in their faces,
　　　Proceeded to the monarch's deposition,—
　　　This act was follow'd by preferring
　　　　A new Petition
For a new Prince more active and more stirring.
　　　The prayer was heard;
　　　To make quick work,
　　Jove sent them down the Stork,
　　First cousin to the Secretary Bird.
His forte was business and despatch:
　　　At the first snatch
He swallow'd the Polonius of the Pool;
Then following Machiavelli's rule,
He fell upon the poor Marsh-landers,
Conscribing all that he could catch,
Trampling them down into the mud,
Confiscating their guts and blood,
Like a French Prefect sent to Flanders.
The wretched Frogs in their despair
　　　　　Renew'd their prayer;
And Jove in answer thunder'd this decree,—
　　　'Since you could not agree
　　　To live content and free,
I sent you down a King of the best wood,
　　　Suited to your pacific brood;
　　　Your foolish pride
　　　Set him aside;
This second was intended for a curse,—
Be satisfied—or I shall find a worse.'

# WILLIAM WORDSWORTH

## 1770–1850

### FROM THE LATIN OF CATULLUS

351                        *Carmina*, V

Cp.
Ralegh
Jonson
Crashaw
Landor

My Lesbia let us love and live,
And to the winds my Lesbia give
Each cold restraint, each boding fear
Of Age and all her saws severe.
Yon sun now posting to the main
Will set—but 'tis to rise again;
But we, when once our [      ] light
Is set, must sleep in endless night.
Then come, with whom alone I live,
A thousand kisses take or give,
Another thousand—to the store
Add hundreds—then a thousand more,
And when they to a million mount
Let Confusion take the account,
That you, the number never knowing,
May continue still bestowing,
That I for joys may never pine
That never can again be mine.

### FROM THE LATIN OF MICHELANGELO

352 Yes! hope may with my strong desire keep pace,
And I be undeluded, unbetrayed;
For if of our affections none finds grace
In sight of Heaven, then, wherefore hath God made
The world which we inhabit? Better plea
Love cannot have, than that in loving thee
Glory to that eternal Peace is paid,
Who such divinity to thee imparts
As hallows and makes pure all gentle hearts.

338

His hope is treacherous only whose love dies
With beauty, which is varying every hour;
But, in chaste hearts uninfluenced by the power
Of outward change, there blooms a deathless flower,
That breathes on earth the air of paradise.

## FROM THE LATIN OF THOMAS WHARTON THE YOUNGER

353     Come, gentle Sleep, Death's image though thou art,
Come share my couch nor speedily depart;
How sweet thus living without life to lie,
Thus without death how sweet it is to die.

# SIR WALTER SCOTT

1771–1832

## FROM THE GERMAN OF
## JOHANN WOLFGANG VON GOETHE

354          *The Erl-King*

O who rides by night thro' the woodland so wild?
It is the fond father embracing his child;
And close the boy nestles within his loved arm,
To hold himself fast, and to keep himself warm.

'O father, see yonder! see yonder!' he says;
'My boy, upon what dost thou fearfully gaze?'
'O, 'tis the Erl-King with his crown and his shroud.'
'No, my son, it is but a dark wreath of the cloud.'

### THE ERL-KING SPEAKS

'O come and go with me, thou loveliest child;
By many a gay sport shall thy time be beguiled;
My mother keeps for thee full many a fair toy,
And many a fine flower shall she pluck for my boy.'

'O father, my father, and did you not hear
The Erl-King whisper so low in my ear?'
'Be still, my heart's darling—my child, be at ease;
It was but the wild blast as it sung thro' the trees.'

### ERL-KING

'O wilt thou go with me, thou loveliest boy?
My daughter shall tend thee with care and with joy;
She shall bear thee so lightly thro' wet and thro' wild,
And press thee, and kiss thee, and sing to my child.'

'O father, my father, and saw you not plain
The Erl-King's pale daughter glide past thro' the rain?'
'O yes, my loved treasure, I knew it full soon;
It was the grey willow that danced to the moon.'

### ERL-KING

'O come and go with me, no longer delay,
Or else, silly child, I will drag thee away.'
'O father! O father! now, now, keep your hold,
The Erl-King has seized me—his grasp is so cold!'

Sore trembled the father; he spurr'd thro' the wild,
Clasping close to his bosom his shuddering child;
He reaches his dwelling in doubt and in dread,
But, clasp'd to his bosom, the infant was dead.

# SAMUEL TAYLOR COLERIDGE

### 1772–1834

#### FROM THE GERMAN (ANONYMOUS)

355        *Westphalian Song*

When thou to my true love com'st
   Greet her from me kindly;
When she asks thee how I fare?
   Say, folks in Heaven fare finely.

When she asks, 'What! Is he sick?'
  Say, dead!—and when for sorrow
She begins to sob and cry,
  Say, I come to-morrow.

FROM THE GERMAN OF FRIEDRICH VON SCHILLER

356                  *The Visit of the Gods*

          Never, believe me,
          Appear the Immortals,
            Never alone:
Scarce had I welcomed the sorrow-beguiler,
Iacchus! but in came boy Cupid the smiler;
Lo! Phœbus the glorious descends from his throne!
They advance, they float in, the Olympians all!
          With divinities fills my
            Terrestrial hall!
          How shall I yield you
          Due entertainment,
            Celestial quire?
Me rather, bright guests! with your wings of upbuoyance
Bear aloft to your homes, to your banquets of joyance,
That the roofs of Olympus may echo my lyre!
Hah! we mount! on their pinions they waft up my soul!
          O give me the nectar!
          O fill me the bowl!

          Give him the nectar!
          Pour out for the poet,
            Hebe! pour free!
Quicken his eyes with celestial dew,
That Styx the detested no more he may view,
And like one of us Gods may conceit him to be!
Thanks, Hebe! I quaff it! Io Pæan, I cry!
          The wine of the Immortals
            Forbids me to die!

341

# WALTER SAVAGE LANDOR

1775–1864

## EXPANDED FROM THE GREEK OF SAPPHO

**357**
Cp.
Young

Mother, I cannot mind my wheel;
　My fingers ache, my lips are dry:
Oh! if you felt the pain I feel!
　But Oh, who ever felt as I?

No longer could I doubt him true;
　All other men may use deceit:
He always said my eyes were blue,
　And often swore my lips were sweet.

## FROM THE LATIN OF CATULLUS

**358**

### *Carmina*, V
*To Lesbia*

Cp.
Ralegh
Jonson
Crashaw
Wordsworth

Yes! my Lesbia! let us prove
All the sweets of life in love.
Let us laugh at envious sneers;
Envy is the fault of years.
Vague report let us despise;
Suns may set and suns may rise:
We, when sets *our* twinkling light,
Sleep a long-continued night.
Make we then, the most of this—
Let us kiss, and kiss, and kiss.
While we thus the night employ,
Envy cannot know our joy.
So, my Lesbia! let us prove
All the sweets of life in love.

359          *Carmina*, XXXIX

Egnatius has fine teeth, and those
Eternally Egnatius shows.
Some criminal is being tried
For murder; and they open wide.
A widow wails her only son;
Widow and him they open on.
'Tis a disease, I'm very sure,
And wish 'twere such as you could cure,
My good Egnatius! for what's half
So silly as a silly laugh?

360          *Carmina*, LXXV

Cp.
Brown
Swift

None could ever say that she,
Lesbia! was so loved by me.
Never all the world around
Faith so true as mine was found:
If no longer it endures
(Would it did!) the fault is yours.
I can never think again
Well of you: I try in vain:
But—be false—do what you will—
Lesbia! I must love you still.

361          *Carmina*, LXXXV

Cp.
Lovelace
Pound

I love and hate. Ah! never ask why so!
I hate and love—and that is all I know.
I see 'tis folly, but I feel 'tis woe.

# FRANCIS HOWES

## 1776–1844

### FROM THE LATIN OF HORACE

*from* Epistles, Book I, 7

### To Maecenas

Your kindness, sir, to me, is really kind;—
Not like the boons of some Calabrian hind
With fulsome zeal that will not be repressed
Forcing his pears upon the sated guest.
'Come, eat them, pray!'—'I've eaten all I would.'
'Then pocket what you please.'—'You're very good.
Your infant tribe would deem them no bad store.
I'm as obliged as if I took a score.'
'Well please yourself; but know, what you decline
Will fall ere night a portion to the swine.'
   The spendthrift and the fool are so polite,
They give to others what they hate or slight;
And where love's seed is sown with hand so rude,
No wonder if the crop's ingratitude.

*

   Philippus, for his pleadings famed afar,
Alert and bold, returning from the Bar
About the hour of two one sultry day,
And now complaining that the length of way
Grew for his years too much, espied ('tis said)
A smug-faced cit beneath a barber's shed
Paring his nails with easy unconcern;—
Then called his lackey—'Boy, step in and learn
Who this may be—his family—his fame—
Where he resides—and what's his patron's name.'
The lad (by name Demetrius) lacked not skill
Or promptness to despatch his master's will.
He flies—returns—informs him in a trice,
'Twas one Vulteius Mena, pure from vice,
Of humble means, by trade an auctioneer,
Who bustled to and fro to raise the gear,

Lounged when his daily toils were at an end,
Was fain to get, but not afraid to spend;—
Mixed with acquaintance of his own degree,
Had a fixed dwelling, and enjoyed with glee
The public shows; or, when his work was done,
In Mars's field at tennis would make one.
'Troth, I should like to know the wight; go, say
I should be glad he'd dine with me to-day.'
Mena, the message heard, in mute surprise
Stares, and can scarce believe his ears and eyes;
Begs his devout acknowledgments,—in sum
Feels flattered and obliged, but cannot come.
'How! does the wretch then slight me?'—'Even so,
And through contempt or shyness answers, no.'
Next morning, as Philippus strolls along,
He 'spies Vulteius to a tunic'd throng
Vending cheap wares, and having crossed the street,
Makes toward his client and is first to greet.
He, humbly bowing, pleads the ties of trade
And business, that he had not early paid
His compliments; ev'n now, in toils immersed,
Is shocked to think he had not hailed him first.
'On one condition be your pleas allowed—
Dine with me to-day.'—'Sir, I shall be proud.'
'Enough—you'll come at the ninth hour; till which
Go, ply your trade and labour to be rich.'
The hour arrives—he goes—and having said
Some wisdom and some foolery, hies to bed.
Day after day when thus he kindly took
The flattering bait and nibbled round the hook,
A morning dangler now and constant guest;
What time the Latian festival gives rest
To wrangling law-courts, he's invited down
To see his patron's seat not far from town,
Perched in the chaise, he lauds in terms most high
The golden crops, green lawns, and Sabine sky.
Philippus, much diverted all the while,
Sees his scheme work and sees it with a smile,
Resolved with all chance pastime care to drown.
In short, seven thousand sesterces paid down,
With seven more proffered at an easy rate,
Tempt him to buy and farm a snug estate.

'Tis bought; and (not to spin my story out)
The smart cit drops into the rustic lout;—
He prattles of his tilth and vines—prepares
His elms—and launches in a sea of cares,
Stung to the quick with gain's delusive itch
And pining with the thirst of waxing rich.
Soon after (mark the change!) night-plunderers seize
His lambs; his she goats perish with disease;
Now blighted harvests mock his hopes; and now
The jaded ox drops dead beneath his plough.
Teased with his losses, cursing fortune's spite,
Snatching his nag at the mid hour of night,
Half-frantic to his patron's seat he goes,
Unshorn, with squalid garb that speaks his woes.
'How now!' Philippus cries, 'Your looks are such,
I fear you drudge too hard and toil too much.'
'Troth, patron! to this merit I've no claim;
Wretched I am, and that's my proper name.
Then oh! by all the ties of faith and love,
By all your boons, and by the powers above,
Kind sir! I do conjure you and implore,
Replace me in my pristine state once more.'
  The moral of my tale is briefly this:
Let him who finds that he has changed amiss,
And that his promised joy turns out but pain,
With all convenient speed change back again!
'Tis a sound rule that each man has his pleasure,
And each should mete himself by his own measure.

FROM THE ITALIAN OF TASSO

363            *Aminta*, Chorus I

O lovely age of gold!
Not that the rivers rolled
With milk, or that the woods wept honeydew;
Not that the ready ground
Produced without a wound,
Or the mild serpent had no tooth that slew;
Not that a cloudless blue
For ever was in sight,
Or that the heaven, which burns
And now is cold by turns,
Looked out in glad and everlasting light;
No, nor that even the insolent ships from far
Brought war to no new lands nor riches worse than war:

But solely that that vain
And breath-invented pain,
That idol of mistake, that worshipped cheat,
That Honour,—since so called
By vulgar minds appalled,—
Played not the tyrant with our nature yet.
It had not come to fret
The sweet and happy fold
Of gentle human-kind;
Nor did its hard law bind
Souls nursed in freedom; but that law of gold,
That glad and golden law, all free, all fitted,
Which Nature's own hand wrote,—What pleases is permitted.

Then among streams and flowers
The little winged powers
Went singing carols without torch or bow;
The nymphs and shepherds sat
Mingling with innocent chat

Sports and low whispers; and with whispers low,
Kisses that would not go.
The maiden, budding o'er,
Kept not her bloom uneyed,
Which now a veil must hide,
Nor the crisp apples which her bosom bore;
And oftentimes, in river or in lake,
The lover and his love their merry bath would take.

'Twas thou, thou, Honour, first
That didst deny our thirst
Its drink, and on the fount thy covering set;
Thou bad'st kind eyes withdraw
Into constrained awe,
And keep the secret for their tears to wet;
Thou gather'dst in a net
The tresses from the air,
And mad'st the sports and plays
Turn all to sullen ways,
And putt'st on speech a rein, in steps a care.
Thy work it is,—thou shade, that wilt not move,—
That what was once the gift is now the theft of Love.
Our sorrows and our pains,
These are thy noble gains.
But, O, thou Love's and Nature's masterer,
Thou conqueror of the crowned,
What dost thou on this ground,
Too small a circle for thy mighty sphere?
Go, and make slumber dear
To the renowned and high;
We here, a lowly race,
Can live without thy grace,
After the use of mild antiquity.
Go, let us love; since years
No truce allow, and life soon disappears;
Go, let us love; the daylight dies, is born;
But unto us the light
Dies once for all; and sleep brings on eternal night.

## FROM THE ITALIAN OF FRANCESCO REDI

364          *from* Bacchus in Tuscany

### 'Bacchus's Opinion of Wine, and Other Beverages'

Give me, give me Buriano,
Trebbiano, Colombano,—
Give me bumpers, rich and clear!
'Tis the true old Aurum Potabile,
Gilding life when it wears shabbily:
Helen's old Nepenthe 'tis
That in the drinking
Swallowed thinking,
And was the receipt for bliss.
Thence it is, that ever and ay,
When he doth philosophize,
Good old glorious Rucellai
Hath it for light unto his eyes;
He lifteth it, and by the shine
Well discerneth things divine:
Atoms with their airy justles,
And all manner of corpuscles;
And, as through a crystal skylight,
How morning differeth from evening twilight;
And further telleth us the reason why go
Some stars with such a lazy light, and some with a vertigo.

O, how widely wandereth he,
Who in search of verity
Keeps aloof from glorious wine!
Lo, the knowledge it bringeth to me!
For Barbarossa, this wine so bright,
With its rich red look and its strawberry light,
So inviteth me,
So delighteth me,
I should infallibly quench my inside with it,
Had not Hippocrates
And old Andromachus
Strictly forbidden it
And loudly chidden it,
So many stomachs have sickened and died with it.

Yet, discordant as it is,.
Two good biggins will not come amiss;
Because I know, while I'm drinking them down,
What is the finish and what is the crown.
A cup of good Corsican
Does it at once;
Or a glass of old Spanish
Is neat for the nonce:
Quackish resources are things for a dunce.

Talk of Chocolate!
Talk of Tea!
Medicines made—ye gods!—as they are,
Are no medicines made for me.
I would sooner take to poison
Than a single cup set eyes on
Of that bitter and guilty stuff ye
Talk of by the name of Coffee.
Let the Arabs and the Turks
Count it 'mongst their cruel works:
Foe of mankind, black and turbid,
Let the throats of slaves absorb it.
Down in Tartarus,
Down in Erebus,
'Twas the detestable Fifty invented it;
The Furies then took it
To grind and to cook it,
And to Proserpina all three presented it.
If the Mussulman in Asia
Doats on a beverage so unseemly,
I differ with the man extremely.

*

There's a squalid thing, called Beer:
The man whose lips that thing comes near
Swiftly dies; or falling foolish,
Grows, at forty, old and owlish.
She that in the ground would hide her,
Let her take to English Cider:
He who'd have his death come quicker,
Any other Northern liquor.
Those Norwegians and those Laps
Have extraordinary taps:

Those Laps especially have strange fancies;
To see them drink,
I verily think,
Would make me lose my senses.
But a truce to such vile subjects,
With their impious, shocking objects.
Let me purify my mouth
In a holy cup o' th' South;
In a golden pitcher let me
Head and ears for comfort get me,
And drink of the wine of the vine benign
That sparkles warm in Sansovine.

# LORD GEORGE GORDON BYRON

## 1788–1824

### A BURLESQUE FROM THE GREEK OF EURIPIDES

365　　*The Nurse's Dole in the Medea*

Oh how I wish that an embargo
Had kept in port the good ship Argo!
Who, still unlaunch'd from Grecian docks,
Had never pass'd the Azure rocks;
But now I fear her trip will be a
Damn'd business for my Miss Medea, &c. &c.

### FROM THE LATIN OF MARTIAL

366　　*Epigrams*, Book I, 1

He unto whom thou art so partial,
Oh, reader! is the well-known Martial,
The Epigrammatist: while living,
Give him the fame thou wouldst be giving;
So shall he hear, and feel, and know it—
　　Post-obits rarely reach a poet.

## FROM THE LATIN OF THE EMPEROR HADRIAN

367     *Hadrian's Address to his Soul when Dying*

Cp.
Prior
Cunningham
Stevie Smith

Ah! gentle, fleeting, wav'ring sprite,
Friend and associate of this clay!
     To what unknown region borne,
Wilt thou now wing thy distant flight?
No more with wonted humour gay,
     But pallid, cheerless, and forlorn.


# PERCY BYSSHE SHELLEY

### 1792–1822

### FROM THE GREEK

368          from *Homer's Hymn to Mercury*
                (Authorship and date uncertain)

... Seized with a sudden fancy for fresh meat,
He in his sacred crib deposited
     The hollow lyre, and from the cavern sweet
Rushed with great leaps up to the mountain's head,
     Revolving in his mind some subtle feat
Of thievish craft, such as a swindler might
Devise in the lone season of dun night.

Lo! the great Sun under the ocean's bed has
     Driven steeds and chariot—the child meanwhile strode
O'er the Pierian mountains clothed in shadows,
     Where the immortal oxen of the God
Are pastured in the flowering unmown meadows,
     And safely stalled in a remote abode.—
The archer Argicide, elate and proud,
Drove fifty from the herd, lowing aloud.

368 The archer Argicide] Mercury

He drove them wandering o'er the sandy way,
    But, being ever mindful of his craft,
Backward and forward drove he them astray,
    So that the tracks which seemed before, were aft;
His sandals then he threw to the ocean spray,
    And for each foot he wrought a kind of raft
Of tamarisk, and tamarisk-like sprigs,
And bound them in a lump with withy twigs.

And on his feet he tied these sandals light;
    The trail of whose wide leaves might not betray
    His track; and then, a self-sufficing wight,
Like a man hastening on some distant way,
    He from Pieria's mountain bent his flight;
But an old man perceived the infant pass
Down green Onchestus heaped like beds with grass.

The old man stood dressing his sunny vine:
    'Halloo! old fellow with the crookèd shoulder!
You grub those stumps? before they will bear wine:
    Methinks even you must grow a little older:
Attend, I pray, to this advice of mine:
    As you would 'scape what might appal a bolder—
Seeing, see not—and hearing, hear not—and—
If you have understanding—understand.'

So saying, Hermes roused the oxen vast;
    O'er shadowy mountain and resounding dell,
And flower-paven plains, great Hermes passed;
    Till the black night divine, which favouring fell
Around his steps, grew gray, and morning fast
    Wakened the world to work, and from her cell
Sea-strewn, the Pallantean Moon sublime
Into her watch-tower just began to climb.

Now to Alpheus he had driven all
    The broad-foreheaded oxen of the Sun;
They came unwearied to the lofty stall
    And to the water-troughs which ever run
Through the fresh fields—and when with rushgrass tall,
    Lotus and all sweet herbage, every one
Had pastured been, the great God made them move
Towards the stall in a collected drove.

A mighty pile of wood the God then heaped,
  And having soon conceived the mystery
Of fire, from two smooth laurel branches stripped
  The bark, and rubbed them in his palms;—on high
Suddenly forth the burning vapour leaped
  And the divine child saw delightedly.—
Mercury first found out for human weal
Tinder-box, matches, fire-irons, flint and steel...
[*Mercury slaughters two of the cattle and apportions them among
the gods, then returns to his cradle.*]

                                    ... meanwhile the day

Aethereal born arose out of the flood
  Of flowing Ocean, bearing light to men.
Apollo passed toward the sacred wood,
  Which from the inmost depths of its green glen
Echoes the voice of Neptune,—and there stood
  On the same spot in green Onchestus then
That same old animal, the vine-dresser,
Who was employed hedging his vineyard there.

Latona's glorious Son began:—'I pray
  Tell, ancient hedger of Onchestus green,
Whether a drove of kine has passed this way,
  All heifers with crooked horns? for they have been
Stolen from the herd in high Pieria,
  Where a black bull was fed apart, between
Two woody mountains in a neighbouring glen,
And four fierce dogs watched there, unanimous as men.

'And what is strange, the author of this theft
  Has stolen the fatted heifers every one,
But the four dogs and the black bull are left:—
  Stolen they were last night at set of sun,
Of their soft beds and their sweet food bereft.—
  Now tell me, man born ere the world begun,
Have you seen anyone pass with the cows?'—
To whom the man of overhanging brows:

'My friend, it would require no common skill
  Justly to speak of everything I see:
On various purposes of good or ill
  Many pass by my vineyard,—and to me
'Tis difficult to know the invisible
  Thoughts, which in all those many minds may be:—
Thus much alone I certainly can say,
I tilled these vines till the decline of day,

'And then I thought I saw, but dare not speak
  With certainty of such a wondrous thing,
A child, who could not have been born a week,
  Those fair-horned cattle closely following,
And in his hand he held a polished stick:
  And, as on purpose, he walked wavering
From one side to the other of the road,
And with his face opposed the steps he trod.'

Apollo hearing this, passed quickly on—
  No wingèd omen could have shown more clear
That the deceiver was his father's son.
  So the God wraps a purple atmosphere
Around his shoulders, and like fire is gone
  To famous Pylos, seeking his kine there,
And found their track and his, yet hardly cold,
And cried—'What wonder do mine eyes behold!

'Here are the footsteps of the hornèd herd
  Turned back towards their fields of asphodel;—
But *these* are not the tracks of beast or bird,
  Gray wolf, or bear, or lion of the dell,
Or manèd Centaur—sand was never stirred
  By man or woman thus! Inexplicable!
Who with unwearied feet could e'er impress
The sand with such enormous vestiges?

'That was most strange—but this is stranger still!'
  Thus having said, Phoebus impetuously
Sought high Cyllene's forest-cinctured hill,
  And the deep cavern where dark shadows lie,
And where the ambrosial nymph with happy will
  Bore the Saturnian's love-child, Mercury—
And a delightful odour from the dew
Of the hill pastures, at his coming, flew.

355

And Phoebus stooped under the craggy roof
    Arched over the dark cavern:—Maia's child
Perceived that he came angry, far aloof,
    About the cows of which he had been beguiled;
And over him the fine and fragrant woof
    Of his ambrosial swaddling-clothes he piled—
As among fire-brands lies a burning spark
Covered, beneath the ashes cold and dark.

There, like an infant who had sucked his fill
    And now was newly washed and put to bed,
Awake, but courting sleep with weary will,
    And gathered in a lump, hands, feet, and head,
He lay, and his belovèd tortoise still
    He grasped and held under his shoulder-blade.
Phoebus the lovely mountain-goddess knew,
Not less her subtle, swindling baby, who

Lay swathed in his sly wiles.

## FROM THE GREEK OF PLATO

369 *To Stella*

Thou wert the morning star among the living,
    Ere thy fair light had fled;—
Now, having died, thou art as Hesperus, giving
    New splendour to the dead

370 *Kissing Helena*

Kissing Helena, together
    With my kiss, my soul beside it
        Came to my lips, and there I kept it,—
For the poor thing had wandered thither,
    To follow where the kiss should guide it,
        Oh, cruel I, to intercept it!

## FROM THE GREEK ANTHOLOGY

371 *Spirit of Plato*

Eagle! why soarest thou above that tomb?
To what sublime and star-ypaven home
    Floatest thou?—
I am the image of swift Plato's spirit.
Ascending heaven; Athens doth inherit
    His corpse below.

## FROM THE GREEK OF MOSCHUS

372    Pan loved his neighbour Echo—but that child
    Of Earth and Air pined for the Satyr leaping;
The Satyr loved with wasting madness wild
    The bright nymph Lyda,—and so three went weeping.
As Pan loved Echo, Echo loved the Satyr,
    The Satyr, Lyda; and so love consumed them.—
And thus—to each which was a woful matter—
    To bear what they inflicted Justice doomed them;
For, inasmuch as each might hate the lover,
    Each, loving, so was hated. Ye that love not
Be warned—in thought turn this example over,
    That when ye love, the like return ye prove not.

373    When winds that move not its calm surface sweep
The azure sea, I love the land no more;
The smiles of the serene and tranquil deep
Tempt my unquiet mind.—But when the roar
Of Ocean's grey abyss resounds, and foam
Gathers upon the sea, and vast waves burst,
I turn from the drear aspect to the home
Of earth and its deep woods, where interspersed,
When winds blow loud, pines make sweet melody.
Whose house is some lone bark, whose toil the sea,
Whose prey the wondering fish, an evil lot
Has chosen.—But I my languid limbs will fling
Beneath the plane, where the brook's murmuring
Moves the calm spirit, but disturbs it not.

## FROM THE ITALIAN OF CAVALCANTI

374      *Sonnet: Guido Cavalcanti to Dante*

Returning from its daily quest, my Spirit
Changed thoughts and vile in thee doth weep to find:
It grieves me that thy mild and gentle mind
Those ample virtues which it did inherit
Has lost. Once thou didst loathe the multitude
Of blind and madding men—I then loved thee—
I loved thy lofty songs and that sweet mood
When thou wert faithful to thyself and me.
I dare not now through thy degraded state
Own the delight thy strains inspire—in vain
I seek what once thou wert—we cannot meet
And we were wont. Again and yet again
Ponder my words: so the false Spirit shall fly
And leave to thee thy true integrity.

## FROM THE ITALIAN OF DANTE

375   *Sonnet: Dante Alighieri to Guido Cavalcanti*

Guido, I would that Lapo, thou, and I,
Led by some strong enchantment, might ascend
A magic ship, whose charmed sails should fly
With winds at will where'er our thoughts might wend,
So that no change, nor any evil chance
Should mar our joyous voyage; but it might be
That even satiety should still enhance
Between our hearts their strict community:
And that the bounteous wizard then would place
Vanna and Bice and my gentle love
Companions of our wandering, and would grace
With passionate talk, wherever we might rove,
Our time, and each were as content and free
As I believe that thou and I should be.

PERCY BYSSHE SHELLEY

376 *The First Canzone of the Convito*

Ye who intelligent the third Heaven move,
Hear the discourse which is within my heart,
Which cannot be declared, it seems so new;
The Heaven whose course follows your power and art,
O gentle creatures that ye are, out of
The state in which I find myself, me drew,
And therefore may I dare to speak to you,
Even of the life which now I live—and yet
I pray that ye will hear me when I cry,
And tell of my own heart this novelty,
How the lamenting spirit moans in it;
And how a voice there murmurs against her
Who came on the refulgence of your sphere.

A sweet thought, which was once the life within
My heavy heart, many a time and oft
Went up before our Father's feet, and there
It saw a glorious lady throned aloft,
And its sweet talk of her my soul did win
So that it said, 'Thither I too will fare'.
That thought is fled, and one doth now appear
Which tyrannizes me with such fierce stress
That my heart trembles—you may see it leap—
And on another lady makes me keep
Mine eyes, and say, 'Who would have blessedness,
Let him but look upon that lady's eyes,
Let him not fear the agony of sighs.'

This lowly thought, which once would talk with me
Of a bright seraph sitting crowned on high,
Found such a cruel foe, it died, and so
My spirit wept—the grief is not even now [gone by]—
And said, 'Alas for me, how swift could flee
That piteous thought which did my life console!'
And the afflicted one questioning
Mine eyes, if such a lady saw they never
And why they would
I said, 'Beneath her eyes might stand for ever
He whom direct regards must kill with awe.'

To have known their power stood me in little stead—
Those eyes have looked on me and I am dead.

'Thou art not dead—but thou has[t] wanderèd,
Thou soul of ours, who thus thyself dost fret,'
A spirit of gentle love beside me said,
'For that fair lady whom thou dost regret
Hath so transformed the life which once she led,
Thou fearest it—so worthless art thou made.
And see how meek, how pitiful, how staid
Yet courteous in her majesty she is;
And still call her     woman in thy thought
Her, whom if thou thyself deceivest not,
Thou wilt behold decked with such loveliness,
That thou wilt cry: 'Only Lord, lo there
Thy handmaiden—do what thou wilt with her!'

My song, I fear that thou wilt find but few
Who fitly shall conceive thy reasoning,
Of such hard matter dost thou entertain;
Whence, if by misadventure, chance should bring
Thee to base company (as chance may do),
Quite unaware of what thou dost contain,
I prithee, comfort thy sweet self again,
My last delight! tell them that they are dull,
And bid them own that thou art beautiful.

[Left unrevised]


377        The Purgatorio, Canto XXVIII

           *Matilda Gathering Flowers*

Earnest to explore within and all around
The divine wood, whose thick green living woof
Tempered the young day to the sight, I wound

Up the [green] slope, beneath the [forest's] roof
With slow soft steps, leaving the abrupt steep
And the                                    aloof.

A gentle air which had within itself
No motion struck upon my forehead bare,
The soft stroke of a continuous wind

In which the passive leaves tremblingly were
All bent towards that [part], where earliest
That sacred hill obscures the morning air;

Yet were they not so shaken from their rest
But that the birds, perched on the utmost spray,
[Incessantly] renewing their blithe quest

With perfect joy received the early day,
Singing within the glancing leaves, whose sound
Kept one low burthen to their roundelay,

Such as from bough to bough gathers around
The pine forest on bleak Chiassi's shore,
When Aeolus Scirocco has unbound.

My slow steps had already borne me o'er
Such space within the antique wood, that I
Perceived not where I entered any more;

When lo, a stream whose little waves went by,
Bending towards the left the grass that grew
Upon its bank, impeded suddenly

My going on—waters of purest hue
On earth, would appear turbid and impure
Compared with this, whose unconcealing dew

Dark, dark [yet] clear moved under the obscure
Eternal shades, whose                    [glooms]
The rays of moon or sunlight ne'er endure.

I moved not with my feet, but amid the glooms
I pierced with my charmed sight, contemplating
The mighty multitude of fresh May blooms;

And then appeared to me, even like a thing
Which suddenly for blank astonishment
Dissolves all other thought,

A solitary woman, and she went
Singing and gathering flower after flower
With which her way was painted and besprent.

Bright lady, who if looks had ever power
To bear [firm] witness of the heart within,
Dost bask under the beams of love, come lower

[Towards] this bank, I prithee let me win
Thus much of thee, that thou shouldst come anear
So I may hear thy song; like Proserpine

Thou seemest to my fancy, singing here
And gathering flowers, at that time when
She lost the spring and Ceres her ... more dear.

## FROM THE GERMAN OF JOHANN WOLFGANG GOETHE

### Faust

378  *The Chorus of the Archangels*

*Raphael*
The Sun makes music as of old
    Amid the rival spheres of Heaven,
On its predestined circle rolled
    With thunder speed: the Angels even
Draw strength from gazing on its glance,
    Though none its meaning fathom may:—
The world's unwithered countenance
    Is bright as at Creation's day.

*Gabriel*
And swift, and swift, with rapid lightness,
    The adornèd earth spins silently,
Alternating Elysian brightness
    With deep and dreadful night; the sea
Foams in broad billows from its deep
    Up to the rocks, and rocks and Ocean,
Onward, with spheres which never sleep,
    Are hurried in eternal motion.

*Michael*

And tempests in contention roar
  From land to sea, from sea to land;
And raging, weave a chain of power,
  Which girds the earth, as with a band.—
A flashing desolation there,
  Flames before the thunder's way;
But thy servants, Lord, revere
  The gentle changes of thy day.

*Chorus of the Three*

The Angels draw strength from thy glance,
  Though no one comprehend thee may:—
Thy world's unwithered countenance
  Is bright as on Creation's day.

379          *Shelley's 'literal' version*

*Raphael*

The sun sounds, according to ancient custom,
  In the song of emulation of his brother-spheres.
And its fore-written circle
  Fulfils with a step of thunder.
Its countenance gives the Angels strength
  Though no one can fathom it.
The incredible high works
  Are excellent as at the first day.

*Gabriel*

And swift, and inconceivably swift
  The adornment of the earth winds itself round
And exchanges Paradise-clearness
  With deep dreadful night.
The sea foams in broad waves
  From its deep bottom up to the rocks
And rocks and sea are torn on together
  In the eternal swift course of the spheres.

*Michael*

And storms roar in emulation
   From sea to land, from land to sea,
And make, raging, a chain
   Of deepest operation round about.
There flames a flashing destruction
   Before the path of the thunderbolt.
But thy servants, lord, revere
   The gentle alternations of thy day.

*Chorus*

Thy countenance gives the Angels strength,
   Though none can comprehend thee:
And all thy lofty works
   Are excellent as at the first day.

# JOHN KEATS

## 1795–1821

### FROM THE FRENCH OF PIERRE DE RONSARD

380    Nature withheld Cassandra in the skies,
    For more adornment, a full thousand years;
    She took their cream of Beauty's fairest dyes,
    And shaped and tinted her above all peers:
    Meanwhile Love kept her dearly with his wings,
    And underneath their shadow filled her eyes
    With such a richness that the cloudy Kings
    Of high Olympus uttered slavish sighs.
    When from the Heavens I saw her first descend,
    My heart took fire, and only burning pains ...
    They were my pleasures—they my Life's sad end;
    Love poured her beauty into my warm veins ...

        [Free and probably unfinished.]

# THOMAS LOVELL BEDDOES

## 1803–1849

### FROM THE GERMAN OF
### WALTHER VON DER VOGELWEIDE

*Song*

I

Under the lime-tree, on the daisied ground,
  Two that I know of made their bed;
There you may see, heaped and scattered round,
  Grass and blossoms, broken and shed,
All in a thicket down in the dale;
        Tandaradei—
Sweetly sang the nightingale.


II

Ere I set foot in the meadow, already
  Some one was waiting for somebody;
There was a meeting—O gracious Lady!
  There is no pleasure again for me.
Thousands of kisses there he took—
        Tandaradei—
See my lips, how red they look!


III

Leaf and blossom he had pulled and piled
  For a couch, a green one, soft and high;
And many a one hath gazed and smiled,
  Passing the bower and pressed grass by;
And the roses crushed hath seen—
        Tandaradei—
Where I laid my head between.

IV

In this love passage, if any one had been there,
  How sad and shamed should I be!
But what were we a-doing alone among the green there,
  No soul shall ever know except my love and me,
And the little nightingale.—
      Tandaradei—
She, I think, will tell no tale.


# ELIZUR WRIGHT

## 1804–1885

### FROM THE FRENCH OF JEAN DE LA FONTAINE

382                *The Wolf and the Dog*

A prowling wolf, whose shaggy skin
(So strict the watch of dogs had been)
    Hid little but his bones,
Once met a mastiff dog astray.
A prouder, fatter, sleeker Tray,
    No human mortal owns.
Sir Wolf in famish'd plight,
      Would fain have made a ration
      Upon his fat relation;
But then he first must fight;
      And well the dog seem'd able
      To save from wolfish table
His carcass snug and tight.
      So, then, in civil conversation
      The wolf express'd his admiration
Of Tray's fine case. Said Tray, politely,
Yourself, good sir, may be as sightly,
      Quit but the woods, advised by me.
      For all your fellows here, I see,
Are shabby wretches, lean and gaunt,
Belike to die of haggard want.
With such a pack, of course it follows,
One fights for every bit he swallows.

Come, then, with me, and share
On equal terms our princely fare.
    But what with you
    Has one to do?
Inquires the wolf. Light work indeed,
Replies the dog; you only need
    To bark a little now and then,
    To chase off duns and beggar men,
To fawn on friends that come or go forth,
Your master please, and so forth;
    For which you have to eat
    All sorts of well-cook'd meat—
Cold pullets, pigeons, savoury messes—
Besides unnumber'd fond caresses.
    The wolf, by force of appetite,
    Accepts the terms outright,
    Tears glistening in his eyes,
    But faring on, he spies
        A gall'd spot on the mastiff's neck.
What's that? he cries. O, nothing but a speck.
A speck? Ay, ay; 'tis not enough to pain me;
Perhaps the collar's mark by which they chain me.
  Chain! chain you! What! run you not, then,
  Just where you please, and when?
    Not always, sir; but what of that?
    Enough for me, to spoil your fat!
    It ought to be a precious price
    Which could to servile chains entice;
    For me, I'll shun them while I've wit.
    So ran Sir Wolf, and runneth yet.

383       *The City Rat and the Country Rat*

      A city rat, one night,
        Did with a civil stoop
      A country rat invite
        To end a turtle soup.

      Upon a Turkey carpet
        They found the table spread,
      And sure I need not harp it
        How well the fellows fed.

The entertainment was
   A truly noble one;
But some unlucky cause
   Disturb'd it when begun.

It was a slight rat-tat,
   That put their joys to rout;
Out ran the city rat;
   His guest, too, scamper'd out.

Our rats but fairly quit,
   The fearful knocking ceased.
Return we, cried the cit,
   To finish there our feast.

No, said the rustic rat;
   To-morrow dine with me.
I'm not offended at
   Your feast so grand and free,—

For I've no fare resembling;
   But then I eat at leisure,
   And would not swap for pleasure
So mix'd with fear and trembling.


384        *The Man and his Image*

*To M. the Duke de la Rochefoucauld*

A man, who had no rivals in the love
   Which to himself he bore,
Esteem'd his own dear beauty far above
   What earth had seen before.
More than contented in his error,
He lived the foe of every mirror.
Officious fate, resolved our lover
From such an illness should recover,
Presented always to his eyes
The mute advisers which the ladies prize;—
Mirrors in parlours, inns, and shops,—
Mirrors the pocket furniture of fops,—

Mirrors on every lady's zone,
From which his face reflected shone.
What could our dear Narcissus do?
From haunts of men he now withdrew,
On purpose that his precious shape
From every mirror might escape.
   But in his forest glen alone,
     Apart from human trace,
     A watercourse,
     Of purest source,
While with unconscious gaze
He pierced its waveless face,
   Reflected back his own.
Incensed with mingled rage and fright,
He seeks to shun the odious sight;
But yet that mirror sheet, so clear and still,
He cannot leave, do what he will.

Ere this, my story's drift you plainly see.
From such mistake there is no mortal free.
    That obstinate self-lover
    The human soul doth cover;
The mirrors follies are of others,
In which, as all are genuine brothers,
Each soul may see to life depicted
Itself with just such faults afflicted;
And by that charming placid brook,
Needless to say, I mean your Maxim Book.

### 385     *The Eagle and the Beetle*

John Rabbit, by Dame Eagle chased,
   Was making for his hole in haste,
When, on his way, he met a beetle's burrow.
     I leave you all to think
     If such a little chink
Could to a rabbit give protection thorough.
   But, since no better could be got,
   John Rabbit there was fain to squat.
   Of course, in an asylum so absurd,
   John felt ere long the talons of the bird.

But first, the beetle, interceding, cried,
Great queen of birds, it cannot be denied,
That, maugre my protection, you can bear
My trembling guest, John Rabbit, through the air
But do not give me such affront, I pray;
And since he craves your grace,
In pity of his case,
Grant him his life, or take us both away;
For he's my gossip, friend, and neighbour.
In vain the beetle's friendly labour;
The eagle clutch'd her prey without reply,
And as she flapp'd her vasty wings to fly,
Struck down our orator and still'd him;
The wonder is she hadn't kill'd him.
The beetle soon, of sweet revenge in quest,
Flew to the old, gnarl'd mountain oak
Which proudly bore that haughty eagle's nest.
And while the bird was gone,
Her eggs, her cherish'd eggs, he broke,
Not sparing one.
Returning from her flight, the eagle's cry,
Of rage and bitter anguish, fill'd the sky.
But, by excess of passion blind,
Her enemy she fail'd to find.
Her wrath in vain, that year it was her fate
To live a mourning mother, desolate.
The next, she built a loftier nest; 'twas vain;
The beetle found and dash'd her eggs again.
John Rabbit's death was thus revenged anew.
The second mourning for her murder'd brood
Was such, that through the giant mountain wood,
For six long months, the sleepless echo flew.
The bird, once Ganymede, now made
Her prayer to Jupiter for aid;
And, laying them within his godship's lap,
She thought her eggs now safe from all mishap;
The god his own could not but make them—
No wretch would venture there to break them.
And no one did. Their enemy, this time,
Upsoaring to a place sublime,
Let fall upon his royal robes some dirt,
Which Jove just shaking, with a sudden flirt,

Threw out the eggs, no one knows whither.
    When Jupiter inform'd her how th' event
    Occurr'd by purest accident,
The eagle raved; there was no reasoning with her;
    She gave out threats of leaving court,
    To make the desert her resort,
    And other braveries of this sort.
      Poor Jupiter in silence heard
      The uproar of his favourite bird.
Before his throne the beetle now appear'd,
And by a clear complaint the mystery clear'd.
The god pronounced the eagle in the wrong.
But still, their hatred was so old and strong,
    These enemies could not be reconciled;
And, that the general peace might not be spoil'd,—
The best that he could do,—the god arranged,
That thence the eagle's pairing should be changed,
To come when beetle folks are only found
    Conceal'd and dormant under ground.


# ELIZABETH BARRETT BROWNING

## 1806–1861

### FROM THE GREEK OF THEOCRITUS

386                 *Idylls*, XI

Cp.
Golding's
Ovid

And so an easier life our Cyclops drew,
    The ancient Polyphemus, who in youth
Loved Galatea while the manhood grew
    Adown his cheeks, and darkened round his mouth.
No jot he cared for apples, olives, roses;
    Love made him mad; the whole world was neglected,
The very sheep went backward to their closes
    From out the fair green pastures, self-directed.
And singing Galatea, thus, he wore
The sunrise down along the weedy shore,
    And pined alone, and felt the cruel wound
Beneath his heart, which Cypris' arrow bore,
    With a deep pang; but, so, the cure was found;

And, sitting on a lofty rock, he cast
His eyes upon the sea, and sang at last:
  'O whitest Galatea, can it be
  That thou shouldst spurn me off who love thee so?
More white than curds, my girl, thou art to see,
More meek than lambs, more full of leaping glee
  Than kids, and brighter than the early glow
On grapes that swell to ripen,—sour like thee!
Thou comest to me with the fragrant sleep,
  And with the fragrant sleep thou goest from me;
  Thou fliest ... fliest as a frightened sheep
  Flies the grey wolf!—yet Love did overcome me,
So long;—I loved thee, maiden, first of all,
  When down the hills (my mother fast beside thee)
I saw thee stray to pluck the summer-fall
  Of hyacinth bells, and went myself to guide thee;
And since my eyes have seen thee, they can leave thee
  No more, from that day's light! But thou ... by Zeus,
Thou wilt not care for *that*, to let it grieve thee!
  I know thee, fair one, why thou springest loose
From my arm round thee. Why? I tell thee, Dear!
  One shaggy eyebrow draws its smudging road
Straight through my ample front, from ear to ear,—
  One eye rolls underneath; and yawning, broad,
Flat nostrils feel the bulging lips too near.
Yet ... ho, ho!—*I*,—whatever I appear,—
  Do feed a thousand oxen! When I have done,
I milk the cows, and drink the milk that's best!
  I lack no cheese, while summer keeps the sun;
And after, in the cold, it's ready prest!
  And then, I know to sing, as there is none
Of all the Cyclops can, ... a song of thee,
Sweet apple of my soul, on love's fair tree,
And of myself who love thee ... till the West
Forgets the light, and all but I have rest.
I feed for thee, besides, eleven fair does,
  And all in fawn; and four tame whelps of bears.
Come to me, Sweet! thou shalt have all of those
  In change for love! I will not halve the shares.

Leave the blue sea, with pure white arms extended
　To the dry shore; and, in my cave's recess,
Thou shalt be gladder for the noonlight ended;
　For here be laurels, spiral cypresses,
Dark ivy, and a vine whose leaves enfold
Most luscious grapes; and here is water cold,
　The wooded Ætna pours down thro' the trees
From the white snows, which gods were scarce too bold
　To drink in turn with nectar. Who with these
　Would choose the salt wave of the lukewarm seas?
Nay, look on me! If I am hairy and rough,
　I have an oak's heart in me; there's a fire
In these grey ashes which burns hot enough;
　And, when I burn for *thee*, I grudge the pyre
No fuel ... not my soul, nor this one eye,—
Most precious thing I have, because thereby
I see thee, Fairest! Out, alas! I wish
My mother had borne me finnèd like a fish,
That I might plunge down in the ocean near thee,
　And kiss thy glittering hand between the weeds,
If still thy face were turned; and I would bear thee
　Each lily white, and poppy fair that bleeds
Its red heart down its leaves!—one gift, for hours
　Of summer,—one for winter; since to cheer thee,
I could not bring at once all kinds of flowers.
Even now, girl, now, I fain would learn to swim,
If stranger in a ship sailed nigh, I wis,—
　That I may know how sweet a thing it is
To live down with you in the Deep and Dim!
Come up, O Galatea, from the ocean,
　And, having come, forget again to go!
As I, who sing out here my heart's emotion,
　Could sit for ever. Come up from below!
Come, keep my flocks beside me, milk my kine,—
　Come, press my cheese, distrain my whey and curd!
Ah, mother! she alone ... that mother of mine ...
　Did wrong me sore! I blame her! Not a word
Of kindly intercession did she address
Thine ear with for my sake; and ne'ertheless
　She saw me wasting, wasting, day by day:
　Both head and feet were aching, I will say,

All sick for grief, as I myself was sick.
  O Cyclops, Cyclops! whither hast thou sent
  Thy soul on fluttering wings? If thou wert bent
On turning bowls, or pulling green and thick
    The sprouts to give thy lambkins, thou wouldst make
      thee
    A wiser Cyclops than for what we take thee.
Milk dry the present! Why pursue too quick
That future which is fugitive aright?
Thy Galatea thou shalt haply find,—
Or else a maiden fairer and more kind;
For many girls do call me thro' the night,
    And, as they call, do laugh out silvery.
    *I*, too, am something in the world, I see!'

While thus the Cyclops love and lambs did fold,
Ease came with song, he could not buy with gold.


FROM THE GERMAN OF HEINRICH HEINE

387        My child, we were two children,
        Small, merry by childhood's law;
        We used to creep to the hen-house,
        And hide ourselves in the straw.

        We crowed like cocks, and whenever
        The passers near us drew—
        Cock-a-doodle! they thought
        'Twas a real cock that crew.

        The boxes about our courtyard
        We carpeted to our mind,
        And lived there both together—
        Kept house in a noble kind.

        The neighbour's old cat often
        Came to pay us a visit;
        We made her a bow and a curtsey,
        Each with a compliment in it.

After her health we asked,
Our care and regard to evince—
(We have made the very same speeches
To many an old cat since).

We also sat and wisely
Discoursed, as old folks do,
Complaining how all went better
In those good old times we knew,—

How love and truth and believing
Had left the world to itself,
And how so dear was the coffee,
And how so rare was the pelf.

The children's games are over,
The rest is over with youth—
The world, the good games, the good times,
The belief, and the love, and the truth.

# EDWARD FITZGERALD

## 1809–1883

### FROM THE PERSIAN OF OMAR KHAYYÁM

388                    from *The Rubáiyát*

#### V*

Iram indeed is gone with all his Rose,
And Jamshyd's Sev'n-ring'd Cup where no one knows;
    But still a Ruby kindles in the Vine,
And many a Garden by the Water blows.

#### VI

And David's lips are lockt; but in divine
High-piping Pehleví, with 'Wine! Wine! Wine!
    Red Wine!'—the Nightingale cries to the Rose
That sallow cheek of hers to' incarnadine.

*

* Pound's 'Tudor indeed is gone and every rose' (Canto LXXX) alludes to
Verses V and VI above.

### XII

A Book of Verses underneath the Bough,
A Jug of Wine, a Loaf of Bread—and Thou
   Beside me singing in the Wilderness—
Oh, Wilderness were Paradise enow!

### XIII

Some for the Glories of This World; and some
Sigh for the Prophet's Paradise to come;
   Ah, take the Cash, and let the Credit go,
Nor heed the rumble of a distant Drum!

### XIV

Look to the blowing Rose about us—'Lo,
Laughing,' she says, 'into the world I blow,
   At once the silken tassel of my Purse
Tear, and its Treasure on the Garden throw.'

### XV

And those who husbanded the Golden grain,
And those who flung it to the winds like Rain,
   Alike to no such aureate Earth are turn'd
As, buried once, Men want dug up again.

\*

### XVII

Think, in this batter'd Caravanserai
Whose Portals are alternate Night and Day,
   How Sultán after Sultán with his Pomp
Abode his destined Hour, and went his way.

### XVIII

They say the Lion and the Lizard keep
The Courts where Jamshyd gloried and drank deep:
   And Bahrám, that great Hunter—the Wild Ass
Stamps o'er his Head, but cannot break his Sleep.

### XIX

I sometimes think that never blows so red
The Rose as where some buried Cæsar bled;
   That every Hyacinth the Garden wears
Dropt in her Lap from some once lovely Head.

XX

And this reviving Herb whose tender Green
Fledges the River-Lip on which we lean—
    Ah, lean upon it lightly! for who knows
From what once lovely Lip it springs unseen!

XXI

Ah, my Belovéd, fill the Cup that clears
TO-DAY of past Regrets and future Fears:
    *To-morrow!*—Why, To-morrow I may be
Myself with Yesterday's Sev'n thousand Years.

XXII

For some we loved, the loveliest and the best
That from his Vintage rolling Time hath prest,
    Have drunk their Cup a Round or two before,
And one by one crept silently to rest.

XXIII

And we, that now make merry in the Room
They left, and Summer dresses in new bloom,
    Ourselves must we beneath the Couch of Earth
Descend—ourselves to make a Couch—for whom?

XXIV

Ah, make the most of what we yet may spend,
Before we too into the Dust descend;
    Dust into Dust, and under Dust to lie,
Sans Wine, sans Song, sans Singer, and—sans End!—

\*

C

Yon rising Moon that looks for us again—
How oft hereafter will she wax and wane;
    How oft hereafter rising look for us
Through this same Garden—and for *one* in vain!

CI

And when like her, oh Sákí, you shall pass
Among the Guests Star-scatter'd on the Grass,
    And in your joyous errand reach the spot
Where I made One—turn down an empty Glass!

# ALFRED, LORD TENNYSON

## 1809–1892

### FROM THE GREEK OF HOMER

## *The Iliad*

389                        (i)

And when they came together in one place,
Then shocked the spears and bucklers and the strength
Of armèd warriors; then the bossy shields
Ground each on each, and huge uproar arose;
And then were heard the vaunts and groans of men
Slaying and being slain, and earth ran blood.
As winter torrents rolling from the hill
And flinging their fierce waters through the clefts
From mighty fountains downward to the gulf
Wherein they dash together; and far away
The shepherd on the mountain hears the sound,
Such the drear roar of battle when they mixt.


390                        (ii)
Cp.  Nor lingered Paris in the lofty house,
Pope But armed himself and all in varied brass
Rushed through the city, glorying in his speed:
As when a horse at manger breaks his band
And riotously rushing down the plain—
Wont in the running river to wash himself
And riot, rears his head and all his mane
Flies back behind him glorying in himself
And galloping to the meadows of the mares—
So ran the son of Priam from the height
Of Ilion, Paris, sunlike all in arms
Glittering.

391
Cp.
Pope

(iii)

So Hector spake; the Trojans roared applause;
Then loosed their sweating horses from the yoke,
And each beside his chariot bound his own;
And oxen from the city, and goodly sheep
In haste they drove, and honey-hearted wine
And bread from out the houses brought, and heaped
Their firewood, and the winds from off the plain
Rolled the rich vapour far into the heaven.
And these all night upon the bridge of war
Sat glorying; many a fire before them blazed:
As when in heaven the stars about the moon
Look beautiful, when all the winds are laid,
And every height comes out, and jutting peak
And valley, and the immeasurable heavens
Break open to their highest, and all the stars
Shine, and the Shepherd gladdens in his heart:
So many a fire between the ships and stream
Of Xanthus blazed before the towers of Troy,
A thousand on the plain; and close by each
Sat fifty in the blaze of burning fire;
And eating hoary grain and pulse the steeds,
Fixt by their cars, waited the golden dawn.

(iv)

392

*Achilles Over the Trench*

So saying, light-foot Iris passed away.
Then rose Achilles dear to Zeus; and round
The warrior's puissant shoulders Pallas flung
Her fringèd ægis, and around his head
The glorious goddess wreathed a golden cloud,
And from it lighted an all-shining flame.
As when a smoke from a city goes to heaven
Far off from out an island girt by foes,
All day the men contend in grievous war
From their own city, but with set of sun
Their fires flame thickly, and aloft the glare
Flies streaming, if perchance the neighbours round
May see, and sail to help them in the war;

So from his head the splendour went to heaven.
From wall to dyke he stept, he stood, nor joined
The Achæans—honouring his wise mother's word—
There standing, shouted, and Pallas far away
Called; and a boundless panic shook the foe.
For like the clear voice when a trumpet shrills,
Blown by the fierce beleaguerers of a town,
So rang the clear voice of Æakidês;
And when the brazen cry of Æakidês
Was heard among the Trojans, all their hearts
Were troubled, and the full-maned horses whirled
The chariots backward, knowing griefs at hand;
And sheer-astounded were the charioteers
To see the dread, unweariable fire
That always o'er the great Peleion's head
Burned, for the bright-eyed goddess made it burn.
Thrice from the dyke he sent his mighty shout,
Thrice backward reeled the Trojans and allies;
And there and then twelve of their noblest died
Among their spears and chariots.

# FROM THE ANGLO-SAXON

393            *Battle of Brunanburh*

I

Athelstan King,
Lord among Earls,
Bracelet-bestower and
Baron of Barons,
He with his brother,
Edmund Atheling,
Gaining a lifelong
Glory in battle,
Slew with the sword-edge
There by Brunanburh,
Brake the shield-wall,
Hewed the lindenwood,
Hacked the battleshield,
Sons of Edward with hammered brands.

II

Theirs was a greatness
Got from their Grandsires—
Theirs that so often in
Strife with their enemies
Struck for their hoards and their hearths and their homes.


III

Bowed the spoiler,
Bent the Scotsman,
Fell the shipcrews
Doomed to the death.
All the field with blood of the fighters
Flowed, from when first the great
Sun-star of morningtide,
Lamp of the Lord God
Lord everlasting,
Glode over earth till the glorious creature
Sank to his setting.


IV

There lay many a man
Marred by the javelin,
Men of the Northland
Shot over shield.
There was the Scotsman
Weary of war.


V

We the West-Saxons,
Long as the daylight
Lasted, in companies
Troubled the track of the host that we hated,
Grimly with swords that were sharp from the grindstone,
Fiercely we hacked at the flyers before us.

### VI

Mighty the Mercian,
Hard was his hand-play,
Sparing not any of
Those that with Anlaf,
Warriors over the
Weltering waters
Borne in the bark's-bosom,
Drew to this island:
Doomed to the death.

### VII

Five young kings put asleep by the sword-stroke,
Seven strong Earls of the army of Anlaf
Fell on the war-field, numberless numbers,
Shipmen and Scotsmen.

### VIII

Then the Norse leader,
Dire was his need of it,
Few were his following,
Fled to his warship:
Fleeted his vessel to sea with the king in it,
Saving his life on the fallow flood.

### IX

Also the crafty one,
Constantinus,
Crept to his North again,
Hoar-headed hero!

### X

Slender warrant had
*He* to be proud of
The welcome of war-knives—
He that was reft of his
Folk and his friends that had
Fallen in conflict,
Leaving his son too
Lost in the carnage,
Mangled to morsels,
A youngster in war!

XI

Slender reason had
*He* to be glad of
The clash of the war-glaive—
Traitor and trickster
And spurner of treaties—
He nor had Anlaf
With armies so broken
A reason for bragging
That they had the better
In perils of battle
On places of slaughter—
The struggle of standards,
The rush of the javelins,
The crash of the charges,
The wielding of weapons—
The play that they played with
The children of Edward.

XII

Then with their nailed prows
Parted the Norsemen, a
Blood-reddened relic of
Javelins over
The jarring breaker, the deep-sea billow,
Shaping their way toward Dyflen again,
Shamed in their souls.

XIII

Also the brethren,
King and Atheling,
Each in his glory,
Went to his own in his own West-Saxonland,
Glad of the war.

XIV

Many a carcase they left to be carrion,
Many a livid one, many a sallow-skin—
Left for the white tailed eagle to tear it, and
Left for the horny-nibbed raven to rend it, and
Gave to the garbaging war-hawk to gorge it, and
That gray beast, the wolf of the weald.

XV

Never had huger
Slaughter of heroes
Slain by the sword-edge—
Such as old writers
Have writ of in histories—
Hapt in this isle, since
Up from the East hither
Saxon and Angle from
Over the broad billow
Broke into Britain with
Haughty war-workers who
Harried the Welshman, when
Earls that were lured by the
Hunger of glory gat
Hold of the land.

# WILLIAM MAKEPEACE THACKERAY

1811–1863

PARAPHRASED FROM THE LATIN OF HORACE

**394**                *Odes*, Book I, 38

Cp.
Smart
Cowper
Hopkins

Dear Lucy, you know what my wish is,—
    I hate all your Frenchified fuss:
Your silly entrees and made dishes
    Were never intended for us.
No footman in lace and in ruffles
    Need dangle behind my arm-chair;
And never mind seeking for truffles,
    Although they be ever so rare.

But a plain leg of mutton, my Lucy,
    I prithee get ready at three:
Have it smoking, and tender and juicy,
    And what better meat can there be?

And when it has feasted the master
   'Twill amply suffice for the maid;
Meanwhile I will smoke my canaster
   And tipple my ale in the shade.


# SIR THEODORE MARTIN

1816–1909

## FROM THE LATIN OF HORACE

395              *Epistles*, Book I, 19

If, O Maecenas, versed in lore antique,
  We may Cratinus trust, that thirsty Greek
Never did yet a water-drinker's song
The general favour win, or keep it long.
For since the day that Bacchus of the pards
With fauns and satyrs classed us crackbrained bards,
It has been rumoured, that the Dulcet Nine
Have mostly in the morning smelt of wine.
So high does Homer wine's delights extol,
Folks will maintain he loved a brimming bowl;
And father Ennius ne'er caught up his lyre
To sing of fights, till wine had lent him fire:
'Ye that drink not, to court or change repair,
But from sweet song I charge you to forbear!'
I spoke; and bards have ever since, men say,
Toped wine all night, and reeked of it all day.
   What! if a man shall mimic Cato's air,
By naked feet, grim looks, and cloak threadbare,
Does he by this embody to our view
Cato's great character and virtues too?
Poor Codrus, bent on passing for a wit,
To give Timagenes back hit for hit,
With so much energy and passion spoke,
That in the effort a blood-vessel broke.

What mere delusion is it which reflects
A man of note by copying his defects?
Yet some would, if perchance my colour fail,
Drink cummin-wine to make themselves look pale.
O servile crew! How oft your antics mean
Have moved my laughter, oh, how oft my spleen!
    I was the first new regions to explore,
And boldly tread where none had trod before.
Who trusts himself, and leaves the beaten track,
Will soon have hosts of followers at his back.
'Twas in my measures Italy first heard
The tones Iambic of the Parian bard.
These and his spirit were my model,—not
The words that drove Lycambes all distraught;
Yet should you deck me not with scantier bays,
Because my style was modelled on his lays.
With her strong numbers Sappho blends a tone
Caught from Archilochus, to swell her own;
So too Alcaeus, though unlike, we know,
Both in his themes and in his rhythmic flow,
He neither seek a sire-in-law, on whose
Vexed head to pour the rancours of his muse,
Nor yet in fierce calumnious distichs chide,
To weave a halter for a faithless bride.
Him, too, till then by Latium's barbs unsung,
I made familiar on our Roman tongue;
And 'tis my pride, that gentle hands and eyes
The strains that else had been unheard of prize.
    Ask you, what makes ungracious readers laud
My works at home, and rail at them abroad?
'Tis that I will not stoop to buy men's votes
By costly dinners, or by cast-off coats;
'Tis that when men of rank their poems read,
I keep away, nor will their merits plead;
'Tis that I hold of no account the cliques
Of fussy pedants, and their sage critiques.
Hence all these tears! Were I to say, 'Indeed,
For very shame I could not dare to read
Before a crowded theatre the small
And flimsy trifles from my pen that fall;'

'Oh, sir,' they'd cry, 'we understand the sneer;
Your works are kept for Jove's imperial ear!
You've such high notions of yourself; from you
Alone distils the pure poetic dew!'
   Retort were dangerous; and my courage quails
At what might happen from my critic's nails.
So, 'The ground does not suit me!' I exclaim,
And crave for a cessation of the game.
For sport like this has oft engendered rude
Intemperate wrangling, and an angry mood,—
That angry mood engendered rooted hate,
War to the knife, and an untimely fate.


# BRANWELL BRONTË

## 1817–1848

### FROM THE LATIN OF HORACE

396           Odes, Book I, 21

#### *To Apollo and Diana*

Virgins, sing the Virgin Huntress;
   Youths, the youthful Phœbus, sing;
Sing Latona, she who bore them
   Dearest to the eternal King:
Sing the heavenly maid who roves
Joyous, through the mountain groves;
She who winding waters loves;
   Let her haunts her praises ring!

Sing the vale of Peneus' river;
   Sing the Delian deity;
The shoulder glorious with its quiver;
   And the Lyre of Mercury.
From our country, at our prayer—
Famine, plague, and tearful war
These, benign, shall drive afar
   To Persia's plains or Britain's sea.

397           ## Odes, Book I, 23

### *To Chloe*

Why, whenever she can spy me,
Like a fawn will Chloe fly me?
Like a fawn, its mother seeking
O'er the hills, through brambles breaking;
Frightened if the breezes move
But a leaflet in the grove;
Or a branch the Zephyr tosses;
Or its path a Lizard crosses;
Nothing can its fear dissemble—
Heart and knees together tremble.
    Stop my love; Thou needst not fear me,
For I follow not to tear thee
Like the Lion, prowling o'er
Far Letulia's savage shore:
Stop—Thy budding charms discover
Tis thy time to choose a lover.

# JOHN CONINGTON

## 1825–1869

### FROM THE LATIN OF HORACE

398      ✳      *Epistles*, Book I, 5

If you can lie, Torquatus, when you take
Your meal, upon a couch of Archias' make,
And sup off potherbs, gathered as they come,
You'll join me, please, by sunset at my home.
My wine, not far from Sinuessa grown,
Is but six years in bottle, I must own:
If you've a better vintage, send it here,
Or take your cue from him who finds the cheer.

My hearth is swept, my household looks its best,
And all my furniture expects a guest.
Forego your dreams of riches and applause,
Forget e'en Moschus' memorable cause;
To-morrow's Caesar's birthday, which we keep
By taking, to begin with, extra sleep;
So, if with pleasant converse we prolong
This summer night, we scarcely shall do wrong.

    Why should the Gods have put me at my ease,
If I mayn't use my fortune as I please?
The man who stints and pinches for his heir
Is next-door neighbour to a fool, I'll swear.
Here, give me flowers to strew, my goblet fill,
And let men call me mad-cap if they will.
O, drink is mighty! secrets it unlocks,
Turns hope to fact, sets cowards on to box,
Takes burdens from the careworn, finds out parts
In stupid folks, and teaches unknown arts.
What tongue hangs fire when quickened by the bowl?
What wretch so poor but wine expands his soul?

    Meanwhile, I'm bound in duty, nothing loth,
To see that nought in coverlet or cloth
May give you cause to sniff, that dish and cup
May serve you as a mirror while you sup;
To have my guests well-sorted, and take care
That none is present who'll tell tales elsewhere.
You'll find friend Butra and Septicius here,
Ditto Sabinus, failing better cheer:
And each might bring a friend or two as well,
But then, you know, close packing's apt to smell.
Come, name your number, and elude the guard
Your client keeps by slipping through the yard.

399            *Epistles*, Book I, 14

Good bailiff of my farm, that snug domain
Which makes its master feel himself again,
Which, though you sniff at it, could once support
Five hearths, and send five statesmen to the court,

Let's have a match in husbandry; we'll try
Which can do weeding better, you or I,
And see if Horace more repays the hand
That clears him of his thistles, or his land.
Though here I'm kept administering relief
To my poor Lamia's broken-hearted grief
For his lost brother, ne'ertheless my thought
Flies to my woods, and counts the distance nought.
You praise the townsman's, I the rustic's state:
Admiring others' lots, our own we hate:
Each blames the place he lives in: but the mind
Is most in fault, which ne'er leaves self behind.
A town-house drudge, for farms you used to sigh;
Now towns and shows and baths are all your cry:
But I'm consistent with myself: you know
I grumble, when to Rome I'm forced to go.
Truth is, our standards differ: what your taste
Condemns, forsooth, as so much savage waste,
The man who thinks with Horace thinks divine,
And hates the things which you believe so fine.
I know your secret: 'tis the cook-shop breeds
That lively sense of what the country needs:
You grieve because this little nook of mine
Would bear Arabian spice as soon as wine;
Because no tavern happens to be nigh
Where you can go and tipple on the sly,
No saucy flute-girl, at whose jigging sound
You bring your feet down lumbering to the ground.
And yet, methinks, you've plenty on your hands
In breaking up these long unharrowed lands;
The ox, unyoked and resting from the plough,
Wants fodder, stripped from elm and poplar bough;
You've work too at the river, when there's rain,
As, but for a strong bank, 'twould flood the plain.
Now have a little patience, you shall see
What makes the gulf between yourself and me:

I, who once wore gay clothes and well-dressed hair,
I, who, though poor, could please a greedy fair,
I, who could sit from mid-day o'er Falern,
Now like short meals and slumbers by the burn:
No shame I deem it to have had my sport;
The shame had been in frolics not cut short.
There at my farm I fear no evil eye;
No pickthank blights my crops as he goes by;
My honest neighbours laugh to see me wield
A heavy rake, or dibble my own field.
Were wishes wings, you'd join my slaves in town,
And share the rations that they swallow down:
While that sharp footboy envies you the use
Of what my garden, flocks, and woods produce.
The horse would plough, the ox would draw the car.
No; do the work you know, and tarry where you are.

# DANTE GABRIEL ROSSETTI

## 1828–1882

### FROM THE ITALIAN OF ST. FRANCIS OF ASSISI

400     *Cantica: Our Lord Christ: of order.* *

Set Love in order, thou that lovest Me.
  Never was virtue out of order found;
And though I fill thy heart desirously,
  By thine own virtue I must keep My ground:
When to My love thou dost bring charity,
  Even she must come with order girt and gown'd.
      Look how the trees are bound
      To order, bearing fruit;
      And by one thing compute,
In all things earthly, order's grace or gain.

* This speech occurs in a long poem on Divine Love, half ecstatic, half
scholastic, and hardly appreciable now. The passage stands well by itself, and is
the only one spoken by our Lord.       (*Rossetti's note*)

All earthly things I had the making of
    Were number'd and were measured then by Me;
And each was order'd to its end by Love,
    Each kept, through order, clean for ministry.
Charity most of all, when known enough,
    Is of her very nature orderly.
            Lo, now! what heat in thee,
            Soul, can have bred this rout?
            Thou putt'st all order out.
Even this love's heat must be its curb and rein.


## FROM THE ITALIAN OF GUIDO GUINICELLI

401         *Canzone: Of the gentle Heart*

Within the gentle heart Love shelters him,
    As birds within the green shade of the grove.
Before the gentle heart, in Nature's scheme,
    Love was not, nor the gentle heart ere Love.
        For with the sun, at once,
So sprang the light immediately; nor was
        Its birth before the sun's.
    And Love hath his effect in gentleness
        Of very self; even as
    Within the middle fire the heat's excess.

The fire of Love comes to the gentle heart
    Like as its virtue to a precious stone;
To which no star its influence can impart
    Till it is made a pure thing by the sun;
        For when the sun hath smit
From out its essence that which there was vile,
        The star endoweth it.
And so the heart created by God's breath
        Pure, true, and clean from guile,
A woman, like a star, enamoureth.

In gentle heart Love for like reason is
  For which the lamp's high flame is fann'd and bow'd:
Clear, piercing bright, it shines for its own bliss;
  Nor would it burn there else, it is so proud.
      For evil natures meet
With Love as it were water met with fire,
      As cold abhorring heat.
Through gentle heart Love doth a track divine,—
      Like knowing like; the same
As diamond runs through iron in the mine.

The sun strikes full upon the mud all day;
  It remains vile, nor the sun's worth is less.
'By race I am gentle,' the proud man doth say:
  He is the mud, the sun is gentleness.
      Let no man predicate
That aught the name of gentleness should have,
      Even in a king's estate,
Except the heart there be a gentle man's.
      The star-beam lights the wave,—
Heaven holds the star and the star's radiance.

God, in the understanding of high Heaven,
  Burns more than in our sight the living sun;
There to behold His Face unveil'd is given;
  And Heaven, whose will is homage paid to One,
      Fulfils the things which live
In God, from the beginning excellent.
      So should my lady give
That truth which in her eyes is glorified,
      On which her heart is bent,
To me whose service waiteth at her side.

My lady, God shall ask, 'What dared'st thou?'
  (When my soul stands with all her acts review'd);
'Thou passed'st Heaven, into My sight, as now,
  To make Me of vain love similitude.
      To Me doth praise belong,
And to the Queen of all the realm of grace
      Who endeth fraud and wrong.'
Then may I plead: 'As though from Thee he came,

Love wore an angel's face:
Lord, if I loved her, count it not my shame.'


FROM THE ITALIAN OF PIER MORONELLI
DA FIORENZA

402      *Canzonetta: A bitter Song to his Lady*

O Lady amorous,
Merciless lady,
Full blithely play'd ye
These your beguilings.
So with an urchin
A man makes merry,—
In mirth grows clamorous,
Laughs and rejoices,—
But when his choice is
To fall aweary,
Cheats him with silence.
This is Love's portion:—
In much wayfaring
With many burdens
He loads his servants;
But at the sharing,
The underservice
And overservice
Are alike barren.
As my disaster
Your jest I cherish,
And well may perish.
Even as a falcon
Is sometimes taken
And scantily cautell'd;
Till when his master
At length to loose him,
To train and use him,
Is after all gone,—
The creature's throttled
And will not waken.
Wherefore, my lady,
If you will own me,

O look upon me!
If I'm not thought on,
At least perceive me!
O do not leave me
So much forgotten!

If, lady, truly
You wish my profit,
What follows of it
Though still you say so?—
For all your well-wishes
I still am waiting.
I grow unruly,
And deem at last I'm
Only your pastime.
A child will play so,
Who greatly relishes
Sporting and petting
With a little wild bird:
Unaware he kills it,—
Then turns it, feels it,
Calls it with a mild word,
Is angry after,—
Then again in laughter
Loud is the child heard.

O my delightful
My own my lady,
Upon the Mayday
Which brought me to you
Was all my haste then
But a fool's venture?
To have my sight full
Of you propitious
Truly my wish was,
And to pursue you
And let love chasten
My heart to the centre.
But warming, lady,
May end in burning.
Of all this yearning

What comes, I beg you?
In all your glances
What is't a man sees?—
Fever and ague.

## FROM THE ITALIAN OF NICCOLÒ DEGLI ALBIZZI

403    *Prolonged Sonnet: When the Troops were
          returning from Milan*

If you could see, fair brother, how dead beat
    The fellows look who come through Rome today,—
    Black yellow smoke-dried visages,—you'd say
They thought their haste at going all too fleet.
Their empty victual-waggons up the street
    Over the bridge dreadfully sound and sway;
    Their eyes, as hang'd men's, turning the wrong way;
And nothing on their backs, or heads, or feet.
One sees the ribs and all the skeletons
    Of their gaunt horses; and a sorry sight
Are the torn saddles, cramm'd with straw and stones.
    They are ashamed, and march throughout the night;
Stumbling, for hunger, on their marrowbones;
    Like barrels rolling, jolting, in this plight.
Their arms all gone, not even their swords are saved;
And each as silent as a man being shaved.

## FROM THE ITALIAN OF DANTE

404    *Sestina: Of the Lady Pietra degli Scrovigni*

To the dim light and the large circle of shade
I have clomb, and to the whitening of the hills,
There where we see no colour in the grass.
Natheless my longing loses not its green,
It has so taken root in the hard stone
Which talks and hears as though it were a lady.

Utterly frozen is this youthful lady,
Even as the snow that lies within the shade;
For she is no more moved than is the stone
By the sweet season which makes warm the hills
And alters them afresh from white to green,
Covering their sides again with flowers and grass.

When on her hair she sets a crown of grass
The thought has no more room for other lady;
Because she weaves the yellow with the green
So well that Love sits down there in the shade,—
Love who has shut me in among low hills
Faster than between walls of granite-stone.

She is more bright than is a precious stone;
The wound she gives may not be healed with grass:
I therefore have fled far o'er plains and hills
For refuge from so dangerous a lady;
But from her sunshine nothing can give shade,—
Not any hill, nor wall, nor summer-green.

A while ago, I saw her dressed in green,—
So fair, she might have wakened in a stone
This love which I do feel even for her shade;
And therefore, as one woos a graceful lady,
I wooed her in a field that was all grass
Girdled about with very lofty hills.

Yet shall the streams turn back and climb the hills
Before Love's flame in this damp wood and green
Burn, as it burns within a youthful lady,
For my sake, who would sleep away in stone
My life, or feed like beasts upon the grass,
Only to see her garments cast a shade.

How dark soe'er the hills throw out their shade,
Under her summer-green the beautiful lady
Covers it, like a stone cover'd in grass.

# DANTE GABRIEL ROSSETTI

## FROM THE FRENCH OF FRANÇOIS VILLON

405        *The Ballad of Dead Ladies*

Cp.
Sidney
 Goodsir
 Smith

Tell me now in what hidden way is
    Lady Flora the lovely Roman?
Where's Hipparchia, and where is Thais,
    Neither of them the fairer woman?
    Where is Echo, beheld of no man,
Only heard on river and mere,—
    She whose beauty was more than human? ...
But where are the snows of yester-year?

Where's Héloise, the learned nun,
    For whose sake Abeillard, I ween,
Lost manhood and put priesthood on?
    (From Love he won such dule and teen!)
    And where, I pray you, is the Queen
Who willed that Buridan should steer
    Sewed in a sack's mouth down the Seine? ...
But where are the snows of yester-year?

While Queen Blanche, like a queen of lilies,
    With a voice like any mermaiden,—
Bertha Broadfoot, Beatrice, Alice,
    And Ermengarde the lady of Maine,—
    And that good Joan whom Englishmen
At Rouen doomed and burned her there,—
    Mother of God, where are they then? ...
But where are the snows of yester-year?

Nay, never ask this week, fair lord,
    Where they are gone, nor yet this year,
Save with thus much for an overword,—
    But where are the snows of yester-year?

# GEORGE MEREDITH

1828–1909

FROM THE GERMAN OF EDUARD MÖRICKE

406               *Beauty Rohtraut*

What is the name of King Ringang's daughter?
    Rohtraut, Beauty Rohtraut!
And what does she do the livelong day,
Since she dare not knit and spin alway?
O hunting and fishing is ever her play!
And, heigh! that her huntsman I might be!
I'd hunt and fish right merrily!
        Be silent, heart!

And it chanced that, after this some time,—
    Rohtraut, Beauty Rohtraut,—
The boy in the Castle has gained access,
And a horse he has got and a huntsman's dress,
To hunt and to fish with the merry Princess;
And, O! that a king's son I might be!
Beauty Rohtraut I love so tenderly.
        Hush! hush! my heart.

Under a grey old oak they sat,
    Beauty, Beauty Rohtraut!
She laughs: 'Why look you so slyly at me?
If you have heart enough, come, kiss me.'
Cried the breathless boy, 'Kiss thee?'
But he thinks, kind fortune has favoured my youth;
And thrice he has kissed Beauty Rohtraut's mouth.
        Down! down! mad heart.

Then slowly and silently they rode home,—
  Rohtraut, Beauty Rohtraut!
The boy was lost in his delight:
'And, wert thou Empress this very night,
I would not heed or feel the blight;
Ye thousand leaves of the wild wood wist
How Beauty Rohtraut's mouth I kiss'd.
    Hush! hush! wild heart.'


# CHARLES STUART CALVERLEY
## 1831–1884

### FROM THE GREEK OF THEOCRITUS

407            *The Fishermen*

ASPHALION. A COMRADE.

Want quickens wit: Want's pupils needs must work,
O Diophantus: for the child of toil
Is grudged his very sleep by carking cares:
Or, if he taste the blessedness of night,
Thought for the morrow soon warns slumber off.
  Two ancient fishers once lay side by side
On piled-up sea-wrack in their wattled hut,
Its leafy wall their curtain. Near them lay
The weapons of their trade, basket and rod,
Hooks, weed-encumbered nets, and cords and oars,
And, propped on rollers, an infirm old boat.
Their pillow was a scanty mat, eked out
With caps and garments: such the ways and means,
Such the whole treasury of the fishermen.
They knew no luxuries: owned nor door nor dog;
Their craft their all, their mistress Poverty:
Their only neighbour Ocean, who for aye
Round their lorn hut came floating lazily.

# CHARLES STUART CALVERLEY

Ere the moon's chariot was in mid-career,
The fishers girt them for their customed toil,
And banished slumber from unwilling eyes,
And roused their dreamy intellects with speech:

ASPHALION. They say that soon flit summer-nights away,
Because all lingering is the summer day:
Friend, it is false; for dream on dream have I
Dreamed, and the dawn still reddens not the sky.
How? am I wandering? or does night pass slow?

HIS COMRADE. Asphalion, scout not the sweet summer so.
'Tis not that wilful seasons have gone wrong,
But care maims slumber, and the nights seem long.

A. Didst thou e'er study dreams? For visions fair
I saw last night; and fairly thou should'st share
The wealth I dream of, as the fish I catch.
Now, for sheer sense, I reckon few thy match;
And, for a vision, he whose motherwit
Is his sole tutor best interprets it.
And now we've time the matter to discuss:
For who could labour, lying here (like us)
Pillowed on leaves and neighboured by the deep,
Or sleeping amid thorns no easy sleep?
In rich men's halls the lamps are burning yet;
But fish come alway to the rich man's net.

C. To me the vision of the night relate;
Speak, and reveal the riddle to thy mate.

A. Last evening, as I plied my watery trade,
(Not on an o'erfull stomach—we had made
Betimes a meagre meal, as you can vouch)
I fell asleep; and lo! I seemed to crouch
Among the boulders, and for fish to wait,
Still dangling, rod in hand, my vagrant bait.
A fat fellow caught it: (e'en in sleep I'm bound
To dream of fishing, as of crusts the hound:)
Fast clung he to the hooks; his blood outwelled;
Bent with his struggling was the rod I held:

401

I tugged and tugged: my efforts made me ache:
'How, with a line thus slight, this monster take?'
Then gently, just to warn him he was caught,
I twitched him once; then slacked and then made taut
My line, for now he offered not to run;
A glance soon showed me all my task was done.
'Twas a gold fish, pure metal every inch,
That I had captured. I began to flinch:
'What if this beauty be the sea-king's joy,
Or azure Amphitritè's treasured toy!'
With care I disengaged him—not to rip
With hasty hook the gilding from his lip:
And with a tow-line landed him, and swore
Never to set my foot on ocean more,
But with my gold live royally ashore.
So I awoke: and, comrade, lend me now
Thy wits, for I am troubled for my vow.

C. Ne'er quake: you're pledged to nothing, for no prize
You gained or gazed on. Dreams are naught but lies.
Yet may this dream bear fruit; if, wide-awake
And not in dreams, you'll fish the neighbouring lake.
Fish that are meat you'll there mayhap behold,
Not die of famine, amid dreams of gold.


## FROM THE GERMAN OF HEINRICH HEINE

408      I crave an ampler, worthier sphere;
        I'd liefer bleed at every vein
Than stifle 'mid these hucksters here,
        These lying slaves of paltry gain.

They eat, they drink; they're every whit
        As happy as their type, the mole;
Large are their bounties—as the slit
        Through which they drop the poor man's dole.

With pipe in mouth they go their way,
        With hands in pockets; they are blest
With grand digestions: only *they*
        Are such hard morsels to digest!

The hand that's red with some dark deed,
  Some giant crime, were white as wool
Compared with these sleek saints, whose creed
  Is paying all their debts in full.

Ye clouds that sail to far-off lands,
  O waft me to what clime ye will!
To Lapland's snows, to Lybia's sands,
  To the world's end—but onward still!

Take me, O clouds! They ne'er look down;
  But (proof of a discerning mind)
One moment hung o'er Hamburg town,
  The next they leave it leagues behind.

# WILLIAM MORRIS

1834–1896

## with Eiriks Magnusson

### FROM THE OLD NORSE

## The Elder Edda

*409*  *The First Lay of Gudrun:
'Gudrun Laments over Sigurd'*

Once looked Gudrun—
One look only,
And saw her lord's locks
Lying all bloody,
The great man's eyes
Glazed and deadly,
And his heart's bulwark
Broken by sword-edge.

Back then sank Gudrun,
Back on the bolster,
Loosed was her head array,
Red did her cheeks grow,
And the rain-drops ran
Down over her knees.

Then wept Gudrun,
Giuki's daughter,
So that the tears flowed
Through the pillow;
As the geese withal
That were in the homefield,
The fair fowls the may owned,
Fell a-screaming.

Then spake Gullrond,
Giuki's daughter:
'Surely knew I
No love like your love
Among all men,
On the mould abiding;
Naught wouldst thou joy in
Without or within doors,
O my sister,
Save beside Sigurd.'

Then spoke Gudrun,
Giuki's daughter:
'Such was my Sigurd
Among the sons of Giuki,
As is the king leek
O'er the low grass waxing,
Or a bright stone
Strung on band,
Or a pearl of price
On a prince's brow.

Once was I counted
By the king's warriors
Higher than any
Of Herjan's mays;
Now am I as little
As the leaf may be,
Amid wind-swept wood
Now when dead he lieth.'

410    *Part of the Lay of Sigrdrifa*

Now this is my first counsel,
    That thou with thy kin
Be guiltless, guileless ever,
    Nor hasty of wrath,
    Despite of wrong done—
Unto the dead good that doeth.

    Lo the second counsel,
    That oath thou swearest never,
But trusty oath and true:
    Grim tormenting
    Gripes troth-breakers;
Cursed wretch is the wolf of vows.

    This is my third rede,
    That thou at the Thing
Deal not with the fools of folk;
    For unwise man
    From mouth lets fall
Worser word than well he wotteth.

    Yet hard it is
    That holding of peace
When men shall deem thee dastard,
Or deem the lie said soothly;
But woeful is home-witness,
Unless right good thou gettest it.
    Ah, on another day
    Drive the life from out him,
And pay the liar back for his lying.

Now behold the fourth rede:
  If ill witch thee bideth,
Woe-begetting by the way,
  Good going further
  Rather than guesting,
Though thick night be on thee.

  Far-seeing eyes
  Need all sons of men
Who wend in wrath to war;
  For baleful women
  Bide oft by the highway,
Swords and hearts to soften.

  And now the fifth rede:
  As fair as thou seest
Brides on the bench abiding,
  Let not love's silver
  Rule over thy sleeping;
Draw no woman to kind kissing!

  For the sixth thing, I rede
  When men sit a-drinking
Amid ale-words and ill-words,
  Deal thou naught
  With the drunken fight-staves,
For wine stealeth wit from many.

  Brawling and drink
  Have brought unto men
Sorrow sore oft enow;
  Yea, bane unto some,
  And to some weary bale;
Many are the griefs of mankind.

  For the seventh, I rede thee,
  If strife thou raisest
With a man right high of heart,
  Better fight a-field
  Than burn in the fire
Within thine hall fair to behold.

The eighth rede that I give thee:
  Unto all ill look thou,
And hold thine heart from all beguiling;
  Draw to thee no maiden,
  No man's wife bewray thou,
Urge them not to unmeet pleasure.

  This is the ninth counsel:
  That thou have heed of dead folk
Whereso thou findest them a-field;
  Be they sick-dead,
  Be they sea-dead,
Or come to ending by war-weapons.

  Let bath be made
  For such men foredone,
Wash thou hands and feet thereof,
  Comb their hair and dry them
  Ere the coffin has them;
Then bid them sleep full sweetly.

  This for the tenth counsel:
  That thou give trust never
Unto oaths of foeman's kin,
Be'st thou bane of his brother,
Or hast thou felled his father;
Wolf in young son waxes,
Though he with gold be gladdened.

  For wrong and hatred
  Shall rest them never,
Nay, nor sore sorrow.
  Both wit and weapons
  Well must the king have
Who is fain to be the foremost.

  The last rede and eleventh:
  Unto all ill look thou,
And watch thy friends' ways ever.
  Scarce durst I look
  For long life for thee, king:
Strong trouble ariseth now already.

407

411    from *The Short Lay of Sigurd*

[Brynhild's last request to Gunnar. Having engineered the death of Sigurd whom she loves and who brought her as wife to Gunnar, she kills herself and makes this request.]

'And now one prayer
Yet pray I of thee—
The last word of mine
Here in the world—
So broad on the field
Be the burg of the dead
That fair space may be left
For us all to lie down,
All those that died
At Sigurd's death!

'Hang round that burg
Fair hangings and shields,
Web by Gauls woven,
And folk of the Gauls:
There burn the Hun King
Lying beside me.

'But on the other side
Burn by the Hun King
Those who served me
Strewn with treasure;
Two at the head,
And two at the feet,
Two hounds therewith,
And two hawks moreover:
Then is all dealt
With even dealing.

'Lay there amidst us
The ring-dight metal,
The sharp-edged steel,
That so lay erst;
When we both together
Into one bed went,
And were called by the name
Of man and wife.

'Never, then, belike
Shall clash behind him
Valhall's bright door
With rings bedight:
And if my fellowship
Followeth after,
In no wretched wise
Then shall we wend.

'For him shall follow
My five bondmaids,
My eight bondsmen,
No borel folk:
Yea, and my fosterer,
And my father's dower
That Budli of old days
Gave to his dear child.

'Much have I spoken,
More would I speak,
If the sword would give me
Space for speech;
But my words are waning,
My wounds are swelling—
Naught but truth have I told—
—And now make I ending.'

# ALGERNON CHARLES SWINBURNE

## 1837–1909

### FROM THE FRENCH OF FRANÇOIS VILLON

412        *The Ballad of Villon and Fat Madge*

''Tis no sin for a man to labour in his vocation.'
'The night cometh, when no man can work.'

What though the beauty I love and serve be cheap,
   Ought you to take me for a beast or fool?
All things a man could wish are in her keep;
   For her I turn swashbuckler in love's school.
   When folk drop in, I take my pot and stool
And fall to drinking with no more ado.
I fetch them bread, fruit, cheese, and water, too;
   I say all's right so long as I'm well paid;
'Look in again when your flesh troubles you,
   Inside this brothel where we drive our trade.'

But soon the devil's among us flesh and fell,
   When penniless to bed comes Madge my whore;
I loathe the very sight of her like hell.
   I snatch gown, girdle, surcoat, all she wore,
   And tell her, these shall stand against her score.
She grips her hips with both hands, cursing God,
Swearing by Jesus' body, bones, and blood,
   That they shall not. Then I, no whit dismayed,
Cross her cracked nose with some stray shiver of wood
   Inside this brothel where we drive our trade.

When all's up she drops me a windy word,
   Bloat like a beetle puffed and poisonous:
Grins, thumps my pate, and calls me dickey-bird,
   And cuffs me with a fist that's ponderous.
   We sleep like logs, being drunken both of us;
Then when we wake her womb begins to stir;
To save her seed she gets me under her
   Wheezing and whining, flat as planks are laid:
And thus she spoils me for a whoremonger
   Inside this brothel where we drive our trade.

Blow, hail or freeze, I've bread here baked rent free!
Whoring's my trade, and my whore pleases me;
   Bad cat, bad rat; we're just the same if weighed.
We that love filth, filth follows us, you see;
Honour flies from us, as from her we flee
   Inside this brothel where we drive our trade.*

     * I bequeath likewise to fat Madge
       This little song to learn and study;
      By God's head she's a sweet fat fadge,
       Devout and soft of flesh and ruddy;
      I love her with my soul and body,
      So doth she me, sweet dainty thing.
       If you fall in with such a lady,
      Read it, and give it her to sing.

413      *The Complaint of the Fair Armouress*

I

Meseemeth I heard cry and groan
   That sweet who was the armourer's maid;
For her young years she made sore moan,
   And right upon this wise she said;
     'Ah fierce old age with foul bald head,
To spoil fair things thou art over fain;
   Who holdeth me? who? would God I were dead!
Would God I were well dead and slain!

II

'Lo, thou hast broken the sweet yoke
   That my high beauty held above
All priests and clerks and merchant-folk;
   There was not one but for my love
   Would give me gold and gold enough,
Though sorrow his very heart had riven,
   To win from me such wage thereof
As now no thief would take if given.

### III

'I was right chary of the same,
   God wot it was my great folly,
For love of one sly knave of them,
   Good store of that same sweet had he;
   For all my subtle wiles, perdie,
God wot I loved him well enow;
   Right evilly he handled me,
But he loved well my gold, I trow.

### IV

'Though I gat bruises green and black,
   I loved him never the less a jot;
Though he bound burdens on my back,
   If he said "Kiss me and heed it not"
   Right little pain I felt, God wot,
When that foul thief's mouth, found so sweet,
   Kissed me—Much good thereof I got!
I keep the sin and the shame of it.

### V

'And he died thirty year agone.
   I am old now, no sweet thing to see;
By God, though, when I think thereon,
   And of that good glad time, woe's me,
   And stare upon my changed body
Stark naked, that has been so sweet,
   Lean, wizen, like a small dry tree,
I am nigh mad with the pain of it.

### VI

'Where is my faultless forehead's white,
   The lifted eyebrows, soft gold hair,
Eyes wide apart and keen of sight,
   With subtle skill in the amorous air;
   The straight nose, great nor small, but fair,
The small carved ears of shapeliest growth,
   Chin dimpling, colour good to wear,
And sweet red splendid kissing mouth?

VII

'The shapely slender shoulders small,
  Long arms, hands wrought in glorious wise,
Round little breasts, the hips withal
  High, full of flesh, not scant of size,
  Fit for all amorous masteries;
*** ***** *****, *** *** ****** **** ***
  ******* ***** ** **** ***** ******
** * ***** ****** ** **** *****?


VIII

'A writhled forehead, hair gone grey,
  Fallen eyebrows, eyes gone blind and red,
Their laughs and looks all fled away,
  Yea, all that smote men's hearts are fled;
  The bowed nose, fallen from goodlihead;
Foul flapping ears like water-flags;
  Peaked chin, and cheeks all waste and dead,
And lips that are two skinny rags;


IX

'Thus endeth all the beauty of us.
  The arms made short, the hands made lean,
The shoulders bowed and ruinous,
  The breasts, alack! all fallen in;
  The flanks too, like the breasts, grown thin;
** *** *** ***** *****, *** ** **!
  For the lank thighs, no thighs but skin,
They are specked with spots like sausage-meat.


X

'So we make moan for the old sweet days,
  Poor old light women, two or three
Squatting above the straw-fire's blaze,
  The bosom crushed against the knee,
  Like faggots on a heap we be,
Round fires soon lit, soon quenched and done;
  And we were once so sweet, even we!
Thus fareth many and many an one.'

[published censored]


413

414    *The Dispute of the Heart and Body of*
*François Villon*

Who is this I hear?—Lo, this is I, thine heart,
    That holds on merely now by a slender string.
Strength fails me, shape and sense are rent apart,
    The blood in me is turned to a bitter thing,
    Seeing thee skulk here like a dog shivering.—
Yea, and for what?—For that thy sense found sweet.—
What irks it thee?—I feel the sting of it.—
    Leave me at peace.—Why?—Nay now, leave me at peace;
I will repent when I grow ripe in wit.—
    I say no more.—I care not though thou cease.—

What art thou, trow?—A man worth praise, perfay.—
    This is thy thirtieth year of wayfaring.—
'Tis a mule's age.—Art thou a boy still?—Nay.—
    Is it hot lust that spurs thee with its sting,
    Grasping thy throat? Know'st thou not anything?—
Yea, black and white, when milk is specked with flies,
I can make out.—No more?—Nay, in no wise.
    Shall I begin again the count of these?—
Thou art undone.—I will make shift to rise.—
    I say no more.—I care not though thou cease.—

I have the sorrow of it, and thou the smart.
    Wert thou a poor mad fool or weak of wit,
Then might'st thou plead this pretext with thine heart;
    But if thou know not good from evil a whit,
    Either thy head is hard as stone to hit,
Or shame, not honour, gives thee most content.
What canst thou answer to this argument?—
    When I am dead I shall be well at ease.—
God! what good hope!—Thou art over eloquent.—
    I say no more.—I care not though thou cease.—

Whence is this ill?—From sorrow and not from sin.
    When Saturn packed my wallet up for me
I well believe he put these ills therein.—
    Fool, wilt thou make thy servant lord of thee?
    Hear now the wise king's counsel; thus saith he:

All power upon the stars a wise man hath;
There is no planet that shall do him scathe.—
    Nay, as they made me I grow and I decrease.—
What say'st thou?—Truly this is all my faith.—
    I say no more.—I care not though thou cease.—

Wouldst thou live still?—God help me that I may!—
Then thou must—What? turn penitent and pray?—
Read always—What?—Grave words and good to say;
    Leave off the ways of fools, lest they displease.—
Good; I will do it.—Wilt thou remember?—Yea.—
Abide not till there come an evil day.
    I say no more.—I care not though thou cease.

# GERARD MANLEY HOPKINS

## 1844–1889

### FROM THE LATIN OF HORACE

**415**

## *Odes*, Book I, 38

Cp.
Smart
Cowper
Thackeray

Ah child, no Persian—perfect art!
Crowns composite and braided bast
They tease me. Never know the part
    Where roses linger last.

Bring natural myrtle, and have done:
Myrtle will suit your place and mine:
And set the glasses from the sun
    Beneath the tackled vine.

**416**

## *Odes*, Book III, 1

Cp.
Cowley

Tread back—and back, the lewd and lay!—
Grace guard your tongues!—what never ear
Heard yet, the Muses' man, today
I bid the boys and maidens hear.

Kings herd it on their subject droves
But Jove's the herd that keeps the kings—
Jove of the Giants: simple Jove's
Mere eyebrow rocks this round of things.

Say man than man may more enclose
In rankèd vineyards; one with claim
Of blood to our green hustings goes;
One with more conscience, cleaner fame;

One better backed comes crowding by:—
That level power whose word is Must
Dances the balls for low or high:
Her urn takes all, her deal is just.

Sinner who saw the blade that hung
Vertical home, could Sicily fare
Be managed tasty to that tongue?
Or bird with pipe, viol with air

Bring sleep round then?—sleep not afraid
Of country bidder's calls or low
Entries or banks all over shade
And Tempe with the west to blow.

Who stops his asking mood at par
The burly sea may quite forget
Nor fear the violent calendar
At Haedus-rise, Arcturus-set,

For hail upon the vine nor break
His heart at farming, what between
The dog-star with the fields abake
And spitting snows to choke the green.

Fish feel their waters drawing to
With our abutments: there we see
The lades discharged and laded new,
And Italy flies from Italy.

But fears, fore-motions of the mind,
Climb quits: one boards the master there
On brazèd barge and hard behind
Sits to the beast that seats him—Care.

O if there's that which Phrygian stone
And crimson wear of starry shot
Not sleek away; Falernian-grown
And oils of Shushan comfort not,

Why .     .     .     .     .
     .     .     .     .     .     .
Why should I change a Sabine dale
For wealth as wide as weariness?

*[Left incomplete]*

# ALFRED EDWARD HOUSMAN
## 1859–1936

### FROM THE LATIN OF HORACE

417            Odes, Book IV, 7

*Diffugere Nives*

Cp.
Johnson

The snows are fled away, leaves on the shaws
   And grasses in the mead renew their birth,
The river to the river-bed withdraws,
   And altered is the fashion of the earth.

The Nymphs and Graces three put off their fear
   And unapparelled in the woodland play.
The swift hour and the brief prime of the year
   Say to the soul, *Thou wast not born for aye.*

Thaw follows frost; hard on the heel of spring
   Treads summer sure to die, for hard on hers
Comes autumn with his apples scattering;
   Then back to wintertide, when nothing stirs.

417

But oh, whate'er the sky-led seasons mar,
    Moon upon moon rebuilds it with her beams;
Come *we* where Tullus and where Ancus are
    And good Aeneas, we are dust and dreams.

Torquatus, if the gods in heaven shall add
    The morrow to the day, what tongue has told?
Feast then thy heart, for what thy heart has had
    The fingers of no heir will ever hold.

When thou descendest once the shades among,
    The stern assize and equal judgment o'er,
Not thy long lineage nor thy golden tongue,
    No, nor thy righteousness, shall friend thee more.

Night holds Hippolytus the pure of stain,
    Diana steads him nothing, he must stay;
And Theseus leaves Pirithous in the chain
    The love of comrades cannot take away.


## POEMS FROM THE AMERICAN INDIAN

# DANIEL G. BRINTON

### 1837–1899

### FROM THE DELAWARE

418        from *Walam Olum* or *Red Score*

I

After the Seizer there were ten chiefs, and there was much warfare
    south and east.
After them, the Peaceable was chief at Snake land.
After him, Not-Black was chief, who was a straight man.
After him, Much-Loved was chief, a good man.
After him, No-Blood was chief, who walked in cleanliness.
After him, Snow-Father was chief, he of the big teeth.
After him, Tally-Maker was chief, who made records.
After him, Shiverer-with-Cold was chief, who went south to the corn
    land.

After him, Corn-Breaker was chief, who brought about the planting of
    corn.
After him, the Strong-Man was chief, who was useful to the chieftains.
After him, the Salt-Man was chief; after him the Little-One was chief.
There was no rain, and no corn, so they moved further seaward.
At the place of caves, in the buffalo land, they at last had food, on a
    pleasant plain.
After the Little-One came the Fatigued; after him, the Stiff-One.
After him, the Reprover; disliking him, and unwilling to remain,
Being angry, some went off secretly, moving east.

2

A great land and a wide land was the east land,
A land without snakes, a rich land, a pleasant land.
Great Fighter was chief, toward the north.
At the Straight river, River-Loving was chief.
Becoming-Fat was chief at Sassafras land.
All the hunters made wampum again at the great sea.
Red-Arrow was chief at the stream again.
The Painted-Man was chief at the Mighty Water.
The Easterners and the Wolves go northeast.
Good-Fighter was chief, and went to the north.
The Mengwe, the Lynxes, all trembled.
Again an Affable was chief, and made peace with all.
All were friends, all were united, under this great chief.
Great-Beaver was chief, remaining in Sassafras land.
White-Body was chief on the sea shore.
Peace-Maker was chief, friendly to all.
He-Makes-Mistakes was chief, hurriedly coming.
At this time whites came on the Eastern sea.

# WASHINGTON MATTHEWS

## 1843–1905

### FROM THE NAVAJO

419            *Magpie Song* (gambling song)

The magpie! The magpie! Here underneath
In the white of his wings are the footsteps of morning.
It dawns! It dawns!


420                *Song to Promote Growth*

Truly in the East
The white bean
And the great corn-plant
Are tied with the white lightning.
Listen! It approaches!*
The voice of the bluebird is heard.

Truly in the East
The white bean
And the great squash
Are tied with the rainbow.
Listen! It approaches!
The voice of the bluebird is heard.


421            *The Song of Bekotsidi*

[This is the song that was chanted by the god Bekotsidi to bless the animals that
he was shaping during the Navajo genesis]

Now Bekotsidi, that am I. For them I make.
Now child of Day Bearer am I. For them I make.
Now Day Bearer's beam of blue. For them I make.
Shines on my feet and your feet too. For them I make.
Horses of all kinds now increase. For them I make.
At my fingers' tips and yours. For them I make.
Beasts of all kinds now increase. For them I make.
The bluebirds now increase. For them I make.

*the rain

Soft goods of all kinds now increase. For them I make.
Now with the pollen they increase. For them I make.
Increasing now, they will last forever. For them I make.
In old age wandering on the trail of beauty. For them I make.
To form them fair, for them I labor. For them I make.


# FRANCES DENSMORE

1867–1957


## FROM THE CHIPPEWA

422                         *Song*

Now and then there will arise,
Out of the waters,
My Midé brothers,
The otters.


423                     *The Sky Clears*

Verily
The sky clears
When my Midé drum
Sounds
For me.
Verily
The waters are smooth
When my Midé drum
Sounds
For me.


424                     *Spring Song*

As my eyes search the prairie
I feel the summer in the spring.


422 Midé] the Midéwiwin was a medicine society.

425            *The Noise of the Village*

              Whenever I pause—
                   The noise
                   Of the village.


426            *Song of the Thunders*

              Sometimes I,
              I go about pitying myself
              While I am carried by the wind
              Across the sky


427            *Song of the Trees*

              The wind
                   Only
                   I am afraid of.


428            *The Approach of the Storm*

              From the half
              Of the sky
              That which lives there
              Is coming, and makes a noise.


429            *A Loon I Thought It Was*

              A loon I thought it was,
              But it was my love's splashing oar.
              To Sault Ste. Marie he has departed,
              My love has gone on before me,
              Never again can I see him.
              A loon I thought it was,
              But it was my love's splashing oar.

## FROM THE PAPAGO

430 *Healing Song*

The sun is rising,
At either side a bow is lying.
Beside the bows are lion-babies.
The sky is pink,
That is all.

The moon is setting,
At either side are bamboos for arrow-making.
Beside the bamboos are wildcat babies,
They walk uncertainly,
That is all.

## FROM THE PAWNEE

431 *Dream Song*

Beloved, it is good,
He is saying quietly,
The thunder, it is good.

## FROM THE ACOMAN

432 *Butterfly Song*

Butterfly, butterfly, butterfly, butterfly,
Oh, look, see it hovering among the flowers,
It is like a baby trying to walk and not knowing how to go.
The clouds sprinkle down the rain.

## FROM THE YUMAN

433 The water bug is drawing the shadows of the evening toward
   him on the water

# FRANK RUSSELL

1868–1903

434      *Song of the Fallen Deer*

At the time of the White Dawn;
    At the time of the White Dawn,
I arose and went away.
    At Blue Nightfall I went away.

I ate the thornapple leaves
    And the leaves made me dizzy.
I drank the thornapple flowers
    And the drink made me stagger.

The hunter, Bow-Remaining,
    He overtook and killed me,
Cut and threw my horns away.
    The hunter, Reed-Remaining,
He overtook and killed me,
    Cut and threw my feet away.

Now the flies become crazy
    And they drop with flapping wings.
The drunken butterflies sit
    With opening and shutting wings.

435      *Foot Race Song*

Many people have gathered together,
    I am ready to start in the race,
And the Swallow with beating wings
    Cools me in readiness for the word.

Far in the west stands the black mountain
    Around which our racers ran at noon.
Who is this man running with me,
    The shadow of whose hands I see?

# THOMAS HARDY

## 1840–1928

### FROM THE GREEK OF SAPPHO

**436**

Cp.
Young

## *Sapphic Fragment*

'Thou shalt be—Nothing.'—OMAR KHAYYÁM.
'Tombless, with no remembrance.'—W. SHAKESPEARE.

Dead shalt thou lie; and nought
Be told of thee or thought,
For thou hast plucked not of the Muses' tree:
And even in Hades' halls
Amidst thy fellow-thralls
No friendly shade thy shade shall company!

### FROM THE LATIN OF CATULLUS

**437**

## *Carmina*, XXXI

(After passing Sirmione, April 1887)

Sirmio, thou dearest dear of strands
That Neptune strokes in lake and sea,
With what high joy from stranger lands
Doth thy old friend set foot on thee!
Yea, barely seems it true to me
That no Bithynia holds me now,
But calmly and assuringly
Around me stretchest homely Thou.

Is there a scene more sweet than when
Our clinging cares are undercast,
And, worn by alien moils and men,
The long untrodden sill repassed,
We press the pined for couch at last,
And find a full repayment there?
Then hail, sweet Sirmio; thou that wast,
And art, mine own unrivalled Fair!

# LADY AUGUSTA GREGORY

### 1859–1932

#### FROM THE IRISH

438 *The Hag of Beare*

Ebb-tide to me as to the sea; old age brings me reproach; I used to wear a shift that was always new; to-day, I have not even a cast one.

It is riches you are loving, it is not men; it was men we loved in the time we were living.

There were dear men on whose plains we used to be driving; it is good the time we passed with them; it is little we were broken afterwards.

When my arms are seen it is long and thin they are; once they used to be fondling, they used to be around great kings.

The young girls give a welcome to Beltaine when it comes to them; sorrow is more fitting for me; an old pitiful hag.

I have no pleasant talk; no sheep are killed for my wedding; it is little but my hair is grey; it is many colours I had over it when I used to be drinking good ale.

I have no envy against the old, but only against women; I myself am spent with old age, while women's heads are still yellow.

The stone of the kings on Feman; the chair of Ronan in Bregia; it is long since storms have wrecked them, they are old mouldering gravestones.

The wave of the great sea is speaking; the winter is striking us with it; I do not look to welcome today Fermuid son of Mugh.

I know what they are doing; they are rowing through the reeds of the ford of Alma; it is cold is the place where they sleep.

The summer of youth where we were has been spent along with its harvest; winter age that drowns everyone, its beginning has come upon me.

It is beautiful was my green cloak, my king liked to see it on me; it is noble was the man that stirred it, he put wool on it when it was bare.

Amen, great is the pity; every acorn has to drop. After feasting with shining candles, to be in the darkness of a prayer-house.

I was once living with kings, drinking mead and wine; to-day I am drinking whey-water among withered old women.

There are three floods that come up to the dun of Ard-Ruide:
a flood of fighting-men, a flood of horses, a flood of the hounds of
Lugaidh's son.

The flood-wave and the two swift ebb-tides; what the flood-wave
brings you in, the ebb-wave sweeps out of your hand.

The flood-wave and the second ebb-tide; they have all come as
far as me, the way that I know them well.

The flood-tide will not reach to the silence of my kitchen;
though many are my company in the darkness, a hand has been
laid upon them all.

My flood-tide! It is well I have kept my knowledge. It is Jesus
Son of Mary keeps me happy at the ebb-tide.

It is far is the island of the great sea where the flood reaches
after the ebb: I do not look for floods to reach to me after the
ebb-tide.

There is hardly a little place I can know again when I see it;
what used to be on the flood-tide is all on the ebb to-day!

# DOUGLAS HYDE

## 1860–1949

### FROM THE IRISH

439               *The Roman Earl*

No man's trust let woman claim,
    Not the same as men are they;
Let the wife withdraw her face
    When ye place the man in clay.

Once there was in Rome an earl
    Cups of pearl did hold his ale,
Of this wealthiest earl's mate
    Men relate a famous tale.

So it chanced that of a day
    As they lay at ease reclined,
He in jest pretends to die,
    Thus to try her secret mind.

'Och! Ochone, if you should die,
　　Never I would be myself;
To the poor of God I'd give
　　All my living, lands and pelf.

'Then in satin stiff with gold,
　　I would fold thy fair limbs still,
Laying thee in gorgeous tomb,'
　　Said the woman bent on ill.

Soon the earl, as if in death,
　　Yielded up his breath to try her;
Not one promise kept his spouse
　　Of the vows made glibly by her.

Jerked into a coffin hard,
　　With a yard of canvas coarse;
(To his hips it did not come);
　　To the tomb they drove the corse.

Bravely dressed was she that day,
　　On her way to Mass and grave;
To God's Church and needy men,
　　Not one penny piece she gave.

Up he starts, the coffined man,
　　Calls upon his wife aloud,
'Why am I thus thrust away,
　　Almost naked, with no shroud?'

Then as women do when caught
　　In a fault, with ready wit
Answered she upon the wing—
　　Not one thing would she admit:

'Winding-sheets are out of date,
　　All men state it. Clad like this,
When the judgment trump shall sound,
　　You shall bound to God and bliss.

'When in shrouds they trip and stumble
 You'll be nimble then as erst,
Hence I shaped thee this short vest,
 You'll run best and come in first.'

Trust not to a woman's faith,
 'Tis a breath, a broken stem;
Few whom they do not deceive,
 Let him grieve that trusts to them.

Though full her house of linen web,
 And sheets of thread spun full and fair
(A warning let it be to us)
 She left her husband naked there.

Spake the prudent earl—'In sooth
 Woman's truth ye here behold;
Now let each his coffin buy,
 Ere his wife shall get his gold.

'When death wrestles for his life
 Let his wife not hear him moan;
Great though be his pain and fear,
 Let her hear not sigh nor groan.'

# WILLIAM BUTLER YEATS

## 1865–1939

### ADAPTED FROM THE GREEK OF SOPHOCLES

440    *from* Oedipus at Colonus

*Colonus' Praise*

CHORUS: Come praise Colonus' horses, and come praise
 The wine-dark of the wood's intricacies,
 The nightingale that deafens daylight there,
 If daylight ever visit where,

Unvisited by tempest or by sun,
Immortal ladies tread the ground
Dizzy with harmonious sound,
Semele's lad a gay companion.

And yonder in the gymnasts' garden thrives
The self-sown, self-begotten shape that gives
Athenian intellect its mastery,
Even the grey-leaved olive-tree
Miracle-bred out of the living stone;
Nor accident of peace nor war
Shall wither that old marvel, for
The great grey-eyed Athena stares thereon.

Who comes into this country, and has come
Where golden crocus and narcissus bloom,
Where the Great Mother, mourning for her daughter
And beauty-drunken by the water
Glittering among grey-leaved olive-trees,
Has plucked a flower and sung her loss;
Who finds abounding Cephisus
Has found the loveliest spectacle there is.
Because this country has a pious mind
And so remembers that when all mankind
But trod the road, or splashed about the shore,
Poseidon gave it bit and oar,
Every Colonus lad or lass discourses
Of that oar and of that bit;
Summer and winter, day and night,
Of horses and horses of the sea, white horses.

FROM THE LATIN OF JONATHAN SWIFT

441            *Swift's Epitaph**

Swift has sailed into his rest;
Savage indignation there
Cannot lacerate his breast.
Imitate him if you dare,
World-besotted traveller; he
Served human liberty.

* The first and fifth line are Yeats's invention.

# ARTHUR SYMONS

1865–1945

## FROM THE FRENCH OF PAUL VERLAINE

442         *A la Promenade*

The sky so pale, and the trees, such frail things,
Seem as if smiling on our bright array
That flits so light and grey upon the way
With indolent airs and fluttering as of wings.

The fountain wrinkles under a faint wind,
And all the sifted sunlight falling through
The lime-trees of the shadowy avenue
Comes to us blue and shadowy-pale and thinned.

Faultlessly fickle and yet fond enough,
With fond hearts not too tender to be free,
We wander whispering deliciously,
And every lover leads a lady-love,

Whose imperceptible and roguish hand
Darts now and then a dainty tap, the lip
Revenges on an extreme finger-tip,
The tip of the left little finger, and,

The deed being so excessive and uncouth,
A duly freezing look deals punishment,
That in the instant of the act is blent
With a shy pity pouting in the mouth.

443         *Cortège*

A silver-vested monkey trips
And pirouettes before the face
Of one who twists a kerchief's lace
Between her well-gloved finger-tips.

A little negro, a red elf,
Carries her drooping train, and holds
At arm's-length all the heavy folds,
Watching each fold displace itself.

The monkey never lets his eyes
Wander from the fair woman's breast,
White wonder that to be possessed
Would call a god out of the skies.

Sometimes the little negro seems
To lift his sumptuous burden up
Higher than need be, in the hope
Of seeing what all night he dreams.

She goes by corridor and stair,
Still to the insolent appeals
Of her familiar animals
Indifferent or unaware.


444          *Femme et Chatte*

They were at play, she and her cat,
And it was marvellous to mark
The white paw and the white hand pat
Each other in the deepening dark.

The stealthy little lady hid
Under her mittens' silken sheath
Her deadly agate nails that thrid
The silk-like dagger-points of death.

The cat purred primly and drew in
Her claws that were of steel filed thin:
The devil was in it all the same.

And in the boudoir, while a shout
Of laughter in the air rang out,
Four sparks of phosphor shone like flame.

# EDWIN ARLINGTON ROBINSON

## 1869–1935

### FROM THE GREEK OF POSEIDIPPOS

445              *Doricha*

So now the very bones of you are gone
Where they were dust and ashes long ago;
And there was the last ribbon you tied on
To bind your hair, and that is dust also;
And somewhere there is dust that was of old
A soft and scented garment that you wore—
The same that once till dawn did closely fold
You in with fair Charaxus, fair no more.

But Sappho, and the white leaves of her song,
Will make your name a word for all to learn,
And all to love thereafter, even while
It's but a name; and this will be as long
As there are distant ships that will return
Again to your Naucratis and the Nile.


# SIR EDWARD MARSH

## 1872–1953

### FROM THE FRENCH OF JEAN DE LA FONTAINE

446           *The Hag and the Slavies*

There was a Hag who kept two Chambermaids;
So well they spun that the Three Sister Spinners,
Compared with them, were bunglers and beginners,
And her sole study was to give them work.
The moment Phœbus left his watery bed,
Up wheel, up distaffs, spin, spin, spin,
Morning out and evening in,
She kept 'em at it like a Turk.

433

The moment Eos raised her golden head,
A shabby cock would crow his punctual note:
The Hag, still shabbier, from her pallet leaping,
Would huddle on a greasy petticoat,
Light a cracked lamp, and scurry to the bed
Where the poor slaves with all their might
Were fiercely, ravenously sleeping.
One stretched an arm, one opened half an eye,
And both with concentrated spite
Swore through their teeth that the damned cock should die.
   No sooner said than done—that scrannel crow
Was hushed; but did the assassins profit? No—
The Hag became her own alarum,
And lest the hour should slip her unbeknown,
Began to hustle harum-scarum
Almost before the pair had lain them down.

Thus oft a struggle to escape
But lands us in a still worse scrape:
To exchange the cock for old Sibylla
Was *From Charybdis into Scylla*.


# WALLACE STEVENS

## 1879–1955

### FROM THE FRENCH OF JEAN LE ROY

447    I feel an apparition,
       at my back,
       an ebon wrack,
       of more than man's condition,
       that leans upon me there;
       and then in back, one more;
       and then, still farther back,
       still other men aligned;
       and then, toujours plus grands, immensities of night,
       who, less and less defined
       by light
       stretch off in the black:

ancestors from the first days of the world.

Before me, I know more,
one smaller at the first, and then one smaller still,
and more and more, that are my son and then his sons.

They lie buried in dumb sleep,
or bury themselves in the future.

And for the time, just one exists:
I.
Just one exists and I am time,
the whole of time.
I am the whole of light.
My flesh alone, for the moment, lives,
my heart alone gives,
my eyes alone have sight.
I am emblazoned, the others, all, are black.
I am the whole of light!
And those behind and those before
are only routineers of rounding time.
In back, they lie perdu in the black: the breachless grime,
(just one exists and I am time)
of an incalculable ether that burns and stings.

My will alone commands me: I am time!
Behind they passed the point of man,
before they are not embryo—I, only, touch with prime.
And that will last long length of time,
think what you will!

I am between two infinite states
on the mid-line dividing,
between the infinite that waits
and the long–abiding,
at the golden spot, where the mid-line swells
and yields to a supple, quivering, deep
inundation.

What do we count? All is for us that live!
Time, even time, and the day's strength and beam.
My fellows, you that live around me,
are you not surprised to be supreme,
on the tense line, in this expanse
of dual circumstance?
And are you not surprised to be the base
to know that, without you, the scale of lives
on which the eternal poising turns
would sink upon death's pitty under-place?
And are you not surprised to be the very poles?

Let us make signals in the air and cry aloud.
We must leave a wide noise tolling
in the night;
and in the deep of time,
set the wide wind rolling.


# WILLIAM CARLOS WILLIAMS

## 1883–1963

### FROM THE GREEK OF SAPPHO

**448**

Cp.
Sidney

Peer of the gods is that man, who
face to face, sits listening
to your sweet speech and lovely
                laughter.

It is this that rouses a tumult
in my breast. At mere sight of you
my voice falters, my tongue
                is broken.

Straightway, a delicate fire runs in
my limbs; my eyes
are blinded and my ears
                thunder.

# *vanee*
## *iters'*
## *rence*

# 9, 1990
# *f the South*
# *ennessee*

*tion, and Playwriting.*

| | |
|---|---|
| mmond | Tim O'Brien |
| owe | Monroe Spears |
| Irwin | Robert Stone |
| ustice | Peter Taylor |
| Lytle | Jarvis Thurston |
| Martin | |

James Stone was awarded the 1988 Robert Fitzgerald Translation Prize for these
He is currently a graduate student in clinical psychology at the Massachusetts S
a Fellowship at the NEH Literary Translation Institute at University of California,
Fragments 31, 2, 137, 168B, 34, 55, 42, 47, 48, 94, and 105 are presented in the ord

# SAPPHO: Selected
# translated from th
# by James Stone

*ονκ οιδ οττι θεω· δνο μοι τα νοημματα*

I don't know what I want: my mind split in two.

He gleams like a god that
man who sits beside you and
up close abandons himself to
       your honeyed voice

and tantalizing laughter which
rattle the heart in my ribcage;
a glimpse of you is all it
       takes to mute me;

yet so quietly is the tongue
mangled while lean flames race
under the skin, eyes peer
       in a void, bees whir

in the brain

chill the bone, tremors seize
every limb; now paler than parched weed
I appear little

by little in my loss to have died;

tested in every way since even . . .
. . . . . . . . . . that penniless man


**C**ome down from the sky.

Leave Crete, come here to our pure
temple, a haven of apple orchards,
and altars spiraled in frankincensed
curls of smoke.

Here the cool waters call
the yawning fruit tree limbs while
heavy-headed roses toss their shade and trembling
leaves trickle sleep,

here where stallions fed a glade
nurtures spring bloom; breathing winds
spirit our circle with smiles . . . . .
. . . . . .

Here and now, you . . . Cypris, take hold . . .
share, in goblets laced with gold,
this potion that blends these ritual
delights.

rs, and agents will take part.

olarships available.

, DIRECTOR
 write or call:
ssociate Director
CE, 310F St. Luke's Hall
 — (615) 598-1141

*Se*
*W*
*Cor*

**July 17**
**University**
**Sewanee**

*Workshops in Poetry*

Peter Davison        Wendy
Ellen Douglas        Tir
Mona Van Duyn     John
Marianne Gingher   Dona
Emily Grosholz      And
                   Char

Additional writers, critics,

Fellowships and

WYATT PR
For inforr
William Clarks
SEWANEE WRITERS' CON
SEWANEE, TN 3

s of Sappho from the ancient Greek.
ofessional Psychology. In 1989 he was awarded

ppearance.

# Fragments
# Ancient Greek

I have to tell you this, but self-
respect stops me short . . . . . .
. . . . . . . . . . . . . . . . .
. . . . . . . . . . . . . . . . .
If ever you felt the need to speak
what's respectable or even decent and
not stir up gossip with your tongue, in-
sult would not stream from your eyes—
you might be talking sense.

The moon has drifted off.
And the Pleiades. In the middle
of night, hour slides into hour.
I drift alone asleep.

Neighbors of the gentle moon stars
appear in a fluster to disappear
whenever she rises fully revealed
bathing the earth in silver light.

When you lie on a slab stretched out dead,
no one will requi    thing of you
or both           have said,
                  seed;
                  o
                  d.

Sweat pours out: a trembling hunts
me down. I grow paler
than dry grass and lack little
      of dying.


# EZRA POUND

## 1885–1973

### FROM THE ITALIAN OF GUIDO CAVALCANTI

449          *Sonnet VII*

Who is she that comes, makyng turn every man's eye
And makyng the air to tremble with a bright clearenesse
That leadeth with her Love, in such nearness
No man may proffer of speech more than a sigh?

Ah God, what she is like when her owne eye turneth, is
Fit for Amor to speake, for I can not at all;
Such is her modesty, I would call
Every woman else but an useless uneasiness.

No one could ever tell all of her pleasauntness
In that every high noble vertu leaneth to herward,
So Beauty sheweth her forth as her Godhede;

Never before was our mind so high led,
Nor have we so much of heal as will afford
That our thought may take her immediate in its embrace.

                            [Revised version]

## FROM THE PROVENÇAL OF ARNAUT DANIEL

450                             *Alba*

When the nightingale to his mate
Sings day-long and night late
My love and I keep state
In bower,
In flower,
'Till the watchman on the tower
Cry:

        'Up! Thou rascal, Rise,
        I see the white
           Light
           And the night
              Flies.'

## FROM THE CHINESE OF WU-TI
### via the English of H. A. Giles

451                           *Liu Ch'e*

The rustling of the silk is discontinued,
Dust drifts over the court-yard,
There is no sound of footfall, and the leaves
Scurry into heaps and lie still,
And she the rejoicer of the heart is beneath them:

A wet leaf that clings to the threshold.

### FROM THE CHINESE
via the notes of Ernest Fenollosa

## Cathay

**452**　　*Song of the Bowmen of Shu* (Anon.)

Cp.
'Pick a fern'
(later version)

Here we are, picking the first fern-shoots
And saying: When shall we get back to our country?
Here we are because we have the Ken-nin for our
　　foemen,
We have no comfort because of these Mongols.
We grub the soft fern-shoots,
When anyone says 'Return', the others are full of
　　sorrow.
Sorrowful minds, sorrow is strong, we are hungry and
　　thirsty.
Our defence is not yet made sure, no one can let his
　　friend return.
We grub the old fern-stalks.
We say: Will we be let to go back in October?
There is no ease in royal affairs, we have no comfort.
Our sorrow is bitter, but we would not return to our
　　country.
What flower has come into blossom?
Whose chariot? The General's.
Horses, his horses even, are tired. They were strong.
We have no rest, three battles a month.
By heaven, his horses are tired.
The generals are on them, the soldiers are by them.
The horses are well trained, the generals have ivory
　　arrows and quivers ornamented with fish-skin.
The enemy is swift, we must be careful.
When we set out, the willows were drooping with spring,
We come back in the snow,
We go slowly, we are hungry and thirsty,
Our mind is full of sorrow, who will know of our grief?

453        *The Beautiful Toilet* (Anon.)

Blue, blue is the grass about the river
And the willows have overfilled the close garden.
And within, the mistress, in the midmost of her youth,
White, white of face, hesitates, passing the door.
Slender, she put forth a slender hand;

And she was a courtezan in the old days,
And she has married a sot,
Who now goes drunkenly out
And leaves her too much alone.

454        *The River Merchant's Wife: a Letter* (Li Po) *701–62*

While my hair was still cut straight across my forehead
I played about the front gate, pulling flowers.
You came by on bamboo stilts, playing horse,
You walked about my seat, playing with blue plums.
And we went on living in the village of Chokan:
Two small people, without dislike or suspicion.

At fourteen I married My Lord you.
I never laughed, being bashful.
Lowering my head, I looked at the wall.
Called to, a thousand times, I never looked back.

At fifteen I stopped scowling,
I desired my dust to be mingled with yours
Forever and forever and forever.
Why should I climb the look out?

At sixteen you departed,
You went into far Ku-to-yen, by the river of swirling eddies,
And you have been gone five months.
The monkeys make sorrowful noise overhead.

You dragged your feet when you went out.
By the gate now, the moss is grown, the different mosses,
Too deep to clear them away!
The leaves fall early this autumn, in wind.
The paired butterflies are already yellow with August
Over the grass in the West garden;
They hurt me. I grow older.
If you are coming down through the narrows of the river Kiang,
Please let me know beforehand,
And I will come out to meet you
                              As far as Cho-fu-Sa.

455    *Poem by the Bridge at Ten-Shin* (Li Po)

March has come to the bridge head,
 Peach boughs and apricot boughs hang over a thousand gates,
At morning there are <u>flowers to cut the heart</u>,
 And evening drives them on the eastward-flowing waters.
Petals are on the gone waters and on the going,
          And on the back-swirling eddies,
But to-day's men are not the men of the old days,
Though they hang in the same way over the bridge-rail.
The sea's colour moves at the dawn
And the princes still stand in rows, about the throne,
And the moon falls over the portals of Sei-go-yo,
And clings to the walls and the gate-top.
With head gear glittering against the cloud and sun,
The lords go forth from the court, and into far borders.
They ride upon dragon-like horses,
Upon horses with head-trappings of yellow metal,
And the streets make way for their passage.
          Haughty their passing,
Haughty their steps as they go in to great banquets,
To high halls and curious food,
To the perfumed air and girls dancing,
To clear flutes and clear singing;
To the dance of the seventy couples;
To the mad chase through the gardens.
Night and day are given over to pleasure
And they think it will last a thousand autumns,
          Unwearying autumns.

For them the yellow dogs howl portents in vain,
And what are they compared to the lady Riokushu,
    That was cause of hate!
Who among them is a man like Han-rei
    Who departed alone with his mistress,
With her hair unbound, and he his own skiffsman!


456    *The Jewel Stairs' Grievance** (Li Po)

The jewelled steps are already quite white with dew,
It is so late that the dew soaks my gauze stockings,
And I let down the crystal curtain
And watch the moon through the clear autumn.


457    *Lament of the Frontier Guard* (Li Po)

By the North Gate, the wind blows full of sand,
    Lonely from the beginning of time until now!
    Trees fall, the grass goes yellow with autumn.
    I climb the towers and towers
        to watch out the barbarous land:
Desolate castle, the sky, the wide desert.
There is no wall left to this village.
Bones white with a thousand frosts,
High heaps, covered with trees and grass;
Who brought this to pass?
Who has brought the flaming imperial anger?
Who has brought the army with drums and with kettle-drums?
Barbarous kings.
A gracious spring, turned to blood-ravenous autumn,
A turmoil of wars-men, spread over the middle kingdom,
Three hundred and sixty thousand,
And sorrow, sorrow like rain.
Sorrow to go, and sorrow, sorrow returning.

---

* Jewel stairs, therefore a palace. Grievance, therefore there is something to complain of. Gauze stockings, therefore a court lady, not a servant who complains. Clear autumn, therefore he has no excuse on account of weather. Also she has come early, for the dew has not merely whitened the stairs, but has soaked her stockings. The poem is especially prized because she utters no direct reproach. (*Pound's note*)

Desolate, desolate fields,
And no children of warfare upon them,
      No longer the men for offence and defence.
Ah, how shall you know the dreary sorrow at the
      North Gate,
With Rihaku's name forgotten,
And we guardsmen fed to the tigers.

458     *South-Folk in Cold Country* (Anon.)

The Dai horse neighs against the bleak wind of Etsu,
The birds of Etsu have no love for En, in the north,
Emotion is born out of habit.
Yesterday we went out of the Wild-Goose gate,
Today from the Dragon-Pen.*
Surprised. Desert turmoil. Sea sun.
Flying snow bewilders the barbarian heaven.

Lice swarm like ants over our accoutrements.
Mind and spirit drive on the feathery banners.
Hard fight gets no reward.
Loyalty is hard to explain.
Who will be sorry for General Rishogu,
      the swift moving,
Whose white head is lost for this province?

A TRAVESTY OF PROPERTIUS' LATIN

459     *Homage to Sextus Propertius*

I

Shades of Callimachus, Coan ghosts of Philetas,
It is in your grove I would walk,
I who come first from the clear font
Bringing the Grecian orgies into Italy,
      and the dance into Italy.

---

* i.e., we have been warring from one end of the empire to the other, now east, now west, on each border. (*Pound's note*)

443

Who hath taught you so subtle a measure,
                    in what hall have you heard it;
What foot beat out your time-bar,
                    what water has mellowed your whistles?


Out-weariers of Apollo will, as we know, continue their
        Martian generalities,
        We have kept our erasers in order.
A new-fangled chariot follows the flower-hung horses;
A young Muse with young loves clustered about her
                    ascends with me into the æther, ...
And there is no high-road to the Muses.


Annalists will continue to record Roman reputations,
Celebrities from the Trans-Caucasus will belaud Roman celebrities
And expound the distentions of Empire,
But for something to read in normal circumstances?
For a few pages brought down from the forked hill unsullied?
I ask a wreath which will not crush my head.
            And there is no hurry about it;
I shall have, doubtless, a boom after my funeral,
Seeing that long standing increases all things
                            regardless of quality.
And who would have known the towers
                    pulled down by a deal-wood horse;
Or of Achilles withstaying waters by Simois,
Or of Hector spattering wheel-rims,
Or of Polydmantus, by Scamander, or Helenus and
        Deiphoibos?
Their door-yards would scarcely know them, or Paris.
Small talk O Ilion, and O Troad
                            twice taken by Oetian gods,
If Homer had not stated your case!


And I also among the later nephews of this city
                    shall have my dog's day
With no stone upon my contemptible sepulchre;
My vote coming from the temple of Phoebus in Lycia,
        at Patara,
And in the meantime my songs will travel,
And the devirginated young ladies will enjoy them
                    when they have got over the strangeness,

For Orpheus tamed the wild beasts—
                    and held up the Threician river;
And Cithaeron shook up the rocks by Thebes
                and danced them into a bulwark at his pleasure,
And you, O Polyphemus? Did harsh Galatea almost
Turn to your dripping horses, because of a tune, under Aetna?
We must look into the matter.
Bacchus and Apollo in favour of it,
There will be a crowd of young women doing homage to
            my palaver,
Though my house is not propped up by Taenarian columns
            from Laconia (associated with Neptune and Cerberus),
Though it is not stretched upon gilded beams;
My orchards do not lie level and wide
                        as the forests of Phaeacia
                        the luxurious and Ionian,
Nor are my caverns stuffed stiff with a Marcian vintage,
My cellar does not date from Numa Pompilius,
Nor bristle with wine jars,
Nor is it equipped with a frigidaire patent;
Yet the companions of the Muses
            will keep their collective nose in my books,
And weary with historical data, they will turn to my
            dance tune


Happy who are mentioned in my pamphlets,
        the songs shall be a fine tomb-stone over their
                            beauty.
            But against this?
Neither expensive pyramids scraping the stars in their
                            route,
Nor houses modelled upon that of Jove in East Elis,
Nor the monumental effigies of Mausolus,
                    are a complete elucidation of death.


Flame burns, rain sinks into the cracks
And they all go to rack ruin beneath the thud of the
                            years.
Stands genius a deathless adornment,
                    a name not to be worn out with the years.


445

## A CONDENSATION OF HOMER
### via the Renaissance Latin of Andreas Divus

460                          from *The Odyssey*, Book XI

And then went down to the ship,
Set keel to breakers, forth on the godly sea, and
We set up mast and sail on the swart ship,
Bore sheep aboard her, and our bodies also
Heavy with weeping, and winds from sternward
Bore us out onward with bellying canvas,
Circe's this craft, the trim-coifed goddess.
Then sat we amidships, wind jamming the tiller,
Thus with stretched sail, we went over sea till day's end.
Sun to his slumber, shadows o'er all the ocean,
Came we then to the bounds of deepest water,
To the Kimmerian lands, and peopled cities
Covered with close-webbed mist, unpierced ever
With glitter of sun-rays
Nor with stars stretched, nor looking back from heaven
Swartest night stretched over wretched men there.
The ocean flowing backward, came we then to the place
Aforesaid by Circe.
Here did they rites, Perimedes and Eurylochus,
And drawing sword from my hip
I dug the ell-square pitkin;          .
Poured we libations unto each the dead,
 First mead and then sweet wine, water mixed with white flour.
 Then prayed I many a prayer to the sickly death's-heads;
As set in Ithaca, sterile bulls of the best
For sacrifice, heaping the pyre with goods,
A sheep to Tiresias only, black and a bell-sheep.
Dark blood flowed in the fosse,
Souls out of Erebus, cadaverous dead, of brides
Of youths and of the old who had borne much;
Souls stained with recent tears, girls tender,
Men many, mauled with bronze lance heads,
Battle spoil, bearing yet dreory arms,
These many crowded about me; with shouting,
Pallor upon me, cried to my men for more beasts;
Slaughtered the herds, sheep slain of bronze;

Poured ointment, cried to the gods,
To Pluto the strong, and praised Proserpine;
Unsheathed the narrow sword,
I sat to keep off the impetuous impotent dead,
Till I should hear Tiresias.
But first Elpenor came, our friend Elpenor,
Unburied, cast on the wide earth,
Limbs that we left in the house of Circe,
Unwept, unwrapped in sepulchre, since toils urged other.
Pitiful spirit. And I cried in hurried speech:
'Elpenor, how art thou come to this dark coast?
Cam'st thou afoot, outstripping seamen?'
            And he in heavy speech:
'Ill fate and abundant wine. I slept in Circe's ingle.
Going down the long ladder unguarded,
I fell against the buttress,
Shattered the nape-nerve, the soul sought Avernus.
But thou, O King, I bid remember me, unwept, unburied,
Heap up mine arms, be tomb by sea-bord, and inscribed:
*A man of no fortune, and with a name to come.*
And set my oar up, that I swung mid fellows.'

And Anticlea came, whom I beat off, and then Tiresias Theban,
Holding his golden wand, knew me, and spoke first:
'A second time? why? man of ill star,
Facing the sunless dead and this joyless region?
Stand from the fosse, leave me my bloody bever
For soothsay.'
            And I stepped back,
And he strong with the blood, said then: 'Odysseus
Shalt return through spiteful Neptune, over dark seas,
Lose all companions.' Then Anticlea came.
Lie quiet Divus. I mean, that is Andreas Divus,
In officina Wecheli, 1538, out of Homer.
And he sailed, by Sirens and thence outward and away
And unto Circe.

FROM THE ITALIAN OF GUIDO CAVALCANTI

461 *Donna Me Prega*

A lady asks me
      I speak in season
She seeks reason for an affect, wild often
That is so proud he hath Love for a name

Who denys it can hear the truth now
Wherefore I speak to the present knowers
Having no hope that low-hearted

      Can bring sight to such reason
Be there not natural demonstration
      I have no will to try proof-bringing
Or say where it hath birth

What is its virtu and power
Its being and every moving
Or delight whereby 'tis called 'to love'
Or if man can show it to sight.

Where memory liveth,
      it takes its state
Formed like a diafan from light on shade

Which shadow cometh of Mars and remaineth
Created, having a name sensate,
Custom of the soul,
      will from the heart;

Cometh from a seen form which being understood
Taketh locus and remaining in the intellect possible
Wherein hath he neither weight nor still-standing,

Descendeth not by quality but shineth out
Himself his own effect unendingly
Not in delight but in the being aware
Nor can he leave his true likeness otherwhere.

He is not vertu but cometh of that perfection
Which is so postulate not by the reason
But 'tis felt, I say.

Beyond salvation, holdeth his judging force
Deeming intention to be reason's peer and mate,
Poor in discernment, being thus weakness' friend

Often his power cometh on death in the end,
Be it withstayed
          and so swinging counterweight
Not that it were natural opposite but only

Wry'd a bit from the perfect,
Let no man say love cometh from chance
Or hath not established lordship
Holding his power even though
          Memory hath him no more.

Cometh he to be
          when the will
From overplus
Twisteth out of natural measure,
Never adorned with rest Moveth he changing colour
Either to laugh or weep
Contorting the face with fear
          resteth but a little

Yet shall ye see of him That he is most often
With folk who deserve him
And his strange quality sets sighs to move
Willing man look into that forméd trace in his mind
And with such uneasiness as rouseth the flame.

Unskilled can not form his image,
He himself moveth not, drawing all to his stillness,
Neither turneth about to seek his delight
Nor yet to seek out proving
Be it so great or so small.

He draweth likeness and hue from like nature
So making pleasure more certain in seeming
Nor can stand hid in such nearness

Beautys be darts tho' not savage
Skilled from such fear a man follows
Deserving spirit, that pierceth.
Nor is he known from his face
But taken in the white light that is allness
Toucheth his aim

Who heareth, seeth not form
But is led by its emanation.

Being divided, set out from colour,
Disjunct in mid darkness
Grazeth the light, one moving by other,
Being divided, divided from all falsity
Worthy of trust
From him alone mercy proceedeth.  .

Go, song, surely thou mayest
Whither it please thee
For so art thou ornate that thy reasons
Shall be praised from thy understanders,
With others hast thou no will to make company.


## FROM THE CHINESE BOOK OF RITES

462 Know then:
        Toward summer when the sun is in Hyades
Sovran is Lord of the Fire
        to this month are birds.
with bitter smell and with the odour of burning
To the hearth god, lungs of the victim
        The green frog lifts up his voice
          and the white latex is in flower
In red car with jewels incarnadine
        to welcome the summer
In this month no destruction
        no tree shall be cut at this time

Wild beasts are driven from field
      in this month are simples gathered.
The empress offers cocoons to the Son of Heaven
      Then goes the sun into Gemini
Virgo in mid heaven at sunset
      indigo must not be cut
No wood burnt into charcoal
      gates are all open, no tax on the booths.
Now mares go to grazing,
      tie up the stallions
Post up the horsebreeding notices
        Month of the longest days
Life and death are now equal
      Strife is between light and darkness
Wise man stays in his house
      Stag droppeth antlers
Grasshopper is loud,
      leave no fire open to southward.
Now the sun enters Hydra, this is the third moon of summer
Antares of Scorpio stands mid heaven at sunset
Andromeda is with sunrise
      Lord of the fire is dominant
To this month is SEVEN,
      with bitter smell, with odour of burning
Offer to gods of the hearth
      the lungs of the victims
Warm wind is rising, cricket bideth in wall
Young goshawk is learning his labour
      dead grass breedeth glow-worms.
In Ming T'ang HE bideth
      in the west wing of that house
Red car and the sorrel horses
      his banner incarnadine.
The fish-ward now goes against crocodiles
To take all great lizards, turtles, for divination,
sea terrapin.
The lake warden to gather rushes
      to take grain for the *manes*
to take grain for the beasts you will sacrifice
to the Lords of the Mountains
      To the Lords of great rivers

Inspector of dye-works, inspector of colour and broideries
see that the white, black, green be in order
let no false colour exist here
black, yellow, green be of quality
          This month are trees in full sap
Rain has now drenched all the earth
          dead weeds enrich it, as if boil'd in a bouillon.
Sweet savour, the heart of the victim
yellow flag over Emperor's chariot
          yellow stones in his girdle.
Sagittarius in mid-course at sunset
          cold wind is beginning. Dew whitens.
Now is cicada's time,
          the sparrow hawk offers birds to the spirits.
Emperor goes out in war car, he is drawn by white horses,
white banner, white stones in his girdle
eats dog and the dish is deep.
          This month is the reign of Autumn
Heaven is active in metals, now gather millet
          and finish the flood-walls
Orion at sunrise.
          Horses now with black manes.
Eat dog meat. This is the month of ramparts.
Beans are the tribute, September is end of thunder
The hibernants go into their caves.
          Tolls lowered, now sparrows, they say, turn into oysters
The wolf now offers his sacrifice.
               Men hunt with five weapons,
They cut wood for charcoal.
          New rice with your dog meat.
First month of winter is now
          sun is in Scorpio's tail
at sunrise in Hydra, ice starting
The pheasant plunges into Houai (great water)
          and turns to an oyster
Rainbow is hidden awhile.
          Heaven's Son feeds on roast pork and millet,
Steel gray are stallion.
          This month winter ruleth.
The sun is in the archer's shoulder
          in crow's head at sunrise
Ice thickens. Earth cracks. And the tigers now move to mating.

452

Cut trees at solstice, and arrow shafts of bamboo.
Third month, wild geese go north,
        magpie starts building,
Pheasant lifteth his voice to the Spirit of Mountains
The fishing season is open,
        rivers and lakes frozen deep
Put now ice in your ice-house,
        the great concert of winds
Call things by the names. Good sovereign by distribution
Evil king is known by his imposts.

FROM THE CHINESE OF THE CLASSIC ANTHOLOGY
DEFINED BY CONFUCIUS

463        Pine boat a-shift
        on drift of tide,
        for flame in the ear, sleep riven,
        driven; rift of the heart in dark
        no wine will clear,
        nor have I will to playe.

        Mind that's no mirror to gulp down all 's seen,
        brothers I have, on whom I dare not lean,
        angered to hear a fact, ready to scold.

        My heart no turning-stone, mat to be rolled,
        right being right, not whim nor matter of count,
        true as a tree on mount.

        Mob's hate, chance evils many, gone through,
        aimed barbs not few;
        at bite of the jest in heart
        start up as to beat my breast.

        O'ersoaring sun, moon malleable
        alternately
        lifting a-sky to wane;
        sorrow about the heart like an unwashed shirt, I
        clutch here at words,
        having no force to fly.

464 *Pedlar*

Hill-billy, hill-billy come to buy
silk in our market, apparently?
toting an armful of calico.

Hill-billy, hill-billy, not at all
but come hither to plot my fall,
offering cloth for raw silk and all,
till I went out over the K'i
to Tun Mount, in fact, quite willingly,
and then I asked for a notary.
I said: It's O.K. with me,
we could be spliced autumnally,
> be not offended.

Autumn came, was waiting ended?
I climbed the ruin'd wall, looked toward Kuan pass.
On the Kuan frontier no man was.
I wept until you came,
trusted your smiling talk.   One would.
You said the shells were good and the stalks all clear.
You got a cart
and carted off me and my gear.

> *Let doves eat no more mulberries*
> *While yet the leaves be green,*
> *And girls play not with lustful men,*
> *Who can play and then explain,*
>> *for so 'tis usèd,*
>> *and girls be naught excusèd.*

The mulberry tree is bare,
yellow leaves float down thru the air,
Three years we were poor,
now K'i's like a soup of mud,
the carriage curtains wet, I ever straight
and you ambiguous
with never a grip between your word and act.

Three years a wife, to work without a roof,
up with the sun and prompt to go to bed,
never a morning off. I kept my word.
You tyrannize, Brothers unaware,
if told would but grin and swear
(with truth, I must confess):
If I'm in trouble, well, I made the mess.

'Grow old with you,' whom old you spite,
K'i has its banks and every swamp an edge.
Happy in pig-tails, laughed to hear your pledge,
sun up, sun up, believing all you said,
who in your acts reverse
(as a matter of course)
all that you ever said
and for the worse,
an end.

465   Wide, Ho?
A reed will cross its flow;
Sung far?
One sees it, tip-toe.
Ho strong?
The blade of a row-boat cuts it so soon.
Sung far? I could be there
(save reverence) by noon
     (did I not venerate
     Sung's line and state.)*

466    *Toujours la Politesse*

'That turn 'll get her.' I said.
We were loafing about under Nao,
each in his hunting gig
after a brace of wild pig;
You bowed and replied: 'Yours, better!'

* Said to be by the divorced wife of Huan of Sung, after her son's accession, decorum forbidding her to return to court. (*Pound's note*)

'Some cut.' I said.
We had come to the meet at Dog Hill,
two boar for the kill. You said,
with a bow: 'And yours, now!'

We met on the south slope of Nao,
wolves the game this time,
the exchange of the same lightness,
save that you said bowing: 'Majesterial!'
a huntsman not to be outdone in politeness.

467                    *Fraternitas*

Splendour recurrent
in cherry-wood,
in all the world there is
nothing like brotherhood.

Brothers meet
in death and sorrow;
broken line, battle heat,
Brothers stand by;

In a pinch they collaborate
as the ling bird's vertebrae
when friends of either
protractedly just sigh.

Wrangle at home, unite outside
when friends of either are ready of course
to help either with anything
'short of brute force.'

And peril past, there be those who
let brothers stew
in their own juice
as unfriends born, of no immediate use.

Set out the dishes
serve the wine,
let brothers dine tonight
with boyhood appetite.

Wife and childer together be
as sound of lutes played concurrently;
there's a deeper tone in fraternity
when elder and younger rise to agree.

Calm over earth, under sky
so be thy hearth and house as they should be:
probe to the utmost plan,
here the sincerity to rest a man.

468

Cp.
'Song
of the
Bowmen
of Shu'
(no. 452)

Pick a fern, pick a fern, ferns are high,
'Home,' I'll say: home, the year's gone by,
no house, no roof, these huns on the hoof.
Work, work, work, that's how it runs,
We are here because of these huns.

Pick a fern, pick a fern, soft as they come,
I'll say 'Home.'
Hungry all of us, thirsty here,
no home news for nearly a year.

Pick a fern, pick a fern, if they scratch,
I'll say 'Home,' what's the catch?
I'll say 'Go home,' now October's come.
King wants us to give it all,
no rest, spring, summer, winter, fall,
Sorrow to us, sorrow to you.
We won't get out of here till we're through.

When it's cherry-time with you,
we'll see the captain's car go thru,
four big horses to pull that load.
That's what comes along our road,
What do you call three fights a month,
and won 'em all?

Four car-horses strong and tall
and the boss who can drive 'em all
as we slog along beside his car,
ivory bow-tips and shagreen case
to say nothing of what we face
sloggin' along in the Hien-yün war.

Willows were green when we set out,
it's blowin' an' snowin' as we go
down this road, muddy and slow,
hungry and thirsty and blue as doubt
(no one feels half of what we know).

469

Fine fish to net,
ray, skate;
Milord's wine is
heavy and wet.

Fish to trap,
beam, tench,
Milord has wine
to drink and quench.

Fine fish to trap,
carp and mud-fish,
Milor' has' wine
in quantities'h.

Food in plenty
say good food
Plenty of food
all of it good,

This the song each guest agrees on:
Milor's good food all fits the season.

1

470  For an officer
in the old Capital, fox fur
(yellow) his manner without pretense;
his speech made sense
                    Ergo ten thousand now
                    yearn to return to Chou.


2

In the old Capital scholars all
wore wide plaited leaf hats and small
silk caps (black), the ladies' hair
was of a neatness that appeared unaided,
                    the present hair-dos
                    leave my heart unpersuaded.


3

In the old Capital officers wore ear-plugs fittingly
of seu stones (common jade) and the dames seemed
as to the manner born of Yin or Ki.
None such do we see pass
                    today, and my heart is
                    as smothered beneath wild grass.


4

The scholars' sash ends in the older court
had a certain grace in severity,
their ladies' side hair curved like a scorpion's tail,
something to follow, tho' we never see.


5

There was no fuss about the fall
of the sash ends, there was just that much to spare
and it fell, and ladies' hair
curved, just curved and that was all
                    the like of which, today, is never met;
                    And I therefore
                    express regret.

1

471 For deep deer-copse beneath Mount Han
hazel and arrow-thorn make an even, orderly wood;
A deferent prince
seeks rents in fraternal mood.

2

The great jade cup holds yellow wine,
a fraternal prince can pour
blessing on all his line.

3

High flies the hawk a-sky,
deep dives the fish,
far, far, even thus amid distant men
shall a deferent prince have his wish.

4

The red bull stands ready, and
clear wine is poured,
may such rite augment the felicity
of this deferent lord.

5

Thick oaks and thorn give folk fuel to spare,
a brotherly prince shall energize
the powers of air.

6

And as no chink is between vine-grip and tree
thick leaf over bough to press,
so a fraternal lord seeks abundance
only in equity,
in his mode is no crookedness.

472
Full be the year, abundant be the grain,
high be the heaps composed in granaries,
robust the wine for ceremonial feast
and lack to no man be he highest or least,
neither be fault in any rite here shown
so plenteous nature shall inward virtue crown.

## FROM THE GREEK OF SOPHOCLES

473    Choruses from *Women of Trachis*: Khoros 4

[Herakles, having put on the poisoned robe
sent by Daysair, is carried home.]

KHOROS (*declaimed*):                                (*Str. 1*)

TORN between griefs, which grief shall I lament,
which first? Which last, in heavy argument?
One wretchedness to me in double load.

DEATH'S in the house,                           (*Ant. 1*)
           and death comes by the road.

(*sung*)                                      (*Str. 2*)

THAT WIND might bear away my grief and me,
Sprung from the hearth-stone, let it bear me away.
God's Son is dead,
       that was so brave and strong,
And I am craven to behold such death
   . Swift on the eye,
Pain hard to uproot,
       and this so vast
A splendour of ruin.

THAT NOW is here. (*Ant. 2*)
As Progne shrill upon the weeping air,
'tis no great sound.
      These strangers lift him home,
with shuffling feet, and love that keeps them still.
The great weight silent
      for no man can say
If sleep but feign
      or Death reign instantly.


### Khoros 5

KHOROS (*low cello merely sustaining the voice*):

OYEZ: (*Str. 1*)
Things foretold and forecast:
Toil and moil.
God's Son from turmoil shall
—when twelve seed-crops be past—
be loosed with the last,
      his own.
Twining together, godword found good,
Spoken of old,
      as the wind blew, truth's in the flood.
We and his brood see in swift combine,
      here and at last that:
Amid the dead is no servitude
      nor do they labour.

(*contrabassi & drums muffled*)

LO, beneath deadly cloud (*Ant. 1*)
Fate and the Centaur's curse, black venom spread,
Dank Hydra's blood
Boils now through every vein, goad after goad
from spotted snake to pierce the holy side,
nor shall he last to see a new day's light,
Black shaggy night descends
      as Nessus bade.

WHAT MOURNFUL case                                        (*Str. 2*)
> who feared great ills to come,
New haste in mating threatening her home,
Who hark'd to reason in a foreign voice
Entangling her in ravage out of choice.
Tears green the cheek with bright dews pouring down,
Who mourns apart, alone
Oncoming swiftness in o'erlowering fate
To show what wreck is nested in deceit.

LET the tears flow.                                               (*Ant. 2*)
> Ne'er had bright Herakles in his shining
Need of pity till now
> whom fell disease burns out.
How swift on Oechal's height
> to take a bride.
Black pointed shaft that shielded her in flight,
Attest
That
Kupris stood by and never said a word,
Who now flares here the contriver
manifest ...
and indifferent.

### FROM THE LATIN OF CATULLUS

## *Carmina*, LXXXV

**474**

Cp.
Lovelace
Landor

I hate and love. Why? You may ask but
It beats me. I feel it done to me, and ache.

# H. D. (HILDA DOOLITTLE)

## 1886–1961

FROM THE GREEK OF EURIPIDES

475       Chorus from *Iphigeneia in Aulis*

And Pergamos,
city of the Phrygians,
ancient Troy
will be given up to its fate.
They will mark the stone-battlements
and the circle of them
with a bright stain.
They will cast out the dead—
a sight for Priam's queen to lament,
and her frightened daughters.

And Helen, child of Zeus,
will cry aloud for the mate
she has left in that Phrygian town.

May no child of mine,
nor any child of my child
ever fashion such a tale,
as the Phrygians shall murmur,
as they stoop at their distaffs,
whispering with Lydians,
splendid with weight of gold—

'Helen has brought this.
They will tarnish our bright hair.
They will take us as captives
for Helen—born of Zeus,
when he sought Leda with bird-wing
and touched her with bird-throat—
if men speak truth.

'But still we lament our state,
the desert of our wide courts,
even if there is no truth
in the legends cut on ivory,
nor in the poets
nor the songs.'


# MARIANNE MOORE

## 1887–1972

### FROM THE FRENCH OF JEAN DE LA FONTAINE

476          *The Fox and the Crow*

On his airy perch among the branches
    Master Crow was holding cheese in his beak.
Master Fox, whose pose suggested fragrances,
    Said in language which of course I cannot speak,
        'Aha, superb Sir Ebony, well met.
How black! who else boasts your metallic jet!
        If your warbling were unique,
        Rest assured, as you are sleek,
One would say that our wood had hatched nightingales.'
All aglow, Master Crow tried to run a few scales,
        Risking trills and intervals,
Dropping the prize as his huge beak sang false.
The fox pounced on the cheese and remarked, 'My dear sir,
    Learn that every flatterer
    Lives at the flattered listener's cost:
A lesson worth more than the cheese that you lost.'
        The tardy learner, smarting under ridicule,
Swore he'd learned his last lesson as somebody's fool.

477 *The Wolf and the Stork*

Wolves can outeat anyone;
Indeed at a festivity,
Such gluttony second to none
Almost ended fatally
When a bone choked a wolf as he gulped what he ate;
But happily since he was inarticulate,
A stork chanced to hear him groan,
Was besought by frowns to run and peer,
And ah, had soon relieved the beast of the bone;
Then, having done him a service, had no fear,
So asked him how compensate her.
'Compensate?' he inquired with bared teeth,
'A humorist, I infer!
You should be glad that you draw breath.
Thrust your beak down my throat and you somehow
escaped death?
Be off. You are unappreciative;
Shun my paws if you care to live.'

478 *The Donkey and the Lapdog*

Don't ape what must be born in one;
You'll become a clown of awkwardness:
A boor by birth is never less,
Whatever his caparison.
Just a few upon whom Heaven smiled indulgently,
Seem blessed with the art of pleasing naturally—
An art better not assisted;
So let us not be the donkey in my tale,
Who hoped to seem more lovable
By proffering endearments which would be resisted.
He said to himself, 'Why not the same
As that lapdog? Because he's a scrap of a thing,
Have master and mistress been flattering
And petting him the instant he came,
Whereas I'm drubbed till the cudgels sing?
His paw goes up, wheedling some benefit;
He's kissed and promptly overrated.

If that's all one must do to be a favourite,
      It's not too complicated.'
      So since initiated,
He lumbered up as his master shook with merriment,
      Raised a hoof which use had dented,
And dealt his master's chin a blow that was well meant,
To the music of a bray's accompaniment:
A dainty match for boorish intrepidity.
'Oh! oh! What a caress! and what a melody!'
Master shouted, 'Martin haste. This beast is pestilent!'
Cudgel-Martin rushed forth, made the tune different,
      And that ended the comedy.


479        *The Rat and the Elephant*

I fear that appearances are worshipped throughout France:
      Whereas pre-eminence perchance
      Merely means a pushing person.
      An extremely French folly—
A weakness of which we have more than our share—
Whereas false pride, I'd say, has been the Spaniard's snare.
      To be epigrammatical,
      They're foolish folk; we're comical.
      Well, I've put us in this tale
      Which came to mind as usable.
A mite of a rat was mocking an elephant
As it moved slowly by, majestically aslant,
      Valued from antiquity,
      Towering in draped solemnity
      While bearing along in majesty
      A queen of the Levant—
      With her dog, her cat, and sycophant,
Her parakeet, monkey, anything she might want—
      On their way to relics they wished to see.
      But the rat was not one whom weight could daunt
And asked why observers should praise mere size.
'Who cares how much space something occupies?'

He said. 'Size does not make a thing significant!
All crowding near an elephant? Why must I worship him?
Servile to brute force at which mere tots might faint?
Should persons such as I admire his heavy limb?
       I pander to an elephant!'
       About to prolong his soliloquy
       When the cat broke from captivity
       And instantly proved what her victim would grant:
       That a rat is not an elephant.

# ELIZABETH DARYUSH

## 1887–1977

### FROM THE PERSIAN OF JALĀL UD DIN RŪMI

480      I am your mother, your mother's mother,
I am your father, his father also;
look on me, see each living ancestor;
it is well you should understand your kin,
should learn who your body's bound to, should know
who they are whose house you are prisoned in.

I am your dear spouse, your wife, your husband,
I am nearer to you than your own folk,
I am what you loved, freely chose, the friend
you cannot leave – ev'n in the tomb I wait
to be your soul's only companion.... Look,
if you dare, on your mind's eternal mate.

# THOMAS STEARNS ELIOT

## 1888–1965

### FROM HIS OWN FRENCH

481                    *Death by Water*

Phlebas the Phoenician, a fortnight dead,
Forgot the cry of gulls, and the deep sea swell
And the profit and loss.
                          A current under sea
Picked his bones in whispers. As he rose and fell
He passed the stages of his age and youth
Entering the whirlpool.
                          Gentile or Jew
O you who turn the wheel and look to windward,
Consider Phlebas, who was once handsome and tall as you.


### FROM THE FRENCH OF SAINT-JOHN PERSE

482                    from *Anabasis*

#### IV

Such is the way of the world and I have nothing but good to say
of it.—Foundation of the City. Stone and bronze. Thorn fires at
dawn
   bared these great
   green stones, and viscid like the bases of temples, of latrines,
   and the mariner at sea whom our smoke reached saw that the
earth to the summit had changed its form (great tracts of burnt-
over land seen afar and these operations of channelling the living
waters on the mountains).
   Thus was the City founded and placed in the morning under
the labials of a clear sounding name. The encampments are razed
from the hills! And we who are there in the wooden galleries,
   head bare and foot bare in the freshness of the world,
   what have we to laugh at, but what have we to laugh at,
as we sit, for a disembarkation of girls and mules?

and what is there to say, since the dawn, of all this people under sail?—Arrivals of grain! ... And the ships taller than Ilion under the white peacock of the sky, having crossed the bar, hove to

in this deadwater where floats a dead ass. (We must ordain the fate of this pale meaningless river, colour of grasshoppers crushed in their sap.)

In the great fresh noise of the yonder bank, the blacksmiths are masters of their fires! The cracking of whips in the new streets unloads whole wainsful of unhatched evils. O mules, our shadows under the copper sword! four restive heads knotted to the fist make a living cluster against the blue. The founders of asylums meet beneath a tree and find their ideas for the choice of situations. They teach me the meaning and the purpose of the buildings: front adorned, back blind; the galleries of laterite, the vestibules of black stone and the pools of clear shadow for libraries; cool places for wares of the druggist. And then come the bankers blowing into their keys. And already in the streets a man sang alone, one of those who paint on their brow the cipher of their god. (Perpetual crackling of insects in this quarter of vacant lots and rubbish.) ... And this is no time to tell you, no time to reckon our alliances with the people of the other shore; water presented in skins, commandeering of cavalry for the dockworks and princes paid in currency of fish. (A child sorrowful as the death of apes—one that had an elder sister of great beauty—offered us a quail in a slipper of rose-coloured satin.)

... Solitude! the blue egg laid by a great sea-bird, and the bays at morning all littered with gold lemons!—Yesterday it was! The bird made off!

Tomorrow the festivals and tumults, the avenues planted with podded trees, and the dustmen at dawn bearing away huge pieces of dead palmtrees, fragment of giant wings.... Tomorrow the festivals,

the election of harbour-masters, the voices practising in the suburbs and, under the moist incubation of storms,

the yellow town, casque'd in shade, with the girls' waist cloths hanging at the windows.

\*    \*    \*

... At the third lunation, those who kept watch on the hill-tops folded their canvas. The body of a woman was burnt in the sands. And a man strode forth at the threshold of the desert—profession of his father: dealer in scent-bottles.

[Revised version. Hiatus marks in original.]


# ARTHUR WALEY

## 1889–1966

### FROM THE CHINESE

483 *The Ejected Wife*

Entering the Hall, she meets the new wife;
Leaving the gate, she runs into former husband.
Words stick; does not manage to say anything.
Presses hands together: stands hesitating.
Agitates moon-like fan, sheds pearl-like tears,
Realises she loves him as much as ever—
Present pain never come to an end.


484

Yellow dusk: messenger fails to appear.
Restraining anger, heart sick and sad.
Turn candle towards bed-foot;
Averting face—sob in darkness.


485

In her boudoir, the young lady,—unacquainted with grief.
Spring day,—best clothes, mounts shining tower.
Suddenly sees at the dyke's head, the changed colour of the willows.
Regrets she made her dear husband go to win a fief.*

---

*She urged him to enlist out of vanity, hoping to become a sort of Lady of the Manor. (*Waley's note*)

486 *Plucking the Rushes*

[A boy and girl are sent to gather rushes for thatching]

Green rushes with red shoots,
Long leaves bending to the wind—
You and I in the same boat
Plucking rushes at the Five Lakes.
We started at dawn from the orchid-island;
We rested under the elms till noon.
You and I plucking rushes
Had not plucked a handful when night came!

FROM THE CHINESE OF PO CHÜ-I

487 *Lazy Man's Song*

I could have a job, but am too lazy to choose it,
I have got land, but am too lazy to farm it.
My house leaks; I am too lazy to mend it.
My clothes are torn; I am too lazy to darn them.
I have got wine, but I am too lazy to drink;
So it's just the same as if my cup were empty.
I have got a lute, but am to lazy to play;
So it's just the same as if it had no strings.
My family tells me there is no more steamed rice;
I want to cook, but am too lazy to grind.
My friends and relatives write me long letters;
I should like to read them, but they're such a bother to open.
I have always been told that Hsi Shu-yeh
Passed his whole life in absolute idleness.
But he played his lute and sometimes worked at his forge;
So even *he* was not so lazy as I.

488 *Starting Early from the Ch'U-Ch'êng Inn*

Washed by the rain, dust and grime are laid;
Skirting the river, the road's course is flat.
The moon has risen on the last remnants of night;
The travellers' speed profits by the early cold.

In the great silence I whisper a faint song;
In the black darkness are bred sombre thoughts.
On the lotus-bank hovers a dewy breeze;
Through the rice furrows trickles a singing stream.
At the noise of our bells a sleeping dog stirs;
At the sight of our torches a roosting bird wakes.
Dawn glimmers through the shapes of misty trees ...
For ten miles, till day at last breaks.

489            *Eating Bamboo-Shoots*

My new Province is a land of bamboo-groves:
Their shoots in spring fill the valleys and hills.
The mountain woodman cuts an armful of them
And brings them down to sell at the early market.
Things are cheap in proportion as they are common;
For two farthings I buy a whole bundle.
I put the shoots in a great earthen pot
And heat them up along with boiling rice.
The purple skins broken—like an old brocade;
The white skin opened—like new pearls.
Now every day I eat them recklessly;
For a long time I have not touched meat.
All the time I was living at Lo-yang
They could not give me enough to suit my taste.
Now I can have as many shoots as I please;
For each breath of the south-wind makes a new bamboo!

490            *Invitation to Hsiao Ch'U-Shih*

            (Written when Governor of Chung-Chou)

Within the Gorges there is no lack of men;
They are people one meets, not people one cares for.
At my front door guests also arrive;
They are people one sits with, not people one knows.
When I look up, there are only clouds and trees;
When I look down—only my wife and child.
I sleep, eat, get up or sit still;
Apart from that, nothing happens at all.

But beyond the city Hsiao the hermit dwells,
And with *him* at least I find myself at ease.
For *he* can drink a full flagon of wine
And is good at reciting long-line poems.
Some afternoon, when the clerks have gone home,
At a season when the path by the river bank is dry,
I beg you, take up your staff of bamboo-wood
And find your way to the parlour of Government House.

491 *The Cranes*

The western wind has blown but a few days;
Yet the first leaf already flies from the bough.
On the drying paths I walk in my thin shoes;
In the first cold I have donned my quilted coat.
Through shallow ditches the floods are clearing away;
Through sparse bamboos trickles a slanting light.
In the early dusk, down an alley of green moss,
The garden-boy is leading the cranes home.

FROM THE CHINESE OF SU TUNG-P'O

492 *On the Birth of his Son*

Families, when a child is born
Want it to be intelligent.
I, through intelligence,
Having wrecked my whole life,
Only hope the baby will prove
Ignorant and stupid.
Then he will crown a tranquil life
By becoming a Cabinet Minister.

# JOHN PEALE BISHOP

## 1892–1944

### FROM THE GREEK OF EUENOS

493

*To a Swallow*

Cp.
Cowper

Relish honey. If you please
Regale yourself on Attic bees.
But spare, O airy chatterer,
Spare the chattering grasshopper!

Winging, spare his gilded wings,
Chatterer, his chatterings.
Summer's child, do not molest
Him the summer's humblest guest.

Snatch not for your hungry young
One who like yourself has sung—
For it is neither just nor fit
That poets should each other eat.


# HUGH MACDIARMID

## 1892–1978

### FROM THE GERMAN OF RUDOLF LEONHARD

494

*The Dead Liebknecht*

His corpse owre a' the city lies
In ilka square and ilka street
His spilt bluid floods the vera skies
And nae hoose but is darkened wi't.

The factory horns begin to blaw
Thro' a' the city, blare on blare,

475

The lowsin' time o' workers a',
Like emmits skailin' everywhere.

And wi' his white teeth shinin' yet
The corpse lies smilin' underfit.

## FROM THE CRETAN

### *Under the Greenwood Tree*

495

A sodger laddie's socht a hoose,
A hoose and toon to bide in.
He's fund a road but never a hoose
Or toon the haill warld wide in.

And syne he's come to an auld green tree
—Then wae for a sodger loon
Wha's tint his way frae the battlefield
And here maun lay him doon.

There's brainches here for his graith o' war,
A root to tether his horse,
And a shaddaw for a windin' sheet
To row aboot his corse.

### *The Robber*

496

A robber cam' to my hoose
And theft was a' his ploy,
Nor gowd nor siller could he find
And sae he stow my joy.

He stow the kisses frae my mou'
And mony a lauch and tear,
And syne begood upon my bluid
And toomed it vera near.

494 lowsin'] loosing      underfit] underfoot
495 graith]gear, equipment
496   begood] began     toomed] emptied

## HUGH MACDIARMID

I gied him a' he wanted
And mebbe a wee thing mair,
I dinna ken what a' he took
But that's no' here nor there.

For aye he gied for a' he took,
And better gied than took,
And I've a bonnie laddie noo
And breists for him to sook.


# BASIL BUNTING

1900–

## FROM THE PERSIAN OF FIRDOSI

497    When the sword of sixty comes nigh his head
give a man no wine, for he is drunk with years.
Age claps a stick in my bridle-hand:
substance spent, health broken,
forgotten the skill to swerve aside from the joust
with the spearhead grazing my eyelashes.

The sentinel perched on the hill top
cannot see the countless army he used to see there:
the black summit's deep in snow
and its lord himself sinning against the army.

He was proud of his two swift couriers:
lo! sixty ruffians have put them in chains.
The singer is weary of his broken voice,
one drone for the bulbul alike and the lion's grousing.

Alas for flowery, musky, sappy thirty
and the sharp Persian sword!
The pheasant strutting about the briar,
pomegranate-blossom and cypress sprig!
Since I raised my glass to fifty-eight
I have toasted only the bier and the burial ground.

I ask the just Creator
so much refuge from Time
that a tale of mine may remain in the world
from this famous book of the ancients
and they who speak of such matters weighing their words
think of that only when they think of me.

## FROM THE PERSIAN OF RUDAKI

498

Came to me—
   Who?
She.
   When?
In the dawn, afraid.

   What of?
Anger.
   Whose?
Her father's.
   Confide!

I kissed her twice.
   Where?
On her moist mouth.
   Mouth?

No.
   What, then?
Cornelian.
   How was it?
Sweet.

# ROY CAMPBELL

1901–1957

FROM THE SPANISH OF SAN JUAN DE LA CRUZ

499          *Upon a Gloomy Night*

Upon a gloomy night,
With all my cares to loving ardours flushed,
(O venture of delight!)
With nobody in sight
I went abroad when all my house was hushed.

In safety, in disguise,
In darkness up the secret stair I crept,
(O happy enterprise)
Concealed from other eyes
When all my house at length in silence slept.

Upon that lucky night
In secrecy, inscrutable to sight,
I went without discerning
And with no other light
Except for that which in my heart was burning.

It lit and led me through
More certain than the light of noonday clear
To where One waited near
Whose presence well I knew,
There where no other presence might appear.

Oh night that was my guide!
Oh darkness dearer than the morning's pride,
Oh night that joined the lover
To the beloved bride
Transfiguring them each into the other.

Within my flowering breast
Which only for himself entire I save
He sank into his rest
And all my gifts I gave
Lulled by the airs with which the cedars wave.

Over the ramparts fanned
While the fresh wind was fluttering his tresses,
With his serenest hand
My neck he wounded, and
Suspended every sense with its caresses.

Lost to myself I stayed
My face upon my lover having laid
From all endeavour ceasing:
And all my cares releasing
Threw them amongst the lilies there to fade.

500     from *Coplas about the soul which suffers
with impatience to see God*

I live without inhabiting
Myself—in such a wise that I
Am dying that I do not die.

Within myself I do not dwell
Since without God I cannot live.
Reft of myself, and God as well,
What serves this life (I cannot tell)
Except a thousand deaths to give?
Since waiting here for life I lie
And die because I do not die.

This life I live in vital strength
Is loss of life unless I win You:
And thus to die I shall continue
Until in You I live at length.
Listen (my God!) my life is in You
This life I do not want, for I
Am dying that I do not die.

Thus in your absence and your lack
How can I in myself abide
Nor suffer here a death more black
Than ever was by mortal died.
For pity of myself I've cried
Because in such a plight I lie
Dying because I do not die.


## FROM THE FRENCH OF CHARLES BAUDELAIRE

501
### *The Giantess*

Of old when Nature, in her verve defiant,
Conceived each day some birth of monstrous mien,
I would have lived near some young female giant
Like a voluptuous cat beside a queen;

To see her body flowering with her soul
Freely develop in her mighty games,
And in the mists that through her gaze would roll
Guess that her heart was hatching sombre flames;

To roam her mighty contours as I please,
Ramp on the cliff of her tremendous knees,
And in the solstice, when the suns that kill

Make her stretch out across the land and rest,
To sleep beneath the shadow of her breast
Like a hushed village underneath a hill.


502
### *The Seven Old Men*
#### To Victor Hugo

Ant-seething city, city full of dreams,
Where ghosts by daylight tug the passer's sleeve.
Mystery, like sap, through all its conduit-streams,
Quickens the dread Colossus that they weave.

One early morning, in the street's sad mud,
Whose houses, by the fog increased in height,
Seemed wharves along a riverside in flood:
When with a scene to match the actor's plight,

Foul yellow mist had filled the whole of space:
Steeling my nerves to play a hero's part,
I coaxed my weary soul with me to pace
The backstreets shaken by each lumbering cart.

A wretch appeared whose tattered, yellow clothing,
Matching the colour of the raining skies,
Could make it shower down alms—but for the loathing
Malevolence that glittered in his eyes.

The pupils of his eyes, with bile injected,
Seemed with their glance to make the frost more raw.
Stiff as a sword, his long red beard projected,
Like that of Judas, level with his jaw.

He was not bent, but broken, with the spine
Forming a sharp right-angle to the straight,
So that his stick, to finish the design,
Gave him the stature and the crazy gait

Of a three-footed Jew, or crippled hound.
He plunged his soles into the slush as though
To crush the dead; and to the world around
Seemed less of an indifferent than a foe.

His image followed him (back, stick, and beard
In nothing differed) spawned from the same hole,
A centenarian twin. Both spectres steered
With the same gait to the same unknown goal.

To what foul plot was I exposed? of what
Humiliating hazard made the jeer?
For seven times (I counted) was begot
This sinister, self multiplying fear!

Let him mark well who laughs at my despair
With no fraternal shudder in reply ...
Those seven loathsome monsters had the air,
Though rotting through, of what can never die.

Disgusting Phoenix, his own sire and father!
Could I have watched an eighth instalment spawn
Ironic, fateful, grim—nor perished rather?
But from that hellish *cortège* I'd withdrawn.

Perplexed as drunkards when their sight is doubled,
I locked my room, sick, fevered, chilled with fright:
With all my spirit sorely hurt and troubled
By so ridiculous yet strange a sight.

Vainly my reason for the helm was striving:
The tempest of my efforts made a scorn.
My soul like a dismasted wreck went driving
Over a monstrous sea without a bourn.


# JAMES BLAIR LEISHMAN

## 1902–1963

### FROM THE GERMAN OF FRIEDRICH HÖLDERLIN

503         *Half of Life*

With yellow pears leans over,
And full of run-wild roses,
The land into the lake,
You gracious swans,
And, drunk with kisses,
You dip your heads
In the sacredly-sober water.

Where shall I gather though,
When winter comes, the flowers, and where
The dappling shine
And shadow of earth?
The walls will stand
Speechless and cold, the wind-swung
Weather-vanes clatter.

504        *Ripe, Being Plunged into Fire ...*

Ripe, being plunged into fire, being boiled,
Being proved upon the earth, are fruits, and a decree is
That all shall therein like serpents,
Prophetic, dreaming on
The hills of Heaven. And many
A thing must, like a burden
Of faggots on the shoulder,
Be clung to. But evil are
The ways. And most perversely,
Like horses, run the captured
Elements and ancient
Laws of earth. With ever
A hankering after unrestraint. Many a thing though
Has to be clung to. And faith is needed.
Ahead of us though and behind us we will not
Try to look, but let ourselves be rocked as
In swaying bark on the sea.

FROM THE GERMAN OF RAINER MARIA RILKE

505        *Annunciation*

(Words of the Angel)

You are not nearer God than we,
and we are far at best,
yet through your hands most wonderfully
his glory's manifest.
From woman's sleeves none ever grew
so ripe, so shimmeringly:
I am the day, I am the dew,
you, Lady, are the Tree.

Pardon, now my long journey's done,
I had forgot to say
what he who sat as in the sun,
grand in his gold array,
told me to tell you, pensive one
(space has bewildered me).
I, the beginner, have begun,
you, Lady, are the Tree.

I spread my wings out wide and rose,
the space around grew less;
your little house quite overflows
with my abundant dress.
But still you keep your solitude
and hardly notice me:
I'm but a breeze within the wood,
you, Lady, are the Tree.

The angels tremble in their choir,
grow pale, and separate:
never were longing and desire
so vague and yet so great.
Something perhaps is going to be
that you perceived in dream.
Hail to you! for my soul can see
that your are ripe and teem.
You lofty gate, that any day
may open for our good:
you ear my longing songs assay,
my word—I know now—lost its way
in you as in a wood.

And thus your last dream was designed
to be fulfilled by me.
God looked at me: he made me blind ...

You, Lady, are the Tree.

*Sonnets to Orpheus: Second Part*

IV

This is the creature there has never been.
They never knew it, and yet, none the less,
they loved the way it moved, its suppleness,
its neck, its very gaze, mild and serene.

Not there, because they loved it, it behaved
as though it were. They always left some space.
And in that clear unpeopled space they saved
it lightly reared its head, with scarce a trace

of not being there. They fed it, not with corn,
but only with the possibility
of being. And that was able to confer

such strength, its brow put forth a horn. One horn.
Whitely it stole up to a maid,—to *be*
within the silver mirror and in her.

XVII

Where, in what ever-blissfully watered gardens, upon what trees,
out of, oh, what gently dispetalled flower-cups do these
so strange-looking fruits of consolation mature?
Delicious, when, now and then, you pick one up in the poor

trampled field of your poverty. Time and again you find
yourself lost in wonder over the size of the fruit,
over its wholesomeness, over its smooth, soft rind,
and that neither the heedless bird above nor jealous worm at
        the root

has been before you. Are there, then, trees where angels will
        congregate,
trees invisible leisurely gardeners so curiously cultivate,
that, without being ours, they bear for us fruits like those?

Have we, then, never been able, we shadows and shades,
with our doing that ripens too early and then as suddenly fades,
to disturb that even-tempered summer's repose?

# STEVIE SMITH

## 1903–1971

### FROM THE LATIN OF THE EMPEROR HADRIAN

507      *The Emperor Hadrian to his Soul*

Cp.
Prior
Byron
Cunningham

Little soul so sleek and smiling
Flesh's friend and guest also
Where departing will you wander
Growing paler now and languid
And not joking as you used to?

# FRANK O'CONNOR

## 1903–1966

### FROM THE IRISH OF BRYAN MERRYMAN

508      from *The Midnight Court*

*'The Lament of the Unmarried Girl'*

Every night when I went to bed
I'd a stocking of apples beneath my head;
I fasted three canonical hours
To try and come round the heavenly powers;
I washed my shift where the stream was deep
To hear a lover's voice in sleep;
Often I swept the woodstack bare,
Burned bits of my frock, my nails, my hair,
Up the chimney stuck the flail,
Slept with a spade without avail;
Hid my wool in the lime-kiln late
And my distaff behind the churchyard gate;
I had flax on the road to halt coach or carriage
And haycocks stuffed with heads of cabbage,
And night and day on the proper occasions
Invoked Old Nick and all his legions;

But 'twas all no good and I'm broken-hearted
For here I'm back at the place I started;
And this is the cause of all my tears
I am fast in the rope of the rushing years,
With age and need in lessening span,
And death beyond, and no hopes of a man.
But whatever misfortunes God may send
May He spare me at least that lonesome end,
Nor leave me at last to cross alone
Without chick nor child when my looks are gone
As an old maid counting the things I lack
Scowling thresholds that warn me back!
God, by the lightning and the thunder,
The thought of it makes me ripe for murder!
Every idiot in the country
With a man of her own has the right to insult me.
Sal' has a slob with a well-stocked farm,
And Molly goes round on a husband's arm,
There's Min and Margery leaping with glee
And never done with their jokes at me.
And the bounce of Sue! and Kitty and Anne
Have children in droves and a proper man,
And all with their kind can mix and mingle
While I go savage and sour and single.


### 'The Husband's Lament'

I lived alone as happy as Larry
Till I took it into my head to marry,
Tilling my fields with an easy mind,
Going wherever I felt inclined,
Welcomed by all as a man of price,
Always ready with good advice.
The neighbours listened—they couldn't refuse
For I'd money and stock to uphold my views—
Everything came at my beck and call
Till a woman appeared and destroyed it all:
A beautiful girl with ripening bosom,
Cheeks as bright as apple-blossom,
Hair that glimmered and foamed in the wind,
And a face that blazed with the light behind;

A tinkling laugh and a modest carriage
And a twinkling eye that was ripe for marriage.
I goggled and gaped like one born mindless
Till I took her face for a form of kindness,
Though that wasn't quite what the Lord intended
For He marked me down like a man offended
For a vengeance that wouldn't be easy mended
With my folly exposed and my comfort ended.

Not to detain you here all day
I married the girl without more delay,
And took my share in the fun that followed.
There was plenty for all and nothing borrowed.
Be fair to me now! There was no one slighted;
The beggarmen took the road delighted;
The clerk and mummers were elated;
The priest went home with his pocket weighted.
The lamps were lit, the guests arrived;
The supper was ready, the drink was plied;
The fiddles were flayed, and, the night advancing,
The neighbours joined in the sport and dancing.
A pity to God I didn't smother
When first I took the milk from my mother,
Or any day I ever broke bread
Before I brought that woman to bed!
For though everyone talked of her carouses
As a scratching post of the publichouses
That as sure as ever the glasses would jingle
Flattened herself to married and single,
Admitting no modesty to mention,
I never believed but 'twas all invention.
They added, in view of the life she led,
I might take to the roads and beg my bread,
But I took it for talk and hardly minded—
Sure, a man like me could never be blinded!—
And I smiled and nodded and off I tripped
Till my wedding night when I saw her stripped,
And knew too late that this was no libel
Spread in the pub by some jealous rival—
By God, 'twas a fact, and well-supported:
I was a father before I started!

So there I was in the cold daylight,
A family man after one short night!
The women around me, scolding, preaching,
The wife in bed and the baby screeching.
I stirred the milk as the kettle boiled
Making a bottle to give the child;
All the old hags at the hob were cooing
As if they believed it was all my doing—
Flattery worse than ever you heard:
'Glory and praise to our blessed Lord,
Though he came in a hurry, the poor little creature,
He's the spit of his da in every feature....'


# CELIA and LOUIS ZUKOFSKY

the latter 1904–1978

### FROM THE LATIN OF CATULLUS

509              *Carmina*, VIII

Miss her, Catullus? don't be so inept to rail
at what you see perish when perished is the case.
Full, sure once, candid the sunny days glowed, solace,
when you went about it as your girl would have it,
you loved her as no one else shall ever be loved.
Billowed in tumultuous joys and affianced,
why you would but will it and your girl would have it.
Full, sure, very candid the sun's rays glowed solace.
Now she won't love you: you, too, don't be weak, tense, null,
squirming after she runs off to miss her for life.
*Said* as if you meant it: *obstinate, obdurate.*
Vale! puling girl. I'm Catullus, *obdurate,*
I don't require it and don't beg uninvited:
won't you be doleful when no one, no one! begs you,
scalded, every night. Why do you want to live now?
Now who will be with you? Who'll seee that you're lovely?
Whom will you love now and who will say that you're his?
Whom will you kiss? Whose morsel of lips will you bite?
But you, Catullus, your destiny's *obdurate.*

510 *Carmina*, XL

What demented malice, my silly Ravidus,
eggs your pricked conceit into my iambics?
What god not too benign that you invoked would
care dream your parrot's skit of ire and ruckus?
And it wants to purr in the public vulva?
What wish to live it up, be noticed—apt as
air is, squandering in my love's amorous
vice longer than you wished it, marred but poignant.


# KENNETH REXROTH

## 1905–

### FROM THE GREEK OF SAPPHO

511 ... about the cool water
the wind sounds through sprays
Cp.
Young          of apple, and from the quivering leaves
Davenport      slumber pours down ...


### FROM THE GREEK OF ANYTE

512 I, Hermes, have been set up
Where three roads cross, by the windy
Orchard above the grey beach.
Here tired men may rest from travel,
By my cold, clean, whispering spring.


### FROM THE GREEK OF ANTIPATER OF SIDON

513 Never again, Orpheus
Will you lead the enchanted oaks,
Nor the rocks, nor the beasts
That are their own masters.
Never again will you sing to sleep

The roaring wind, nor the hail,
Nor the drifting snow, nor the boom
Of the sea wave.
You are dead now.
Led by your mother, Calliope,
The Muses shed many tears
Over you for a long time.
What good does it do us to mourn
For our sons when the immortal
Gods are powerless to save
Their own children from death?

### FROM THE GREEK OF SIMONIDES

514
Cp.
Bowles

Stranger, when you come to
Lakedaimon, tell them we lie
Here, obedient to their will.

### FROM THE GREEK

515    *The Last Utterance of the Delphic Oracle\**

Go tell the King: The daedal
Walls have fallen to the earth
Phoibos has no sanctuary,
No prophetic laurel, no
Speaking spring. The garrulous
Water has dried up at last.

\* Probably a forgery by a pagan attached to the old religion or by a Christian
attempting to expose the futility of Apollo and his oracle.

# SAMUEL BECKETT

1906–

FROM THE SPANISH OF RAMÓN LÓPEZ VELARDE

*My Cousin Agueda*

My godmother invited my cousin
Agueda to spend the day
with us, and my cousin
came with a conflicting
prestige of starch and fearful
ceremonious weeds.

Agueda appeared, sonorous
with starch, and her green eyes
and ruddy cheeks protected
me against the fearsome
weeds.

       I was a small boy,
knew O was the round one,
and Agueda knitting,
mild and persevering,
in the echoing gallery,
gave me unknown shivers.
(I think I even owe her the heroically
morbid habit of soliloquy.)

At dinner-time in the quiet
shadowy dining-room,
I was spellbound by the brittle
intermittent noise of dishes
and the caressing timbre
of my cousin's voice.

       Agueda was
(weeds, green pupils, ruddy cheeks)
a polychromatic basket of
apples and grapes
in the ebony of an ancient cupboard.

## The Malefic Return

Better not to go back to the village,
to the ruined Eden lying silent
in the devastation of the shrapnel.

Even to the mutilated ash-trees,
dignitaries of the swelling dome,
the lamentations must be borne of
the tower riddled in the slinging winds.

And on the chalk of all
the ghostly hamlet's walls
the fusillade engraved
black and baneful maps,
whereon the prodigal son might trace,
returning to his threshold,
in a malefic nightfall,
by a wick's petrol light,
his hopes destroyed.

When the clumsy mildewed key
turns the creaking lock,
in the ancient
cloistered porch
the two chaste gyps
medallions will unseal narcotic lids,
look at each other and say: 'Who is that?'

And I shall enter on intruding feet,
reach the fatidic court
where a well-curb broods
with a skin pail dripping
its categoric drop
like a sad refrain.

If the tonic, gay, inexorable sun
makes the catechumen fountains boil
in which my chronic dream was wont to bathe;
if the ants toil;
if on the roof the crawy call resounds

and grows aweary of the turtle-doves
and in the cobwebs murmurs on and on;
my thirst to love will then be like a ring
imbedded in the slabstone of a tomb.

The new swallows, renewing
with their new potter beaks
the early nests;
beneath the signal opal
of monachal eventides
the cry of calves newly calved
for the forbidden exuberant udder
of the cud-chewing Pharaonic cow
who awes her young;
belfry of new-aspiring peal;
renovated altars;
loving love
of well-paired pairs;
betrothals of young
humble girls, like humble kales;
some young lady
singing on some piano
some old song;
the policeman's whistle . . .
. . . and a profound reactionary sorrow.


FROM THE FRENCH OF PAUL ELUARD

518                    *Lady Love*

She is standing on my lids
And her hair is in my hair
She has the colour of my eye
She has the body of my hand
In my shade she is engulfed
As a stone against the sky

She will never close her eyes
And she does not let me sleep
And her dreams in the bright day
Make the suns evaporate
And me laugh cry and laugh
Speak when I have nothing to say


# EDWARD MERYON WILSON

## 1906–

### FROM THE SPANISH OF LUIS DE GÓNGORA

## The First Solitude

519  *'The young Pilgrim finds Refuge with
the Goatherds'*

O hermitage well found
Whatever hour it be!
Temple of Pales, Flora's granary!
No artificer new
Models designed for thee, or sketches drew,
Adjusting to the skies' concavity
An edifice sublime; for here reveal
The woods of oak and broom
Thy poor and modest room,
In which, instead of steel,
Pure Innocence can keep
The shepherd safe and sound—
More than his pipe, the sheep.
O hermitage well found
Whatever hour it be!

'Here no ambitious care
Can dwell, hydroptic of the empty air;
Nor Envy with her food,
The Egyptian serpent's brood;
Nor monster with a woman's face that springs
Out of a bestial body, who persuades—
Sphinxlike—the new Narcissus of our glades

496

To follow echoes and desert the springs;
Nor she who wastes in shows impertinent
The gunpowder that Time so meanly lent,
  O foolish Courtesy!
At whom the honest villagers may laugh
  Over their crooked staff.
  O well found hermitage
  Whatever hour it be!


  'Nor does thy threshold know
  Of Adulation bland,
Syren of royal palaces, whose sand
  So many vessels greet;
Of a canorous dream the trophies sweet.
Nor turning now her feathered sphere around
Is Pride seen here, while Flattery gilds her feet;
And Favour falls not to the foam below
On wings of wax from false security.
  O hermitage well found
  Whatever hour it be!'


## 520 *'The River compared to an Oratorical Sentence'** 

Though much a little map unfolds, more still—
Far more—is that which now dissolving mists
The sun confounds and distances deny;
Dumb Wonder speaks by silence, her blind eye
Follows the river, son of that same hill,
  Whose prolix discourse twists
Benevolent to tyrannise the plain.
Its borders lined with many an orchard lawn,
*If not with petals stolen from the Dawn,*
*The stream flows straight while it does not aspire*
*The heights with its own crystals to attain;*
*Flies from itself to find itself again,*
*Is lost, and searching for its wanderings,*
*Both errors sweet and sweet meanderings*
*The waters make with their lascivious fire;*

---

* Later abbreviated: italics indicate Góngora's first version.

And, linking buildings in its silver force,
*With bowers crowned, majestically flows*
*Into abundant branches, there to wind*
*'Mid isles that green parentheses provide*
*In the main period of the current's course;*
From the high cavern where it first arose,
Until the liquid jasper, there to find
All memory lost and forfeited all pride.


521                    *'The Wedding Feast'*

They all arrived, and then with generous show,
Civil magnificence, her father grave
To mountain and to lowland peasants gave
        Abundant rustic food
        That on great tables stood.

The graceful artifice of doubling may
Itself as crisp white statuary enfold
In damasked tablecloths from Flanders' shore;
But here domestic linen Ceres bore,
Offering too the fruit, preserved in hay,
Sweet apples, that in Atalanta's way
        Had been a rein of gold.

Food, that to poison and lewd appetite
        Was unknown equally,
They served. Confused Bacchus did not try
In burnished silver, no, nor shining gold
        His liquor to supply,
The pallid rubies and the topaz bright
        In simple glass behold.


*Wilson's notes:*
521 The pallid rubies and the topaz bright] the wine in the glasses was
between the colour of rubies and topazes, hence it was the colour of pale
rubies or bright topaz.

To abate the greedy stomachs' genial fire
The gentle waxy cheeses might desire,
    (And Oh! when these were pressed
How white the rustic milk-maid's hand did seem
That veins alone distinguished from the cream!)
The coy imprisoned nut and wrinkled quince
Unto like task in vain themselves addressed,
Only the savoury olives could aspire
To appease the drunken flood, like that long since.

The tables cleared, to the canorous sound
Of her before a nymph but now a reed,
Six mountain girls, six from the plains around,
    Triad of graces these
Four times repeated in twelve maidens, see,
—Their shoulders gleaming with the subtle gold
That woven nacre guarded from the breeze—
Now entered dancing to that melody,
And a sweet muse among them—if indeed
Parnassus can such rustic maids enfold:—

    'Live happily,' she said,
'A long but never prolix term of life,
If prolix, only in the bonds of love,
    Live ever man and wife.
May silver's splendour be the vital thread
(Excelling too the whiteness of the snow)
That fatal Clotho cards for you above,
From her high distaff to her spindle low.

    'May soon the answer be
    The shouts of Fortune's praise
    To all your industry;
Let all be fertile on unequal days,
    That every grateful field
May beaten gold or pressed out nectar yield;
    So shall your plough and hoe
    Too great a harvest know.

Their shoulders gleaming ... from the breeze] the subtle gold of their hair
was kept from the wind by ribbons of the colour of mother of pearl.
Clotho] one of the three Fates
Beaten gold or pressed out nectar] threshed ears of corn and wine.

'Its purple spikes and holm-oaks, let the mount,
Before your vagrant goats, proceed to count,
Or herds of cattle, for whose number great
The branding iron shall never touch or late.

'Then may the flocks of lambs your district rears
    In number far surpass
The pearls of dew and shoots of slender grass;
As many as the foam the river bears
Be then the fleeces, victims to your shears.

'So many be the shelters, although rude
Their manufacture, that your bees enfold,
So many Springs deflowered by them be told,
That as Arabia, perfumes' mother, sees
Sweating their fragrant gums her sacred trees,
So shall your skeps through every pore exude
    Their sweet and liquid gold.

'Prosperous then, but not with spumy show
May your good fortune be, nor yet to know
Envy fomenting in your villages
Asps more than in the world of deepest woe.
'Twixt opulence and hard necessities,
Avoiding either evil, may the years
Furnish their modest fortune to your sons.
    For though the mighty towns
Adorn themselves with obelisks, their crowns
Are to the rays of Jupiter displayed
    Even more than to the sun's;
The thunderbolt the rustic hovel spares
    But fires the forest glade.

'And may the fatal hour your bones receive
When swans in whiteness either one shall be,
And in the labourers' tranquillity:
Your epitaph shall travellers undeceive
Who in few letters many years shall see.'

Its purple spikes ... or late] let the mount rather proceed to count its
purple spikes and holm-oaks than your numerous vagrant goats, and herds
of cattle; the cattle that are so numerous that they cannot all be branded,
or at least, they will be branded later than they should have been.

# WYSTAN HUGH AUDEN

## 1907–1973

### with Paul B. Taylor

**FROM THE ICELANDIC**

from *The Words of the All-Wise*

[Alvis the dwarf comes up out of the darkness of the dwarves' world to claim
    a daughter of Thor in marriage, but is tricked by him.]

THOR    Say, Dwarf, for it seems to me
            There is nothing you do not know:
        What is earth called, the outstretched land,
            In all the worlds there are?

ALVIS   *Earth* by men, *The Fold* by gods,
            Vanes call it *The Ways*,
        Giants *Ever-green*, elves *Growing*,
            High gods call it *Clay*.

THOR    What is heaven called, that all know,
            In all the worlds there are?

ALVIS   *Heaven* by men, *The Arch* by gods,
            *Wind-Weaver* by vanes,
        By giants *High-Earth*, by elves *Fair-Roof*,
            By dwarves *The Dripping Hall*.

THOR    What is the moon called, that men see,
            In all the worlds there are?

ALVIS   *Moon* by men, *The Ball* by gods,
            *The Whirling Wheel* in Hel,
        *The Speeder* by giants, *The Bright One* by dwarves,
            By elves *Tally-of-Years*.

THOR    What is sol called, that is seen by men,
            In all the worlds there are?

ALVIS    Sol by men, *Sun* by gods,
        By dwarves, *Dvalin's Doll*,
        By giants *Everglow*, by elves *Fair-Wheel*,
        *All-Bright* by sons of gods.

THOR    What are clouds called, that carry rain,
        In all the worlds there are?

ALVIS    *Clouds* by men, *Hope-of-Showers* by gods,
        *Wind-Ships* by vanes,
        By giants *Drizzle-Hope*, by elves *Weather-Might*,
        In Hel *Helmet-of-Darkness*.

THOR    What is wind called, that widely fares
        In all the worlds there are?

ALVIS    *Wind* by men, *Woe-Father* by gods,
        By holy powers *The Neigher*,
        *The Shouter* by giants, *Traveling-Tumult* by elves,
        *Squall-Blast* they call it in Hel.

THOR    What is calm called, that cannot stir,
        In all the worlds there are?

ALVIS    *Calm* by men, *Stillness* by gods,
        *Idle-Wind* by vanes,
        *Over-Warmth* by giants, by elves *Day-Quiet*,
        And *Day-Rest* by dwarves.

THOR    What is sea called, that is crossed by men,
        In all the worlds there are?

ALVIS    *Sea* by men, *Still-Main* by gods,
        The vanes call it *Wave*,
        *Eel-Home* by giants, by elves *Water-Charm*,
        *The Dark Deep* by dwarves.

THOR    What is fire called, so fierce to men,
        In all the worlds there are?

vanes] vanir, i.e. fertility gods

ALVIS *Fire* by men, *Flame* by gods,
  *The Flickering One* by vanes,
 *The Wolfish* by giants, *All-Burner* by elves,
  In Hel *The Corpse-Destroyer*.

THOR What is forest called, that flourishes for men,
  In all the worlds there are?

ALVIS *Forest* by men, *Field's-Mane* by gods,
  By heroes *Mountain Sea-Weed*,
 *Fire-Wood* by giants, *Fair-Bough* by elves,
  By vanes *Wand-of-Charms*.

THOR What is night called, that Nor fathered,
  In all the worlds there are?

ALVIS *Night* by men, *The Dark* by gods,
  By holy powers *The Hood*,
 *Unlight* by giants, by elves *Sleep-Pleasure*,
  By dwarves *Spinner-of-Dreams*.

THOR What is the seed called, that is sown by men,
  In all the worlds there are?

ALVIS *Brew* by men, *Barley* by gods,
  Vanes call it *The Growth*,
 *Oats* by giants, by elves *Water-Charm*,
  In Hel they call it *The Drooping*.

THOR What is ale called, that is quaffed by men,
  In all the worlds there are?

ALVIS *Ale* by men, *Beer* by gods,
  The vanes call it *Strength*,
 *Water-Pure* by giants, *Mead* in Hel,
  *Feast* by Sutting's Sons.

THOR Never have I met such a master of lore
  With such a wealth of wisdom.
 I talked to trick you, and tricked you I have:
  Dawn has broken, Dwarf,
  Stiffen now to stone.

# ROBERT GARIOCH

1908–

## FROM THE ITALIAN (ROMANESCO) OF
## GIUSEPPE BELLI

523

### Campidoglio

This is Campidojo, whaur Titus ran
his retail mairket, selling Jewish folk,
and here's whit they cry the Tarpeian Rock
whaur Cleopatra coupit her guidman.

Marcus Aurelius thair, aa spick and span
in his topcoat, fearing nae tempest-shock,
says Abbot Fea, keeper of antique trock,
sall turn to gowd, believe it if ye can.

Jist hae a guid luik at the mannie's face
and at the horse's rump, I think ye'll say
that ye can glisk a kinna yellie trace.

Whan the haill thing turns gowd, as weill it may,
that spells the end of even the statue's base,
because it shaws we're gey near Judgment-day.

524

### Judgment Day

Fowre muckle angels wi their trumpets, stalkin
til the fowre airts, sall aipen the inspection;
they'll gie a blaw, and bawl, ilk to his section,
in their huge voices: 'Come, aa yese, be wauken.'

coupit] tipped     trock] smallwares     glisk] glimpse
kinna] kind of     gey] very
524 muckle] big     airts] directions

Syne sall crawl furth a ragment, a haill cleckin
of skeletons yerkt out fir resurrection
to tak again their ain human complexion,
like choukies gaitheran roun a hen that's clockan.

And thon hen sall be Gode the blissit Faither;
he'll pairt the indwellars of mirk and licht,
tane doun the cellar, to the ruiff the tither.

Last sall come angels, swarms of them, in flicht,
and, like us gaean to bed without a swither,
they will blaw out the caunnles, and guid-nicht.

525          *Sanct Christopher II*

Sanct Christopher's a muckle sanct and strang,
faur bigger nor a Glesca stevedore,
wha, owre some river, barefuit, on his lang
shanks, yuistae cairry folk frae shore to shore.

Maybe thon river he wad aye owregang
wes a smaa burn, or dub left frae a shouer;
that's aa I ken about it, richt or wrang;
I tell ye jist whit I wes tellt afore.

Yae day he cairried a wee boy. Nae suiner
did he wyde in, but he wes near owreharl'd;
muckle Sanct Christopher begood to founer.

'By Christ! whit kinna trick is this?' he snarled.
'Son, ye're an aafie wecht, a richt wee wunner!
whit's this I hae upon my back; the Warld?'

syne] then      choukies] chicks
swither] hesitation
525  aafie] awful      wecht] weight      wunner] wonder

# A. L. LLOYD
## 1908–

FROM THE SPANISH OF
FEDERICO GARCÍA LORCA

526      Lament for Ignacio Sánchez Mejías
         *Cogida and Death*

At five in the afternoon.
It was exactly five in the afternoon.
A boy brought the white sheet
*at five in the afternoon.*
A frail of lime already prepared
*at five in the afternoon.*
The rest was death and death alone
*at five in the afternoon.*

The wind bore away the cotton gauze
*at five in the afternoon*
And the oxide scattered crystal and nickel
*at five in the afternoon.*
Now the dove and the leopard are struggling
*at five in the afternoon.*
And a thigh with a desolate horn
*at five in the afternoon.*
The sound of the strings begins
*at five in the afternoon.*
The bells of arsenic and steam
*at five in the afternoon.*
Groups of silence in the corners
*at five in the afternoon.*
And, the bull alone is left high-hearted!
*at five in the afternoon.*
Just as the snowy sweat broke out
*at five in the afternoon.*
When the bullring was covered in iodine
*at five in the afternoon.*
death laid its eggs in the wound
*at five in the afternoon.*

*At five in the afternoon.*
*At exactly five o'clock in the afternoon*
A coffin on wheels is his bed
*at five in the afternoon.*
Bones and flutes sound in his ears
*at five in the afternoon.*
Already the bull is bellowing within his head
*at five in the afternoon.*
The room is iridescent with agony
*at five in the afternoon.*
Now from afar comes gangrene
*at five in the afternoon,*
a lily-trumpet through greenish groins
*at five in the afternoon*
His wounds blazed like suns
*at five in the afternoon,*
and the rabble shattered the windows
*at five in the afternoon.*
At five in the afternoon.
Ay, that terrible five o'clock in the afternoon!
It was five by all the clocks!
It was five in the shadow of the afternoon!

# JAMES VINCENT CUNNINGHAM

## 1911–

### FROM THE GREEK OF SKYTHINOS

527 And now you're ready who while she was here
Hung like a flag in a calm. Friend, though you stand
Erect and eager, in your eye a tear,
I will not pity you, or lend a hand.

# JAMES VINCENT CUNNINGHAM

A.D 40-104

## FROM THE LATIN OF MARTIAL

528

### *Epigrams*, Book II, 5

Believe me, sir, I'd like to spend whole days,
Yes, and whole evenings in your company,
But the two miles between your house and mine
Are four miles when I go there to come back.
You're seldom home, and when you are deny it,
Engrossed with business or with yourself.
Now, I don't mind the two-mile trip to see you;
What I do mind is going four to not to.

## FROM THE LATIN OF THE EMPEROR HADRIAN

529
Cp.
Prior
Byron
Stevie Smith

My little soul, my vagrant charmer,
The friend and house-guest of this matter,
Where will you now be visitor
In naked pallor, little soul,
And not so witty as you were?

## FROM THE LATIN OF JANUS VITALIS PANORMITANUS
## (GIANO VITALE)

530

### *Rome*

Cp.
Spenser

You that a stranger in mid-Rome seek Rome
And can find nothing in mid-Rome of Rome,
Behold this mass of walls, these abrupt rocks,
Where the vast theatre lies overwhelmed.
Here, here is Rome! Look how the very corpse
Of greatness still imperiously breathes threats!
The world she conquered, strove herself to conquer,
Conquered that nothing be unconquered by her.
Now conqueror Rome's interred in conquered Rome,
And the same Rome conquered and conqueror.
Still Tiber stays, witness of Roman fame,
Still Tiber flows on swift waves to the sea.
Learn hence what Fortune can: the unmoved falls
And the ever-moving will remain forever.

# JAMES VINCENT CUNNINGHAM

FROM THE LATIN OF GEORGE BUCHANAN

531 The Pope from penance purgatorial
   Freed some, but Martin Luther freed them all.


532 Neaera when I'm there is adamant,
   And when I'm not there is annoyed,
   And not from tenderness and sentiment
   But that my pain is unenjoyed.


# CZESLAW MILOSZ

## 1911–

### FROM THE POLISH OF ZBIGNIEW HERBERT

533    *Elegy of Fortinbras*

           *for C.M.*

Now that we're alone we can talk prince man to man
though you lie on the stairs and see no more than a dead ant
nothing but black sun with broken rays
I could never think of your hands without smiling
and now that they lie on the stone like fallen nests
they are as defenceless as before The end is exactly this
The hands lie apart The sword lies apart The head apart
and the knight's feet in soft slippers

You will have a soldier's funeral without having been a soldier
the only ritual I am acquainted with a little
There will be no candles no singing only cannon-fuses and
  bursts
crepe dragged on the pavement helmets boots artillery horses
  drums drums I know nothing exquisite
those will be my manoeuvres before I start to rule
one has to take the city by the neck and shake it a bit

Anyhow you had to perish Hamlet you were not for life
you believed in crystal notions not in human clay
always twitching as if asleep you hunted chimeras
wolfishly you crunched the air only to vomit
you knew no human thing you did not know even how to
　　breathe

Now you have peace Hamlet you accomplished what you
　　had to
and you have peace The rest is not silence but belongs to me
you chose the easier part an elegant thrust
but what is heroic death compared with eternal watching
with a cold apple in one's hand on a narrow chair
with a view of the ant-hill and the clock's dial

Adieu prince I have tasks a sewer project
and a decree on prostitutes and beggars
I must also elaborate a better system of prisons
since as you justly said Denmark is a prison
I go to my affairs This night is born
a star named Hamlet We shall never meet
what I shall leave will not be worth a tragedy

It is not for us to greet each other or bid farewell we live on
　　archipelagos
and that water these words what can they do what can they
　　do prince

# GEORGE JOHNSTON

1913–

## FROM THE ICELANDIC

## from *The Saga of Gisli*

[Gisli, outlawed, tells his wife, Aud, of his dream of the
seven fires and of his good dream woman.]

534

'Wife, land of the wave fire,
Where I came were flaming
Seven fires to my sorrow,
Stern, in the hall burning;
Bench crews rose and bowed there
From board seats to greet me;
In return I answered
Old meet words of greeting.

Bend your eyes, band goddess
Bade me, glad spender,
Fires, your life foretelling,
Furnish the hall, burning.
Years are few of yearning
Yet, until a better
Time for you, storm tamer,
Treader of sword weather.

Let your heart from learning
Lightness, and in right wise,
Schooled by good scalds, said she,
Seek the best, unresting.
Worst lot for the waster
Of wave fire, brave spender,
Ever, to know evil
Is, men say, in wisdom.

*Translator's Notes on the Kennings (poetic diction):*
land of the wave fire] wave fire is gold, whose land is a woman.
band goddess] woman        spender] (generous) man
storm tamer, treader of sword weather] warrior, man
waster of wave fire] waster of gold, (generous) man

Hold your blade from bloodshed,
Be not first to stir them
Nor press them, promise me,
The proud gods of slaughter.
Help the blind and handless,
And heed this, ring-speeder,
Low the mocker's fame lies
And lame-harmer's name, low.'


[Gisli's dream of the good dream woman and the noble house.]

535           'Goddess of threads gladly
On her grey steed prayed me
Rise up, praise-rune maker,
Ride away beside her.
Golden one, of seagull's
Ground, in weakness found me;
To help me and heal me
Her grave promise gave me.

Splendid sea-flame goddess
Showed me, ode-contriver,
Where, for my worn body
And will, lay a pillow.
Linen goddess led me
Lo, where sleep would know me;
No hilled pallet held me;
My head, sweetly bedded.


ring-speeder] (generous) man

535 goddess of threads] woman     praise-rune maker] poet
golden one, of seagull's ground] woman. Probably seagull's ground,
i.e. sea, is a half-kenning for gold, stemming from a full kenning for gold of
the type, fire of the sea.
sea-flame goddess] goddess of gold, woman     linen goddess] woman

Hither, when death's heavy
Handblow has unmanned you,
Said then that sweet lady,
Shall the valkyr bring you.
Adder's earth and other
Old rich treasure told here
And my self you solely
Sovereign shall govern.'


# CHARLES H. SISSON

1914–

## IMITATED FROM THE LATIN OF HORACE

536 *Carmen Saeculare*

O sun, and moonlight shining in the woods,
The best things in heaven, always to be worshipped
As long as they give us exactly what we want

Now, at this season when selected girls
And the boys who are about to venture upon them,
Though still in bud, sing what will please London,

As you bring out one day and conceal another
Shine on the arms and legs and make them brown.
May all you see be greater than we are.

The time will come to open thighs in child-birth.
Gently, supervising god, look after the mothers.
Bringing to light is the true meaning of genitals.

Could you bring up these children without laws?
The statute-book is crowded, what wonder therefore
If all that interests them is an obscure kindness?


535 adder's earth] gold

A hundred and ten years it may easily be
Before songs and games which come as speedily
As these three days, ah, and delicious nights.

You have sung truthfully enough, O fates.
Once it was ordained that everything should be stable
And will be again, but not now, or for ever.

Rich in apples, yes, and seething with cattle,
The succulent earth is dressed in barley whiskers.
And grow plump, embryo, from the natural gifts.

The sun will shine, as long as the boys are suppliant,
That will keep sickness away; and you girls,
Listen, for the moon will hear you if you do.

If you made London, as before it Engelland,
The Jutes cóming over in ships, but only to be Romans,
Part of that remnant to join this one

The ways that have led here are multifarious,
Even Brutus from Troy, our ancestors believed,
But whatever they left they found better here.

You cannot credit the wish, that the young should be teachable
And old age quiet. Yet it is these wishes
Spring from the earth at last, when the country flowers.

Might you not even remember the old worship?
I could name ancestors, it is not done any more.
It remains true that, before you are king, you must win.

We have been through it all, victory on land and sea,
These things were necessary for your assurance.
The King of France. Once there was even India.

Can you remember the expression 'Honour'?
There was, at one time, even Modesty.
Nothing is so dead it does not come back.

There is God. There are no Muses without him.
He it is who raises the drug-laden limbs
Which were too heavy until he stood at Saint Martin's.

It is he who holds London from Wapping to Richmond,
May he hold it a little longer, Saint George's flag
Flap strenuously in the wind from the west country.

Have you heard the phrase: 'the only ruler of princes'?
Along the Thames, in the Tower, there is the crown.
I only wish God may hear my children's prayers.

He bends now over Trafalgar Square.
If there should be a whisper he would hear it.
Are not these drifting figures the chorus?


# DOUGLAS YOUNG

## 1913–

### FROM THE GREEK OF SAPPHO

I

**537**

Cp.
Landor

Minnie, I canna caa my wheel,
or spin the oo or twyne the tweel.
It's luve o a laddie whammles me.
Ech, the wanchancie glamarie.

2

**538**

Cp.
Rexroth
Davenport

Caller rain frae abune
reeshles amang the epple-trees:
the leaves are soughan wi the breeze,
and sleep faas drappan doun.

537 minnie] mother    caa] drive    oo] wool    tweel] cloth
wanchancie] uncanny
538   reeshles] rustles

### 3

**539**

Cp.
Hardy

Deid sall ye ligg, and ne'er a memorie
sall onie hain, or ae regret for ye,
sin that ye haena roses o Pierie.
In Hades' howff a gangrel ghaist ye'll flee,
amang derk ghaists stravaigan sichtlesslie.

## FROM THE FRENCH OF PAUL VALÉRY

**540**       from *The Kirkyaird by the Sea*

Steekit, consecrat, fou o fire but fuel,
a fragment o yird offered to the licht's rule,
I like this place, wi its brands' royal waves,
biggit frae gowd and stane and derk-leaved glades,
whaur fouth o marble sooms owre fouth o shades,
thonder the leal sea sleeps atour my graves.

C'wa, my grand bitch! gar misbelievers skail!
When I'm my lane smilean I tell my tale
o ferlie sheep lang I hae herdit here,
the whyte flock o thir my laigh lown lairs.
Keep aff the doos wi their auld-farrant airs,
and thowless dreams, and angels gleg to speir.

Aince here, the future is but indolence.
The golloch-scartit drouth liggs here intense.
Aathing brunt up, forduin, taen intil air,
intil ane essence stark ayont our thocht....
Life becomes merchless, fou wi want o ocht,
wershness is douce, the spreit is clear and rare.

539  roses o Pierie] the Muses' flowers
howff] resort (used especially of churchyards, public houses)
stravaigan] wandering
540  steekit] closed       but] without
brands] torches       fouth] abundance
sooms] floats       leal] faithful       gar] make       skail] scatter
ferlie] mysterious       laigh lown lairs] low quiet graves       auld-farrant] sage
gleg to speir] quick to ask, inquisitive       golloch-scartit] insect-scratched
drouth] drought       forduin] exhausted       stark] strong
merchless] infinite       wershness] bitterness       douce] sweet

The dernit deid ligg cozy in this yird,
that warms and dries their mystery interred.
Midday abune, Midday without a steer
thinks in himsel, self-congruent, cordial. . . .
Thou complete heid and perfect coronal,
I am the secret change inside you here.

You've nane but me to haud in check your fears.
My penitence, compulsion, douts and fears
the flaw to tash your diamant's majestie.
But in their nicht, wechtit wi marble stane,
a drowie fowk doun at the tree-ruits lain
hae sideit wi you in slaw solemnitie.

They hae dwyneit intil a thick nonentitie,
the reid clay drank the whyte identitie,
the gift o life has gane intil the fleurs.
Whaur are the deid anes' turns o phrase we kent,
their individual sauls, their personal sclent?
The larva spins in the tears' auld course.

Kittlit lassies' skreighins, blyth and keen,
bricht whyte teeth, blue and greetan een,
the loesome breist whaur the reid lowelicht lay,
the bluid that leams frae the surrendered mou,
the final gifts, the hands that guaird them true,
aa gangs to grund and comes again in play.

dernit] hidden     yird] earth     drowie] indistinct     kittlit] tickled
                skreighins] cries     leams] shines

# SIDNEY GOODSIR SMITH

## 1915–

### FROM THE FRENCH OF TRISTAN CORBIÈRE

**541**     from *The Gangrel Rymour and the Pairdon of Sanct Anne*

*'The Ballad-singer'*

But ae braithless note,
An echo trummlan on the wind,
Comes to brash the drizzenan drune
O' this stravaigan limbo-grund.

A human bouk, that's rairan,
Stands by the Calvarie;
It looks like ane half-blind;
Wi nae tyke and but ae ee. . . .

It's a gangrel rymour
That gies the fowk, for a farden,
*The Ballant o the Vagabone Yid*,
*Abelard*, or *The Magdalen*.

Breathan like a dredgie,
Like a dredgie o hunger itsel,
And, dreich as a day wantan breid,
Dowilie, its wail. . . .

541  brash] assault, bruise      drizzenan drune] plaintive lowing
stravaigan limbo-grund] wandering purgatory      bouk] shape, bulk
dredgie] dirge      dreich] wearisome      dowilie] woebegone

## SIDNEY GOODSIR SMITH

Wae bird, wantan fedder or nest,
It sings as it breathes,
Round the puirs'-houses o granite
Vaigan whar instinct leads....

Doutless it can speak tae,
And, juist as it sees, can think:
Afore it aye the hie road...
And, when there's tuppence, there's drink;

A woman, it looks; wae's me!—her clouts
Hing frae her, wi twine upkiltit:
Her black tooth hauds a pipe, gane out...
—Life's aye some consolation intil't!

Her name?—She's cried Miserie.
Hap saw her birth, and yerth
Will see her daith ... nae
Differ—for the maist pairt.

Gin ye suld meet wi her, makar,
Wi her auld sodjer's poke:
It's our sister ... gie her—it's holidays—
A bit baccy, for a smoke!

Ye'll see her runklie face runkle
Wi a smile, as in a tree;
And her sca'd hand will mak
A true sign o the Corse for ye.

yerth] earth     makar] poet     runkle] wrinkle     sca'd] scrofulous

# DAVID GASCOYNE

1916–

## FROM THE GERMAN OF FRIEDRICH HÖLDERLIN

*Patmos*

The God is near, and
                    difficult to grasp.
But danger fortifies the rescuing power.
In sombre places dwell the eagles; the Alps' sons
Go fearless forth upon the roads of the abyss
Across lightly constructed bridges. And since all round
    there press
The peaks of time, and those so close
In love, are worn out on the separate heights,
Then give us the innocent waters,
O give us the innocent waters,
O give us wings, that with the truest thought
We may fly yonder and return to this same place.

I spoke thus. And then rose
A guardian spirit, carried me away
More swiftly and still further than I dreamed,
Far from my house and home.
And as I passed, the light of dawn
Glowed on the shady woods and longed-for streams
Of my own land. I knew the earth no more.
And soon, with mysterious freshness shining
And rapidly growing beneath the footsteps of the sun,
In golden haze there blossomed forth
In a thousand peaks, a thousand glittering spires,

Asia, before my eyes. I blindly sought
For some familiar image,
A stranger to those wide streets where there descends
From Tmolus to the sea the Pactolus adorned with gold,
And the Taurus rises with the Messogis,
And the flowering garden like a peaceful fire,

But in the light on high, the silver snow
And sign of immortal life, on the unscaled wall
The age-old ivy grows, and on living pillars
Of cedar and of laurel
Stand the solemn palaces the Gods have built.

And all around the Asiatic gates,
Calling out here and there from the sea's uncertain plain,
There murmur the unshadowed roads:
But the pilot knows the islands.
When I heard
That Patmos was among the nearest isles,
I longed to disembark
And to approach its gloomy caves.
For it is not like Cyprus rich with springs
Or any of the other islands, it is not
In proud display that Patmos stands

But like a poor house full of hospitality,
And when from a wrecked ship, or weeping
For his lost land or for an absent friend
A stranger comes, she listens with good will;
And all her children, and the voices of the hot groves,
And the place where the sand falls, and where the fields
    are cracked,
And all the sounds
Hear him, and all resounds again
With love for the man's plaint.
Thus it was one day that she took in care
The belov'd of God, the seer
Who in his happy youth had gone

With the All-Highest's Son, inseparable from Him...

# TOM SCOTT

## 1916–

### FROM THE FRENCH OF FRANÇOIS VILLON

**543**       *Ballat O the Leddies O Langsyne*

Cp.
Rossetti

Tell me whaur, in whit countrie
Bides Flora nou, yon Roman belle?
Whaur Thais, Alcibiades be,
Thon sibbit cuisins: can ye tell
Whaur clettaran Echo draws pell-mell
Abuin some burn owrehung wi bine
Her beautie's mair nor human spell—
Ay, whaur are the snaws o langsyne?

Whaur's Heloise, yon wyce abbess
For wham Pete Abelard manless fell,
Yet lovin aye, at Sanct Denys
Wrocht out his days in cloistrit cell?
And say whaur yon queen is as well
That ordrit Buridan ae dine
Be seckt and cuist in the Seine to cool—
Ay, whaur are the snaws o langsyne?

Queen Blanch, as pure's the flouer-de-lys,
Whase voice nae siren's could excel,
Bertha Braid-fuit, Beatrice, Alys,
Ermbourg wha hent the Maine hersel?
Guid Joan of Arc, the lass they tell
The Inglish brunt at Rouen hyne—
Whaur are they, Lady, I appeal?
Ay, whaur are the snaws o langsyne?

Prince, this week I cannae well,
Nor this year, say whaur nou they shine:
Speir, ye'll but hear the owrecome swell—
Ay, whaur are the snaws o langsyne?

sibbit cuisins] blood-cousins     seckt] sacked     cuist] cast
hyne] distant     Speir] enquire     owrecome] refrain

544                    *Ballat O the Hingit*

Brither-men wha eftir us live on,
Harden no your herts agin us few,
But petie the puir chiels ye gove upon,
And God mair likely your fauts will forhou.
Five or sax o's strung up here ye view,
Our tramorts, doutless pampert yince wi stew,
Theirsels are suppit, tho gey wersh the brew.
When our banes til dust and ashes faa,
Dinna lauch at the sinners dree sic rue,
But pray the Lord hes mercy on us aa.

And gif we caa ye 'brethren', dinna scorn
The humble claim, evin tho it's true
It's juist we swing. Weill ye ken nae man born
No aa the time is blessed wi mense enou.
Sae, for our cause, guid-hertit brethren, sue
Wi the Virgin's Son they hingit on Calvarie's bou,
That grace devall afore our juidgment's due
And snek us up in time frae hell's gret maw.
Sen we are deid, ye needna girn at's nou,
But pray the Lord hes mercy on us aa.

We hae been washed and purifee'd by rain.
The sun hes tanned our hides a leathery hue.
Craws and pyes hae pykit out our een,
And barbered ilka stibble-chin and brou.
Nae peace we ken the twenty-fowr hours throu,
For back and furth, whiles braid-on, whiles askew,
Wi ilka wind that blaws we twist and slue;
Mair stoggit nor straeberries, and juist as raw.
See til it *ye* never mell wi sic a crew,
And pray the Lord shaws mercy til us aa.

gove] stare        forhou] forgive        tramorts] corpses
   gey wersh] rather sour        dree] endure        mense] good-sense
devall] descend        snek] snatch        girn] complain        stoggit] pitted
                    mell] mingle

TOM SCOTT

Prince Jesus, wha haud aa mankind in feu,
Watch Satan duisna reive us serfs frae you;
Wi him we'll byde nae langer nor we awe.
Guid-fellae-men, dinnae ye mock us nou,
But pray the Lord shaws mercy til us aa.


# ROBERT LOWELL

## 1917–1977

### FROM THE LATIN OF JUVENAL

545

from *The Vanity of Human Wishes*
A version of Juvenal's Tenth Satire
(*For William Arrowsmith*)

#### 'Sejanus'

Cp.
Vaughan
Gifford
Dryden

How many men are killed by Power, by Power
and Power's companion, Envy! Your long list
of honors breaks your neck. Statues follow
the rope and crash, the axe cuts down the two-
wheeled chariot's wheels and snaps the horse's legs.
Fierce hiss the fires, the bellows roar, the head,
all-popular and adored by all once, burns—
Sejanus crackles, and his crude bronze face,
the second in the world, melts down to jars,
frying pans, basins, platters, chamber pots.
Hang out your streamers, lead the great chalked bull
to the high altar at the Capitol—
men lead Sejanus on a hook, and all
rejoice. 'What flannel lips he has! No man,
I tell you, ever loved this man!' 'But tell us,
what was his crime, friend? Who were the informers?
What witness swore away his life?' 'No witness!
A wordy long epistle came from Capri.'
'Tiberius spoke, enough, I'll hear no more.'

But what about the Roman mob? Their rule
is always follow fortune and despise
the fallen. One thing's certain, if the gods
had spared Sejanus, if some accident
had choked Tiberius in his green old age,
the mob would hail Sejanus Caesar now.

### 'Hannibal'

Throw Hannibal on the scales, how many pounds
does the great captain come to? This is he
who found the plains of Africa too small,
rich Carthage with her mercenary grip
stretched from Gibraltar to the steaming Nile
and back to Ethiopia, her stud
for slaves and elephants. He set his hand
firmly on Spain, then scaled the Pyrenees;
when snows, the Alps, and Nature blocked his road,
he derricked rocks, and split the mountainsides
with vinegar. Now Italy is his;
the march goes on. 'Think nothing done,' he says,
'until my Punic soldiers hack through Rome,
and plant my standard over the Suburva's
whorehouses.' What a face for painters! Look,
the one-eyed leader prods his elephant!
And what's the end? O glory! Like the others,
he is defeated, then the worried flight,
the great, world-famous client cools his heels
in royal anterooms, and waits on some
small despot, sleeping off a drunken meal.
What is the last day of this mighty spirit
whose valor turned the known world on its head?
Not swords, or pikes, or legions—no, not these,
his crown for Cannae and those seas of blood
is poison in a ring. March, madman, cross
the Alps, the Tiber—be a purple patch
for schoolboys, and a theme for declamation!

FROM THE ITALIAN OF DANTE

546     *Brunetto Latini, 'Inferno', Canto XV*
(For Lillian Hellman)

And now we walked along the solid mire
above a brook whose fuming mist protected
water and banks from the surrounding fire.
Just as the men of Flanders threw up huge
earthworks to stop the sea that always threatens
their fields and cattle between Ghent and Bruges,
or Paduans along the Brenta spread
out dykes to shield their towns and towers against
spring thawing the Carinzian watershed—
on such a plan the evil engineer,
whoever he was, had laid his maze of dykes,
though on a smaller scale, and with less care.
By now we'd gone much deeper underground,
and left the bleeding wood so far behind
I'd have seen nothing, if I'd looked around.

We met a company of spirits here,
trooping below us on the sand. Each one
stared closely at our faces. As men peer
at one another under the new moon,
or an old tailor squints into his needle,
these puckered up their brows and glowered. Soon,
I saw a man whose eyes devoured me, saying,
'This is a miracle.' He seized my sleeve,
and as I felt his touch, I fixed my eyes
with such intensity on his crusted face
that its disfigurement could not prevent
my recognizing who he was. 'Oh, Oh,'
I answered groaning, as I stretched my hand
to touch his arm, 'are you here Ser Brunetto?'
He answered, 'Do not be displeased, my Son,
if Brunetto Latini turn and walk a little
downward with you, and lets this herd pass on.'
Then I, 'I'll go with you, or we can sit
here talking as we used to in the past,
if you desire it, and my guide permit.'

'O Son,' he answered, 'anyone who stands
still a moment will lie here a hundred years,
helpless to brush the sparks off with his hands.
Move on, I'll follow. Soon enough I must
rejoin my little group of friends who walk
with me lamenting their eternal lust.'
Then since I dared not leave my bank and move
over the flames of his low path, I bent
my head to walk with reverence and love.
Then he, 'What brings you here before your day?
Is it by accident, or Providence?
Who is this man who guides you on your way?'
I answered, 'In the world that lies serene
and shining over us, I lost my path,
even before the first young leaves turned green.
Yesterday morning when my steps had come
full circle, this man appeared. He turned me round,
and now he guides me on my journey home.'
'O Son,' said he, 'if you pursue your star,
you cannot fail to reach the glorious harbor.
And if the beautiful world, less sinister,
had let me live a little longer, I too
might have sustained your work and brought you comfort,
seeing how heaven has befriended you.
But that perverted and ungrateful flock
that held the hills with Catiline, and then
descended, hard and sterile as their rock,
to govern Florence, hate you for the good
you do; and rightly! Could they wish to see
the sweet fig ripen on their rotten wood?
Surely, they've earned their reputation: blind,
fratricidal, avaricious, proud.
O root their filthy habits from your mind!
Fortune will load such honors on your back
that Guelph and Ghibelline will hunger for you.
But beat them from the pasture. Let the pack
run loose, and sicken on the carcasses
that heap the streets, but spare the tender flower,
if one should rise above the swamp and mess—
some flower in which the fragile, sacred seed
of ancient Roman virtue still survives
in Florence, that vulture's nest of lies and greed.'

'Master,' I said, 'you would not walk here now
cut off from human nature, if my prayers
had had an answer. I remember how
I loved you, sitting at your knees—all thought
fixed on your fatherly and gentle face,
when in the world, from hour to hour, you taught
me how a man becomes eternal. O
Master, as long as I draw breath and live,
men shall remember you and what I owe.
Your words about my future shall remain
with other prophecies I keep to give
a Lady, who if I reach her, will explain.
This much I know: If I can bear the stings
of my own heavy conscience, I will face
whatever good or evil Fortune brings.
This promise of good fortune has been made
before this; so, let Fortune whirl her wheel
at random, and the peasant work his spade.'

Then Virgil, turning backward with one hand
lifted in wonder, mused at me, and said:
'He who knows how to listen shall understand.'

Dwelling upon his words, I did not stop
eagerly briefing Ser Brunetto, and asked,
'Who are the most illustrious in your group?'
And he, 'It's right to know a few of us,
but fitting I be silent on the rest;
our time's too short to squander on such dross.
In one word, we were scholars in our time,
great men of letters, famous in the world
we soiled and lost for our one common crime.
Priscian goes with us on this dismal turf,
and Francesco d'Accorso; you can see,
if you have any liking for such scurf,
the man the Servants' Servant chose to serve
him on the Arno, then on the Bacchilione,
where he laid down his ill-extended nerve.
I would say more to you, but must not stand
forever talking, speech must have an end.

## ROBERT LOWELL

I see fresh steam is stirring from the sand,
and men I would avoid are coming. Give
me no pity. Read my *Tesoro*. In
my book, my treasure, I am still alive.'

Then he turned back, and he seemed one of those
who run for the green cloth through the green field
at Verona ... and seemed more like the one
who wins the roll of cloth than those who lose.

FROM THE ITALIAN OF GIACOMO LEOPARDI *1798-1837*

547 === *Saturday Night in the Village*

The day
is ready to close;
the girl takes the downward
path homeward from the vineyard,
and jumps from crevice to crevice
like a goat, as she holds a swath
of violets and roses
to decorate her hair and bodice
tomorrow as usual for the Sabbath.

Her grandmother sits,
facing the sun going out,
and spins and starts to reason
with the neighbours, and renew the day,
when she used to dress herself for the holiday
and dance away
the nights—still quick and healthy,
with the boys, companions of her fairer season.

Once again the landscape is brown,
the sky drains to a pale blue,
shadows drop from mountain and thatch,
the young moon whitens.
As I catch
the clatter of small bells,
sounding in the holiday,
I can almost say
my heart takes comfort in the sound.

Children place their pickets
and sentinels,
and splash round and round
the village fountain.
They jump like crickets,
and make a happy sound.
The field-hand,
who lives on nothing,
marches home whistling,
and gorges on the day of idleness at hand.

Then all's at peace;
the lights are out;
I hear the rasp of shavings,
and the rapping hammer
of the carpenter, working all night
by lanternlight—
hurrying and straining himself
to increase his savings
before the whitening day.

This is the most kind
of the seven days; tomorrow, you will wait
and pray for Sunday's boredom and anguish
to be extinguished
in the workdays' grind
you anticipate.

Lively boy,
the only age you are alive
is like this day of joy,
a clear and breathless Saturday
that heralds life's holiday.
Rejoice, my child,
this is the untroubled instant.
Why should I undeceive you?
Let it not grieve you,
if the following day is slow to arrive.

FROM THE FRENCH OF PAUL VALÉRY

548 *Helen*

I am the blue! I come from the lower world
to hear the serene erosion of the surf;
once more I see the galleys bleed with dawn,
and shark with muffled rowlocks into Troy.
My solitary hands recall the kings;
I used to run my fingers through their beards;
I wept. They sang about their shady wars,
the great gulfs boiling sternward from their keels.
I hear the military trumpets, all that brass,
blasting commands to the frantic oars;
the rowers' metronome enchains the sea,
and high on beaked and dragon prows, the gods—
their fixed, archaic smiles stung by the salt—
reach out their carved, indulgent arms to me!

# MARTIN BELL

1918–

FROM THE FRENCH OF JULES LAFORGUE

549 *Winter Coming On*
*A caricature from Laforgue*
For Peter Porter

Fine feelings under blockade! Cargoes just in from Kamschatka!
Rain falling and falling the night falling
And how the wind howls...
Halloween, Christmas, New Year's Day
Sodden in drizzle—all my tall chimneys—
Industrial smoke through the rain!
No sitting down, all the park-benches are wet.
It's finished, I tell you, till next season.
Park-benches wet and all the leaves rust-eaten,
Horns and their echoes—dying, dying...

Rally of rain-clouds! Procession from the Channel—
You certainly spoiled our last free Sunday.

Drizzles:
And in wet woods the spiders' webs
Weigh down with rain-drops: and that's their lot.
O golden delegates from harvest festivals,
Broad suns from cattle-shows,
Where have they buried you?
This evening a sun lies, shagged, on top of the hill,
On a tramp's mattress, rags in the gorse—
A sun as white as a blob of spittle
On tap-room saw-dust, on a litter of yellow gorse,
Of yellow October gorse.
And the horns echo and call to him—
Come back! Won't you come back?
View halloo, Tally-ho ... Gone away.
O oratorio chorus, when will you be done?
Carrying on like mad things...
And there he lies, like a torn-out gland on a neck,
Shivering, with no one by.
Tally-ho, then, and get on with it.
It's good old Winter coming, we know that.
By-passes empty, turnings on main roads
With no Red Riding Hood to be picked up.
Ruts from the wheels of last month's traffic—
Quixotic tram-lines to the rescue of
Cloud-patrols scurrying
Bullied by winds to transatlantic sheep-folds.
Get a move on, it's the well-known season coming, now.
And the wind last night, on top of its form,
Smashing suburban front-gardens—what a mess!
Disturbing my night's sleep with dreams of axes.

These branches, yesterday, had all their dead leaves—
Nothing but compost now, just lying about.
Dear leaves of various shapes and sizes
May a good breeze whirlpool you away
To lie on ponds, decorative,
To glow in the park-keeper's fire,
To stuff ambulance mattresses, comforts
For our soldiers overseas.

Time of year, time of year: the rust is eating,
The rust is gnawing long miles of ennui,
Telegraph-wires along main roads, deserted.

Horns, again horns ... the echoes dying,
Dying ...
Now changing key, going north
With the North Wind, Wagnerian,
Up to all those bloody skalds and Vikings ...

Myself, I can't change key; too many echoes!
What beastly weather! Good-bye autumn, good-bye ripeness ...
And here comes the rain with the diligence of an angel.
Good-bye harvest, good-bye baskets for nutting,
And Watteau picnics under the chestnut trees.
It's barrack-room coughing again,
The landlady's horrible herbal tea—
It's TB in the garden suburb,
All the sheer misery of satellite towns.

Wellingtons, long underwear, cash chemists, dreams,
Undrawn curtains over verandas, shores
Of the red-brick sea of roofs and chimney-pots,
Lamp-shades, tea and biscuits, all the picture papers—
You'll have to be my only loves!
(And known them, have you? ritual more portentous
Than the sad pianos tinkling through the dusk,
The registrar's returns of births and deaths,
In small type weekly in the press.)

No! It's the time of year, and this clown of a planet!
O please let the wind, let the high wind
Unknit the bed-socks Time is knitting herself!
Time of year, things tearing, time of year!
O let me every year, every year, just at this time
Join in the chorus, sound the right sour note.

# EDWIN MORGAN

1920–

## FROM THE HUNGARIAN OF SÁNDOR WEÖRES

550                from *The Lost Parasol*

> I think there is much more in even the smallest creation of God,
> should it only be an ant, than wise men think.
>
> *St. Teresa of Avila*

Where metalled road invades light thinning air,
some twenty steps more and a steep gorge yawns
with its jagged crest, and the sky is rounder there,
    it is like the world's end;
nearer: bushy glade in flower,
farther: space, rough mountain folk;
    a young man called his lover
    to go up in the cool of daybreak,
they took their rest in the grass, they lay down;
the girl has left her red parasol behind.

Wood shades sunshade. Quietness all round.
What can be there, with no one to be seen?
Time pours out its measureless froth and
    the near and the far still unopened
    and midday comes and evening comes,
no midday there, no evening, eternal floods
that swim in the wind, the fog, the light, the world
and this tangle moves off into endlessness
like a gigantic shimmering silk cocoon,
skirted by wells of flame and craters of soot.

Dawn, a pearl-grey ferry, was drifting
    on its bright herd of clouds,
from the valley the first cow-bell came ringing
and the couple walked forward, head by head;
    now their souvenir clings to the shadows,
red silk, the leaves, the green light on it, filtering,
    metal frame, bone handle, button:
    separate thing from the order of men,
    it came home intact, the parasol,
its neighbours rockface and breeze, its land cold soil.

In a sun-rocked cradle which is as massive
as the very first creation itself
    the little one lies, light instrument
on the blue-grey mossy timber of a cliff,
around it the stray whistling, the eternal murmuring
of the forest, vast Turkey-oak, slim hornbeam,
briar-thickets, a thousand sloe-bushes quivering,
noble tranquil ranks of created things,
    and among them only the parasol flares out:
jaunty far-off visitor whose clothes still shout.

Languidly, as if long established there,
    its new home clasps it about:
the rocks hug their squat stonecrops,
above it the curly heliotropes
    cat's-tail veronica,
wild pinks push through cage of thistles,
dragon-fly broods on secret convolvulus,
dries his gauze wings, totters out:
    so life goes on here, never otherwise—
a chink in the leaves, a flash of blue-smiling skies.

The sea-lunged forest breathes at it
    like yesterday, like long ago,
mild smell of the soft nest of a girl.
    Shy green woodpecker and russet
frisky squirrel refused to sit on it,
who knows what it hides: man left it;
but a nosy hedgehog comes up to the ledge,
the prickly loafer, low of leg,
    like a steam puffer patrols round the rock;
puts heart in the woodpecker tapping at his trunk.

The sun stretches out its muscular rays:
you would expect the bell of heaven to crack.
Broad world—so many small worlds find their place
in you! Through the closed parasol's hills and valleys
an oblong speck moves: an ant that drags
the headless abdomen of a locust with rapt
persistence and effort: up to the bare heights,
down to the folds, holding the load tight,
    and turning back at the very end of the way,
floundering up again with the body. Who knows why?

This finger-long journey is not shorter or sillier
than Everything, and its aim is just as hidden.
Look: through the branches you can see the hillside,
there a falcon, a spot on the clear sky,
hangs in the air like a bird of stone:
predator, hanging over from history.
Here, wolf and brown bear were once at home,
crystalline lynx lay in ambush for the innocent.
God wetted a finger, turned a page
and the world had a very different image.


A sky-splitting single-sloped precipice,
its lap a lemon-yellow corrie of sand,
far off a rosy panorama of mist,
curly hills in a ragged mauve cloud-band;
above, the couple stood; below, the sun-wheel
stirred;
in the dawn-flames, so interdependent
they stood, afraid, at the very edge of fate;
boulders rolled from beneath their feet,
they were quarrelling, tearing their hearts,
each of them deaf before the other starts.


In the tangled thicket of their young blood
the luminous world skulks off, sinks;
shame like a rose-branch cut
the boy to the quick:
beyond entreaty, ready to throw himself down to...
His white shirt gestured against the blue,
at the shrubby scarp with its bindweed
he lurched forward, forward
growing smaller and more distant—and his frightened
girl
runs after him through briars, her knee's blood is a pearl.


Tall sedges lean over the gorge
and like a gemmed porch of the depths below
an army of tiny shining shields of weeds
and a thick dark couch of green
cling round the bark of a stump that points no-
where, here their frenzy lost its rage:

they twined together, to ask why, to cry,
like the horned moon the white flash of a thigh;
a hooded boletus at their feet
fattened its spore-crammed belly, not bothering to mate.

\*

In the vault of summer skies, diamond-blue,
an ice-white lace-mist moves in a smile;
over the plain, at the foothills of heaven,
there are dark woolpacks hanging heavy
and truant cloud-lines in crumbling style;
Apollo, body stripped, striding through,
    runs young, strong, and fresh,
hot oil steams on the earth's rough flesh;
in air that rocks both valley and peak,
in empty immensities—a red spot of silk.

The girl of the neglected parasol
is just as small, lost in the broad world,
a tiny insect dropped in a sea-wide flood;
    no one to talk to at all,
wrapping her own soul round her fear,
    she curls up in a curtained room,
and hears a whipped dog whining there
as if there was no misery anywhere,
no other wound to ache in earth or heaven;
or does he howl for all the pain of men?

    Hanging on the sky's arch
      at the lower bank
        the dusk
        is hazy.
The first? How many before? On the lazy
ridge no grass or insect measures it,
neither cuckoo nor cuckoo-spit,
the twilights turn for ever, as created.
At the rock's edge, with forever's speed
the sleek silk vanishes into foaming shade.

# DONALD DAVIE

1922–

## FROM THE POLISH OF ADAM MICKIEWICZ
via the prose version of George Rapall Noyes

551 *The Year 1812*

Year well remembered! Happy who beheld thee!
The commons knew thee as the year of yield,
But as the year of war, the soldiery.

Rumours and skyward prodigies revealed
The poet's dream, the tale on old men's lips,
The spring when kine preferred the barren field.

Short of the acres green with growing tips
They halted lowing, chewed the winter's cud;
The men awaited an apocalypse.

Languid the farmer sought his livelihood
And checked his team and gazed, as if enquiring
What marvels gathered westward while he stood.

He asked the stork, whose white returning wing
Already spread above its native pine
Had raised the early standard of the Spring.

From swallows gathering frozen mud to line
Their tiny homes, or in loud regiments
Ranged over water, he implored a sign.

The thickets hear each night as dusk descends
The woodcock's call. The forests hear the geese
Honk, and go down. The crane's voice never ends.

What storms have whirled them from what shaken seas,
The watchers ask, that they should come so soon?
Or in the feathered world, what mutinies?

For now fresh migrants of a brighter plume
Than finch or plover gleam above the hills,
Impend, descend, and on our meadows loom.

Cavalry! Troop after troop it spills
With strange insignia, strangely armed,
As snow in a spring thaw fills

The valley roads. From the forests long
Bright bayonets issue, as brigades of foot
Debouch like ants, form up, and densely throng;

All heading north as if the bird, the scout,
Had led men here from halcyon lands, impelled
By instincts too imperative to doubt.

War! the war!—a meaning that transpires
To the remotest corner. In the wood
Beyond whose bounds no rustic mind enquires,

Where in the sky the peasant understood
Only the wind's cry, and on earth the brute's
(And all his visitors the neighbourhood),

A sudden glare! A crash! A ball that shoots
Far from the field, makes its impeded way,
Rips through the branches and lays bare the roots.

The bearded bison trembles, and at bay
Heaves to his forelegs, ruffs his mane, and glares
At sudden sparks that glitter on the spray.

The stray bomb spins and hisses; as he stares,
Bursts. And the beast that never knew alarm
Blunders in panic to profounder lairs.

'Whither the battle?'—and the young men arm.
The women pray, 'God is Napoleon's shield,
Napoleon ours', as to the outcome calm.

Spring well remembered! Happy who saw thee then,
Spring of the war, Spring of the mighty yield,
That promised corn but ripened into men.

FROM THE FRENCH OF STÉPHANE MALLARMÉ

552            *Prose for Des Esseintes*

Hyperbole! Can't you arise
From memory, and triumph, grow
Today a form of conjuration,
Robed in an iron folio?

For I establish, by my lore,
Hymns of the heart's enlivened powers,
In products of my patient round,
Arcana, atlases, and flowers.

This way and that we cast our eyes
(I say, we two, and I have cause)
Upon the landscape's many charms,
Sister, comparing them with yours.

The era of authority
Quakes, to hear it idly said
Of this our *midi*, by our twin
Subconscious deeply read,

That to that hundred-irised soil
(And they know if it was at all)
No name is ever blazoned by
Summer's gold trumpet-call.

Aye, in an island that the air
Charged not with vision but with sight,
Each blossom burgeoned wider where
We had not talked as if it might,

And grew so large that each one there
By normal course of nature prinked
In lucid line, a void of air
That from the plots made it distinct.

Glory of long desire, ideas,
All in me lifted up, to see
The family of the iris-eyed
Rise to this new necessity.

But this sister would not go,
In her good sense and tender heart,
Further than smile; which as I heard
I secure my ancient part.

Now as we call a halt to talk
Oh learn from this, litigious wit,
Multiplicate with blooms, the stalk
Throve past our understanding it,

And thriving not as thirls the strand,
Whose lying monotones are bent
On positing a swell to land
Among my young astonishment,

Hearing that map and all that sky
Witnessed for true at each footfall,
By just that wave that was put by
There was (it says) no land at all.

The child puts ecstasy away,
Instructed by the paths she's worn,
And Anastase! you hear her say,
For an eternal parchment born,

Before some sky sees her forebears
Moved to gladness in a tomb,
And Pulchérie, the name it bears,
Is hidden by the enormous bloom.

# MICHAEL HAMBURGER

## 1924–

### FROM THE GERMAN OF PAUL CELAN

553        *Your Hand Full of Hours*

Your hand full of hours, you came to me—and I said:
Your hair is not brown.
So you lifted it lightly on to the scales of grief; it
    weighed more than I ...

On ships they come to you and make it their cargo, then
    put it on sale in the markets of lust—
You smile at me from the depth, I weep at you from the
    scale that stays light.
I weep: Your hair is not brown, they offer brine from
    the sea and you give them curls ...
You whisper: They're filling the world with me now,
    in your heart I'm a hollow way still!
You say: Lay the leafage of years beside you—it's time
    you came closer and kissed me!

The leafage of years is brown, your hair is not brown.

554        *Psalm*

No one moulds us again out of earth and clay,
no one conjures our dust.
No one.

Praise be your name, no one.
For your sake
we shall flower.
Towards
you.

A nothing
we were, are, shall
remain, flowering;
the nothing—, the
no one's rose.

With our pistil soul-bright
with our stamen heaven-ravaged
our corolla red
with the crimson word which we sang
over, o over
the thorn.

555                    *. . . plashes the fountain*

You prayer—, you blasphemy, you
prayer-sharp knives
of my
silence.

You my words being crippled
together with me, you
my hale ones.

And you:
you, you, you
my later of roses
daily worn true and
more true—;

How much, O how much
world. How many
paths.
You crutch, you wing. We—

We shall sing the nursery rhyme, that one,
do you hear, that one
with the hu, with the man, with the human being, the
    one
with the scrub and with
the pair of eyes that lay ready there as
tear-upon-
tear.

556 *Thread Suns*

Thread suns
above the grey-black wilderness.
A tree-
high thought
tunes in to light's pitch: there are
still songs to be sung on the other side
of mankind.

557 *Etched Away From*

Etched away from
the ray-shot wind of your language
the garish talk of rubbed-
off experience—the hundred-
tongued pseudo-
poem, the noem.

Whirled
clear,
free
your way through the human-
shaped snow,
the penitents' snow, to
the hospitable
glacier rooms and tables.

Deep in time's crevasse
by the alveolate ice
waits, a crystal of breath,
your irreversible
witness.

558 *Leap-Centuries*

Leap-centuries, leap-
seconds, leap-
births, novembering, leap-
deaths,

stacked in honeycomb troughs,
'bits
on chips',

the menora poem from Berlin

(Unasylumed, un-
archived, un-
welfare-attended? A-
live?),

reading stations in the late word,

saving flame points
in the sky,

comb lines under fire,

feelings, frost-
mandrelled,

cold start
with haemoglobin.


559 *Irish*

Give me the right of way
over the corn steps into your sleep,
the right of way
over the sleep path,
the right to cut peat
on the heart slope,
tomorrow.

# ALAN NEAME

1924–

### FROM THE FRENCH OF JEAN COCTEAU

560                                        from *Leoun*

### I

Leoun I dreamed on the night of the 28th.
Padding with lioness paws across the night
She walked, Leoun, between the burnt-out fires.
Greek actors walk in clogs with comparable poise.

### II

Leoun went forward until bedworthy dawn.
Skilfully walking on the night went Leoun.
Leoun walked on the night itself, I mean.

### III

The dream hung in my head and Leoun in my dream.
Hearse and mutes were hard put to keep up with her
The roundabout twisted its corded copper
The robot scanned her shepherded footfall
All seemed to turn yet nothing moved at all
For, expert in the properties of mirrors, Leoun
Climbed backwards up the ladder the rain let down.

### IV

She straddled the bodies of showmen asleep.
Halted. Counted her enemies. Thought deep.
Under her cloak hid the Head of Holophernes
(You see, this head was the lamp for her journeys
Deaf blind frightful with its brilliant beam)
And resumed the course designed by my dream.

### V

That's how she walked, relentless Leoun,
For Leoun walking was chameleon,
Taking form and colour from everywhere she trod
Moving with the grace of a thief on the job.

### VI

She walked on the fringe of the Dew's eye-lash.
Her undertaking was unspeakably rash
For at the jetty-corner and from cardinal points
The soldiery of morning patrolled the battlements.

### VII

Monuments on the ages drifting
Sported their light rig of scaffolding.
History was marking houses with an X.
The queen was at the chymist buying a portpest.
Lurid in mauve patches between the bridges flowed
The virgin-seeming waters, often enough widowed,
And Leoun Leoun at the foot of the quay wall
Went on her way with disguised footfall.

### VIII

Where the streetlamps were out painted women were towed
By stark naked cyclists to the pretty crossroad
While heedless of its human cattle the city held
Its great palm open under a sky ciphered with gold.

\*

### XXXI

Tristram may linger for the horn's lament
Leoun despises him and laughs at his distress.
She and the Zeitgeist walk abreast.
I dream her and I contain the dream.
Yet I still cannot tell Leoun's final aim.
Flat on my bed how could I follow her?
No. I can only snuff her out altogether.

### XXXII

Snuff her out? Can a Leoun really die?
What does her name mean? What does the sleeper do?
He lies. Offers himself for a dream-stage.
Now the dream fills me as water fills a sponge.

\*

### XXXIV

The sleeper gives nothing of his own.
My dream makes a mere passage for Leoun,
Knowing my impotence my sole reward.
I have no means to trap her off her guard.
Who can tell whence Leoun or whither away?

### XXXV

So plied Gradiva through the streets of Pompeii
With a grace somewhat reminiscent of Leoun
So on the water pranced the Colleoun
So the Commendatorè kicked the ground agape
So trod the Vénus d'Ille with brazen step
So flew Icarus plumed with artifice.

\*

### LVIII

Leoun pierced further under the soulless vault.
No landmark from the known world marked her route.
A hero lying asleep with his limbs straddled wide
Composed valley rock wood rampart and mountainside.
The swallows were nesting in the hollows of his arms.
For his arms flung apart left his armpits unarmed
And below in a tangled grove between his legs
The cockbird slept brooding on his eggs.

### LIX

Leoun untouched by a grace so ignoble
Strode through his vineyard fallow-land and grove.
And I followed Leoun in my turn to trample
The body of the hero dismasted by love.

### LX

'Twas Renaldo fallen prey to Armida's devices
Sleeping in the fragrance of his dewy fleeces.
Biceps shoulderblade breastbone thigh and hip
Littered the warm snow where the heroes sleep.

## LXI

Armida in the veil of a lawful bride
And taller than a shot-tower surveyed fallen pride.
Chaste after love, her great body locked up,
She slept on her feet by her own true love.

\*

## CV

Palace of Don Juan Rampart of Elsinor
Your walking dead would leave me less dismayed
Than the Palais-Royal's girdling arcade
And less dismayed at your grandees from Hell
Than the familiar noise of its iron grills.
They pull them down of an evening. Raise them at dawn.
One of these iron curtains shattered my dream.

\*

## CXIII

Let me go: I shall write whatever I fancy!
Aren't you sick of pulling out my hair
And knotting it tight to the top of your lyre?

## CXIV

Let me go! Let me go! I abhor your frenzy
My hair strung in hatred to the lyre
And the assizes where flayed I expire.

\*

## CXIX

If you are plotting my more ingenious torture
Can I sleep at the end untroubled by any dream?
You write? And your books are read, may I ask, by whom?
Does a world exist where I shall not have to speak?
Need I tremble there at Leoun and her panther-feet?
Need I tremble there at the Muse with claws like a lion?

## CXX

Need I tremble there at the sky with its thousand million
Eyes intent on pulling our whole world down?
Your forbidden city is truly an open town
Where I can evade the shame of offering fight?
Someone is watching me.
                    Look out.
                              Keep quiet.

# PETER WHIGHAM

## 1925–

### FROM THE LATIN OF CATULLUS

561                              *Attis*

Plunging towards Phrygia over violent water
shot on the wood-slung Berecynthian coast
Attis with urgent feet treads the opaque ground
of the Goddess, his wits fuddled, stung with phrenetic
itch, slices his testicles off with a razor-
flint, sees the signs of new blood spotting
the earth, knows arms, legs, torse, sans
male members and
                    SHE
ecstatically snatches in delicate hands
the hand-drum of Cybebe, the hand-drum
of forest rites and Cybebe's torture
with nervous fingers taps the hollowed hide
shakes it and shaking summons the Mother's Brood:
'Ololugmos!
              To Cybebe's thickets!
                          You have found the strange coast.
Ololugmos!
              Stamp in my footprints!
                          You are tied to my tether.
Ololugmos!
              Capsized in my currents—
                          unsexing yourselves
in my Love-hate.

Ololugmos! Break the close thicket,
with rabid abandon brighten Dindymia's face
Stamp on Cybebe's ground
              stamp where the drum shudders
stamp where the cymbals clang
               where the flute drones
where the Maenads convulsively toss their ivied heads
where the protracted scream signals the Maenad rite—
the carlines flit restlessly in the grove
—Come with your quick triple step,
              Ololugmos!'
As Attis speaks
        the trembling tongues of her neophytes
rise with the drum beats,
            the concave cymbals begin clanging.
They head for green Ida.
          Attis is a frenzied steer.
She gasps
      goaded by yoke-hate
bursts through the holy grove,
           the throbbing drums
the foot-mad Gallae, stream in her wake....
And the touch of Cybebe's bower brings lassitude.
Fatigue lowers their lids. They are foodless.
Investing apathy unstrings the manic pitch.
They sleep.
        Then when the sun's manifold hooves splinter
darkness, and the eyes from the gold mask sweep sky &
  earth
& the wild sea, Sleep takes a nimble drive from wak-
   ing Attis into the expectant arms of his paramour
                —Pasithea.
At once, shedding the night's tranquillity, Attis
relives the pictures in her heart,
           freed from the maelstrom,
unclouded, recognises the rootless place where she has come,
her thoughts turned inside out, goes headlong back
to the beach, where she cries to Attica she has lost
for ever ... looks over the brutal water
that stares back at her through her tears:
'Attica mother & maker, I
like a grateless housecarl fleeing

his mesne, footloose among Ida's
snows among the wood & rock lairs
with the boar caves for an icy hearth,
have I stripped myself of my patrimony
friends, goods, kin?
                 Are these ungreek landscapes
my new life-home?
                 Where is Attica?
Where can the pupil open with Attica?
The storm has lifted
                 and there is no *piazza*,
where is the stadium? the wrestling ring? the gymnasium
—a fallen life left to tread sorrow.
What have I not known? What shape not been?
A synthetic woman:
                 once man, once lad, once boy.
Once the flower of the athletes.
                 Once the pride of the young wrestlers.
My doors & thresholds were warm with friends.
The house full of blossoms greeting
the morning separation from the lover's couch.
And now, I, but part "I",
                 a plucked torse
a Maenad
     familiar of the gods
               huscarl of Cybebe,
tethered under these obsessive peaks
rooting with the tree-stag & the boar
                 in the snow woods,
the pain at Attis' heart outweighs the Attis rage.'
As the words fly from the pink mouth
they lodge in Cybebe's ears
who stoops to the fear-of-flocks
unyokes the left-hand lion
and whispers:
         'Attis is truant. Hound Attis hither.
Infect her with fear & desire
for Cybebe's pale. Lash at yourself with
your tail-knot. Drown the whole mountain
with roaring. Let the red mane dreadfully
cloud the brute neck.'
               She looses the leash.

The beast self-scourges its flanks
bounds through the brushwood, bursts
on the white-lined sands, appearing
where delicate Attis still stands by the sea.
The demented creature flees to Cybebe's wold
her life-space doomed spent in Cybebe's thrall.

'Great Cybebe, Mother Goddess, Berecynthian Queen,
avert your fury from Catullus' house
goad others to your actions,
others trap in the snarl of frenzy.'

# CHRISTOPHER LOGUE

## 1926–

### ADAPTED FROM THE GREEK OF HOMER

562    *from* Patrocleia (The Iliad, Book XVI)

*'Wearing Achilles' Armour, Patroclus, along with the*
*Myrmidons, attacks the Trojans'*

*Hornets occasionally build their nests near roads.*
*In the late Spring they breed; feeding their grubs*
*And feeding off the sticky spit the grubs exude.*
*Now and again a child pokes a stick into the nest*
*And stirs. The hornets swarm. Jab, jabbing their*
*Insect poison in its eyes and flesh.*
*Often the swollen child dies that night. Sometimes*
*They menace passers-by instead.*

But the Myrmidons made no mistake.

Swarming up and off the beach Patroclus swung them left
At the ditch: keeping it on their right they streamed
Along the camp's main track; on one side, the embankment;
On the other, ships—a line of slender necking
With the huts clutched under the tense black hulls.
Things were so close a man could hardly see in front of him,
And Patroclus on the foot-plate of his chariot, cried—
   'FOR ACHILLES!'
As the two sides closed.

The Trojans lay across the ship,
Most of them busy seeing that it burned.
Others slid underneath and were so occupied
Knocking away the chocks that kept it upright
They did not see Patroclus swoop
Out of nowhere on their necks.
    But those above did.
Between the time it takes to dip and light a match
Achilles' helmet loomed under their wretched chins,
With Myrmidons splayed out on either side
Like iron wings.
    Dropping the pitch
They grabbed up javelins, knives—boathooks, too—oh,
    Anything to keep Achilles off!
Have he and Agamemnon patched things up?
    Likely enough ...
And are we covered from the rear?


    Patroclus aimed where they were thickest.
That is to say, around a Macedonian
Chariot commander called Pyraykemese,
Tough, one of Troy's best. But as Patroclus aimed
The ship's mast split from stem to peak—Aoi!—and fell
Lengthwise across the incident.
    Its fat waist clubbed the hull's top strake,
And the whole ship flopped sideways.
Those underneath got crunched.
And howling Greeks ran in
To stick the others as they slithered down
Into their lap.
    But not you, Pyraykemese; no,
Heaven had something special up its sleeve for you.
Because the mast's peak hit the ground no more than six
Foot from Patroclus' chariot hub, the horses shied,
Spoiling his cast. Nothing was lost. God blew the javelin straight
At Pyraykemese as he pitched downwards twenty feet,
Headfirst, back arched, belly towards the Greeks—who laughed—
The tab-ends of his metal kilt dangling across his chest.
    Whether it was the fall that scared him,
Or the vague flare Patroclus' javelin made
As it drifted through the morning air towards
His falling body like a yellow-headed bird,

We do not know. Suffice to say he shrieked until,
Mid-air, the cold bronze apex sank
Between his teeth and tongue,
Parted his brain, pressed on, and skewered him
Against the upturned hull.
  His dead jaw gaped. His soul,
Crawled off his tongue and vanished into sunlight ...

### 'Apollo defeats Patroclus'

  His hand came out of the east,
And in his wrist lay eternity.
And every atom of his mythic weight
Was poised between his fist and bent left leg,
And it hit the small of your back, Patroclus ...
  Your eyes leant out. Achilles' helmet rang
Far and away beneath the cannon-bones of enemy horses,
And Achilles' breastplate (five copper plys
Mastered with even bronze) split like a pod.
And you were footless ... staggering ... amazed
Between the clumps of dying, dying yourself,
Dazed by the brilliance in your eyes
And the noise, like weirs heard far away.
  So you staggered, blind eyes open,
Dabbling your astounded fingers in the vomit
On your chest.
  And all the Trojans lay and stared at you,
Propped themselves up and stared at you,
Feeling themselves as blest as you felt cursed.
All of them just lay and stared
Except a boy called Euphorbus.
  He took his chance and cast.
The javelin went through both your calves,
Stitching your knees together, and you fell
(Not noticing the pain) and tried to crawl
Towards the fleet, and—even now—snatching
Euphorbus' ankle—Ah!—and got it? No ...
Not a boy's ankle that you got,
But Hector's

Standing above you,
His bronze mask smiling down into your face,
Putting his spear through ... ach, and saying,
    'Why tears, Patroclus?
Did you hope to melt Troy down
And make our women carry home the ingots for you?
    I can imagine it!
You and your marvellous Achilles sitting,
Him with his upright finger wagging, saying,
*"Don't show your face in here again, Patroclus,*
*Unless it's red with Hector's blood."*
    You fool.
You weak, impudent, silly little fool.'
    And Patroclus,
Shaking his voice out of his body, says
    'Big mouth,
Remember it took three of you to kill me.
A god, a boy, and last of all, a hero!
    I can hear Death
Calling my name and yet,
Somehow it sounds like *"Hector"*
    And when I close my eyes
I see Achilles' face with Death's voice coming out of it.'

Saying these things Patroclus died.
And as his soul went through the sand like water,
Hector withdrew his spear and said
    *'Perhaps.'*


# CHRISTOPHER MIDDLETON

## 1926–

### FROM THE GERMAN OF PAUL CELAN

563                          *The Jugs*

At the long tables of time
the jugs of God carouse.
They drink empty the eyes that see and the eyes of the blind,
the hearts of the mastering shadows,

the hollow cheek of the evening.
They are the most mighty carousers:
they carry empty and full alike to their mouths
and do not flow over like you or like me.

564                    *Fugue of Death*

Black milk of daybreak we drink it at nightfall
we drink it at noon in the morning we drink it at night
drink it and drink it
we are digging a grave in the sky it is ample to lie there
A man in the house he plays with the serpents he writes
he writes when the night falls to Germany your golden hair
    Margarete
he writes it and walks from the house the stars glitter
    he whistles his dogs up
he whistles his Jews out and orders a grave to be dug in the
    earth
he commands us strike up for the dance

Black milk of daybreak we drink you at night
we drink in the mornings at noon we drink you at nightfall
drink you and drink you
A man in the house he plays with the serpents he writes
he writes it and walks from the house the stars glitter
    Margarete
Your ashen hair Shulamith we are digging a grave in the sky
    it is ample to lie there

He shouts stab deeper in earth you there and you others you
    sing and you play
he grabs at the iron in his belt and swings it and blue are his
    eyes
stab deeper your spades you there and you others play on for
    the dancing

Black milk of daybreak we drink you at nightfall
we drink you at noon in the mornings we drink you at nightfall
drink you and drink you
a man in the house your golden hair Margarete
your ashen hair Shulamith he plays with the serpents

He shouts play sweeter death's music death comes as a
   master from Germany
he shouts stroke darker the strings and as smoke you shall
   climb to the sky
then you'll have a grave in the clouds it is ample to lie there

Black milk of daybreak we drink you at night
we drink you at noon death comes as a master from Germany
we drink you at nightfall and morning we drink you and drink you
a master from Germany death comes with eyes that are blue
with a bullet of lead he will hit in the mark he will hit you
a man in the house your golden hair Margarete
he hunts us down with his dogs in the sky he gives us a grave
he plays with the serpents and dreams death comes as a master
   from Germany

your golden hair Margarete
your ashen hair Shulamith.

# OMAR POUND

## 1926–

### FROM THE PERSIAN OF IBN HAZM AL-ANDALUSI

565          *Twice times then is now*

You ask how old am I
bleached by the sun
my teeth all gone.
How old am I?

I have no guide
no calendar inside
except a smile
and little kiss
she gave me
by surprise
upon my brow.

And now,
that little while
is all my life
and all reality,
how long or brief
it seems to be.

# GUY DAVENPORT

## 1927–

### FROM THE GREEK OF SAPPHO

I

**566**

Cp.
Rexroth
Young

Come out of Crete
And find me here,
Come to your grove,
Mellow apple trees
And holy altar
Where the sweet smoke
Of libanum is in
Your praise,

Where leaf melody
In the apples
Is a crystal crash,
And the water is cold.
All roses and shadow,
This place, and sleep
Like dusk sifts down
From trembling leaves.

Here horses stand
In flowers and graze.
The wind is glad
And sweet in its moving.
Here, Kypris [          ]
Pour nectar in the golden cups
And mix it deftly with
Our dancing and mortal wine.

567    *'The Marriage of Hector and Andromache'*

Crying Asia! that famous place,
The messenger came from his dust.
Crying Ektor! the winded runner
Silver with sweat, laughing, Ektor!
Ektor comes from that famous Asia,
From its strange towns with his friends.
They bring home a black-eyed girl
From Theba the high on the Plakia,
The graceful, the young Andrómakha.
They come in the ships on the ocean.
For gifts they bring wrist-chains of gold,
And purple coats and silver jars,
And carved toys incredibly strange,
And things made of ivory.

So the runner said.
                    Quick with astonishment,
Ektor's father shouted for his friends,
And told the coming the city over.
Ilos' boys put wheels to the high carts
And hitched the mules. Wives and girls
Came to stand with Priam's daughters.
Bachelors led the chariot horses;
Charioteers like gods sang commands.

A long parade sings its way from the sea.
The flutes are keen and the drums tight;
Charmed air holds the young girls' songs.
Along the way the people bring them bowls
Of cassia, cups of olibanum and myrrh.
Dancing grandmothers shout the marriage song.
Men and boys march and sing to Páon,
To Apollo of the harp, archer of archers,
And sing that Ektor and Andrómakha
Are like two of the gods together.

568

3

[                                    ]
[            ] that labor [               ]
[        ] a face to remember in wonder [
[                    ]

[                ] to sing [                    ]
[                    ] to storm wind [            ]
[                ] and no pain [                ]
[                        ]

[            ] I urge [                ]
Gongyla [                    ] harp
[                        ] whose longing again
Hovers on wings

Around your loveliness. For when she sees
The long pleats of your dress in their moving
She catches her breath at the beauty,
And I laugh for joy.

Goddess born from the sea at Kypros
Thus I pray [                        ]
That [                            ]
I long [                ].


FROM THE LATIN OF ARCHILOCHUS

I

569
This island,
            garlanded with wild woods,
      Lies in the sea
            like the backbone of an ass.

### 2

570
Like Odysseus under the ram
You have clung under your lovers
And under your love of lust,
Seeing nothing else for this mist,
Dark of heart, dark of mind.

### 3

571
Decks awash,
Mast-top dipping,
And all
Balanced on the keen edge
Now of the wind's sword,
Now of the wave's blade.

### 4

572
May he lose his way on the cold sea
And swim to the heathen Salmydessos,
May the ungodly Thracians with their hair
Done up in a fright on the top of their heads
Grab him, that he know what it is to be alone
Without friend or family. May he eat slave's bread
And suffer the plague and freeze naked,
Laced about with the nasty trash of the sea.
May his teeth knock the top on the bottom
As he lies on his face, spitting brine,
At the edge of the cold sea, like a dog.
And all this it would be a privilege to watch,
Giving me great satisfaction as it would,
For he took back the word he gave in honor,
Over the salt and table at a friendly meal.

# WILLIAM S. MERWIN

1927–

## FROM THE FRENCH OF GUILLAUME APOLLINAIRE

573        *The Mirabeau Bridge*

Under the Mirabeau Bridge the Seine
Flows and our love
Must I be reminded again
How joy came always after pain

Night comes the hour is rung
The days go I remain

Hands within hands we stand face to face
While underneath
The bridge of our arms passes
The loose wave of our gazing which is endless

Night comes the hour is rung
The days go I remain

Love slips away like this water flowing
Love slips away
How slow life is in its going
And hope is so violent a thing

Night comes the hour is rung
The days go I remain

The days pass the weeks pass and are gone
Neither time that is gone
Nor love ever returns again
Under the Mirabeau Bridge flows the Seine

Night comes the hour is rung
The days go I remain

## with Clarence Brown

### FROM THE RUSSIAN OF OSIP MANDELSTAM

574 *Batyushkov**

An idler with a wand for a walking stick,
gentle Batyushkov lives with me,
strides down the alleys into Zamost'e,
sniffs a rose, sings Zafna—

nothing has ever been lost!
I believe I bowed when I met him,
and pressed his pale cold glove
like a man with a fever.

He smiled a little, I pronounced Thank you,
too shy to say any more.
No one else could trace those sounds,
no other waves sound the same.

He was bringing with him our anguish
and our great richness, and he was muttering:
the noise of making a poem, the bell of brotherhood,
the soft patter of tears,

still mourning for Tasso. And he answered me
'I can't get a taste for praise.
Only the grape-flesh of poetry
ever cooled my tongue.'

You that live in cities with city friends
would scarcely believe it:
eternal dreams, blood samples
pouring from one glass to the next.

---

*Konstantine Nikolaevich Batyushkov (1787–1855), a contemporary of
Pushkin, was one of the greatest of Russian poets. 'The Dying Tasso' is among
his best known poems. The name Zafna occurs in his poem 'Istochnik' (The
Spring), 1810. Zamost'e is a town to the south-east of Lublin. (*Translator's
note*)

575 *Ariosto*

Ariosto—no one in Italy more delightful—
these days has a frog in his throat.
He amuses himself with the names of fish,
he rains nonsense into the seas.

Like a musician with ten cymbals,
forever breaking in on his own music,
he leads us backwards and forwards, himself quite lost
in the maze of chivalric scandals.

A Pushkin in the language of the cicadas,
with a Mediterranean haughtiness to his melancholy,
he leaves his hero struggling with the preposterous,
and shudders, and is another man.

He says to the sea: roar but don't think!
To the maiden on the rock: lie there without bedclothes!
We've heard too little—tell us again,
while there's blood in the veins, and a roar in the ears.

O lizard city with a crust for a heart, and no soul,
Ferrara, give birth to more of such men!
While there's blood in the veins, hurry, tell the story
so often told, once more from the beginning.

It's cold in Europe. Italy is in darkness.
And power—it's like having to swallow a barber's hand.
But he goes on improving his act, playing
the great man smiling out of the window

at the lamb on the hill, the monk on his donkey,
the Duke's men-at-arms silly with wine
and the plague and garlic,
the baby dozing under a net of flies.

I love his desperate leisure,
his babble, the salt and sugar of his words,
the sounds happily conspiring in twos and threes.
Why should I want to split the pearl?

Ariosto, maybe this age will vanish
and we'll pour your azure and our Black Sea together
into one wide fraternal blue.
We too know it well. We've drunk mead on its shore.


# CHARLES TOMLINSON

## 1927–

## with Henry Gifford

### FROM THE SPANISH OF ANTONIO MACHADO
*1875- 1939*

576    *Lament of the Virtues and Verses on Account
of the Death of Don Guido*

It was pneumonia
finally carried away
Don Guido, and so the bells
(*din-dan*) toll for him the whole day.

Died Don Guido
gentleman; when younger
great at gallantry and roistering,
a minor talent in the bullring—
older, his prayers grew longer.

This Sevillan gentleman
kept (so they say)
a seraglio, was apt
at managing a horse
and a master
at cooling manzanilla.

When his riches dwindled
it was his obsession
to think that he ought to think
of settling in quiet possession.
And he settled
in a very Spanish way
which was—to marry

a maiden of large fortune
and to repaint his blazons,
to refer to the traditions of
'this house of ours',
setting a measure
to scandals and amours
and damping down the expenditure on pleasure.

He became, great pagan
that he was,
brother in a fraternity;
on Holy Thursday could be seen
disguised
(the immense candle in his hand)
in the long robe of a Nazarene.

Today
you may hear the bell
say that the good Don Guido
with solemn face
tomorrow must go
the slow road to the burial place.
For ever and for always
gone, good Don Guido ...
'What have you left?' some will say—
I ask, 'What have you taken
to the world in which you are today?'

Your love for braid
and for silks and gold
and the blood of bulls and the fume that rolled
from off the altars.

To good Don Guido and his equipage
bon voyage!

The here
and the there,
cavalier,
show in your withered face,
confess the infinite:
the nothingness.

Oh the thin cheeks
yellow
and the eyelids, wax,
and the delicate skull
on the bed's pillow!

Oh end of an aristocracy!
The beard on breast
lies limp and hoary,
in the rough serge
of a monk he's dressed;
crossed, the hands that cannot stir
and the Andalusian gentleman
on his best behaviour.

## FROM THE ITALIAN OF LUCIO PICCOLO

577 *Veneris Venefica Agrestis*

She springs from the ground-clinging thicket, her face
—gay now, now surly—bound in a black
kerchief, a shrivelled chestnut it seems: no fine fleece
the hair that falls loose, but a lock
of curling goat-hair; when she goes by
(is she standing or bending?) her gnarled and dark
foot is a root that suddenly juts from the earth and walks.
   Be watchful she does not offer you her cup of bark,
its water root-flavoured that tastes of the viscid leaf,
either mulberry or sorb-apple, woodland fruit that flatters with lies
the lips but the tongue ties.
   She governs it seems
the force of rounding moons
that swells out the rinds of trees
and alternates the invincible ferments,
flow of the sap and of the seas ...
   Pronubial, she, like the birds that bring
seeds from afar: arcane
the breeds that come of her grafting.
   And the mud walls of the unstable
cottage where the nettle grows
with gigantic stalk, are her realms of shadows:
she ignites the kindlings in the furnaces of fable.

And round the door, from neighbouring orchard ground
the fumes that rise
are the fine, unwinding muslins of her sibiline vespers.
    She appears in the guise
of the centipede among the darknesses
by water-wheels that turn
no more in the maidenhair fern.
    She is the mask that beckons
and disappears, when the light
of the halfspent wicks
makes voracious the shadows in the room where
they are milling by night, working at the presses,
and odours of crushed olives are in the air,
kindled vapours of grapejuice; and lanterns come
swayed to the steps of hobnailed boots.
    The gestures of those who labour
in the fields, are accomplices
in the plots she weaves:
the stoop of those who gather up dry leaves
and acorns ... and the shoeless tread and measured bearing
under burdened head, when you cannot see
the brow or the olives of the eyes
but only the lively mouth ... the dress
swathes tight the flanks, the breasts, and has comeliness—
passing the bough she leaves behind
an odour of parching ...
or the gesture that raises the crock
renewed at the basin of the spring.
    She bends, drawing a circle:
her sign sends forth
the primordial torrent out of the fearful earth
(and the foot that presses the irrigated furrow
and the hand that lifts
the spade—power of a different desire summons them now);
she draws strength
from the breaths of the enclosures,
the diffused cries, the damp and burning
straw of the litters, the blackened
branches of the vine, and the shadow that gives back
the smell of harnesses of rope and sack,
damp baskets, where who stands
on the threshold can descry

the stilled millstone, hoes long used to the grip of rural hands:
the rustic shade ferments with ancestral longings.
  Rockroses, thistles, pulicaria, calaminths—scents
that seem fresh and aromatic, are
(should your wariness pall) the lures
of a spiral that winds-in all,
(night bites into silver
free of all alloy of sidereal ray) she will
blur in a fume of dust the gentle hill-curve.
  Now, she's in daylight, one hand against an oak,
the other hangs loose—filthy and coaxing,
her dress black as a flue-brush . . .
and the sudden rush of wind
over the headland, sets at large, lets flow
in a flood a divine
tangle of leaves and flourishing bough.
  The heat, too, promises, discloses
freshness, vigour of the breath that frees
peach and the bitter-sweet
odour of the flowering almond tree; under coarse leaf
are fleshy and violent mouths, wild offshoots,
between the ferns' long fans
obscure hints of mushroom growths,
uncertain glances of water glint through the clovers,
and a sense of bare
original clay is there
near where the poplar wakes unslakeable thirst
with its rustling mirages of streams
and makes itself a mirror of each breeze,
where, in the hill's shade,
steep sloping
the valley grows
narrow and closes
in the mouth of a spring
among delicate mosses.
  If, for a moment,
cloud comes to rest
over the hill-crest or the valley threshold,
in the living shade
the shaft of that plough now shows
which shakes which unflowers unleafs
the bush and the forest rose.

### FROM THE SPANISH OF OCTAVIO PAZ

578           *Landscape*

Rock and precipice,
More time than stone, this
Timeless matter.

Through its cicatrices
Falls without moving
Perpetual virgin water.

Immensity reposes here
Rock over rock,
Rocks over air.

The world's manifest
As it is: a sun
Immobile, in the abyss.

Scale of vertigo:
The crags weigh
No more than our shadows.

# JOHN MONTAGUE

### 1929–

### after Kuno Meyer

### FROM THE IRISH

579       *The Vision of MacConglinne*

The vision that appeared
Splendidly to me, I now
    Relate to all;
Carved from lard, a coracle
In a port of New Milk Lake
    On the world's calm sea.

We climbed that handsome boat,
Over ocean's heaving way
   Set out bravely;
Our oars as we leaned
Raised the sea's harvest
   Of honeyed algae.

The fort we reached was beautiful—
Thick breastworks of custard
   Above the lake
Fresh butter for a drawbridge
A moat of wheaten bread
   A bacon palisade.

Stately and firmly placed
On strong foundations, it seemed
   As I entered
Through a door of dried beef
A threshold of well-baked bread
   Walls of cheese-curd.

Sleek pillars of ripe cheese
And fleshed bacon posts
   In alternate rows;
Fine beams of yellow cream
Thin rafters of white spice
   Held up the house.

Spurting behind, a spring of wine
Beer and ale flowing in streams
   And tasty pools;
From a well-head of nectar
A crest of creamy malt ran
   Over the floor.

An estuary of juicy pottage,
Winking with oozy fat, lay
   Next the sea:
A hedge of butter to guard,
Under blossoms of mantling lard,
   The wall outside.

### JOHN MONTAGUE

A row of flowering apple-trees,
An orchard in pink-topped bloom
   Before the nearest hill:
A forest of lanky leeks,
Of scallions and carrot clumps
   Under the back sill.

Within, a welcoming household
Of ruddy, well-fleshed men
   About the fire;
Seven necklaces of tangy cheese
Seven strings of tripe, dangling
   About each neck.

Swathed in a mantle of beefy fat
Beside his well proportioned wife
   I glimpsed the Chief:
Before the mighty cauldron's mouth
Crouched the Dispenser, his flesh fork
   Upon his back.


# PETER PORTER

## 1929–

### FROM THE GREEK OF LUCILIUS 39-65 AD

580    Lean Gaius, who was thinner than a straw
And who could slip through even a locked door,
Is dead, and we his friends are twice bereft,
In losing him and finding nothing left
To put into the coffin: what they'll do
In Hades with a creature who is too
Shadowy to be a Shade, God knows,
But when we bear him to his last repose,
We'll make it stylish—mourners, black crêpe, bier,
The lot, and though he won't himself appear,
His empty coffin's progress will be pious—
THE DEATH OF NOTHING, FUNERAL OF GAIUS!

## FROM THE LATIN OF MARTIAL

581        *Epigrams*, Book I, 43

What a host you are, Mancinus;
there we were, all sixty of us,
last night, decently invited guests
and this was the order of dishes
you pampered us with:
    NO late-gathered grapes
    NO apples sweet as honeycomb
    NO ponderous ripe pears lashed to the branch
    NO pomegranates the colour of blowing roses
    NO baskets of best Sassina cheese
    NO Picenian jars of olives

Only a miserable boar so small
a dwarf could have throttled it
one-handed. And nothing to follow,
no dessert, no sweet, no pudding, nothing...

We were the spectres, this was the feast,
a boar fit for the arena, duly
masticated by us—

I don't want to see you struggle
in your turn for a share of the crackling—
no, imitate instead
that poor devil Charidemus
who was shredded in the ring—
rather than miser eats boar
lets have boar eats miser:
*bon appetit*, my host of nothings,
I can almost feel the tushes in your throat.

582          *Epigrams*, Book II, 52

Dasius, chucker-out
at the Turkish Baths,
is a shrewd assessor;
when he saw big-titted
Spatale coming, he decided
to charge her entry for three
persons. What did she do?
Paid with pride of course.

583          *Epigrams*, Book IV, 18

Near the Vipsanian columns where the aqueduct
    drips down the side of its dark arch,
the stone is a green and pulsing velvet
    and the air is powdered with sweat
from the invisible faucet: there winter
    shaped a dagger of ice, waiting till
a boy looked up at the quondam stalactites,
    threw it like a gimlet through his throat
and as in a murder in a paperback the clever
    weapon melted away in its own hole. Where
have blood and water flowed before from one wound?
    The story is trivial and the instance holy—
what portion of power has violent fortune
    ever surrendered, what degraded circumstance
will she refuse? Death is everywhere
    if water, the life-giving element,
will descend to cutting throats.

# ELAINE FEINSTEIN

## 1930–

## with Angela Livingstone

### FROM THE RUSSIAN OF MARINA TSVETAYEVA

584          from *The Poem of the End*

I didn't want this, not
    this (but listen, quietly,
to want is what bodies do
    and now we are ghosts only).

And yet I   didn't say it
    though the time of the train is set
and the sorrowful honour of leaving
    is a cup given to women

or perhaps in madness I
    misheard you   polite liar:
is this the bouquet that you give your
    love, this blood-stained honour?

Is it? Sound follows
    sound clearly: was it good-bye
you said? (as sweetly casual
    as a handkerchief dropped without

thought) in this battle
    you are Caesar (What an
insolent thrust, to put the
    weapon of defeat, into my hand

like a trophy). It continues. To
    sound in my ears. As I bow.
—Do you always pretend
    to be forestalled in breaking?

Don't deny this, it
    is a vengeance of Lovelace
a gesture that does you credit
    while it lifts the flesh

576

from my bones, Laughter    the laugh of
  death. Moving. Without desire.
That is for others now
  we are shadows to one another.

Hammer the last nail in
  screw up the lead coffin.
—And now a last request.
  —Of course. Then say nothing

about us    to those who will
  come after me. (The sick
on their stretchers talk of spring.)
  —May I ask the same thing?

      —Perhaps I should give you a ring?
       —No. Your look is no longer open.
      The stamp left on your heart
       would be the ring on your hand.

      So now    without any scenes
       I must swallow, silently, furtively.
      —A book then? No, you give those
       to everyone, don't even write them

      books...

So now    must    be no
so now    must    be no
must be no crying

In wandering tribes of
fishermen brothers
drink without crying

dance without crying
their blood is hot, they
pay without crying

pearls in a glass
melt, as they run their
world    without crying

577

Now I am going and this
Harlequin gives his
Pierrette a bone like
a piece of contempt

He throws her the honour
of ending the curtain, the last
word when one inch of lead in
the breast would be hotter and better

Cleaner. My    teeth
press my lips. I can
stop myself crying

pressing the sharpness
into the softest
so/ without crying

so tribes of nomads
die without crying
burn without crying.

So tribes of fishermen
in ash and song can
hide their dead man.


# TED HUGHES

1930–

with János Csokits

FROM THE HUNGARIAN OF JÁNOS PILINSZKY

585            *The Desert of Love*

A bridge, and a hot concrete road—
the day is emptying its pockets,
laying out, one by one, all its possessions.
You are quite alone in the catatonic twilight.

A landscape like the bed of a wrinkled pit,
with glowing scars, a darkness which dazzles.
Dusk thickens. I stand numb with brightness
blinded by sun. This summer will not leave me.

Summer. And the flashing heat.
The chickens stand, like burning cherubs,
in the boarded-up, splintered cages.
I know their wings do not even tremble.

Do you still remember? First there was the wind.
And then the earth. Then the cage.
Flames, dung. And now and again
a few wing-flutters, a few empty reflexes.

And thirst. I asked for water—
Even today I hear that feverish gulping,
and helplessly, like a stone, bear
and quench the mirages.

Years are passing. And years. And hope
is like a tin-cup toppled into the straw.

586               *Fable*

*Detail from his KZ-Oratorio: Dark Heaven*

Once upon a time
there was a lonely wolf
lonelier than the angels.

He happened to come to a village.
He fell in love with the first house he saw.

Already he loved its walls
the caresses of its bricklayers.
But the windows stopped him.

In the room sat people
Apart from God nobody ever
found them so beautiful
as this child-like beast.

So at night he went into the house.
He stopped in the middle of the room
and never moved from there any more.

He stood all through the night, with wide eyes
and on into the morning when he was beaten to death.


# JON STALLWORTHY

1935–

## with Peter France

### FROM THE RUSSIAN OF ALEXANDER BLOK

587         *A Red Glow in the Sky*

A red glow in the sky, the dead night underground.
The pine trees imprison me in their dark density,
but unmistakeably there comes the sound
of a far distant, undiscovered city.

You will make out houses in heavy rows,
and towers, and the silhouette of buttresses,
and gardens behind stone walls sombre with shadows,
and arrogant ramparts of ancient fortresses.

Unmistakeably from submerged centuries
The piercing mind makes ready for dawning
the long forgotten roar of silted cities
and the rhythm of life returning.

588        from *Dances of Death*

II

Night, street, a lamp, a chemist's window,
a senseless and dim light. No doubt
in a quarter century or so
there'll be no change. There's no way out.

You'll die, and just the same as ever
begin the dance again. A damp
night, frozen ripples on the river,
a chemist's shop, a street, a lamp.


# CHRISTOPHER PILLING

## 1936–

### FROM THE FRENCH OF TRISTAN CORBIÈRE

589        from *Litany of Sleep*

I have sawn sleep apart! MACBETH.

YOU who snore with your sleeping wife so near,
RUMINANT! do you know this sigh: INSOMNIA?
—Have you seen Night and winged Sleep who's flown
Into the night, leaving you at the threshold, alone
—Not a friendly wing-beat from that midnight butterfly—
Alone in the pitch-pot whose lid has no eye?
—Have you been out in a boat? ... Thought is the swell
Resifting the shingle: my head ... your creel.
—Have you let a balloon take you up?—No?—well,
That's insomnia.—A big jolt from a heel,
Like that!—You see the flickering of strange candles:
A woman, a Halo of sunshine, archangels ...
And, night having brought day to the brink,
You wake up doggo, not having slept a wink.

SLEEP! listen to me: I shall speak very softly:
Sleep.—Baldachin for those with no canopy!

YOU who soar with the Albatross when storms blow,
And perch on honest night-caps of calico!
SLEEP!—For quite silly virgins, a white Pillow!
And for well-developed ones, a secret Overflow!
—Downy mattress for those who suffer polio!
Black Bag where, to hide their heads, the hounded go!
Prowler of the outer boulevards! Gigolo!
Country where the dumb wake to let their people know!
Caesura of the long line, and Rhyme for Sappho!

SLEEP—Grizzly Werewolf! Black Sleep in a smokescreen!
SLEEP!—Fragrant lace round a Wolf of velveteen!
Kiss from the Faire Unknowne, and Kiss from your heart's Queen!
—SLEEP! Thief of night! Frisking cat's paw become serene!
Redolence from graves rising to heaven unseen!
Cinderella's coach picking up each Magdalene!
Confessor Obscene to each pious still-born cailín!

YOU who come, like a dog, to lick the stigmata
Of the one racked by death on his hurdle, the martyr!
O forced smile of the crisis that's lost its aura!
SLEEP! Constant North-East breeze! Vapours of Aurora!

\*

HUGE Milch-Cow whose moon-calves we appear!
Ark where boa sloughs its skin like hobo or deer!
Glittering rainbow! Real for false! False for real!
What the boor calls time out when he's full of beer!
Witch in tawdry woollen tunic from Bohemia!
Tityrus trying reed-pipes in the shade of an alder!
Time bearing a chibouk in place of a reaper!
Atropos putting a drop of oil on her shear!
Clotho putting a hank of flax on her spindle!
Cat playing with Lachesis's clew of wool!

SLEEP!—Manna of grace to the disgraced heart!
..............................................................................................

SLEEP, ON WAKING, SAYS TO ME: YOU HAS SAWN ME APART.
..............................................................................................

# KEITH BOSLEY

1937–

FROM THE FRENCH OF STÉPHANE MALLARMÉ

590          *The Glazier*

The pure sun puzzled
By too bright a pack
Takes its shirt dazzled
Off the glazier's back.

591          *Album Leaf*

Suddenly half in jest
Young lady who beguiled
Made a discreet request
To hear my woodnotes wild

It strikes me that this test
Held in so fair a place
Has its points when I paused
To look you in the face

Yes that vain breath I kept
Out to the last limit
In gouty fingers gripped
Lacks means to emulate

Your most natural clear
Child's laugh that charms the air.

# TONY HARRISON

## 1937–

### FROM THE GREEK OF PALLADAS

592      Loving the rituals that keep men close,
Nature created means for friends apart:

pen, paper, ink, the alphabet,
signs for the distant and disconsolate heart.

593      Racing, reckoning fingers flick
at the abacus. Death's double-quick
comptometer works out the sums.

The stiffening digits, the rigid thumbs
still the clicking. Each bead slides
like a soul passing over, to the debit side.

594      Poor devil that I am, being so attacked
by wrath in fiction, wrath in fact.

Victim of wrath in literature and life:

1. The *Iliad* and 2. the wife!

595      Grammar commences with a 5-line curse:
*Wrath*'s first and *fatal*'s second verse;
then *sufferings*. The third verse sends
many men to various and violent ends,

594–5 Palladas was a *grammatikos*, a sort of secondary teacher who taught pupils to commit to memory as much of Homer as possible. The point of these two poems depends on that fact and on the opening lines of the *Iliad*.
(*Harrison's note*.)

and then the fourth and fifth expose
men to Zeus's anger, dogs and crows.

Sad study, grammar! Its whole content's
one long string of accidents!

596   When you send out invitations, don't ask me.
It's rare fillets that I like not filigree.
A piece of pumpkin each! The table creaks
not with the weight of food but your antiques.

Save your *soirées* for connoisseurs who'll notch
their belts in tighter for a chance to watch
the long procession of your silverware,
for art's sake happy just to starve and stare,
and, for some fine piece to goggle at, forego
all hope of eating, if the hallmarks show.

# JAMES GREENE

## 1938–

### FROM THE RUSSIAN OF OSIP MANDELSTAM

597             *Notre Dame*

Where a Roman judged a foreign people
A basilica stands and, first and joyful
Like Adam once, an arch plays with its own ribs:
Groined, muscular, never-unnerved.

From outside, the bones betray the plan:
Flying buttresses decide
That cumbersome mass shall never crush the wall:
Onslaught of a crashing vault is hindered.

Elemental labyrinth, unfathomable forest,
The Gothic soul's rational abyss,
Egyptian power with Christian shyness,
Where perpendicular is potentate.

But the more attentively I studied,
Notre Dame, your monstrous ribs, your stronghold,
The more I thought: I too one day will create
Beauty from cruel weight.

598                          'Phaedra'

—How the splendour of these veils and of this dress
Weighs me down in my disgrace!

    —In stony Troezen there will be
    An imperishable shriek,
    The royal stairs
    Will redden,
    .....................
    .....................
    And a black sun rise
    For the amorous mother.

—Oh if it were rancour seething in my breast—
But you see—the confession broke from my own lips.

    —In the white light of noon
    Phaedra burns with a black flame.
    In the white light of noon
    A baleful taper smoulders.
    Beware, Hippolytus, your sun-struck mother:
    Phaedra—the night—makes eyes at you
    In the white light of noon.

—With my black love I have sullied the sun...
..........................................................................................

—Scared, we do not dare
To succour the imperial grief.
Stung by Theseus,
Night fell on him.
With our burial song
We shall bring the dead home
And cool the black sun
Of a savage, insomniac, passion.

599      Not yet dead, not yet alone,
A beggar-woman my companion,
I am delighted by the immense plains,
And the haze, and hunger, and snow-storms.

I live in lovely poverty, opulent privation—
Alone and peaceful and consoled.
These days and nights are blessed,
This sinless labour mellifluous.

Unhappy he whom, like his shadow,
The dog's bark scares and the wind makes hay of.
And poor indeed he who, half-alive,
Begs favour of a shadow.

# MICHAEL ALEXANDER

## 1941–

### FROM THE EARLY ENGLISH

600      *The Seafarer*

The tale I frame shall be found to tally:
the history is of myself.
              Sitting day-long
at an oar's end clenched against clinging sorrow,
breast-drought I have borne, and bitternesses too.

I have coursed my keel through care-halls without end
over furled foam, I forward in the bows
through the narrowing night, numb, watching
for the cliffs we beat along.
                              Cold then
nailed my feet, frost shrank on
its chill clamps, cares sighed
hot about heart, hunger fed
on a mere-wearied mind.
                              No man blessed
with a happy land-life is like to guess
how I, aching-hearted, on ice-cold seas
have wasted whole winters; the wanderer's beat,
cut off from kind....
hung with hoar-frost.
                              Hail flew in showers,
there was no sound there but the slam of waves
along an icy sea. The swan's blare
my seldom amusement; for men's laughter
there was curlew-call, there were the cries of gannets,
for mead-drinking the music of the gull.
To the storm striking the stone cliffs
gull would answer, eagle scream
from throats frost-feathered. No friend or brother
by to speak with the despairing mind.

This he little believes whose life has run
sweet in the burgs, no banished man,
but well-seen at wine-round, my weariness of mind
on the ways stretching over the salt plains.
Night thickened, and from the north snowflakes;
hail fell on the frost-bound earth,
coldest of grains.

                              Now come thoughts
knocking my heart, of the high waves,
clashing salt-crests, I am to cross again.
Mind-lust maddens, moves as I breathe
soul to set out, seek out the way
to a far folk-land flood-beyond.

For no man above mould is so mood-proud,
so thoroughly equipped, so quick to do,
so strong in his youth, or with so staunch a lord
that before seafaring he does not fear a little
whither the Lord shall lead him in the end.
His heart is not in harping nor in the having of rings,
has no delight in women nor the world's gladnesses
nor can think of any thing outside the thrash of waves,
sea-struck, is distracted, stillness lost.

The thriving of the treeland, the town's briskness,
a lightness over the leas, life gathering,
everything urges the eagerly mooded
man to venture on the voyage he thinks of,
the faring over flood, the far bourn.
And the cuckoo calls him in his care-laden voice,
scout of summer, sings of new griefs
that shall make breast-hoard bitter.
                                Blithe heart cannot know,
through his happiness, what hardships they suffer
who drive the foam-furrow furthest from land.
Spirit breaks from the body's chest
to the sea's acres; over earth's breadth
and whale's range roams the mind now,
homes to the breast hungry and thirsty.

Cuckoo's dirge drags out my heart,
whets will to the whale's beat
across wastes of water: far warmer to me
are the Lord's kindnesses than this life of death
lent us on land.
                I do not believe
earthly estate is everlasting:
three things that all ways threaten a man's peace
and one before the end shall overthrow his mind;
either illness or age or the edge of vengeance
shall draw out the breath from the doom-shadowed.
Wherefore, for earl whosoever, it is afterword,
the praise of livers-on, that, lasting, is best:
won in the world before wayfaring,
forged, framed here, in the face of enmity,
in the Devil's spite: deeds, achievements.

That after-speakers should respect the name
and after them angels have honour toward it
for always and ever. From those everlasting joys
the daring shall not die.

                         Days are soon over,
on earth imperium with the earl's hand fails;
kings are not now, kaisers are not,
there are no gold-givers like the gone masters
who between them framed the first deeds in the world,
in their lives lordly, in the lays renowned.
That chivalry is changed, cheer is gone away,
it is a weaker kind who wields earth now,
sweats for its bread. Brave men are fewer,
all excellence on earth grows old and sere
as now does every man over the world;
age fares against him, his face bleaches
and his thatch thins: had a throng of friends
of noble houses, knows now they all
are given to the ground. That grieves his white head.
Once life is going, this gristle slackens;
nothing can pain or please flesh then,
he cannot stir a finger, fix his thinking.
A man may bury his brother with the dead
and strew his grave with the golden things
he would have him take, treasures of all kinds,
but gold hoarded when he here lived
cannot allay the anger of God
towards a soul sin-freighted.

# ACKNOWLEDGEMENTS

The editor and publishers gratefully acknowledge permission to reproduce copyright poems in this book.

Michael Alexander: 'The Seafarer' from *The Earliest English Poems* translated by Michael Alexander (Penguin Classics 1966) (© Michael Alexander, 1966). Reprinted by permission of Penguin Books Ltd.

Samuel Beckett: 'Lady Love' from *Collected Poems in English and French* (© 1977 Samuel Beckett). Reprinted by permission of John Calder (Publishers) Ltd, and Grove Press, Inc. 'My Cousin Agueda' and 'The Malefic Return' from *Anthology of Mexican Poetry* (1970) (© 1958 by Indiana University Press). Reprinted by permission of John Calder (Publishers) Ltd, and Indiana University Press.

Martin Bell: 'Winter Coming On' from *Collected Poems* (1966). Reprinted by permission of Macmillan, London and Basingstoke.

John Peale Bishop: 'To a Swallow' from *The Collected Poems of John Peale Bishop*, edited by Allen Tate (Copyright 1933, 1941, 1948 by Charles Scribner's Sons). Reprinted by permission of Charles Scribner's Sons.

Keith Bosley: 'The Glazier' and 'Album Leaf' from *Mallarmé: the Poems* (Penguin) (Translation © Keith Bosley 1977). Reprinted by permission of the author.

Clarence Brown and William S. Merwin: 'Batyushkov' and 'Ariosto' from *Mandelstam: Selected Poems* (© Clarence Brown and William S. Merwin 1973). Reprinted by permission of Oxford University Press, and Atheneum Publishers.

Basil Bunting: 'When the sword of sixty comes nigh his head' and 'Came to me—Who?' both from *Collected Poems* (© Basil Bunting 1978). Reprinted by permission of Oxford University Press.

Roy Campbell: 'Upon a Gloomy Night' and 'Coplas About the Soul Which Suffers With Impatience to See God' from *Poems* (Harvill Press) (Copyright © Roy Campbell 1951). 'The Giantess' and 'The Seven Old Men' from *Fleurs du Mal* (Harvill Press) (Copyright © Roy Campbell 1952). Reprinted by permission of Hughes Massie Limited.

James Vincent Cunningham: 'And now you're ready ...', 'Epigrams, Book II, 5', 'My little soul, my vagrant charmer ...', 'The Pope', 'Rome' and 'Neaera when I'm there is adamant' all from *Collected Poems and Epigrams* (Swallow Press) (© 1971 by J. V. Cunningham). Reprinted by permission of The Ohio University Press.

Elizabeth Daryush: 'I am your mother ...' from *Collected Poems* (© Elizabeth Daryush 1976). Reprinted by permission of Carcanet Press Limited.

Donald Davie: 'The Year 1812' from *The Forests of Lithuania* (1959). Reprinted by permission of The Marvell Press. 'Prose for Des Esseintes' (© 1980 by Donald Davie) is appearing for the first time in this anthology and is reprinted by permission of the author.

# ACKNOWLEDGEMENTS

Guy Davenport: 'This island ...', 'Like Odysseus under the ram ...', 'Decks awash ...' and 'May he lose his way on the cold sea ...' from *Carmina Archilochi: The Fragments of Archilochos* (1964) (Copyright 1964 by The Regents of the University of California). Reprinted by permission of the University of California Press. 'Come out of Crete ...', 'The Marriage· of Hector and Andromache' and a fragment commencing 'that labor ... a face to remember ...' from *Sappho, Poems and Fragments* (1965). Reprinted by permission of The University of Michigan Press.

Hilda Doolittle: 'Chorus from Iphigeneia in Aulis' from *The Collected Poems of H.D.* (Copyright © 1925, 1953 by Norman Holmes Pearson). Reprinted by permission of New Directions, New York for the Estate of Norman Holmes Pearson.

Thomas Stearns Eliot: 'Death by Water' from *The Waste Land* and also from *Collected Poems 1909–1962* (Copyright 1936 by Harcourt, Brace Jovanovich, Inc. Copyright © 1963, 1964 by T. S. Eliot). 'Anabasis' from *Anabasis* Copyright 1938 by Harcourt, Brace Jovanovich, Inc. Copyright 1966 by Esme Valerie Eliot). All reprinted by permission of Faber & Faber Ltd., and Harcourt, Brace Jovanovich, Inc.

Elaine Feinstein: Extract from 'The Poem of the End' from *Selected Poems of Tsvetayeva* (OUP 1971) Reprinted by permission of Olwyn Hughes on behalf of Elaine Feinstein.

Robert Garioch: 'Campidoglio', 'Judgment Day' and 'Sanct Christopher II' from *Collected Poems* (1977). Reprinted by permission of Macdonald Publishers.

David Gascoyne: 'Patmos' from *Hölderlin's Madness* (1938). Reprinted by permission of J. M. Dent & Sons Ltd.

James Greene: 'Notre Dame', 'Phaedra' and 'Not yet dead, not yet alone' from *Mandelstam: Poems* (1977). Reprinted by permission of Paul Elek Ltd.

Lady Augusta Gregory: 'The Hag of Beare' from *The Kiltartan Books* (1972). Reprinted by permission of Colin Smythe Ltd, publishers of the Coole Edition of Lady Gregory's work.

Michael Hamburger: 'Your Hand Full of Hours' and 'Psalm' from *Nineteen Poems* (Carcanet Press 1972) (Copyright © 1972 Michael Hamburger). 'Thread Suns', 'Etched Away From', 'Leap-Centuries', 'Irish' and '... plashes the fountain' from *Paul Celan: Selected Poems* (Penguin 1972). Reprinted by permission of the author.

Tony Harrison: 'Loving the Rituals', 'Poor devil that I am ...', 'When You Send Out Invitations', 'Racing, reckoning fingers ...', 'Grammar Commences', from *Palladas: Poems* (copyright © 1975 Tony Harrison). Reprinted by permission of Anvil Press Poetry.

Gerard Manley Hopkins: 'Odes, Book I, 38—'Ah Child, no Persian ...', 'Odes, Book III, 1—'Tread back—and back ...', from *The Poems of Gerard Manley Hopkins* (4th edn. 1967 ed. W. H. Gardner and N. H. Mackenzie. Published by Oxford University Press for the Society of Jesus). Reprinted by permission of Oxford University Press.

## ACKNOWLEDGEMENTS

A. E. Housman: 'Diffugere Nives' from the Latin of Horace in *Collected Poems* (Copyright 1936 by Barclays Bank Ltd. Copyright © 1964 by Robert E. Symons). Reprinted by permission of The Society of Authors as literary representatives of the Estate of A. E. Housman, Jonathan Cape Ltd, and Holt, Rinehart and Winston.

Ted Hughes: 'The Desert of Love' and 'Fable—Detail from his KZ-Oratorio: Dark Heaven' from *Selected Poems: J. Pilinszky* (Copyright © 1976 James Pilinszky/translations Ted Hughes 1976). Reprinted by permission of Carcanet Press Ltd.

Douglas Hyde: 'The Roman Earl' from *Love Songs of Connaught* (1972). Reprinted by permission of the Irish Academic Press and the grandchildren of Douglas Hyde.

George Johnston: Extract from *The Saga of Gisli* (ed. Peter Foote, Everyman's Library Series, 1963). Reprinted by permission of J. M. Dent & Sons Ltd, and the University of Toronto Press.

James Blair Leishman: 'Annunciation', and 'Sonnets to Orpheus: Second Part' IV and XVII from *Rilke's Sonnets to Orpheus* (2nd edn. 1946). Reprinted by permission of St. John's College, Oxford and The Hogarth Press. Also reprinted by permission of W. W. Norton & Company, Inc. publishers of *Translations from the Poetry of Rainer Maria Rilke* by M. D. Herter Norton (Copyright 1938 by W. W. Norton & Co. Inc., Copyright renewed 1966 by M. D. Herter Norton) and *Sonnets to Orpheus* (Copyright 1942 by W. W. Norton & Company Inc. Copyright renewed 1970 by M. D. Herter Norton). Extracts from 'Half of Life' and 'Ripe, Being Plunged into Fire' from *Selected Poems of Hölderlin* (2nd edn. 1954). Reprinted by permission of the literary estate of J. B. Leishman and the Hogarth Press.

A. L. Lloyd: From 'Lament for Ignacio Sánchez Mejías' from the Spanish of Federico García Lorca in *Lament for the Death of a Bull Fighter and Other Poems* (1937, 1953) (All rights reserved). Reprinted by permission of New Directions, New York.

Christopher Logue: Extracts from *Patrocleia* (copyright © 1962 by Christopher Logue). Reprinted by permission of Hope, Leresche and Sayle.

Robert Lowell: 'Saturday Night in the Village' and 'Helen' from *Imitations* (1971) (Copyright © 1958, 1959, 1960, 1961 by R. Lowell). 'The Vanity of Human Wishes' and 'Brunetto Latini, "Inferno, Canto XV"' from *Near the Ocean* (1967) (Copyright © 1963, 1965, 1966, 1967 by Robert Lowell). Reprinted by permission of Faber & Faber Ltd, and Farrar, Straus & Giroux, Inc.

Hugh MacDiarmid: 'The Dead Liebknecht', 'Under the Greenwood Tree' and 'The Robber', from *Collected Poems* (1962) (© Christopher Murray Grieve 1948, 1962). Reprinted by permission of Macmillan Publishing Co. Inc.

Sir Edward Marsh: 'The Hag and the Slavies' from *The Fables of La Fontaine* (1931). Reprinted by permission of William Heinemann Ltd.

## ACKNOWLEDGEMENTS

William S. Merwin: 'The Mirabeau Bridge' from *Selected Translations* (1968). Reprinted by permission of Atheneum Publishers, and David Higham Associates Ltd. (Copyright 1948, 1949, 1950, 1954, © 1956, 1957, 1958, 1959, 1960, 1961, 1962, 1965, 1966, 1967, 1968 by W. S. Merwin.)

Christopher Middleton: 'The Jugs' and 'Fugue of Death' from *Selected Poems: Paul Celan* (Penguin 1972). Reprinted by permission of the author.

Czeslaw Milosz: 'Elegy of Fortinbras' from *Postwar Polish Poetry* (1966) (Copyright © 1961 by Encounter Ltd). Reprinted by permission of Doubleday & Co. Inc.

John Montague: Extract from 'The Vision of MacConglinne' after Kuno Meyer from *Faber Book of Irish Verse* (1974). Reprinted by permission of A. D. Peters & Co. Ltd.

Marianne Moore: 'The Fox and the Crow', 'The Wolf and the Stork', 'The Donkey and the Lapdog' and 'The Rat and the Elephant' from *The Fables of La Fontaine* (1965) (Copyright © 1964 by Marianne Moore. All rights reserved). Reprinted by permission of Viking Penguin Inc.

Edwin Morgan: 'The Lost Parasol' from *Selected Poems of Weöres and Juhász*, translated by Edwin Morgan and David Wevill (Penguin Modern European Poets, 1970) (© Sándor Weöres, 1970. © Edwin Morgan, 1970). Reprinted by permission of Penguin Books Ltd.

Alan Neame: Extracts from 'Leoun' (21 Stanzas). First appeared in *Agenda*, Vol. 2, Nos. 2 & 3, December–January 1960–1. Reprinted by permission of *Agenda*.

Frank O'Connor: 'The Midnight Court' from *Kings, Lords and Commons* (Macmillan 1961). Reprinted by permission of A. D. Peters & Co. Ltd.

Christopher Pilling: 'Litany of Sleep' from *These Jaundiced Loves* (Harry Chambers/Peterloo Poets 1980) (Copyright © 1980 by Christopher Pilling). Reprinted by permission of the author.

Peter Porter: 'Lean Gaius who was thinner than a Straw' from *The Greek Anthology* (Allen Lane 1973). Reprinted by permission of the author. 'What a host you are, Mancinus', 'Dasius, chucker-out' and 'Near the Vipsanian columns' from *After Martial* (© OUP 1972). Reprinted by permission of Oxford University Press.

Ezra Pound: 'Women of Trachis' an extract from *Women of Trachis* (Copyright © 1957 by Ezra Pound), 'Canto I, Odyssey Book XI—a condensation of Homer', 'Canto XXXVI, Donna Me Prega' and 'Canto LIII' from the Chinese Book of Rites, are all reprinted from *The Cantos of Ezra Pound* (Copyright 1934, 1940 by Ezra Pound). 'Alba' from *Langue d'Or* and 'Liu Ch'e' both from *Selected Poems* and also from *Personae* (Copyright © 1954 by Ezra Pound). 'Song of the Bowmen of Shu', 'The Beautiful Toilet', 'The River Merchant's Wife: a letter', 'Poem by the Bridge at Ten-Shin', 'The Jewel Stairs' Grievance', 'Lament of the Frontier Guard', 'South-Folk in Cold Country' and 'Homage to Sextus Propertius' (I. 'Shades of Callimachus') are all from *Collected Shorter Poems* and also from *Personae* (Copyright 1926 by E. Pound). All the above poems are reprinted by permission of Faber & Faber

# ACKNOWLEDGEMENTS

Ltd. and New Directions, New York. 'Pine Boat a-shift', 'Pedlar', 'Wide, Ho?', 'Toujours la Politesse', 'Fraternitas', 'Pick a fern ...', 'Fine fish to net', 'For an Officer', 'For deep deer-copse beneath Mount Han' and 'Full be the year' all from *The Classic Anthology Defined by Confucius*. Reprinted by permission of Faber & Faber Ltd and Harvard University Press.

Omar S. Pound: 'Twice Times Then Is Now' from *Arabic and Persian Poems* in English (Copyright © 1970 by Omar S. Pound). Reprinted by permission of New Directions, New York.

Kenneth Rexroth: '... about the cool water', 'I, Hermes, have been set up', 'Never Again, Orpheus', 'Stranger, when you come to' and 'The Last Utterance of the Delphic Oracle' from *Poems from the Greek Authors* (1962). Reprinted by permission of the University of Michigan Press.

Edwin Arlington Robinson: 'Doricha' from *Collected Poems* (New York: Macmillan, 1937). Reprinted by permission of Macmillan Publishing Co., Inc.

Tom Scott: 'Ballat O the Leddies O Langsyne' and 'Ballat O the Hingit' from 'Seeven Poems O Maister Francis Villon' (Peter Russell, The Pound Press). Reprinted by permission of the author.

Charles H. Sisson: 'Carmen Saeculare' from *In The Trojan Ditch* (© 1974 C. H. Sisson). Reprinted by permission of Carcanet Press Limited.

Sidney Goodsir Smith: 'The Ballad Singer' an extract from 'The Gangrel Rymour and the Pairdon of Sanct Anne' from *The Collected Poems* (Copyright © John Calder (Publishers) Ltd 1975). Reprinted by permission of John Calder Ltd. and Mrs Hazel Goodsir Smith.

Stevie Smith: 'The Emperor Hadrian to his soul' from *Collected Poems* (Allen Lane 1975). Reprinted by permission of James MacGibbon executor.

Jon Stallworthy and Peter France: 'A Red Glow in the Sky' and 'Dances of Death II' from *Poems of Alexander Blok* (1974). Reprinted by permission of Eyre & Spottiswoode (Publishers) Ltd.

Wallace Stevens: 'I Feel an Apparition' an extract from 'Moment of Light' (Copyright © 1957 by Elsie Stevens and Holly Stevens) from *Opus Posthumous* (1957). Reprinted by permission of Faber & Faber Ltd, and Alfred A. Knopf, Inc.

Arthur Symons: 'A la Promenade', 'Cortège' and 'Femme et Chatte' from *Collected Poems* (Secker & Warburg 1924) (© Mr H. F. Read). Reprinted by permission of Mr H. F. Read.

Paul B. Taylor & W. H. Auden: 'The Words of the All-Wise' (copyright © 1967, 1968, 1969 by Paul B. Taylor and W. H. Auden) from *The Elder Edda: A Selection* (1969). Reprinted by permission of Faber & Faber Ltd, and Random House, Inc.

Charles Tomlinson: 'Lament of the Virtues and Verses on Account of the Death of Don Guido' from *Selected Poems*, (© Charles Tomlinson 1978). 'Veneris Venefica Agrestis' from *Written on Water* © OUP 1972). Reprinted by permission of Oxford University Press.

# ACKNOWLEDGEMENTS

Arthur Waley: 'The Ejected Wife', 'Plucking the Rushes', 'Lazy Man's Song', 'Starting Early from the Ch'U-Ch'êng Inn', 'Eating Bamboo-Shoots', 'Invitation to Hsiao Ch'U-Shih', 'The Cranes', and 'On the Birth of his Son' (Copyright 1919 and renewed 1947 by Arthur Waley) all from *Chinese Poems* (Allen & Unwin 1976) and also from *Translations from the Chinese* (Random House, 1971). The above poems are reprinted by permission of George Allen & Unwin (Publishers) Ltd, and Random House, Inc. 'Yellow Dusk' and 'In Her Boudoir' from *Chinese Poems* (1976). Reprinted by permission of George Allen & Unwin (Publishers) Ltd.

Peter Whigham: 'Plunging towards Phrygia over violent water' from *The Poems of Catullus* (Penguin Classics, 1966) (© Peter Whigham, 1966). Reprinted by permission of Penguin Books Ltd.

William Carlos Williams: 'Peer of the gods is that man' from *Paterson*, Book V, ii (Copyright © 1958 by William Carlos Williams). Reprinted by permission of New Directions, New York.

Edward Meryon Wilson: 'The Young Pilgrim Finds Refuge with the goatherds', 'The River Compared to an Oratorical Sentence' and 'The Wedding Feast' extracts from 'The First Solitude' all from *The Solitudes of Luis Góngora* (1965). Reprinted by permission of Cambridge University Press.

William Butler Yeats: 'Swift's Epitaph' (Copyright 1933 by Macmillan Publishing Co. Inc., renewed 1961 by Bertha Georgie Yeats) and 'Colonus' Praise' (Copyright 1928 by Macmillan Publishing Co. Inc. renewed 1956 by Georgie Yeats) both from *Collected Poems* (Macmillan, New York 1950). Reprinted by permission of M. B. Yeats, Miss Ann Yeats, Macmillan Co. of London & Basingstoke, and Macmillan Publishing Co., Inc.

Douglas Young 'Minnie, I canna caa my wheel', 'Call rain frae abune', 'Deid sall ye ligg ...' and 'The Kirkyaird by the Sea' from *A Braird o Thistles* (1947). Reprinted by permission of Wm. Mclellan.

Celia and Louis Zukofsky: 'VIII' and 'XL' from *Catullus* (Cape Goliard Press 1969). Reprinted by permission of Jonathan Cape Ltd.

While every effort has been made to secure permission, we may have failed in a few cases to trace the copyright holder. We apologize for any apparent negligence.

# NOTES AND REFERENCES

Translation is done into a given state of the language. Men who write of mushrumps, porpentines or ciperstrees are not well served if we re-translate their verbal concepts into mushrooms, porcupines, and cypress trees. Tyndale's spelling of ciperstrees, for example, does not arise from our own separating habits of mind towards language and things: we have fixed that cypress tree so firmly to botanical fact that our very notion is different from his. Furthermore, I have not attempted in this anthology to impose a consistent spelling on the texts I have used: pleas for consistency often seem to imply that the Tudors (say) simply could not spell, whereas their variant spelling of the same word (and I felt the general reader would relish the flavour of this diversity) indicates a very different sense of language from ours. Spelling sometimes also involves questions of pronunciation, rhythm, phrasing, and metre. As scholars are still puzzling out the rhythmic intentions of some of our earlier poets, a policy of modernization which would affect metre seemed to me unwise.

Thus, with those earlier poets, my policy has been to use as a basis edited old-spelling texts, though one is, of course, to some extent in the hands of one's editor in so far as changes of punctuation may have been introduced. I have removed typographical quirks and have normalized the long s and the use of u's, v's, and i's. Where edited texts were not available, I have sought out what seemed to be the most reliable ones, emending only obvious misprints. Titles or subtitles which I have supplied for poems or extracts are set in quotation marks.

The Notes do not give references for poems by authors whose collected poems are easily available. For details of poems still in copyright, see also the Acknowledgements.

1–11. Gavin Douglas. John Small (ed.), *The Poetical Works* (1874). 1. I.i–18; 2. I.vi.17–61; 3. I.vii.5–35; 4. II.iv.57–96; 5. II.vi.8–22; 6. III.vi.162–80; 7. IV.xii.1–42; 8. VI.v.1–40; 9. VIII.i.1–18; 10. XI.x.16–27; 11. XII.xiv. 103–54.

12–16. William Tyndale. *Five Books of Moses.* Edition of 1530, compared with Tyndale's *Genesis* of 1534. Ed. F. F. Bruce (1967).

17–22. Miles Coverdale. The Psalter of 1539. Introduced by John Earle (1894).

23–37. Sir Thomas Wyatt. Texts from Muir and Thomson (eds.), *The Poems*

(1969). 23. Lines 11–27; 24. Lines 1–28; 28. Wyatt exchanges Petrarch's Euphrates and Tigris for the Thames; 32. The freedom of Wyatt's handling of Petrarch (or perhaps of a phrase from a fifteenth-century imitation of Petrarch) clearly goes beyond translation here: furthermore, he not only transforms but subverts Petrarchan attitudes; 37. Wyatt substitutes Kent for Alamanni's Provence. The earliest appearance of *terza rima* in English except for Chaucer's 'Complaint to his Lady'.

38–45. Henry Howard, Earl of Surrey. Frederick Morgan Padelford (ed.), *The Poems* (1920). 38. II.54–66; 39. IV.553–73; 40. IV.606–17.

46–8. Jasper Heywood. *Seneca/His Tenne Tragedies* (1581), 2 vols., introduced by T. S. Eliot (1927). 46. Lines 37–55; 47. Lines 54–68; 48. Lines 62–77.

49–51. John Studley. Ibid. 49. Lines 16–32; 50. Lines 13–28; 51. Lines 77–88.

52–3. Richard Stanyhurst. *Thee first fo[u]re books of Virgil his Aeneis translated into English heroical verse by Richard Stanyhurst* (1582); 52. I.5–29; 53. III.193–222.

54–62. Arthur Golding. W. H. D. Rouse (ed.), *Shakespeare's Ovid, Being Arthur Golding's Translation of the Metamorphoses* (1961). Facsimile of the 1904 edition. 54. I.610–700; 55. IV.26–38; 56. V.485–502; 57. VII.265–77: cp. *The Tempest*, V.i.35–50 where Shakespeare draws on both the original Latin and Golding's version for Prospero's invocation of the spirits; 58. VIII.245–313; 59. X.426–36; 60 X.689–95; 61. XIII.929–1020; 62. XV.984–1005.

63. George Turberville. *The Heroycal Epistles of the learned Poet Publius Ovidius Naso. Set out and translated by George Tubervile* (1567); lines 1–38.

64–6. Edmund Spenser. 64. Sonnet 3; 65. Sonnet 26; 66. *Fairy Queen*, II. Canto XII, verses 74–5.

68–9. Sir Walter Ralegh. 68. VI.724–9; 69. IV.373–8, 380–1.

71–7. Sir Philip Sidney. 77. Stanzas 1–3, 5–11.

78–82. Mary Herbert, Countess of Pembroke. J. Rathmell (ed.), *The Psalms of Sir Philip Sidney and the Countess of Pembroke* (1963). 79. Stanzas 1–4 only; 80. Stanzas 7–9; 81. Stanzas 6–7, 10–11; 82. Stanzas 7–10.

83–101. George Chapman. Allardyce Nicoll (ed.), *Chapman's Homer, the Iliad, the Odyssey and the Lesser Homerica*, 2 vols., (2nd edn. 1967). 83. II.71–8; 84. IV.449–64; 85. V.518–24; 86. VI.141–7; 87. VI.539–51; 88. XII.289–96; 89. XIII.624–30; 90. III.15–36; 91. III.159–74; 92. VI.506–15; 93. VIII.480–497; 94. V.61–102; 95. V.320–39; 96. V.402–31; 97. VII.152–80; 98. XI.259–82; 99. XXI.62–99; 100. XXII.379–404; 101. XXIII.221–43.

102–4. Sir John Harington. R. McNulty (ed.), *Ludovico Ariosto's 'Orlando*

*Furioso*' (1972). 102. VII, stanzas 9–15, 18–26; 103. XIV.67–70, 72–3; 104. XXIX.29–31.

110. Thomas Underdowne. *Ovid his invective against Ibis* (1569). Lines 137–74.

111–13. Thomas Campion. Percival Vivian (ed.), *Campion's Works* (3rd edn. 1967).

114–39. The Authorized Version 1611. William Aldis Wright (ed.), *The English Bible/In Five Volumes* (1909).

142–3. Edward Fairfax. *Godfrey of Bulloigne or The Recoverie of Jerusalem* (1600). 142. IV, stanzas 27–32; 143. XVI.12–15.

144–52. Ben Jonson. 148. Lines 85–104; 150. VIII.1–20.

153. Sir John Beaumont. Frank Kermode (ed.), *English Pastoral Poetry* (1952). Dryden, who also has a version of this, notes: 'Many of the verses are translated from one of the Sybils, who prophesied of our Saviour's birth.'

154. Drummond of Hawthornden. L. E. Kastner (ed.), *Poetical Works* (1913).

155. Anon. F. Kermode (ed.), *English Pastoral Poetry* (1952).

163. William Strode. Bertram Dobell (ed.), *The Poetical Works* (1907). Published by the editor. Crashaw's *Musickes Duell* (not included here) paraphrases and expands Strada's poem (thus lines 57–156 derive from only 15 of the original—34–49).

164–74. Sir Richard Fanshawe. 164–6. *Horatius Flaccus* (*Quintus*) *selections* (1652). 167 and 174. N. W. Bawcutt (ed.), *Martial: Shorter Poems and Translations* (1964); 168–9. Jeremiah D. M. Ford (ed.), *The Luciad*, trans. R. Fanshawe (1940); Canto II, stanzas 20–3 and 93–100; 170–3. W. E. Simeone (ed.), *Il Pastor Fido* (1964); 170. Act I, ii.664–710; 171. II.vi.2057–88; 172. III.v.2591–600; 173. IV.ix.4179–224; a reply to Tasso. See Leigh Hunt.

178. Sir Matthew Hale. *Contemplations Moral and Divine* (1676).

181. Richard Crashaw. Stanzas 20–4.

183–6. Sir John Denham. 183. From Book XII; 184. II.541–8; 185. IV.118–51.

187. Sir Edward Sherburne. F. J. Van Beeck (ed.), *The Poems and Translations* (*1616–1702*) (1961).

194–204. Abraham Cowley. *The Works* (8th edn. 1684). 197. Lines 23–7; 200. Stanzas 1–2 only.

206–11. Henry Vaughan. 206. Lines 33–60; 208. Lines 1–38; 209. Lines 46–67; 210. Lines 234–87; 211. Book II, 5.

212–18. Thomas Stanley G. M. Crump (ed.), *The Poems and Translations* (1962). 215. Lines 1–24, 55–72.

219–43. John Dryden. 219. I.1–8; 220. I.284–305; 221. I.332–53; 222. I.627–50; 223. I.667–815; 225. I.1–33; 226. I.1–26, 49–94, 171–211, 236–70; 227. I.1–18; 228. I.582–609; 229. IV.251–73; 230. VI.413–32; 231. XI.384–422; 232. XI.741–52. Modelled by Virgil on Homer, but Pope in translating Homer modelled *his* Homer on Dryden's Virgil here. See no. 287; 233. XII.991–1000. 236. I.356–73, 386–424; 237. Lines 537–86; 238. VIII. 11–199; 239. II.268–307; 240. XV.262–77, 296–319, 324–53, 388–413; 241. Lines 1–35, 163–89, 264–85, 430–50, 483–98, 593–609; 242. Lines 85–115; 243. Lines 1–66.

244. Wentworth Dillon, Earl of Roscommon. Jacob Tonson's Horace, 1715.

245. Thomas Flatman. *Poems and Songs* (1686).

246–7. Philip Ayres. *Lyric Poems* (1687).

248. Anthony Horneck. Jacob Tonson's Horace, 1715.

250. Nahum Tate. *Poems* (enlarged edn. 1684).

251–2. John Oldham. *Works*, Vol. 1 (1722). 251. Lines 1–40 only; 252. Lines 1–75.

253–4. Thomas Creech. 253. *The Idylliums of Theocritus with Rapin's Discourse of Pastorals Done Into English* (1684): Lines 1–28, 93–102, 119–32, 173–220; 254. *T. Lucretius Carus … De Natura Rerum done into English verse with notes* (1682): V.275–326.

255–6. Tom Brown. *The Works of Mr Thomas Brown in Prose and Verse*, 3 vols. (1707).

257. George Stepney. Jacob Tonson's Horace, 1715.

258. William Walsh. Cooke (ed.), *The Poetical Works* (1797).

259–62. Matthew Prior. H. Bunker Wright and Munroe K. Spears (eds.), *Matthew Prior: Literary Works* (1959).

263–7. Jonathan Swift. Harold Williams (ed.), *The Poems* (1937). 264. This poem alludes to and condenses Horace.

268–71. William Congreve. Montague Somers (ed.), *The Complete William Congreve* (1923). 268. from Book XXIV; 269. XXIV.1–23; 270. Lines 77–105; 271. Lines 322–52.

272. Joseph Addison. *Ovid's Metamorphoses* (Garth folio edn., 1717): II.136–381.

273. Nicholas Rowe. *Lucan's Pharsalia* (1720): I.227–87.

274. Isaac Watts. *The Psalms of David Imitated in the Language of the New Testament* (1719).

275. Thomas Parnell. *Homerus, Battle of the Frogs and Mice* (1717). Lines 87–130.

276–7. Elijah Fenton. Cooke (ed.), *The Poetical Works* (1798).

278. John Gay. VI.211–39.

279–81. William Diaper. 279. I.849–64; 280. I.914–63; 281. I.1347–62.

282–3. Allan Ramsay. *The Poems* (1819).

284–313. Alexander Pope. 284. IV.478–97; 285. V.637–48; 286. VI.161–86; 287. VI.648–63; 288. X.209–22; 289. XII.329–44; 290. XIII.188–200; 291. XIII.877–84; 292. XVI.312–23; 293. XXII.183–210; 294. III.23–52; 295. III.191–210; 296. VIII.685–708; 297. XII.5–30; 298. XII.371–96; 299. XV.390–421; 300. XVIII. 551–704; 301. XXI.257–316, 327–9; 302. V.56–98; 303. V.310–32; 304. V.403–23; 305. V.542–67; 306; V.616–37; 307. VII.142–75; 308. IX.253–548; 309. X.659–68; 310. XXI.41–62; 311. XXI.427–51; 312. XXII.476–516; 313. XXIV.7–14.

314. Soame Jenyns. *Poems* (1752).

315. Philip Francis. *The Works of Horatius Flaccus*, vol. 1 (1743).

321. Samuel Johnson. Lines 1–18, 36–58; the omitted lines are by Mrs Thrale.

322. Thomas Gray. Lines 11–24.

323. Anon. James McPeek, *Catullus in Strange and Distant Britain*.

326. Christopher Smart. Stanzas 1–10 only.

330–43. William Cowper. *Homer's Iliad and Odyssey*, 2 vols. (3rd edn. 1809). 330. II.515–35; 331. XIII.832–40; 332. XVI.253–6; 333. VIII.634–49; 334. XVI.482–93; 335. V.51–7; 336. XII.263–300.

344. Young Gentlemen of Mr Rule's Academy. *Poetical Blossoms by the Young Gentlemen of Mr Rule's Academy* (1766).

345–6. William Gifford, *The Satires of Decimus Junius Juvenalis* (1802). 345. Lines 49–106, 189–218; 346. Lines 77–111, 204–37, 266–91.

347. William Lisle Bowles. William Tirebuck (ed.), *The Poetical Works of Bowles, Lamb and Hartley Coleridge* (1887).

348–50. John Hookham Frere. W. E. Frere (ed.), *The Works of the Rt. Hon. J. H. Frere*, Vol. II (1874).

357–61. Walter Savage Landor. S. Wheeler (ed.), *The Works* vols. xv, xvi.357: '…perhaps found by Landor in Warton's *Essay on Pope* where it is quoted from Fulvius Ursinus' (Wheeler).

NOTES AND REFERENCES

362. Francis Howes. *The Epodes, Satires and Epistles of Horace. Translated by Francis Howes* (1845); lines 19–32, 73–160.

363. Leigh Hunt. *Amyntas, a Tale of the Woods from the Italian of T.T.* (1820).

364. Thornton Hunt (ed.) *The Poetical Works* (1860).

368–79. Percy Bysshe Shelley. 368. Stanzas xi–xviii, xxx.8–xli. I.374–9. Timothy Webb, *The Violet in the Crucible, Shelley and Translation* (1976).

382–5. Elizur Wright. 'The Fables of La Fontaine' in *Masterpieces of World Literature* (n.d.).

388. Edward Fitzgerald. W. A. Wright (ed.), *Letters and Literary Remains of Edward Fitzgerald*, Vol. III (1889). Stanzas v–vii, xii–xv, xvii–xxiv, c–ci.

389–92. Alfred, Lord Tennyson. 389. IV.446–56; 390. VI.503–14; 391. VIII.542–61; 392. XVIII.202.

394. William Makepeace Thackeray. *Miscellanies in prose and verse*, 4 vols. (1857).

395. Sir Theodore Martin. *The Works of Horace, translated by Sir Theodore Martin* (1881).

396–7. Branwell Brontë. *The Shakespeare Head Brontë: Miscellaneous and Unpublished Writings of Charlotte and Patrick Branwell Brontë*, Vol. II.

398–9. John Conington. *The Satires, Epistles and Art of Poetry of Horace translated into English Verse by John Conington* (1870).

400–5. Dante Gabriel Rossetti. *The Early Italian Poets* (1861).

409–11. William Morris. 409. Stanzas 14–19; 411. Stanzas 65–71.

418–35. American Indian. 418–19, 421, 435. A. Grove Day, *The Sky Clears* (1885); 420, 434. John Bierhorst, *In the Trail of the Wind* (1972).

460–62. Ezra Pound. 460. The Cantos, I.1–71; 461. XXXVI.1–84; 462. LII.48–153.

500. Roy Campbell. Stanzas 1–4 only.

508. Frank O'Connor. Part 1, Lines 276–315, Part 2, Lines 119–84.

519–21. Edward Meryon Wilson. 519. Lines 88–117; 520. Lines 185–207; 521. Lines 831–918.

522. Wystan Hugh Auden, stanzas 10–27.

530. James Vincent Cunningham. Spenser has a version of this via Du Bellay. Pound translated the Du Bellay and Lowell a Spanish version by Quevedo.

540. Douglas Young, stanzas 10–16.

545. Robert Lowell, Lines 58–83, 161–88.

550. Edwin Morgan, stanzas I–II, 15–17.

560. Alan Neame, stanzas i–viii, xxxi–xxxii, xxxiv–xxxv, lviii–lxi, cv–cxiv, cxix–cxx.

562. Christopher Logue, pp. 12–14, 34–5.

589. Christopher Pilling, stanzas 1–5, 27–8.

598. James Greene. Lines 7–8 were deleted by Mandelstam and never restored. All other dots are the translator's.

# INDEX OF TRANSLATED AUTHORS
# AND ANONYMOUS TEXTS

The references are to the numbers of the poems

# INDEX OF TRANSLATED AUTHORS

# INDEX OF TRANSLATORS

The references are to the numbers of the poems